A Companion to the Works of Alfred Döblin

Studies in German Literature, Linguistics, and Culture
Edited by James Hardin
(South Carolina)

Camden House Companion Volumes

The Camden House Companions provide well-informed and up-to-date critical commentary on the most significant aspects of major works, periods, or literary figures. The Companions may be read profitably by the reader with a general interest in the subject. For the benefit of student and scholar, quotations are provided in the original language.

A COMPANION TO THE WORKS OF
Alfred Döblin

Edited by
Roland Dollinger,
Wulf Koepke, and
Heidi Thomann Tewarson

CAMDEN HOUSE

Copyright © 2003 by the Editors and Contributors

All Rights Reserved. Except as permitted under current legislation,
no part of this work may be photocopied, stored in a retrieval system,
published, performed in public, adapted, broadcast, transmitted,
recorded, or reproduced in any form or by any means,
without the prior permission of the copyright owner.

First published 2003 by Camden House
Reprinted in paperback and transferred to digital printing 2010

Camden House is an imprint of Boydell & Brewer Inc.
668 Mt. Hope Avenue, Rochester, NY 14620, USA
www.camden-house.com
and of Boydell & Brewer Limited
PO Box 9, Woodbridge, Suffolk IP12 3DF, UK
www.boydellandbrewer.com

Paperback ISBN-13: 978-1-57113-460-8
Paperback ISBN-10: 1-57113-460-3
Hardback ISBN-13: 978-1-57113-124-9
Hardback ISBN-10: 1-57113-124-8

Library of Congress Cataloging-in-Publication Data

A companion to the works of Alfred Döblin / edited by Roland Dollinger,
  Wulf Koepke, and Heidi Thomann Tewarson.
    p. cm. — (Studies in German literature, linguistics, and culture)
  Includes bibliographical references and index.
  ISBN 1-57113-124-8 (alk. paper)
    1. Döblin, Alfred, 1878-1957 — Criticism and interpretation.
  I. Dollinger, Roland A. (Roland Albert)   II. Koepke, Wulf, 1928-
  III. Tewarson, Heidi Thomann.   IV. Studies in German literature,
  linguistics, and culture (Unnumbered)

PT2607.O35Z644 2003
833'.912—dc21

2003048935

A catalogue record for this title is available from the British Library.

This publication is printed on acid-free paper.

Cover photograph of Döblin in Paris, spring 1935. Photographer unknown.
Courtesy of Schiller-Nationalmuseum/Deutsches Literaturarchiv, Marbach.

Contents

Foreword   vii

Abbreviations and Translations of Titles   ix

Works by Alfred Döblin   xiii

Introduction   1
    Roland Dollinger, Wulf Koepke, Heidi Thomann Tewarson

Early Works

Döblin's Early Collection of Stories, *Die Ermordung einer Butterblume:* Toward a Modernist Aesthetic   23
    Heidi Thomann Tewarson

The Advent of Döblinism: *Die drei Sprünge des Wang-lun* and *Wadzeks Kampf mit der Dampfturbine*   55
    David Dollenmayer

Works of the Weimar Period

The Fall of Wallenstein, or the Collapse of Narration? The Paradox of Epic Intensity in Döblin's *Wallenstein*   75
    Neil H. Donahue

Technology and Nature: From Döblin's *Berge Meere und Giganten* to a Philosophy of Nature   93
    Roland Dollinger

"Arzt und Dichter": Döblin's Medical, Psychiatric, and Psychoanalytical Work   111
    Veronika Fuechtner

Döblin's Berlin: The Story of Franz Biberkopf   141
Gabriele Sander

Döblin's Engagement with the New Media: Film, Radio and Photography   161
Erich Kleinschmidt

Döblin's Political Writings during the Weimar Republic   183
Wulf Koepke

Exile and Return to Europe

Döblin, the Critic of Western Civilization: The *Amazon* Trilogy   193
Helmut F. Pfanner

Döblin's *November 1918*   215
Helmuth Kiesel

Döblin and Judaism   233
Klaus Müller-Salget

Robinson the Castaway: Döblin's Christian Faith as Reflected in His Autobiography *Schicksalsreise* and His Religious Dialogues *Der unsterbliche Mensch* and *Der Kampf mit dem Engel*   247
Christoph Bartscherer

The Tragedy of Truth: Döblin's Novel *Hamlet oder Die lange Nacht nimmt ein Ende*   271
Wolfgang Düsing

Bibliography   291

Notes on the Contributors   299

Index   301

Foreword

IT IS OUR HOPE as editors that this Companion volume will serve not merely as another reminder that Alfred Döblin was an important modernist writer, but rather that it will provoke curiosity and provide insight into the many aspects of his work and life. Perhaps more than his contemporaries Thomas and Heinrich Mann, Hugo von Hofmannsthal, and Franz Kafka, Döblin grappled with the idea of becoming modern, exploring it in both his fictional and his theoretical and essayistic writings. And, more than Gottfried Benn, the other prominent contemporary physician/poet, Döblin actively participated in the medical, psychiatric, and psychoanalytical debates of the time. The reasons for his eclipse as a writer and a politically active intellectual are manifold. In part, they are attributable to the stylistic and thematic complexities of his writings and his often contradictory and extreme positions; in part, however, the reasons lie in the times. The collapse of the Weimar Republic, the burning of his books and the years of exile in Switzerland, Paris, and California, as well as a vain attempt to reestablish himself in postwar Germany disrupted a literary career that had finally achieved success in 1929 with the publication of his best-known novel, *Berlin Alexanderplatz*. The conjunction of Döblin's creative impulse and the turbulent and disastrous history of the first half of the twentieth century establish the terms necessary for understanding this complex figure.

The essays in this volume were selected to give a representative overview of Döblin's oeuvre — admittedly a formidable task, given this author's wide-ranging concerns. Written by established Döblin scholars from Germany and the United States, they address major themes, problems, and questions. The essays are not intended to provide a unified viewpoint. Rather, they put forth the diverse perspectives and approaches of our contributors. The editors believe that these multiple points of view will enhance a continuing discussion.

Our thanks go first to our contributors, for their good work and their patience and cooperation during the editing process. We also would like to thank the translators, Kurt A. Beals, Detlev Koepke, Lee Stavenhagen, and Brian Tucker. They acquitted themselves very well of the often difficult task of rendering academic German into English. We are, of course, much indebted to our editors at Camden House. Jim Hardin provided prompt and expert guidance and timely encouragement during the preparation of the manuscript. We also gratefully acknowledge Jim Walker, whose superb copy-editing skills put the finishing touches on this volume. We acknowledge with thanks the work of Jacob Teter, a student of German Studies at Oberlin College, for his help in compiling the bibliography. Finally, we thank Sarah Lawrence College and Oberlin College for their financial support of this project.

The select bibliography features the primary works by Alfred Döblin, their first English translations, and the seminal critical studies that have appeared since the 1970s. Although the secondary literature on this author nowhere approaches the volume of that on Kafka or Thomas Mann, it has nevertheless become too large for inclusion in this volume. Moreover, each article contains a list of Works Cited.

Works by Alfred Döblin are not listed in the Works Cited, but appear as abbreviations followed by the relevant page number or numbers. For the convenience of the reader, we present a list of abbreviations and their titles in alphabetical order together with their English translations following the foreword. There is one exception, however: the Works Cited list for Veronika Fuechtner's article includes medical texts by Döblin that are either unpublished or appeared in medical and psychiatric journals, or as newspaper articles.

Abbreviations and Translations of Titles

	Amazonas (The Amazon)
LoT	*Das Land ohne Tod*
DbT	*Der blaue Tiger*
DnU	*Der neue Urwald*
ASLA	*Autobiographische Schriften und letzte Aufzeichnungen* (Autobiographical Writings)
AzL	*Aufsätze zur Literatur* (Essays on Literature)
BA	*Berlin Alexanderplatz. Die Geschichte vom Franz Biberkopf* (Alexanderplatz, Berlin: The Story of Franz Biberkopf)
BAD	*Berlin Alexanderplatz, Drehbuch* (Berlin Alexanderplatz, Screenplay)
BF	*Die beiden Freundinnen und ihr Giftmord* (The Two Friends and Their Murder by Poison)
BMG	*Berge Meere und Giganten* (Mountains, Seas, and Giants)
B I	*Briefe* (Letters)
B II	*Briefe* II (Letters II)
BW	*Babylonische Wanderung oder Hochmut kommt vor dem Fall* (Babylonian Journey, or Pride Goeth Before the Fall)
DHF	*Drama, Hörspiel, Film* (Drama, Radio, Film)
DMB	*Der deutsche Maskenball* (The German Masked Ball)
EB	*Die Ermordung einer Butterblume. Sämtliche Erzählungen* (Murder of a Buttercup: Complete Stories)
G	*Giganten. Ein Abenteuerbuch* (Giants: An Adventure Saga)
H	*Hamlet oder Die lange Nacht nimmt ein Ende* (Hamlet: Tales of a Long Night)
IN	*Das Ich über der Natur* (Self Over Nature)

JR	*Jagende Rosse, Der schwarze Vorhang und andere frühe Erzählwerke* (Galloping Horses, The Black Curtain, and Other Early Stories)
KdZ	*Kritik der Zeit. Rundfunkbeiträge 1946–1952* (Contemporary Critique: Radio Addresses 1946–1952)
KE	*Der Kampf mit dem Engel* (The Battle with the Angel)
KS-1	*Kleine Schriften 1*: 1902–1921 (Short Writings 1: 1902–1921)
KS-2	*Kleine Schriften 2*: 1922–1924 (Short Writings 2: 1922–1924)
KS-3	*Kleine Schriften 3*: 1925–1933 (Short Writings 3: 1925–1933)
M	*Manas* (Manas)
	November 1918. Eine deutsche Revolution (November 1918: A German Revolution)
N-I	*Bürger und Soldaten 1918*
N-II/1	*Verratenes Volk*
N-II/2	*Heimkehr der Fronttruppen*
N-III	*Karl und Rosa*
OD	*Der Oberst und der Dichter oder Das menschliche Herz* (The Colonel and the Poet, or the Human Heart)
PAe	*Die Pilgerin Aetheria* (Atheria the Pilgrim)
PW	*Pardon wird nicht gegeben* (Men without Mercy)
RP	*Reise in Polen* (Journey to Poland)
SÄPL	*Schriften zu Ästhetik, Poetik und Literatur* (Writings on Aesthetics, Poetics and Literature)
SR	*Schicksalsreise* (Destiny's Journey)
SjF	*Schriften zu jüdischen Fragen* (Writings on the Jewish Question)
SLW	*Schriften zu Leben und Werk* (Writings on Life and Work)
SPG	*Schriften zur Politik und Gesellschaft* (Writings on Politics and Society)
UD	*Unser Dasein* (Our Existence)
UM	*Der unsterbliche Mensch* (Immortal Man)

W		*Wallenstein* (Wallenstein)
WK		*Wadzeks Kampf mit der Dampfturbine* (Wadzek's Battle with the Steam Turbine)
WL		*Die drei Sprünge des Wang-lun* (The Three Leaps of Wang-lun: A Chinese Novel)
WuV		*Wissen und Verändern!* (To Know and to Change!)

Works by Alfred Döblin

(Includes only works published during Döblin's lifetime. When available in English translation, title and date of first publication are given.)

1905   *Gedächtnisstörungen bei der Korsakoffschen Psychose. Inaugural-Dissertation zur Erlangung der medizinischen Doktorwürde.* Berlin: Otto & Emil Klett (doctoral dissertation)

1906   *Lydia und Mäxchen. Tiefe Verbeugung in einem Akt.* Strassburg & Leipzig: Joseph Singer (one-act play)

1908   "Das Stiftsfräulein und der Tod." *Das Magazin* 77: 5–25 (novella)

1910   "Gespräche mit Kalypso. Über die Musik." *Der Sturm* 1 (Hefte 5–17 and 19–23): 34 (1. Gespräch); 42 (2. Gespräch); 50–51 (3. Gespräch); 57–59 (4. Gespräch); 67–69, 76 (5. Gespräch); 83–84, 92–93 (6. Gespräch); 100–101, 108–9, 118–19, 125–26, 134–35 (7. Gespräch); 150, 57–58, 166–67, 173 (8. Gespräch); 182 (10. und letztes Gespräch) (essays on aesthetics)

"Die Tänzerin und der Leib." *Der Sturm* 1 (2): 10 ("The Dancer and the Body," 1972) (novella)

"Die Ermordung einer Butterblume." *Der Sturm* 1 (28): 20–21 and (29): 229 (novella)

"Astralia." *Der Sturm* 1 (31): 244–45 (novella)

"Die falsche Tür," *Der Sturm* 1 (54): 429–30 (novella)

1911   "Die Helferin." *Der Sturm* 2 (62): 493–94 (novella)

"Die Segelfahrt." *Der Sturm* 2 (69): 549–50 (novella)

"Die Verwandlung." *Der Sturm* 2 (73): 581–83 (novella)

"Der Dritte." *Der Sturm* 2 (77): 613–14 and (78): 621–22 (novella)

"Der Ritter Blaubart." *Der Sturm* 2 (85): 676–77 and (86): 683–85 (novella)

"Mariä Empfängnis." *Der Sturm* 2 (88): 700 (novella)

1913 *Die Ermordung einer Butterblume und andere Erzählungen.* Munich and Leipzig: Georg Müller. ("Die Segelfahrt"; "Die Tänzerin und der Leib"; "Astralia"; "Mariä Empfängnis"; "Die Verwandlung"; "Die Helferin"; "Die falsche Tür"; "Die Ermordung einer Butterblume"; "Der Ritter Blaubart"; "Der Dritte"; "Die Memoiren des Blasierten"; "Das Stiftsfräulein und der Tod") (novella collection)

1915 *Die drei Sprünge des Wang-lun, Chinesischer Roman.* Berlin: S. Fischer. (*The Three Leaps of Wang Lun: A Chinese Novel*, 1991) (novel)

1917 *Die Lobensteiner reisen nach Böhmen. Zwölf Novellen und Geschichten.* Munich: Georg Müller (novellas and stories)

1918 *Wadzeks Kampf mit der Dampfturbine.* Berlin: S. Fischer (novel)

1919 *Der schwarze Vorhang. Roman von den Worten und Zufällen.* Berlin: S. Fischer (novel)

1920 *Wallenstein.* Berlin: S. Fischer (novel)

Lusitania. Drei Szenen. In *Die Gefährten* 3 (4): 29–59 (play)

1921 *Der deutsche Maskenball. Von Linke Poot. Zeitglossen.* Berlin: S. Fischer (collection of political articles)

1923 *Die Nonnen von Kemnade. Schauspiel in vier Akten.* Berlin: S. Fischer (play)

1924 *Berge Meere und Giganten.* Berlin: S. Fischer (novel)

Die beiden Freundinnen und ihr Giftmord. Ein Prozeß. Berlin: Die Schmiede (narrative)

1926 *Reise in Polen.* Berlin: S. Fischer (*Journey to Poland*, 1991) (travel report)

1927 *Manas. Epische Dichtung.* Berlin: S. Fischer (epos)

Das Ich über der Natur. Berlin: S. Fischer (philosophical essay)

1928 *Alfred Döblin. Im Buch — zu Haus — auf der Straße.* Berlin: S. Fischer (autobiographical work, together with Oskar Loerke)

1929	*Berlin Alexanderplatz. Die Geschichte vom Franz Biberkopf.* Berlin: Fischer (*Alexanderplatz, Berlin; The Story of Franz Biberkopf,* 1931) (novel)
1931	*Wissen und Verändern! Offene Briefe an einen jungen Menschen.* Berlin: S. Fischer (political letters)
1931	*Die Ehe. Drei Szenen und ein Vorspiel.* Berlin: S. Fischer (play)
1932	*Giganten. Ein Abenteuerbuch.* Berlin: S. Fischer (novel)
1933	*Jüdische Erneuerung.* Amsterdam: Querido (essays on the Jewish question)
	Unser Dasein. Berlin: S. Fischer (philosophical work)
1934	*Babylonische Wandrung oder Hochmut kommt vor dem Fall.* Amsterdam: Querido (novel)
1935	*Pardon wird nicht gegeben.* Amsterdam: Querido (*Men Without Mercy,* 1976) (novel)
	Flucht und Sammlung des Judenvolkes. Aufsätze und Erzählungen. Amsterdam: Querido (essays and stories on the Jewish question)
1937	*Die Fahrt ins Land ohne Tod.* Amsterdam: Querido (novel)
1938	*Der blaue Tiger.* Amsterdam: Querido (novel)
	Die deutsche Literatur (im Ausland seit 1933). Paris: Science et Littérature (literary essay)
1939	*Eine deutsche Revolution. Erzählwerk in drei Bänden.* Band 1: *Bürger und Soldaten 1918.* Stockholm: Bermann-Fischer and Amsterdam: Querido (novel, vol. 1 of *November 1918*)
1946	*Sieger und Besiegte. Eine wahre Geschichte.* New York: Aurora (novel, selections from vols. 1 and 2 of *November 1918*)
	Der unsterbliche Mensch. Ein Religionsgespräch. Freiburg i.Br.: K. Alber (religious work)
	Der Oberst und der Dichter oder Das menschliche Herz. Freiburg i. Br.: K. Alber (religious work)
1947–48	*Das Land ohne Tod. Südamerika-Roman: 1. Das Land ohne Tod, 2. Der blaue Tiger, 3. Der neue Urwald.* Baden-Baden: Keppler (novel, earlier incomplete version of *Amazonas Trilogie*)

1948–50   *November 1918. Eine deutsche Revolution. Erzählwerk.* Munich: K. Alber *Vorspiel und Band 1. Verratenes Volk. Band 2. Heimkehr der Fronttruppen. Band 3. Karl und Rosa. Eine Geschichte zwischen Himmel und Hölle* (*November 1918: A German Revolution,* 2 volumes: *Karl and Rosa; A People Betrayed,* 1983) (novel)

1950   *Schicksalreise. Bericht und Bekenntnis.* Frankfurt am Main: Joseph Knecht (*Destiny's Journey,* 1992) (autobiographical work)

1956   *Hamlet oder Die lange Nacht nimmt ein Ende.* Berlin (East): Rütten & Loening, 1956; Berlin (West): Langen-Müller, 1957 (*Tales of a Long Night; a novel,* 1984) (novel)

Introduction

Roland Dollinger, Wulf Koepke, Heidi Thomann Tewarson

Biographical Overview

ALFRED DÖBLIN (1878–1957) belongs to a generation of German prose writers of extraordinary distinction. The best known among his contemporaries are Heinrich and Thomas Mann, Franz Kafka, Robert Musil, Hermann Broch, Franz Werfel, Erich Maria Remarque, Lion Feuchtwanger, Joseph Roth, Ernst Jünger, Hans Fallada, and Hermann Kesten; not to mention playwrights like Bertolt Brecht, Ernst Toller, Carl Zuckmayer, and Georg Kaiser; and poets like Rainer Maria Rilke, Stefan George, Georg Trakl, Georg Heym, Else Lasker-Schüler, and Gottfried Benn. In this field of enormous literary creativity, Döblin must be regarded as one of the most innovative writers of epic prose. His best-known novel *Berlin Alexanderplatz* was compared with James Joyce's *Ulysses* (written 1914–21) and John Dos Passos's *Manhattan Transfer* (1925). Döblin's oeuvre is by no means limited to novels, but in this genre, he offered a surprising variety of narrative techniques, themes, structures, and outlooks from his first-published "Chinese" novel *Die drei Sprünge des Wang-lun* (1915–16) to his last "Novellenroman" *Hamlet oder Die lange Nacht nimmt ein Ende* (1956). During the intervening fifty years, he published *Wallenstein* (1920), a monumental panorama of the Thirty Years' War; *Berge Meere und Giganten* (1924), a grim view of the future of humankind; *Berlin Alexanderplatz* (1929), his famous big-city epic; *Amazonas* (1937–38), a critique of European colonial imperialism; and *November 1918* (written between 1937 and 1943, but first published in 1948–50), a narrative reflection on the failed revolution in Germany after the First World War and the precedents of Nazism — to name but the most important titles of his multi-faceted work. Although the collected works are now available in over thirty volumes, coming close to a comprehensive edition of all of Döblin's writings, they are still modestly called *Ausgewählte Werke in Einzelbänden*.

Döblin became one of the most prominent figures on the literary scene in Berlin during the Weimar Republic. His productivity was surprising, considering that until 1933 his main occupation remained his medical practice in Berlin. Döblin the writer, whose imagination roamed the world and history, and Döblin the physician, who saw the world with the eyes of a scientific and clinical observer, cannot and should not be separated.

At the same time, Döblin was always troubled by the religious, social, and political implications of his insecure position as a German Jew. Although he felt no affinity to traditional Judaism, he felt a close bond with his Jewish brethren. This feeling of affinity manifested itself in the early 1920s, when, in response to pogrom-like attacks in the Scheunenviertel of Berlin, where the majority of newly arrived Eastern European Jews were concentrated, he traveled to Poland in search of traditional Jewish life. After 1933, he became involved in the "Territorialist" movement, when Jewish emigration turned into an existential question as a result of Hitler's rise to power. However, early on, he realized that he could not find his way back to the God of his forefathers, and in 1941, in Los Angeles, after long years of reading and searching, Döblin, together with his wife and youngest son, converted to Catholicism.

Döblin's political involvement began after his return from the First World War, during which he enlisted as a physician in the German army and served in military hospitals in Alsace-Lorraine. The senseless violence of the war and the physical and psychological suffering of the soldiers moved him deeply. After 1918 his sympathies were leftist and socialist, but he remained aloof from political parties. His later stance can be more accurately described as "anarchist," a position of solidarity with the suffering masses and hostility toward the dictatorial rule of political parties in the name of class warfare. Döblin expressed his plea for overcoming class divisions and achieving social harmony most eloquently in his "open letters to a student" *Wissen und Verändern!* in 1931. His subsequent Christian faith included a strong social commitment and defense of human rights.

There are several events in Döblin's life that marked his destiny. The first was that his father abandoned his family, a wife and five children, and that his mother Sophie, moving to a proletarian district of Berlin, had to survive on handouts from her brothers and her own hard work. When Döblin's own marriage came to a crisis after he met the photographer Yolla Niclas in 1921, he decided not to leave his wife and four sons, mindful of his own childhood. Döblin's school years left hardly any memories except bad ones, and strengthened his life-long opposition against harsh discipline and regimentation. Döblin's forced exile in 1933 after Hitler's ascent to power deprived the writer of his roots and his specific Berlin idiom so masterfully displayed in *Berlin Alexanderplatz*, not to speak of his readers. Although he wrote significant works after 1933, the exile years were a time of loss and isolation, especially so in Los Angeles, 1940–45.

Finally, Döblin's return to Germany in 1945 proved to be a failure, a non-return. He had become a fervent Catholic Christian when his readers expected to find the independent socialist of the 1930s. Like other returning exiles, Döblin experienced a wall of resistance and silence among Germans. This was particularly hurtful to him, as he was among the few who returned early, eager to help in the difficult task of overcoming the catastrophic legacy of Nazism. Eventually, in 1953, Döblin left Germany again. Ironically, his last novel *Hamlet*, published in 1956 after long delays, found a lively reception and, in retrospect, can be considered as the beginning of Döblin's "comeback."

The Basic Paradox

From the outset, the reception of Döblin's works was beset by a strange paradox: he was immediately hailed as an important talent, a genius, an innovative writer, and yet he has remained largely unknown. A number of his books were acclaimed as great literature, but only one novel, *Berlin Alexanderplatz*, has become part of the canon of twentieth-century German literature. It is the only title known to booksellers, book buyers, and borrowers in libraries. While it may not surprise us to learn that Döblin's other texts appeal to relatively few readers and therefore never achieved great popularity, considering their complexities and their demanding style, it is puzzling that scholarly attention, though increasing, lags far behind that paid to the works of Kafka, Thomas Mann, Rilke, and Brecht. Döblin's influence on other writers, both his contemporaries and those who followed, has been insufficiently examined. It is not very helpful to keep quoting Günter Grass as the shining example of a writer who has publicly acknowledged his debt to his "teacher" Döblin.[1] Postwar authors such as Wolfgang Koeppen, Arno Schmidt, and most recently W. G. Sebald (1944–2001), should be considered as well. Sebald, a Döblin scholar in his own right and one of Döblin's harshest critics, was not free of his influence. His writings bear traces of Döblin, even as he was pursuing quite different goals, both thematically and aesthetically. Furthermore, translating Döblin's work has proven to be extremely difficult, owing to his idiomatic language full of allusions and quotations. Even *Berlin Alexanderplatz* did not fare well in other idioms.[2] Döblin may be a writer of international stature; however, the reception of his works was and continues to be essentially limited to a German readership. The great European writer Alfred Döblin is hidden from a large potential audience by his own vernacular.

It is hazardous to speculate on how his German readers perceived his works. Döblin was the witness and victim of radical changes in German society. Those who read his works before 1914 underwent a radical change during and after the First World War. Similarly, the readers who reacquainted themselves with Döblin and his works after 1945 were very different from those who read *Berlin Alexanderplatz* before 1933. Furthermore, before 1933, the writer Alfred Döblin had a commanding presence on the literary scene and was a household name even among those who read his texts only in newspapers and magazines. After 1945, he was a stranger in his homeland, and the publishers treated him as a difficult and forgotten author whose books gathered dust in the warehouses.

After Döblin's death in 1957, appreciation for his rank and significance began to rise, primarily among scholars. In 1978, his hundredth birthday was celebrated with significant editions and publications and the much publicized and successful exhibition in the Deutsches Literaturarchiv, Marbach. Since then, Döblin's works have been available on the book market, a number of them in paperbacks, and he has enjoyed the attention of the academic community. This is due in good part also to Rainer Werner Fassbinder's famous television series of 1979, *Berlin Alexanderplatz.*

Considering the intertwinement of German history and the reception of Döblin's works, it is best to follow their reception chronologically. Most of the information on the reception history is contained in dissertations on specific texts by Döblin and in the "Nachworte" to the volumes of the general edition of his works, *Ausgewählte Werke in Einzelbänden*. Studies of Döblin's standing among his contemporaries, his literary relationships, his impact on other authors as well as on the reading public are urgently needed.[3] While the Döblin-Brecht connection has attracted some attention,[4] little has been written so far on the complex relationship between Thomas Mann und Döblin.

The Avant-Garde before 1914

Although Döblin began writing at an early age, he did not publish his first story until he was thirty, and his first novel did not appear until the age of thirty-seven. He was never a "young" writer. Before his exile in 1933, Döblin did not consider writing his primary occupation, which is surprising considering the size of his literary production. After he abandoned medical research in 1911, he had to devote most of his time to his medical practice.

The first collection of stories, *Die Ermordung einer Butterblume*, was published in 1913. The stories, written between 1904 and 1912, had previously been featured in the magazine *Der Sturm*. As a result Döblin became identified with the avant-garde Expressionism of the *Sturm* circle around Herwarth Walden (1878–1941). Kurt Pinthus (1886–1975) in his review of 1913 saw in these stories the transition from Impressionism to Expressionism. While the echo of this publication was limited, the critics hailed Döblin as a new voice with considerable talent. In spite of a limited reception, Georg Müller of Munich agreed to publish a later collection of novellas, *Die Lobensteiner reisen nach Böhmen*, in 1917. But he waited to distribute the books until the success of Döblin's Chinese novel made his name better known.

Die drei Sprünge des Wang-lun was Döblin's first book published by Samuel Fischer in Berlin, and with it began a long, albeit stormy, relationship between author and publisher that was cut short in 1933. Fischer was one of the major publishers of contemporary literature; he worked hard to establish permanent connections with his authors, among them Thomas Mann (1875–1955), Gerhart Hauptmann (1862–1946), and Hermann Hesse (1877–1962). After an auspicious beginning, when Döblin worked for a short time as the editor of the house organ *Neue Rundschau*, the relationship was punctuated by frequent quarrels. Moreover, most of the books that Döblin wrote after *Wang-lun* did not sell well. Only the big novels *Wallenstein* and *Berge Meere und Giganten* went beyond the original print run. Döblin could never rely on the income from his books except for the short period between the publication of *Berlin Alexanderplatz* and his emigration in 1933. To support his large family, he supplemented the income from his medical practice by writing for various newspapers and magazines. At the time of the publication of *Berlin Alexanderplatz*, the relationship with Samuel Fischer had reached a low point, so that Fischer was ready to rescind the contract. Fortunately, *Berlin Alexanderplatz* turned out to be a big success; it sold more copies during the first weeks than all other books by Döblin combined.

Die drei Sprünge des Wang-lun had been finished in 1913, but was rejected by several publishers before Fischer accepted it. The novel, however, continued to be beset with problems, such as production slowdowns and paper shortages. The book was finally ready in 1915 but not distributed until the spring of 1916. Döblin, who was serving as a physician at the Alsatian front, did not expect much of an echo. To his surprise, however, *Wang-lun* met with a positive response and became his most successful work before *Berlin Alexanderplatz*. *Wang-lun,* moreover, was one of the first texts reissued after 1945. It was promoted by a German book club and issued as one of the first volumes of *Ausgewählte Werke* in 1960, as well as in a paperback edition by the Deutsche Taschenbuch Verlag in 1970. Therefore, the question as to the special appeal of this book arises.

Several factors come together: the fascination with China was particularly strong at the time of its publication, both politically and culturally. Another factor was Döblin's fascinating depiction of mass behavior. Crowd psychology was topical. Crowds were described by writers, shown by artists in their paintings and in advertising, and studied by psychologists. Gustave Le Bon's (1841–1931) *La psychologie des foules* (1895) appeared in a German translation in 1908. In 1915, crowd behavior was new and exciting territory for literature and the arts. Yet more than anything else, it was and still is the idea of *Wu-wei,* of non-violent resistance, that made *Wang-lun* fascinating. Döblin's depiction of the *Wu-wei* movement in eighteenth-century China and his focus on internal problems and contradictions within the movement had a special appeal for contemporary readers. He provided insight into the difficulties surrounding non-violent resistance. This proved intriguing for several generations of readers.[5] For the early critics, *Wang-lun* offered something else as well. They saw it as a new and different kind of novel. Some called it "cubist" and considered it the literary equivalent of modern painting. For others, it was the fulfillment of the Expressionist promise. The general agreement was that this was the most significant novel to be published for quite some time, worthy, according to Ludwig Rubiner's 1917 review in *Zeit-Echo* of being ranked as "world literature" (Schuster/Bode, 38). Yet there were also others who considered it too chaotic, lacking in structure and beauty, a mass of highly interesting material, but without form and meaning. During the turbulent war years, books were read as guides or signposts to a future and better life. Döblin seemed to promise such guidance, but the message was not clear. According to these critics, *Wang-lun* was a disturbing book and of little help for the present (Schuster/Bode, 17–48).

The Early Weimar Years

Following the positive reaction to *Wang-lun* on the part of both the readers and the critics, expectations for subsequent works by Döblin were high. The next novel, however, *Wadzeks Kampf mit der Dampftur-*

bine (1918) was a great disappointment. Similarly, few critics or readers warmed up to the early novel *Der schwarze Vorhang* when Fischer published it in 1919, sixteen years after its completion. Among the few who reacted positively to *Wadzek* were Döblin's fellow writer Oskar Maria Graf (1894–1967), who liked its grotesque humor (Schuster/Bode, 53–54), and Bertolt Brecht, who praised its anti-tragic stance.[6] Döblin "rehabilitated" himself in 1920 with *Wallenstein*, the two-volume novel on the Thirty Years' War, a feat for which he was hailed by Lion Feuchtwanger (1883–1957) in *Die Weltbühne* as "der Homer des Dreißigjährigen Krieges" (Schuster/Bode, 95). Its title, *Wallenstein*, was misleading, for this book was an epic against war, as the critics soon realized. Educated German readers were of course familiar with Friedrich Schiller's trilogy *Wallenstein* (1800), in which Wallenstein appears as a great man and a true tragic hero. They could not help making comparisons, both favorable and unfavorable. Another work fresh on the minds of critics and readers was the historical panorama *Der große Krieg in Deutschland* by Ricarda Huch (1864–1947) (The Great War in Germany, 1912–14). From the beginning, however, *Wallenstein* raised an issue that has stayed with and nagged the reception of Döblin's work ever since: the detailed depiction of a large number of scenes of extreme and barbaric violence. It is true that the war of 1618–48 was known as the most savage conflict in German history prior to the twentieth century. But were these scenes really needed, or did the author relish in such sadistic descriptions? Did he take pleasure in these horrors, or was he appalled, intending them as shock therapy for readers, who had been desensitized by the cruelties of the First World War? To some contemporary readers *Wallenstein* was a pacifist novel. They recognized without difficulty the parallels between the seventeenth century and the present. In general, however, the genre of the historical novel in Germany was to a large extent still determined by the nationalist models of Gustav Freytag's (1816–95) *Die Ahnen* (The Heirs, 1872–78) and Felix Dahn's (1834–1912) *Ein Kampf um Rom* (A Struggle for Rome, 1876–78). Döblin offered something radically different, a critical and not a monumental history, an anti-war novel aimed at the flood of heroic battle accounts and definitely not a nationalistic tribute to German history. The praise for the author's achievement, comparing *Wallenstein* to Tolstoy's *War and Peace* (1864–69), was mixed with reservations over his mannerisms and style. The text was a massive onslaught on the reader, and Lion Feuchtwanger was only one of many critics who wondered if the reading public was ready for this. Ready or not, *Wallenstein* sold reasonably well, and enjoyed a solid reputation as a masterwork. It was noted by most critics that while there was no real individual protagonist in this novel, the central character was not Wallenstein, but Emperor Ferdinand II, whose death is given a mystical religious dimension. Both the character of the emperor and his death are radically different in Döblin's portrayal from the way other writers and historians have seen them. Wallenstein, on the other hand, is characterized by Döblin as anything but a war hero, but rather as a ruthless capitalistic entrepreneur, a fact that irked all nationalist critics, especially in 1920 (Schuster/Bode, 81–112). In light of this demystifying manner of writing German history, it is curious that in 1933, when all of Döblin's books were burned, *Wallenstein* was exempted. The Nazi decision makers cannot have possibly read the text. After 1945, Döblin himself prevented the republication of *Wallenstein*.

When Döblin returned from the Alsace to Berlin in November 1918, he experienced first hand the armistice, the "revolution," and the chaotic events during the early years of the Weimar Republic. He reopened his medical practice and became a keen observer, albeit a skeptical and often disoriented one, of the political and social dynamics in Berlin. He took an active part in the political debates, publishing articles and commentaries, which appeared mostly in *Die Neue Rundschau*, under the pseudonym of "Linke Poot" (left paw). He felt closest to the left wing of the Social Democratic Party, which for some years was a separate party, the USPD or Independent Socialist Democratic Party; unable to resist the pressure from both the newly formed Communist Party on the left and the more conservative majority Social Democrats on the right, it dissolved in 1921. Döblin was highly critical of the Social Democratic governments and the many undesirable social phenomena of corruption and criminality associated with this transition period. The tone and content of the "Linke Poot" glosses are mostly sarcastic, if not bitter. He published them as a collection in 1921 under the title *Der deutsche Maskenball*. Döblin's articles were widely read, although this was a time with many loud voices. When they appeared in book form, they were much criticized and much appreciated. Kurt Tucholsky (1890–1935), writing as "Ignaz Wrobel" in *Die Weltbühne* (Schuster Bode, 116–17), praised them as witty and leftist. All reviewers noted that this leftist commentator was fiercely independent, and that he was also a real Berliner, witty, sharp, and with a lot of sober common sense (Schuster/Bode, 114–17).

Döblin was not a playwright with theatrical talents by inclination, but he wrote a number of formally and thematically interesting plays. None of them was ever a great hit or became part of the repertory, but they were performed and aroused some scandals. *Lusitania* (1919), a play about the fateful sinking of the passenger ship "Lusitania" during the First World War by a German submarine, was performed in Darmstadt in 1926, causing a political scandal, as Nazi protesters wanted to stop the performance, while the majority of the audience resisted. However, the reviewers agreed that it was not a "drama" and did not belong on the stage. It is, indeed, much more suitable as a radio play. *Die Nonnen von Kemnade*, performed in Leipzig in 1923, fared somewhat better. The reviews of the play ranged from enthusiastic praise to total rejection. But the critics and the audience both praised the performance as excellent. Döblin's most topical and substantial play was *Die Ehe* (1930). Modeled on Brecht's epic theater, it was for social and political reasons very controversial. The fact that it was by the author of *Berlin Alexanderplatz* contributed to its notoriety.

In the early 1920s, Döblin became increasingly prominent in the literary circles of Berlin. He continued to write articles and reviews. He gave public readings of his works, and he became active in the Schutzverband deutscher Schriftsteller (SDS), the "Protective Association of German Writers." He was elected its president in 1924. During the years of the galloping inflation Döblin supplemented his income by writing theater reviews and feuilletons for the *Prager Tagblatt*. The "Golden Age" of the Berlin theater looked less than extraordinary to him. Only rarely was he moved to genuine praise.

In the early twenties, when pogrom-like attacks were perpetrated against the Eastern European Jewish immigrants, who lived primarily in Berlin's "Scheunenviertel," Döblin also became involved in Jewish concerns. In 1924 he traveled to Poland to acquaint himself with the Eastern European Jewish communities there, the "Ostjuden." He published his account *Reise in Polen* in 1925 to mostly positive reviews. Criticism came from two sides: the anti-Polish Germans who considered Döblin's sympathy for Jews and Poles unpatriotic, and the Zionists and orthodox Jews who felt that he did not understand "real" Judaism. Döblin was never comfortable with either the champions of traditional Judaism or of Zionism.

Not surprisingly, Döblin was enthusiastic about the new medium of radio, and was one of the first to contribute to radio programs. His first broadcast was on 15 November 1925, very shortly after radio programs were established in Berlin. In 1925 he became part of the "Group 1925," an informal gathering of leftist and communist writers, where he became closely acquainted with Bertolt Brecht. Finally, in 1928, Döblin was elected a member of the Section for Literature of the Prussian Academy of the Fine

Arts. Now a prominent author, Döblin's fiftieth birthday in 1928 was a public event. He himself contributed his first autobiographical account, *Alfred Döblin: Im Buch — Zu Hause — Auf der Straße*, published by Samuel Fischer.

All of these activities ensured that Döblin's name remained well known, and that his novels were reviewed in the major organs, although he was often surrounded by controversy. His reviewers were left bewildered when he published *Berge Meere und Giganten* in 1924, a long, epic work about the future of humankind, a dystopia rather than a utopia, not as much a work of science fiction proper as a writer's fearful fantasy about the destructive tendencies of modern scientific thinking and technology. Fritz Lang's (1890–1976) film *Metropolis* (1926) is a modest fantasy compared to Döblin's visions of the future of civilization. Since 1945, the novel has found more detractors than enthusiasts, but in the twenties, it aroused much attention (Schuster/Bode, 129–50; Sander, 7–69). Döblin considered the plot attractive enough to fashion an abbreviated and simplified version, *Giganten* (1932), but it did not find the hoped-for popular appeal.

Popular Success at Last

Before Döblin scored his one great popular success with *Berlin Alexanderplatz* in 1929, he baffled his readers once more with the verse epic *Manas* (1927). Robert Musil (1880–1942), in the *Berliner Tageblatt* of 10 June 1927, devoted a long and enthusiastic review to this tale drawn from Indian mythology (Schuster/Bode, 187–92). Several other critics, such as Axel Eggebrecht (Schuster/Bode, 178–79), agreed with him, but there were dissonant voices that saw the epic as irrelevant due to its arcane subject matter; they also criticized the style and form of the verse and bemoaned the artificiality of the text. Even academic interest has remained sporadic at best.[7]

Although the great success of *Berlin* Alexanderplatz was perhaps based on a "misunderstanding," as the novel was widely considered a story about the Berlin underworld, the text has found enduring attention among very diverse groups of readers. Inevitably, the politically charged environment of Berlin in the late 1920s gave rise to controversies. For one, there were those who accused Döblin of having copied or plagiarized the techniques of James Joyce's *Ulysses*, the German translation of which appeared in 1925. Döblin himself had reviewed it enthusiastically. When the accusations did not stop, he finally declared that he did not need Joyce to develop his own style and technique. Another reproach centered on the question of linguistic authenticity: how representative of the proletarian Berlin milieu was the language? While most were impressed precisely by what they considered an authentic linguistic representation, there were others, such as the critic Emmanuel Bin Gorion who called it a total fake (Schuster/Bode, 258–64).

The most strident criticism came from the communists. Leftist and communist writers had founded the Bund Proletarisch-Revolutionärer Schriftsteller (BPRS), the Alliance of Proletarian-Revolutionary Writers, and its organ *Die Linkskurve* (Left Curve) attacked the novel in several subsequent articles. One of the critics was Johannes R. Becher (1891–1958), who had been a friend of Döblin and a member of the Gruppe 1925. The main thrust was that the main character Franz Biberkopf was anything but a class-conscious member of the working class, but rather a representative of the "Lumpenproletariat," the jobless and aimless proletarians, and that there was no mention of the crucial role of the German Communist Party or KPD in the district around the Alexanderplatz, where most of the novel's action takes place. Furthermore, the modernist techniques of the novel were nothing but bourgeois aestheticism. This could not possibly be a model for proletarian and revolutionary writing; it was literature of the petty bourgeoisie at its worst.

There were acute political reasons for the aggressive tone of these polemics. The BPRS tried hard to differentiate true proletarian writing from that of the bourgeois fellow travelers. The KPD led a campaign to encourage workers to write up their experiences and create a true "Arbeiterdichtung" (an effort that would be repeated in East Germany in the late 1950s). The goal was a literature by the working class, instead of the earlier "Arbeiterdichtung," written by members of the bourgeoisie who belonged to the German Social Democratic Party or were entirely apolitical. Neither the character of Franz Biberkopf nor the novel as a whole fit any of BPRS's categories. The broad appeal of the book was seen as a danger to the new proletarian writers. The polemics against *Berlin Alexanderplatz* were essentially a prelude to the "Expressionismusstreit," the controversy about avant-garde Expressionist writing, that arose among exile writers in the later 1930s. The German communists accepted Döblin's writings when they deemed his texts useful in their attempts to form "popular front" alliances, but rejected them when they wanted to draw a line between themselves and potential "fellow travelers."

Apart from such polemics, *Berlin Alexanderplatz* generated a wide array of mostly positive criticism. Among these was a review by Walter Benjamin (1892–1940) in *Die Gesellschaft*, which focused both on the montage elements in the depiction of the big city and the stages in the life of Biberkopf (Schuster/Bode, 249–54). The ending was interpreted in different ways: some critics interpreted it positively, as a new beginning for the protagonist, while others saw in it Döblin's characteristic indecisiveness, his lack of political resolve. Besides being a novel about Berlin in the late 1920s, *Berlin Alexanderplatz* is also the story of an unforgettable protagonist, and a book rich in mythical, literary, and political allusions. The popularity of the book prompted Döblin to write a radio play based on it, which was produced but unfortunately never broadcast. In 1931, the first film version of *Berlin Alexanderplatz* was made, with Heinrich George as Biberkopf. Rainer Werner Fassbinder's 1979 television series *Berlin Alexanderplatz* renewed interest in this work and once again underscored the affinity of Döblin's montage style with today's mass media: radio, film, and television. To be sure, Döblin's own characterization of the narrative techniques as "Kinostil" does not reflect a deeper understanding of the new medium of film. While he was open to all technological innovations, Döblin was less interested in the cinema's aesthetic possibilities. For him it remained a mere expression of popular culture.[8]

With his new visibility at a time of increasing economic and political crisis around 1930, Döblin was asked by the student Gustav René Hocke, later a distinguished scholar, for guidance and orientation through the bewildering multitude of political factions and sects. Döblin's answer, in a series of open letters, was published in 1931 under the title of *Wissen und Verändern!* The book provoked a lively discussion, but had few practical results. One of them was a small discussion group that met with Döblin until it had to be disbanded in 1933.[9]

On 29 November, 1930, the Kammerspiele in Munich performed the premiere of Döblin's play *Die Ehe*. The play was also performed in Leipzig and Berlin. The reviewers noted that it was not a play, but rather a "revue," that it showed the influence of Erwin Piscator and Bertolt Brecht, and that it was open propaganda for social change, such as the legalization of abortion. While the performances were praised, the "epic" structure and content were vigorously attacked. One of the most violent attacks on the play was the scathing review by Alfred Kerr (1867–1948) in the *Berliner Tageblatt* of 18 April 1931, ending with a repeated: "Nieder damit. Nieder damit. Nieder damit" (Schuster/Bode, 313–15; the spectrum of voices 305–25). It is noteworthy that in the scandal following the premiere in Munich, Thomas Mann vigorously defended Döblin's play and the preservation of freedom of speech (Schuster/Bode, 322).

Döblin the well-known author of *Berlin Alexanderplatz*, of *Die Ehe*, and of *Wissen und Verändern* was often the subject of controversy, but the "other" Döblin, that is, Döblin the philosopher of nature, remained largely unnoticed. In 1927 he published *Das Ich über der Natur,* based on ideas he had explored earlier in articles and essays. Axel Eggebrecht called it "ein Nebenwerk" (Schuster/Bode, 196), while other reviewers saw connections to *Berge Meere und Giganten* and *Manas,* although the book's message was thought to be unclear. Döblin followed with *Unser Dasein,* a much more complete and convincing treatise. But because it came out in 1933, after Döblin had gone into exile, it too remained practically unnoticed. Herbert Marcuse (1898–1979) wrote a short review for the *Zeitschrift für Sozialforschung* in1933 (Schuster/Bode, 326). His verdict came to this: What Döblin wrote is "not wrong," but remains entirely within the private realm, set apart from what today are deemed historically viable possibilities.

Exile in France

Döblin left Berlin hurriedly in February 1933 and, after a short stay in Switzerland, he settled with his family in France, living in and around Paris. The Döblins obtained French citizenship in 1937. Exile meant, among many other things, the loss of his medical practice, so that for the first time in his life, Döblin was now nothing but an author. Moreover, his readership was severely reduced. He was fifty-four years old when he left Germany. Still, he kept on writing. Fortunately, two new publishing houses were established in Amsterdam, Querido and Allert de Lange, so that until 1939, Döblin was able to publish all of his books, mostly with Querido. They were the novels *Babylonische Wandrung oder Hochmut kommt vor dem Fall* (1934), *Pardon wird nicht gegeben* (1935), *Die Fahrt ins Land ohne Tod* (the first part of *Amazonas,* 1937), *Der blaue Tiger* (the second part of *Amazonas,* 1938), and *Bürger und Soldaten 1918* (the first volume of the planned trilogy *November 1918,* 1939). In Paris, Döblin also wrote on the Jewish question in connection with his engagement for the "Territorialist" movement, which searched for a Jewish homeland other than Palestine. *Jüdische Erneuerung* (1933) and *Flucht und Sammlung des Judenvolkes* (1935) contain his views on this controversial subject. Finally, he wrote a number of seminal essays on literature, including *Die deutsche Literatur (im Ausland seit 1933)* (German Literature Abroad, 1938), "Der historische Roman und wir" (We and the Historical Novel, 1936), and "Prometheus und das Primitive" (1938).

As was to be expected, the critical response to these works was minimal, restricted primarily to the journals published by his fellow exile writers. Interestingly, the ideological controversies emanating from the left during the years before 1933 continued in exile. Moreover, the reviews of Döblin's books clearly reveal shifts within the communist party line between 1933 and 1940. His defenders and champions now came from the liberal left, and were represented by Hermann Kesten (1900–1996) and Ludwig Marcuse (1894–1971).[10] At the same time, none of Döblin's works written at that time, with the possible exception of *Pardon wird nicht gegeben,* reached a broader audience. *Pardon wird nicht gegeben* was translated into English, Italian, and Russian, his only book besides *Berlin Alexanderplatz* to appear in several languages. However, neither of these two novels succeeded on the crucial English-language market. Therefore, while Döblin profited from his reputation and standing during his time in France, he had few prospects as a writer once he reached the United States, after fleeing once again from the advancing German army in 1940. In 1938, he enjoyed for the last time the respect of a larger audience for his pioneering oeuvre, in two celebrations organized in Paris for his sixtieth birthday.

Döblin in America

Döblin had a "life-saving" one-year contract as a scriptwriter for Metro-Goldwyn-Mayer, and this helped him to get to the United States. The contract did not have any lasting results; he was dismissed, like most other exile writers and artists, after one year, and had to rely on the generosity of his more successful colleagues. Since Döblin appeared in the United States as an unknown new writer, American publishers had no reason to be particularly interested in his manuscripts. Therefore, the monumental "narrative work" *November 1918,* completed in 1943, remained unpublished, and even Döblin's account of his escape from France, the first part of his later *Schicksalsreise* (1949), found no place on the book market. His only publications were *The Living Thoughts of Confucius* (1940), for which he wrote the introduction. Additionally, two sections from *November 1918* appeared in German. The Pazifische Presse published *Nocturno,* and Wieland Herzfelde (1896–1988) brought out another section of the novel, titled *Sieger und Besiegte* (Victors and Vanquished, 1946), as a volume in the Aurora series. But even these writings received no response, and Döblin commented sadly that this situation was similar to the very beginning of his career, when he wrote only for himself.

The Postwar Years in Germany

When Döblin returned to Germany in November 1945, he immediately looked for publication outlets to make the works written after 1933 available to the German readership. The difficult conditions at the time — paper shortages, censorship, and the separation of the country into four occupation zones — were not conducive to reintroducing a forgotten writer in a devastated country. Nevertheless, Döblin's activities also included founding the literary journal *Das Goldene Tor* (The Golden Gate, 1946–51), which featured texts by exile authors and young writers who had spent the war years inside Germany, as well as reviews. Between 1946 and 1952, he was also active as a regular political and cultural commentator on radio, which he broadcast under the heading *Kritik der Zeit*.

Döblin's first book published in postwar Germany in which he professed his newfound Christian faith was *Der Oberst und der Dichter oder Das menschliche Herz* (1946). In it, an officer in the German army is confronted by a judge who tries in vain to make the officer recognize his guilt and thus produce a "wirkliche Kapitulation" (*OD*, 17). Although some critics welcomed the book as a necessary work with the purpose of fostering a much-needed moral catharsis of German society after the Second World War, other critics — among them Bertolt Brecht — attacked *Der Oberst und der Dichter* for its moralizing tone and its irritating rhyme. There had been a radical change in Döblin's view of the world. Instead of the underworld of *Berlin Alexanderplatz*, he was now concerned with theological questions of faith and salvation. Likewise, Döblin's *Der unsterbliche Mensch*, which he had already finished in 1943, met with more skepticism than admiration when it was first published in 1946. Imitating the old literary genre of a disputation, Döblin again confronted two persons: a theologically educated, older man teaches Christian "truths" to a young man with an atheist and agnostic worldview. When the autobiographical *Schicksalsreise* appeared in 1949, the readers were therefore prepared for the "new" Döblin. Most of them considered it a very personal document rather than an account of France in the fateful year of 1940. Döblin's description of the religious crisis he had suffered in Mende, on his flight through France, and of his subsequent conversion captivated the reviewers (Schuster/Bode, 417–24). The editions or re-editions of the novels, however, attracted much less attention. *Amazonas*, now in three volumes, did not generate debate as it had in the 1930s, and *November 1918*, which appeared in three volumes between 1948 and 1950, fell victim to the new mood of restoration and the crisis of the publishing industry following the monetary reform in 1948. Moreover, the original first volume, *Bürger und Soldaten 1918*, with its critical depiction of the French takeover of Alsace in November 1918, fell victim to the censorship of the French military government. The first complete four-volume edition of *November 1918* finally appeared in 1978. All in all, Döblin considered his return to Germany a failure (Müller-Salget, 55–65). Once again he left his country and moved to Paris in 1953.

One more unfortunate consequence of Döblin's lack of success was that his last novel *Hamlet oder Die lange Nacht nimmt ein Ende*, completed in 1946, which might have appealed to readers in the immediate postwar years, was rejected by the West German publishers. It appeared finally in 1956 in the GDR, shortly before Döblin's death. Only after meeting with a positive response was it published in the Federal Republic as well. The reactions were varied, but the book generated much debate. Unfortunately, the reviews often had to be combined with Döblin's obituary, as he died in June 1957. The negative comments on *Hamlet* were primarily directed against Döblin's style and language, whereas the story and unusual narrative technique found much interest. For the first time since 1945, there seemed to be an awareness that Alfred Döblin had been a great writer. Karl August Horst, in a detailed analysis of the novel (Schuster/Bode, 428–34), summed up his thoughts with the observation that *Hamlet* constitutes "eine Art Summe aus den Haupttendenzen der zwanziger Jahre" (Schuster/Bode, 434), thus building a bridge from the literature of the 1920s to that of the 1950s.

The Controversy about the Editions

An unfortunate controversy arose about Döblin's work after his death. His close friend Robert Minder, a German professor from Paris, had proposed to edit Döblin's collected works in a critical edition, with the support of the Academy of the Sciences and Literature in Mainz, which Döblin had helped to found. However, Döblin's heirs, his sons, decided against the project and against a cooperation with Minder, for personal and other reasons. Instead, they asked Walter Muschg, a Germanist in Basel, to undertake a more modest enterprise, called *Ausgewählte Werke in Einzelausgaben*. These would be "Leseausgaben" (with an afterword, but without indexes or notes), intended to make Döblin's major works accessible to a larger audience. Muschg began his edition in 1960 and continued it until his death in 1965. While he admired Döblin the writer in general, he considered some of the texts imperfect and made the unfortunate decision to "correct" such imperfections through editorial changes and cuts. The most glaring change happened in his edition of *Amazonas*, where he omitted the entire third part because he considered it unnecessary and aesthetically inferior. On the other hand, Muschg deserves credit for bringing out a sizable number of volumes in a short time, thus drawing attention to this neglected writer. A number of Döblin texts even became available in dtv paperbacks, not only indicating greater reader demand, but also serving to further stimulate interest. These included *Berlin Alexanderplatz, Wang-lun, Hamlet, November 1918*, and even *Berge Meere und Giganten*.

In spite of its valiant efforts, the Walter-Verlag could not bring the works before the public in the same way that Fischer continued to do with those of Thomas Mann and Suhrkamp with those of Bertolt Brecht. Muschg's successor, Heinz Graber, was much more respectful of the original texts; he added editorial notes, factual explanations, and informative afterwords. These editorial policies were continued and extended under the general editorship of Graber's successor Anthony W. Riley. While still called *Ausgewählte Werke*, it is now an almost complete edition of Döblin's works, conforming to rigorous scholarly principles, each volume containing a section entitled "Editorische Nachweise und Anmerkungen." The publication of this wealth of new original and background material in the course of the past three decades has led to a great deal of research and contributed to our understanding of this complex author and his oeuvre. No other writer of his time was concerned with and wrote about such a wide array of issues. His interests spanned not only literature, but also the natural sciences, psychiatry, medicine, philosophy, religion, politics, social policy. With each work, he broke new ground, either thematically or formally. In his novels, he portrayed the present, the immediate and the remote past, as well as the future. It was his lifelong effort to understand the course of human history, which had taken such a disastrous turn. Like his contemporaries Thomas and Heinrich Mann, Franz Kafka, and Gottfried Benn, he was a child of the nineteenth and a witness to the upheavals of the twentieth century. He had a peculiar way of dealing with his time; he was contradictory and provocative, qualities that are reflected throughout his oeuvre.

The articles featured in the present volume attempt to inform the reader of the richness of Döblin's writing. At the same time, they reflect many of the controversies that had their genesis during Döblin's lifetime. The essays have been grouped in order to represent the three major phases of his literary production: early works (1900–1918); works of the Weimar period (1919–1933); and works from the period of his exile and return to Europe (1933–1957). More important than this rather loose periodization is the fact that the themes and concerns appearing in Döblin's early writings established him as an important avant-garde author. They also pervade his later works and, in one way or another, define his entire oeuvre. Among these are first and foremost questions of aesthetics, and several of the essays address in detail the experimental nature of his writing. Other themes relevant to Döblin's entire writing career and taken up in this volume are his view of history, his political, social, and philosophical position, his struggles with religious questions, and the significance of his dual career as a writer and a psychiatrist. The first two articles examine the pioneering aesthetic innovations that marked Döblin as one of the foremost avant-garde writers of the early twentieth century. In her essay on the early story collection *Die Ermordung einer Butterblume,* Heidi Thomann Tewarson traces Döblin's evolution from his rather derivative beginnings to an author committed to what he perceived as the modern reality. She illustrates the literary and philosophical reorientation based on the first of Döblin's many theoretical texts, *Gespräche mit Kalypso. Über die Musik* and, furthermore, shows how Döblin's medical and psychiatric studies impacted on his fiction. The new poetics are revealed in the stories, where the narrator is conspicuously absent and the earlier psychological descriptions have been replaced with an abundance of visual imagery, metaphors, and comparisons. At the same time, they are still imbued with a deep pessimism, a view of the world locked in a permanent struggle. David Dollenmayer's article continues this exploration of aesthetic innovation with regard to Döblin's two novels *Die drei Sprünge des Wang-lun,* which was at the time received as a great modernist work, and *Wadzeks Kampf mit der Dampfturbine,* which was seen by many contemporaries as strange and grotesque rather than funny. He shows the nature and extent of futurism's influence on Döblin as well as his eventual rejection of Marinetti's "manifesto," and the proclamation of his own "Döblinism." Neil Donahue, in his detailed analysis of Döblin's next novel *Wallenstein,* an epic of the Thirty-Years' War but with clear reference to the First World War, similarly considers Döblin's encounter with futurism and Expressionism vis-à-vis his "Döblinism." In *Wallenstein,* Döblin raised his call for a "depersonalized writing" to a new level, and Donahue identifies certain problems with this extreme form of objectivity. His meticulous linguistic and structural analysis reveals that the novel purposely interferes with itself as a narrative, that it becomes primarily "an event of language." The style, instead of serving the narrative, is placed in the foreground.

Aesthetic concerns also play an important role in discussions of the novels after the First World War. Roland Dollinger focuses on Döblin's philosophical ideas informing the monumental futuristic novel *Berge Meere und Giganten,* while at the same time pointing to the formal radicalism and thematic scope of the work. He analyzes the novel within the context of Döblin's philosophy of nature, using a psychoanalytical approach that is also informed by recent feminist scholarship on the history of science. In *Berlin Alexanderplatz,* Döblin abandons some of his earlier positions, most notably, by reinstating an omniscient narrator. In her essay Gabriele Sander shows that, while Franz Biberkopf's fable of initiation forms the core of the work, the montage of various items of realia, such as newspaper clippings, telephone directories, advertisements, popular songs, etc., creates a dense fabric of contemporary discourses and intertextual allusions. Her detailed analysis of the many intertextual references reveals Döblin's impressive use of the intellectual and cultural heritage and of borrowed linguistic and textual materials.

Berlin Alexanderplatz marks the end and culmination of Döblin's middle phase. Until quite recently, most critics have had less regard for Döblin's exile and late works. However, Wolfgang Düsing, in his interpretation of *Hamlet oder Die lange Nacht nimmt ein Ende,* devotes a good part of his essay to this work's complex and innovative poetics. Döblin himself felt that the book could have marked the beginning of a new creative phase, had he been younger. Formally, as Düsing shows, the novel is akin to the "Novellenroman," a term coined by Hermann Broch. It consists of a series of stories enclosed by a frame, whereby the complex interconnections result in a dense epic structure. The stories, told by the various members of the family and their guests, are drawn from myth and literature, allowing for a wealth of interconnecting patterns of identification and interpretation in the search for truth.

In his essay, Erich Kleinschmidt explores Döblin's attitude toward and use of the new media — cinema, radio, and photography. Not surprisingly, the inquisitive modernist followed the development of these new media with great interest. He was, moreover, involved in the filming of several of his works, most notably *Berlin Alexanderplatz,* and he was active in radio broadcasts at various periods during his life. Surprisingly, however, as Kleinschmidt demonstrates, the new media, especially film and photography, remained essentially foreign territory to Döblin; they enriched his writing but did not substantially change it.

Besides questions of aesthetics, the contributors address certain other themes and problems. Among these is Döblin's portrayal of history, which is also revealing of his political attitude at various times. The essays on the historical novels, notably Neil Donahue's on *Wallenstein,* Helmut Pfanner's on *Amazonas,* and Helmuth Kiesel's on *November 1918,* consider the implications of Döblin's "historical fiction." In each novel, the concern with the particular historical period is at the same time an attempt to find answers to the difficult contemporary situation. This was true already of Döblin's "Chinese" novel, *Die drei Sprünge des Wang-lun.* It also applies to *Berge Meere und Giganten,* where Döblin envisions the consequences of an unfettered fascination with science and technology. All these essays examine not only the author's view of history, but also his tendency to intertwine historical facts with elements of mysticism. At the same time, they address another central aspect of Döblin's entire work: the role of the individual in relation to society or nature. Wulf Koepke's essay is devoted to Döblin's political writings published in a number of newspapers and magazines during the turbulent years of the Weimar Republic. He shows Döblin to be, like many of his contemporaries, an intellectual who, in spite of his professed commitment to a humanist socialism, wavered a great deal and ultimately misread the danger of National Socialism before it drove him into exile.

The search for answers to his religious questioning permeates Döblin's entire life and work. The essays by Klaus Müller-Salget on Döblin's relation to Judaism and by Christoph Bartscherer on Döblin's Christian faith in two of his late works take up this topic. The author's Jewish origin, his relations to other Jews, his admiration for the Eastern European Jews whom he visited in Poland in 1924, and his engagement on behalf of Jewish concerns after 1933 are examined, as is his conversion to Catholicism in 1941 and the specific nature of his Catholic convictions. As the essays by Müller-Salget and Bartscherer convincingly show, both Jewish and Christian themes pervade Döblin's works from the beginning.

A final significant topic appearing in the articles concerns the relationship between Döblin's two professions: psychiatry and writing. Veronika Fuechtner's essay provides insight into the fruitful interaction between his medical, political, and fictional writings. She also traces for the first time the development of Döblin's thought in the field of psychiatry and psychoanalysis, his connections to the major figures in the field, and his membership in the "Verein sozialistischer Ärzte." She then examines the short prose work *Die beiden Freundinnen und ihr Giftmord* in light of Döblin's theoretical thinking. Other essays also discuss the impact of psychiatry on his aesthetics as well as on his fiction.

In this manner, the volume offers a comprehensive and nuanced discussion of Döblin's complex oeuvre and thinking. Although his books are not easily accessible to contemporary readers, they have proven their aesthetic and thematic significance for twentieth-century German and, to a lesser degree, world literature. Döblin's memory is best served by responding to his challenging and provocative literary experiments with an open yet critical mind. As editors, we hope that this volume will spark renewed interest in this intriguing writer. His life was inextricably bound to the traumatic eruptions of twentieth-century history, and his work could not help but reflect these epochal events. With all the vehemence, contradiction, and ambivalence of one so immediately caught up in the historical maelstrom, Döblin compels our attention.

Notes

[1] Günter Grass, "Über meinen Lehrer Döblin"; for an analysis see Cepl-Kaufmann.

[2] On the problems of translating *Berlin Alexanderplatz*, see Detken; on the American translation of 1931, see Dollenmayer.

[3] For a sociological study on Döblin's importance for the German book market, see Rusch.

[4] For the relationship between Döblin and Brecht , see Best, Otto Keller, and Tewarson.

[5] Ingrid Schuster, "Die Wirkungen des Wang-lun in der Weimarer Republik."

[6] Brecht, *Tagebücher 1920–22. Autobiographische Aufzeichnungen 1920–54*, 48.

[7] Heinz Graber, who edited the work for *Ausgewählte Werke*, has offered the only thorough study so far: Heinz Graber, *Döblins Epos*; for contemporary reviews, see Schuster/Bode, 176–95.

[8] On the film adaptation of Döblin's documentary novel of 1924, *Die beiden Freundinnen und ihr Giftmord*, see Prangel, "Die Döblinisierung Döblins."

[9] Döblin's first answer from June 1930 in *B I*, 151–61; on the discussion circle, see the circular letters beginning 20 October 1931, *B I*, 166. The critical response to *Wissen und Verändern!* in Schuster/Bode, 267–304.

[10] See Michel Grunewald and Schuster/Bode, 334–36, and 338–40.

Works Cited

Best, Otto F. "'Epischer Roman' und 'dramatischer Roman.' Einige Überlegungen zum Frühwerk von Alfred Döblin und Bertolt Brecht." *Germanistisch-Romanische Monatsschrift* 22 (1972): 281–309.

Brecht, Bertolt. *Tagebücher 1920–22. Autobiographische Aufzeichnungen 1920–54*. Ed. by Herta Ramthun. Frankfurt am Main: Suhrkamp, 1978.

Detken, Anke. *Döblins "Berlin Alexanderplatz" übersetzt: Ein multilingualer kontrastiver Vergleich*. Göttingen: Vandenhoeck & Ruprecht, 1997.

Dollenmayer, David B. "'Wessen Amerikanisch?' Zu Eugene Jolas' Übersetzung von Döblins *Berlin Alexanderplatz*." *Internationale Alfred-Döblin-Kolloquien Münster 1989–Marbach 1991*. Ed. by Werner Stauffacher. Bern: Peter Lang, 1993. 192–205.

Cepl-Kaufmann, Gertrude. "Günter Grass und sein Lehrer Döblin." *Literatur im interkulturellen Dialog: Festschrift für Hans-Christoph Graf v. Nayhauss*. Ed. by Manfred Durzak and Beate Laudenberg. Bern: Peter Lang, 2001. 25–47.

Grass, Günter. "Über meinen Lehrer Döblin." *Akzente* 14, 4 (1967): 290–309; republished in *Über meinen Lehrer Döblin und andere Vorträge*. Berlin: Literarisches Colloquium (LCB Editionen vol. 1), 1968. 7–26.

Grunewald, Michel. "Die Rezeption des Werkes von Alfred Döblin im europäischen Exil (1933–1940)." *Internationales Alfred-Döblin-Kolloquium Paris 1993*. Ed. by Michel Grunewald. Bern: Peter Lang, 1995. 3–23.

Keller, Otto. *Brecht und der moderne Roman: Auseinandersetzung mit den Strukturen der Romane Döblins und Kafka*. Bern and Munich: Francke, 1975.

Müller-Salget, Klaus. "Verfehlte Heimkehr — Alfred Döblin im Deutschland der Nachkriegszeit." *Rückkehr aus dem Exil: Emigranten aus dem Dritten Reich in Deutschland nach 1945. Essays zu Ehren von Ernst Loewy*. Ed. by Thomas Koebner and Erwin Rotermund. Marburg: Wenzel 1990. 55–65.

Prangel, Matthias, "Die Döblinisierung Döblins. Zur Adaption von *Die beiden Freundinnen und ihr Giftmord* durch den Film." *Internationales Alfred-Döblin-Kolloquium Leipzig 1997*. Ed. by Ira Lorf und Gabriele Sander. Bern: Peter Lang, 1999. 67–82.

Rusch, Gebhard. "Die literarische Wirklichkeit Alfred Döblins 1997. Eine Explorationsstudie zur Bedeutung des literarischen Wissens im Buchmarkt." *Internationales Alfred-Döblin-Kolloquium Leipzig 1997*. Ed. by Ira Lorf and Gabriele Sander. Bern: Peter Lang, 1999. 191–210.

Sander, Gabriele, *"An die Grenzen des Wirklichen und Möglichen . . .": Studien zu Alfred Döblins Roman "Berge Meere und Giganten."* Frankfurt am Main: Peter Lang, 1998.

Schuster, Ingrid. "Die Wirkungen des *Wang-lun* in der Weimarer Republik." *Internationale Alfred-Döblin-Kolloquien Basel 1980– New York 1981–Freiburg 1983*. Ed. by Werner Stauffacher. Bern: Peter Lang, 1986. 45–53.

Schuster, Ingrid, and Ingrid Bode, eds. *Alfred Döblin im Spiegel der zeitgenössischen Kritik*. Bern and Munich: Francke, 1973.

Tewarson, Heidi Thomann. "Alfred Döblin und Bertolt Brecht. Aspekte einer literarischen Beziehung." *Monatshefte* 79/2 (1987): 172–85.

Döblin's Early Collection of Stories, *Die Ermordung einer Butterblume:* Toward a Modernist Aesthetic

Heidi Thomann Tewarson

WHEN ALFRED DÖBLIN died in 1957 at the age of seventy-nine, he was all but unknown. His books, confiscated and burned by the Nazis, had not been reissued, and the novels written in exile had found little or no response in postwar Germany. Only the monumental historical novel, *November 1918. Eine deutsche Revolution,* nearly finished at the time of Döblin's return to Europe in 1945, was published in a truncated edition in Munich between 1948 and 1950. His last novel, *Hamlet oder die lange Nacht nimmt ein Ende,* on the other hand, written in 1945, did not find a publisher until 1956.

But at the beginning of the century, Döblin was considered one of the foremost avant-garde writers. Bertolt Brecht (1898–1956) considered him a great prose writer and one of his "two illegitimate fathers" (the other was the playwright Georg Kaiser [1878–1945]) (Sternberg 16). Contemporary writers of quite opposing artistic orientations, such as the expressionist Kasimir Edschmid (pseud. Eduard Schmid, 1890–1966) and the more matter-of-fact novelist Lion Feuchtwanger (1884–1958), also saw Döblin as "ein hervorragend bedeutender Autor," who portrays a "völlig neue Welt" and writes in a language of "meisterhaften Gegenständlichkeit." "Nirgendwo jener Naturalismus, der das Resultat von Studien, mit einiger Psychologie vermengt, wiedergibt" (Schuster/ Bode 25, 29, 50). The usually skeptical novelist Robert Musil (1880–1942), in a lengthy review of Döblin's Indian epos, *Manas: Epische Dichtung* (1926), predicted that this work would become very influential (Schuster/Bode 192). And in 1929, the eminent critic Herbert Ihering suggested that Döblin was really the only German candidate for the Nobel prize in literature (Ihering 446–47).

Because Döblin began to publish in 1910, he is often labeled an Expressionist. In part, this was also due to his association with Herwarth Walden (1878–1941) and his literary magazine, *Der Sturm.* A co-founder, he published most of his early works there,[1] and mingled with many of the other contributors and members belonging to Walden's bohemian circle. His literary beginnings, however, also show many thematic and stylistic affinities with his contemporaries, Hugo von Hofmannsthal (1874–1929), Carl Sternheim (1878–1942), and Thomas Mann (1875–1955). Thus, Döblin's search for a new aesthetic dates back to the turn of the century and emanated from the kinds of problems faced also by this earlier generation. Like the writers of this generation, he confronted and was deeply disturbed by the contradictions within turn-of-the-century society: the conservative and even reactionary political and social forces arrayed against the rising power of the labor movement on the one hand and the radical developments in science, technology, finance, and business on the other. Writers and artists alike became aware that old artistic forms no longer sufficed to represent this rapidly changing reality, and saw, furthermore, that a straightforward representation of reality was no longer sufficient to portray this changed world. In 1901, Hofmannsthal expressed this intellectual disorientation and aesthetic crisis most cogently in his famous "Ein Brief des Philipp Lord Chandos an Francis Bacon" (The Letter of Lord Chandos). It revealed that the crisis was not just formal but extended to language and its conceptual framework, and the entire system of values.

For various reasons discussed below, Döblin was more receptive to modernity and, more important, recognized its relevance for the arts. He bluntly proclaimed, for example, that it was ridiculous to ride the elevated train and listen to Haydn all in one breath. He contrasted Haydn, at that time the most popular representative of the classical heritage, to modern technology and science, such as the wireless telegraph or the newest research in immunology, and made clear that the arts could not afford to ignore these developments (*KS-1,* 93). The observant young Döblin was fascinated by technical and scientific innovation and had no difficulty recognizing that the new technologies, such as the telephone, photography, and especially cinema, offered new possibilities of communication and artistic expression. Sports competed with older forms of entertainment, and the natural and social sciences began to intrude upon everyday life in unprecedented ways. Berlin, the inexorably expanding metropolis, where he grew up, placed the young author at the center of these developments. Not surprisingly, his aesthetic vision evolved from these experiences in combination with the major social and intellectual influences of the time. Döblin's poetic intentions were from the beginning explicitly and consciously polemical.

If the times were imbued with a sense of crisis, Döblin's early experiences were similarly not conducive to establishing a harmonious or confident self. Two traumatic experiences proved pivotal. The breakup of his parents' marriage when Döblin was ten years old, with its attendant poverty and loss of social status, and the notoriously authoritarian, class-conscious, and anti-Semitic Prussian school system induced distinctive psychological and emotional patterns that would determine to a large extent his subsequent social relationships and attitudes. These patterns remained remarkably constant throughout his turbulent life and, as we shall see, manifest themselves in his fiction and his critical and essayistic writings. Ambivalence and tension suffused Döblin's identity — ambivalence vis-à-vis his artistically talented but irresponsible father as well as his business-oriented mother, his Jewish background and the desire to escape through assimilation, his aversion to the Prussian value system and ethos, and his desire to succeed within it. Particularly germane to an understanding of Döblin is the tension between his rebellion against the existing social, that is, bourgeois, order and his ambition to succeed, which necessitated his embrace of the social norms under which he suffered.

Beginnings

Döblin's first attempts at writing occurred during his unhappy student days at the Gymnasium. Defiantly, he penned his first works beneath his school desk. Not surprisingly, they spring from a variety of influences that the young author was absorbing at the time, including contemporary literature, philosophy, science, and even politics. His earliest extant text dates from 1896 and bears the title "Modern." It was as if the eighteen-year-old wanted to signal the seminal role he intended to play in the development of German literary modernism.

The incomplete prose text "Modern," unpublished during his life, is interesting in that, on the one hand, it differs greatly from all his subsequent writings and, on the other, already bears characteristics that would define Döblin's mature works. Rather than serving as an early example of a new kind of writing, "Modern" contains a critique of a society whose ideology and institutions lag sorely behind the demands of the time. Döblin tells the story of Bertha, a young seamstress in search of employment in Berlin. Like so many others, she had come from the countryside, lost her position because of illness, and was now, after weeks of searching, at the point of losing hope and the consolation she had found in her Catholic faith, the Virgin Mary, and Jesus Christ.

Döblin interrupts the narrative with a sociological essay on the position of women in Wilhelminian society. Liberally drawing on August Bebel's (1840–1913) famous study, *Die Frau und der Sozialismus* (Woman and Socialism, 1883),[2] Döblin distinguishes the aristocratic, the bourgeois, and the proletarian woman, and demands equal rights for them. The essay's explicit critique of capitalism and endorsement of socialism allows for an optimistic vision of a future society, where all would have equal rights and duties, where all would have meaningful and pleasurable work. It was the only time that Döblin wrote from so explicit a socialist position and in favor of women's equal status, as we shall see.

In addition to the sociopolitical analysis, Döblin takes up several other issues that must have been important to him at the time. He criticizes the feminine ideal found in modern literature as a gallery of flat, insignificant female characters. "Ihre Gedanken, all ihr Sein ist eine einzige unermeßliche Traum-Schlafseligkeit." The "new woman," he claims, will exist in reality before the modern poets find her (*JR*, 17). He also argues for more openness about sexual matters, a subject that others, including the playwright Frank Wedekind (1864–1918) and the playwright and novelist Arthur Schnitzler (1862–1933), had taken up at that time as well. Bebel, too, acknowledged the importance of the physical nature of man. The young Döblin takes up these concerns, framing them in terms of a struggle between the dictates of society and all powerful nature. He claims that man's animal instincts are not only the only natural thing in our society, but that they are also fundamental, and that whoever dares defy nature by suppressing them will be utterly defeated in this battle (*JR*, 15). He thus prepares the reader for the rather unmotivated change in Bertha's concerns, as he returns to her story. Instead of her struggle against economic ruin, Bertha is now battling a different evil — her sexual desire, awakened by a perfectly decent young man. Sexual love is opposed to the love of Jesus Christ, who appears not in the image of the sufferer for mankind, but as a grandiose figure and her "Supreme Judge." His words resound like the trumpets of the Last Judgment, shattering and crushing her. The reader last sees Bertha at the canal, leaning over the railing, and admitting to herself that she cannot conquer her sexual drive. Here, the manuscript breaks off.

As stated earlier, Bebel and his optimistic outlook soon lost their relevance for the budding author, although he continued to profess certain sympathies for socialism. Other motifs, however, retained their significance or increased in importance. Images of an all-embracing Catholic religion, of the Virgin Mary, and of Jesus carrying the cross regularly reappear. Furthermore, the traditionally gentle and forgiving Jesus Christ is often transformed, as in "Modern," into a rather grand, forbidding, and even avenging figure, rather more in accordance with the god of the Old Testament. Equally pertinent is the concept of all-powerful nature, usually rendered as the supremacy of the instinctual, especially sexual, over the spiritual nature of man, a concept Döblin initially used to criticize the repressive society around him, but which in time took on a force of its own.

In the writings of the next few years, the social world is almost entirely absent. They revolve around the tortured fantasies of an isolated protagonist, alternately contemptuous of or yearning for human companionship and love. Hölderlin (1770–1843) and Nietzsche (1844–1900) have replaced Bebel as Döblin's intellectual patrons. Stylistically and thematically, these early literary endeavors share much with fin-de-siècle literature: the importance of mood (*Stimmung*), the remoteness from social concerns, the elitism of the protagonists. If Döblin criticized the dreamy women of his contemporaries in "Modern," he now portrayed equally dreamy young men in these texts. In his first novel, *Jagende Rosse* (1900), language and theme are very much indebted to Hölderlin's *Hyperion* (1797–99). Hyperion in eighteenth-century Greece, like his author Hölderlin in Germany, despairs of the spiritual poverty and rigidity of his time and yearns for an ideal state, where man, nature, and god can be one, and where the ideal love of a woman will lead to his redemption. Döblin's nameless protagonist similarly aims to soar to the highest heights but is thwarted again and again by his own smallness and limitations. He too longs for unity but finds nothing but division: the dualism between spirit and nature, between life/sexuality and spirituality, between the individual and the collective, and even within himself. He repeatedly laments that he has become a stranger to himself, that he is unlike the others, that he has touched the stars but is ultimately bound to the lowly earth. In the end, he resigns himself to praising the cyclical earthly life "wie es schafft und zerstört," and vaguely resolves to go "zu den Menschen..., meinen Brüdern, meinen Schwestern und Geliebten" (*JR*, 83).

Jagende Rosse, although written for the most part in a highly poetic language, also contains linguistic peculiarities and images that appear strangely out of harmony with the otherwise elegiac, Hölderlin-like tone. They are more in keeping with the sarcasm found in Nietzsche's writings and have been characterized as pre-expressionist.[3] Even more important than the occasional stylistic dissonance in an otherwise epigonal text is something that Döblin may have done unconsciously because the dilemma was as much biographical as aesthetic. But it points most clearly to the modernist path Döblin was soon to take. In *Jagende Rosse,* the first-person narrator/protagonist is anchored neither in space nor time, nor does he seem equipped with any kind of worldview that he then could either endorse or reject. He is without moorings and has recourse to no firm truth. Forever casting about within oppositions and contradictions, he admits: "Bauen werde ich immer . . . In Qual und Fülle drängt es aus mir heraus, rettungslos: das ist die jagende Sehnsucht, die treibt mich seligen, unseligen Ahasver, das sind die göttlichen, irdischen Rosse" (*JR,* 83).[4]

In his second short novel, *Der schwarze Vorhang: Roman von den Worten und Zufällen* (1919), completed in 1902–3, the conflicts Döblin was grappling with in his earlier texts (besides *Jagende Rosse,* there were two novellas, "Adonis" and "Erwachen") emerge more clearly, both in their psychological-autobiographical and their intellectual and philosophical dimensions.[5] The work, complex and multi-layered, testifies to the intellectual, emotional, and aesthetic ferment Döblin was caught up in. There is now a clear separation between the narrator and the protagonist, Johannes, who, to be sure, is once again a dreamy, intellectual, and potentially creative young man in a state of almost complete social isolation and only dimly and guiltily aware of his body. He is introduced reading and quoting from Nietzsche's *Also sprach Zarathustra* (*Thus Spake Zarathustra,* 1883–85). Detached from reality and society, he had resolved to leave all human entanglements — desires, yearnings, amazement — behind him and to reach instead for the free, proud, and cool heights inhabited by a few exceptional individuals like Zarathustra (*JR,* 136). His awakening sexuality, however, hurls him from his lofty heights into the lowly sphere of ordinary human beings. A struggle ensues between Johannes's conscious, rational, and creative self and his sensual/sexual drives, a struggle in which the latter prove to be the absolute victor. He cries out: "Zu arm für die Einsamkeit bin ich, nur Begierde und Liebe bin ich" (*JR,* 142). As in "Modern," sexuality becomes the all powerful drive from which there is no escape. And as before, it is not experienced as an enrichment and brings no happiness. In this novel, it is accompanied not only by feelings of guilt and resentment, but also by violent hatred toward the other sex. The solitary Johannes despairs over his realization that human beings may not rest within themselves, that they are split into man and woman, forever pushed beyond their boundaries toward a strange living thing (*JR,* 128). The strangers are of course the women. Because they are not readily available to him, he comes to see them as his female enemies.

Döblin's women are indeed very different in that they are devoid of intellectual or creative impulses or capacities and are therefore removed from the anxieties and doubts with which their male counterparts are so desperately struggling. They are defined by their sex. Unquestioningly and passively they are at one with life, displaying an instinctive and masochistic readiness to suffer and to sacrifice themselves. Thus, they are at the same time superior and inferior to men. As beings devoid of any intellectual curiosity or talent, they rank far below men. As beings who submit so easily to the laws of nature and life, however, they appear to transcend male limitations. Indeed, they are men's undoing, because men see them as united with those forces of nature against which men wage their hopeless battle. Since women are so alien, men are afraid of them and their own male desires, and these fears gradually turn into hatred, sadism, and violence. The women, in turn, respond with masochism and admissions of shame over being born female.

Johannes's relationship with his beloved, Irene, is a perfect illustration of this scenario. The love story evolves into a battle of the sexes, characterized by extreme sadomasochism (Tewarson, "Frauenfrage," 208–22).[6] Johannes's sadistic impulses are prefigured: initially, he derives sadistic pleasure from watching the severe beating of a schoolmate; next, he finds pleasure in torturing his pet dog to death. Irene is the final victim. He torments her until she loses her peace, her laughter, and smile and eventually, in a reversal of the Penthesilea myth, murders her by sinking his teeth into her neck and drinking her blood. But even now, he feels pursued by the dead girl who has joined with the powers of nature: "Was lächelst du . . . O du Verfluchte. Weit ins Leere habe ich sie abgestoßen, zu den Mächten. [. . .] Oh, ich versteh dein Lächeln, wie ich es immer verstanden habe; nun höhnst du meiner dort . . . Bei den Mächten bist du" (*JR*, 204). He feels compelled to complete his sacrifice, building a pyre and joining her in the flames in order to be with the powers of nature. For Irene, the perfect complement to Johannes, pleasure is coupled with fear and horror (*JR*, 149), and her death is accompanied by feelings of ecstasy (200–201).

On the intellectual and philosophical level, this pathetic story of sexual awakening represents a prevalent theme in turn-of-the-century literature. In its various manifestations it appears as the dichotomy between art and life, between spirit and nature, between free will and biological determinism.[7] By affirming the instinctual side of man, Döblin follows Nietzsche closely. In his *Zur Genealogie der Moral* (*Genealogy of Morals*, 1887), Nietzsche saw modern man's suffering as deriving from his guilty conscience, which in turn was the consequence of man's forced separation from his animal past, the declaration of war against the old instincts, upon which his strength, pleasure, and fertility had rested (312–24). However, Döblin's protagonist falls short of Nietzsche's life-affirming goal. Johannes cannot overcome his suffering and feelings of guilt. Instead of strength and pleasure, he finds despair, and instead of fertility, he finds death and destruction. Döblin's worldview at this point remains deeply pessimistic, even fatalistic.

Joining the forces of nature is a god, reminiscent of the Christ figure in "Modern," who is characterized as "mitleidslos und menschenstolzhassend" (*JR*, 128). It is he who has condemned humans to this desire for each other, who imposed this mark of Cain (*JR*, 128), which Döblin presents in purely negative, social Darwinian terms: "Wir haben nicht Arme, um uns entzückt zu umschlingen, nur uns zu wehren und zu kämpfen gegen das andere und zu töten . . . Jeder Kuss ist ein verfehlter Biss" (199).

Further chipping away at human autonomy and self-worth was the idea that the world was governed by chance. "Die Zufälle wirbeln und reiten durch alle Welt und sind an jedem Orte" (*JR*, 126). Earlier, Johannes had thought that the meaning of life was to be found in emulating the free and proud Zarathustra; now, however, he sees man at the mercy of chance and the meaning of life as insanity. Johannes met Irene purely by chance, and now she, also by chance, has to do penance for her sex, as well as for the fact that love between men and women is not possible. But chance does not rule the world without help. Many things ally themselves with it and give it power, especially words. Döblin is here beginning to examine the conventions of language and the value system imbued within linguistic expression. He was influenced in this quest by the philosopher and cultural critic, Fritz Mauthner (1849–1923), whose *Beiträge zu einer Kritik der Sprache* (Toward a Critique of Language, 1901–2) he greatly admired. Not only did chance play a significant role in Mauthner's philosophical framework — human history is fortuitous, as is the history of language, and even our senses (I, 407), he also maintained that language could not explain the world because it did not depict the world but only a worldview. Language as communication was nothing other than the mutuality of worldviews. Therefore, and this was what especially captivated Döblin, language had no real value, only apparent value (*Scheinwert*), analogous to the way the rules of a game become all the more compelling, the more people submit to them. But language can neither alter nor grasp the world of reality (I, 25). Mauthner also writes of love, specifically the *Liebestrieb*, which can, in civilized persons, be triggered by the mere word *Liebe* (I, 44).

Mauthner's ideas are evident throughout Döblin's text. He had initially given the work the title "Worte and Zufälle" but eventually settled on *Der Schwarze Vorhang: Roman von den Worten und Zufällen*. From the beginning, then, the question of language was present. The solitary Johannes distrusts language. When listening to his schoolmates' easy way with words, he is convinced that this is real life ("fleischgewordenes Schicksal"), the kind of life he yearns for. At the same time, he is horrified at the certainty with which the others speak about people and things. "Er hatte Furcht vor der unerbittlichen Bestimmtheit der Worte, wo er stumm den Dingen lauschte und sich ihnen hingab" (*JR*, 117).[8] After meeting Irene, however, he remembers the word "love," which he alternately calls charming, ridiculous, and stupid, and resolves to play the game (of love). But inside him nothing has changed (*JR*, 150–57). The word "love" with all its traditional associations has nothing to do with the reality as he experiences it, it cannot overcome his isolation. In a letter to a potential publisher, Döblin summarizes the novel as follows:

> Absicht ist: eine Geschichte des Liebestriebes eines Menschen. Wie dieser Trieb aus der natürlichen Isolierung den "Helden" herausdrängt, ihn zu Pflanze, Tier, Freund, schließlich zur "Heldin" und zum Mord an ihr führt, soll psychologisch entwickelt werden. Gegenüberstellung des geläufigen sentimentalen leeren Liebesbegriffs . . . und des inhaltsvollen, des Eigentums- Haß- und Neidtriebes. — Nach ersterm denkt, nach letzterm lebt der "Held." (*B I,* 23)

By bringing together the two rather disparate themes of the novel — the question of sexual love or "Liebestrieb" and the semantic aspects of language — Döblin indicates the direction he is taking aesthetically. Literature now had the task of dealing overtly with those matters that had been touched on (but only generally and subliminally) by German Classicism. The idealized hero striving for perfection, who is enriched and ennobled by the love of a woman, herself more akin to a priestess, muse, or angel than a human being, had lost his validity. Instead, men and women alike were now portrayed according to their allegedly true nature, determined by their instincts, which, however, did not allow for a coming together in mutual understanding or passion. Love was nothing more than the drive for possession and domination, hatred, and envy.

The foregoing discussion shows that Döblin's early texts are complex and multi-layered. The various strands and themes do not necessarily come together and no attempt is made to reconcile them. At this point, they indicate his searching for new ways to grasp reality as he saw and experienced it. It is, however, a characteristic of Döblin's that became more pronounced as his aesthetic intentions became clearer. *Der schwarze Vorhang*, like so many youthful works, is a patchwork of influences from various realms (literature, psychology, philosophy, aesthetics) and is replete with the desperation and hopelessness derived from personal experiences. However, the work retained its importance for Döblin, as he repeatedly sought to publish it. It was first serialized in *Der Sturm* and finally appeared in book form (with some revisions) in 1919.[9]

There is one more dimension that is common to all these early writings — madness. Bertha, in "Modern," is close to going mad as the manuscript breaks off.[10] In *Jagende Rosse*, the narrator/protagonist is driven from madness to madness (*JR*, 57) and later exclaims that the soul yearns for madness, its true home: "nach Wahnsinn lechzt sie, nach Wahnsinn giert sie. Verleumdet hat man den Wahnsinn. Ich weiß es anders. — Sie heben die Beinchen, sie tanzen in der Seele. In der Tiefe der Seele liegen sie gebannt, Kobolde, Fratzen, Teufel, Unholde . . ." (72). The novel's dedication to the mad poet Hölderlin serves as a further indication of Döblin's intense preoccupation with mental aberration. Adonis, in the story bearing the same title, actually descends into madness and drowns himself, joined by his beloved (*JR*, 100). Finally, Johannes, in *Der schwarze Vorhang*, is a clear case of sexual pathology as set forth in the numerous studies of the time as well as in Freudian psychoanalytic theory.[11] The fascination with psychological and sexual pathologies is not exclusive to Döblin's writing. It made its way into literature generally in the form of characters displaying symptoms ranging from weak ego structures (identities) to severe mental illness and perversions. Döblin makes this explicit in his summary of the novel's intention: "Sexual Pathologisches wird also auf ein normalpsychisches Verhalten zurückgeführt, als dessen Verschärfung, und eben durch diese Zurückführung begreiflich und künstlerisch darstellungsfähig" (*B I*, 23). The pathological is presented as the intensification of the normal and therefore acceptable in artistic production. If the reality of madness had been slandered (*JR*, 72) up to now, then it was time to acknowledge it in all its manifestations, without apology.

Reorientation

Döblin's personal interest in the new science of psychology and psychopathology soon took a different turn. For within weeks of graduating from the Gymnasium, he enrolled in medical school, first in Berlin and later in Freiburg, where he became acquainted with the latest ideas in the rapidly evolving natural sciences, neurology, and psychiatry. The study of medicine and, in particular, his specialization in psychiatry had a decisive influence on his intellectual development, including his understanding of human nature and human relations. It also had a marked bearing on his aesthetic intentions. He completed his medical degree in psychiatry in 1905. In the following years he pursued a career as a researcher, first in psychiatry and subsequently in internal medicine.[12]

The psychopathological orientation and especially the approach Döblin pursued in his dissertation, "Gedächtnisstörungen bei der Korsakoffschen Psychose" (Paramnesia in Korsakoff's Psychosis, 1905) established his mode of thought, both in his scientific studies as well as his creative writings, as we shall see. Following in the footsteps of his professor, Alfred Erich Hoche (1865–1943), Döblin approached psychiatry from a psycho-physiological rather than the psychoanalytical perspective. In other words, he sought insight about mental problems on the basis of physiological symptoms or syndromes (Schröter 47–49). His training and subsequent research coincided with important developments in psychiatry, particularly the restructuring of the psychiatric classification system and the questioning of established methodology. Paranoia, for example, was no longer defined as a condition completely at odds with reason and sanity. Quite the contrary, the distinction between sanity and madness became blurred, as the latter was now often determined only by virtue of the patient's institutionalization (Schäffner 17–21). Döblin, during his years as a psychiatrist, made similar observations, and as his scientific writings show, also varied his methodological approach.

Der schwarze Vorhang, although written during his years as a medical student, was still indebted to turn-of-the-century psychopathological ideas. Very soon after completing his degree, however, Döblin's new knowledge in the field of medicine along with the methodological approach became apparent in his literary endeavors. He neither abandoned nor rejected the insights gained from psychoanalytic theory, for they continued to inform his fictional writings, as many psychoanalytically oriented interpretations reveal.[13] But for some time, he felt that an understanding of the physiological rather than the psychic processes would be more rewarding: "Das Dunkel, das um diese Kranken war, wollte ich lichten helfen. Die psychische Analyse, fühlte ich, konnte es nicht tun. Man muß hinein in das Leibliche, aber nicht in die Gehirne, vielleicht in die Drüsen, den Stoffwechsel" (*SLW*, 93). Medical school, as well as the encounter with infirmity, suffering, and death, arrested Döblin's self-absorption as he confronted the reality around him. His earlier autobiographically tinged young male characters, immersed in infinite self-contemplation, disappear; he no longer uses the word "soul" with such monotonous frequency. Additionally, Döblin began to work through some literary theoretical issues.

In his complex yet fascinating text, *Gespräche mit Kalypso: Über die Musik* (1910),[14] Döblin sought answers to fundamental aesthetic questions. Chief among these was the relationship between art and reality. Space does not allow for a detailed discussion of this text; however, the major points, as they relate to Döblin's literary and philosophical reorientation and his progress toward a modernist aesthetics, require attention. *Gespräche mit Kalypso* is also interesting because it represents the first of many theoretical texts Döblin was to write preceding or following the creation of a fictional work, either as a way of clarifying or justifying his ideas.

The dialogues between the goddess Calypso and the musician she held captive on her island[15] are ostensibly about music, but many parts apply explicitly to literature and writing. One of the early discussions concerns the concept of mimesis, with clear reference to Aristotle and his *Poetics* (*SÄPL*, 19). Both the musician and Calypso agree that it is impossible to imitate a thing completely, and therefore reject mimesis as the guiding principle of art. Music, because it is the least imitative of the arts and therefore the freest, effectively illustrates their argument. The musician sets up a hierarchy of arts, ranking the least mimetic at the pinnacle. Well down the hierarchy in descending mimetic order are painting, sculpture, and, without differentiation, drama, dance, and pantomime. Music resides at the top because it doesn't even attempt to imitate reality. Calypso goes one step further, placing the word just above music at the apex of the hierarchy, since the word bears no resemblance whatever to what it represents. In the dialogue between the musician and Calypso, we recognize the semantic problem raised in *Der schwarze Vorhang*. Döblin pursues the question with Calypso's speculation that art could go even further and sever all connections to reality and "sich . . . völlig bezugslos in selbstherrlichen Neubildungen ergehen" (*SÄPL*, 61). The musician recognizes that she is alluding to "pure art" or aestheticism but rejects it. Döblin is quite decidedly turning away from fin-de-siècle aestheticism, with which he too had been flirting. By rejecting both the naturalistic or mimetic as well as the aestheticist approach to art, Döblin theoretically breaks free of earlier traditions.

However, if art was so independent of reality, as the musician and Calypso imply, from where did it derive its meaning? Again taking the example of music, the musician argues that the things themselves sound — by moving and reacting with each other they produce sound. Therefore, the world itself is the greatest musician. From this follows a new position: the artist should step back and refrain from arranging the world according to a conceptual framework but let things sound and speak for themselves. "Im Ton erscheint Beziehung nicht als Begriff, sondern leibhaftig" (*SÄPL,* 26). The artist should furthermore not attempt to interpret feelings but restrict himself to describing the emotions as they appear to the observer. "Es gibt keine Empfindungen. Der Ton ist alles" (*SÄPL,* 29). Music, the musician explains, has no knowledge of feelings, of hatred, pain, sorrow, defiance, anger, or love. It cannot say "I love you, I am proud, I am sad." Its joy is tireless jumping, dancing, jubilation, gentle swaying; its pride is prancing horses, marching armies . . . (*SÄPL,* 72).

Döblin is clearly moving toward a more objective as well as antipsychological approach to literature, one where the author's subjectivity, control over, and authority vis-à-vis his subject matter are curtailed. Instead of a conceptual framework with which to explain and judge the world, he prefers to present it in its variety, richness, and contradictoriness: "Er ist ein großer Realist, der alle Umstände und Nebendinge in Betracht zieht. Wie scharf er viele Beziehungen aufdeckt" (*SÄPL,* 26). The era of authorial omnipotence was over; it was sufficient to consider and uncover relationships without seeking cause and effect. To this end Döblin coined the word *Beziehlichkeit,* or the recognition of multiple relations, which gave meaning to the world and made art comprehensible. The musician admits: "Ich erkenne Gleichmaß, Wiederkehr und Zusammenhang an; einen Sinn hat die Welt, den ihr der Satz der Beziehlichkeit leiht, — weiter aber kann ich nicht, o Kalypso, nur preisen Gleichmaß und Beziehlichkeit und immer preisen den Baum, von dem — mir kein Apfel herunterfällt" (*SÄPL,* 46). Although man's cognitive faculty is limited, the world is no longer governed by chance and therefore no longer meaningless or insane (as in *Der schwarze Vorhang*). The new approach permitted the artist to present the world in its multiplicity without having to hazard a conclusion nor worry about cause and effect. This new acausal writing strategy, as contained in the principle of *Beziehlichkeit,* exemplifies Döblin's transfer of the fundamental methodological insights from psychiatry to the domain of literature. *Beziehlichkeit* was akin to the syndromatic approach in medicine he had adopted from his teacher Hoche; Hoche (and Döblin) also resisted systematizing and classifying psychiatric conditions and, by extension, deriving etiologies (Schröter 47–49).

Philosophically, Döblin remained committed to many of his earlier positions. If, initially, the vitalistic Nietzschean worldview served to reduce the importance of the individual, his scientific training bolstered this position further. Döblin now explicitly rejected the anthropocentric point of view in favor of scientific monism (the doctrine of a unified universe), elements of which appear throughout the text, at times quite naively.[16] Scientific monism of course validated his deterministic perspective:

> Nichts gebe ich mit "Lebensbedingungen," "Wille zum Leben" zu, weil Wille eine Vorwegnahme und blosse Verdoppelung des wirklich Geschehenden ist . . . Tief, aber anscheinend schwer lehrt der einfache Satz und seine Bescheidenheit, die kein Verzicht ist: "der Mensch fällt nicht aus der Welt heraus; die Welt ist; — sie ist so und nicht anders" (*SÄPL,* 38–39)[17]

At the same time, he leaves the door open for human action and creativity by admitting that the world becomes accessible to us only by way of human consciousness and memory. "Wenn ich auch denen, die die Welt an den Menschen binden, nicht beistimmen kann, — sie machen die Welt zur Lüge — so gebe ich doch dies zu: die Welt wird mir nur zugänglich in der Weise der Anerkennung" (*SÄPL,* 37). It is man who recognizes relationships and draws comparisons, and the artist who represents them. Music is composed of material (sound), order (rules), and reality. The musician combines sounds according to rules and imparts bits of reality, modeled after life, which the listener recognizes. Döblin calls this music *sachlich,* or objective (in contrast, for example, to the *Programmusik* of Richard Strauss, 1864–1949). *Sachlichkeit,* with its multiple connotations — objectivity, matter-of-factness, realism — became a guiding principle for Döblin from this point on until the late 1920s, that is, until *Berlin Alexanderplatz: Die Geschichte vom Franz Biberkopf* (1929), the novel in which he reintroduced the explicit and knowing narrator (Tewarson, *Sachlichkeit* 47–117). *Sachlich* or objective writing demanded that the author-narrator refrain from mediating, interpreting, sorting, and judging the events and persons he describes; it further demanded that, rather than providing insight into his characters' psyche, he limit himself to describing observable external manifestations of their inner lives.

The positions Döblin worked out for himself in these dialogues do not constitute a comprehensive poetics, nor are they particularly radical or modernist. But they helped liberate him from the classical traditions, based on mimesis and Enlightenment thinking, that had lost their validity and meaning. Thus, the same principle applied to Döblin's new writing strategy illustrated in his pronouncement about the 1912 futurist exhibit in Berlin: "[Der Futurismus] stellt einen Befreiungsakt dar. Er ist keine Richtung, sondern eine Bewegung. Besser: er ist die Bewegung des Künstlers nach vorwärts" (*KS I,* 116). Later, in his essay, "Berliner Programm" of 1913, he was able to formulate it more precisely: "Die Hegemonie des Autors ist zu brechen; nicht weit genug kann der Fanatismus der Selbstverleugnung getrieben werden. Oder der Fanatismus der Entäußerung: ich bin nicht ich, sondern die Straße, die Laternen, dies und dies Ereignis, weiter nichts" (*AzL*, 18). Thus, the psychological illusion, that is, the concentration on the individual and his or her psychological complexities, must be abandoned in favor of a "depersonalized" kind of writing. Additionally, the love story, what Döblin called the erotic illusion, must give way to the representation of sexual relationships. The stories written during this time (1903–11) illustrate his new attitudes.[18]

The Novellas

Döblin called his early tales novellas, although they bear little resemblance to the traditional nineteenth-century German novella (*EB*, 574). However, this designation and the fact that he referred to them as his children (*B I*, 29), indicate the importance they held for him. Most appeared individually in *Der Sturm* in 1910 and 1911. Subsequently, in 1913, they were published as a collection under the title *Die Ermordung einer Butterblume* (after the novella of the same title), and became famous as a pathbreaking example of Expressionist prose. The stylistic changes are immediately apparent: the narrator seems conspicuously absent; the earlier detailed psychological descriptions give way to an abundance of visual imagery, metaphors, and comparisons and, finally, the lengthy inner monologues (in the first person) are replaced by either direct speech or (third person) interior monologues (*erlebte Rede*). Thematically, the texts now frequently undermine favorite nineteenth-century literary motifs and scenarios as well as traditional male and female representations. Many of Döblin's earlier concerns also reappear, notably the by-now familiar struggle between the individual striving for autonomy and the supremacy of nature. Indeed, this struggle gives the otherwise diverse collection of twelve stories its unity. In some of the stories, it is presented as the tension between free will and biological determinism. In others, it is imbued with a metaphysical dimension (Stegemann 38–51). Additionally, Döblin's encounters with patients in hospitals and asylums became a defining aspect.[19]

> Daß ich nun als Mediziner mich in den Kliniken herumbewegte und beobachtete, ging in merkwürdiger Weise zusammen mit meiner literarischen Neigung, mit dem Phantasieren, und es ergaben sich da die ersten besonderen Verschmelzungen . . . ich wußte nun etwas von Zwangsvorstellungen und anderen geistigen Anomalien. (*SLW*, 359–60)

However, the fates of the scurrilous, pathological, and often paranoid characters populating these novellas are not case histories lifted from his psychiatric practice. A comparison with his notations from the year 1910 at the insane asylum in Regensburg shows the great difference. His limited notes are to daily observations of the patients' physical and physiological states and their, for the most part, progressive deterioration. Moreover, Döblin's perfunctory protocols are indistinguishable from those of his non-writing colleagues.[20] In other words, the medical notations are not potential literary texts *in nuce*. In his fiction, Döblin presents a complete story whereby the often extreme characters begin to make sense by themselves and within their surroundings. They are the result of very specific poetic and philosophical intentions. Döblin was intent on making use of psychiatric knowledge in literature, and vigorously argued that novelists and critics learn from psychiatry rather than psychology, which he rejected as naive. Psychiatry, he maintained, concerned itself with the description of processes and movements, while disregarding questions about "why" and "how" (*SÄPL,* 120). This was the direction he had explored in *Gespräche mit Kalypso* and now pursued in the novellas, where he maintained a consistently and often irritatingly neutral narrative stance.[21] There is not the slightest attempt to find a redeeming aspect to the pathetic characters, their meaningless lives, or the bizarre events or situations in which they are trapped. This is especially true of those tales where pathological characters dominate. To these we shall turn our attention now. They include above all "Das Stiftsfräulein und der Tod," "Die Segelfahrt," "Die Tänzerin und der Leib," and "Die Ermordung einer Butterblume." Others will be considered in relationship to these four novellas.

"Das Stiftsfräulein und der Tod" is one of the earliest tales, dated 1905. It opens with the Stiftsfräulein,[22] a thin, gray-haired woman seated by the window, looking out from behind hyacinth plants into the melting snow outside. Bathed in white light reflected off the snow, she comes to the realization that she will die soon. She reacts to this certainty, the reader is led to infer, by falling into deep apathy, barely eating or talking, and retreating to her room, where she sits stiffly in a corner. When the light fades, a white moon appears at her window, turning away only toward morning. The Stiftsfräulein passes the following day also quite passively, walking through the park, exchanging indifferent phrases with her friend. The next night, however, as the white moon appears, he finds her window shrouded. Within, the bed of the Stiftsfräulein starts swaying, and she, with her fingers clasping onto its edges, is shaking, moaning, and whimpering. From then on, she becomes strangely active and restless, spending her days walking through the secret paths of the park, her eyes fastened on the black bushes, then suddenly fleeing through the black trees back to her room. At night, she moves to the edge of her bed, leaving a space, toward which she periodically reaches out expectantly. With the advancing springtime, she changes once again. She exchanges her black dress for a light blue blouse and white gloves and walks taller and with more bounce. Taking on a girlish and coquettish demeanor, she leaves letters full of flirtatious innuendoes, which begin with "to my dear, strict Lord, Death" under the door and behind the shrubs. While the other ladies in the convent observe her with shock and disapproval, the Stiftsfräulein blossoms. Humming and warbling to herself, she brings masses of spring flowers to her room, arranging them around the picture of the Madonna, but in such a way that her face is completely hidden. One night the long-awaited visitor, death, appears, but not as the imagined bridegroom. Instead, he is a brutal attacker, even a sex murderer (Stegemann 97, 101).

> Mit einem Satz schwang sich der Tod neben sie ins Bett. Da war ein Platz frei . . . Wie ein Bauernlümmel schlug er mit flacher Hand auf ihre Schultern. Da fiel die geballte Faust auf ihre Brust, den Leib, den Leib, und wieder auf den Leib. Ihre Lippen flehten. Ein Würgen kam. Die Zunge fiel in den Rachen zurück. Sie streckte sich.
>
> Da stand der Tod auf und zog das Stiftsfräulein an ihren kalten Händchen hinter sich her zum Fenster hinaus. (*EB*, 110)

Against all the Stiftsfräulein's elaborate preparations and hopes, death arrives not only with pitiless finality but also with extreme and humiliating brutality. She dies unceremoniously, like an animal ("Sie streckte sich").

Döblin is, of course, subverting a familiar topos of literature and art: death variously personified as reaper, as beautiful youth, as friend. An earlier inversion of this topos is Hugo von Hofmannsthal's verse drama, *Der Tor und der Tod* (*The Fool and Death*, 1893), where the protagonist, Claudio, is similarly unprepared when faced with death. Having devoted himself to beauty and the collection of previously functional art objects (musical instruments, religious and ceremonial objects), he is not only unaware of the passing of his life but also of the sufferings he has caused others. When therefore death inexorably claims him, the reader knows Claudio's failings. Moreover, death does not appear with terrifying cruelty. In Döblin's tale, however, the reader is not told anything about the elderly woman's possible failings or the reasons for her limited life. And yet the Stiftsfräulein does not engage the reader's empathy, for the narrator portrays the person, her situation and actions with a cold, clinical glance. Nothing is revealed about her former life, possible psychological motivations, or social constraints. Instead, she pathetically attempts to stop the time and prepare for the "wedding night" she has never had in life. The reader, unassisted by the narrator, can only infer her emotional state from her behavior. But this allegedly neutral narrator is not quite absent and not quite uninvolved. Dignity was not what he had in mind for his character. One need only consider the almost entirely negative adjectives used to characterize her, as well as sentences such as the following: "Oh, der Klumpen wimmerte . . . ," or "Dann saß sie plötzlich zu langem, blöden störrischen Weinen nieder." Another time she is referred to as "Klotz" (*EB*, 104). The black/white color symbolism, too, suggests that Döblin intended more than a mere description of an insignificant life coming to an abrupt end. Death is associated with the color white and light (*weißes Schneelicht, grelles Weiß*), and the moon is described as white. Death furthermore coincides with the return of spring. Black, on the other hand, is associated with the arid life of the Stiftsfräulein; she is dressed in black, fastens her glance on the black bushes and flees through the black trees — black, of course, because they are not yet covered with green leaves. As spring progresses, the Stiftsfräulein seems to affirm the awakening of nature, dressing in light colors and spending her days outside. She replaces the artificially propagated hyacinths in her room with fresh spring flowers. The fact, however, that she has to cover the Madonna's face with the flowers is an indication that she is not on the right path. All these factors point to Döblin's old vitalistic worldview as set forth in the earlier works, imbued now with a metaphysical message — the affirmation of nature as both a supreme and impersonal force that creates and destroys all life, and to which man must submit like any other living organism. The Stiftsfräulein, however, remains stubbornly unreceptive by demanding a meaningful death. Her actions indicate her continued insistence on an individual fate. Consequently, Döblin refers to her as "Klumpen" or "Klotz" and describes her crying as stubborn and stupid.

"Die Segelfahrt," written several years later, is thematically related to "Das Stiftsfräulein und der Tod" and sustained by similar but even more explicit color symbolism. Black stands for life and its entanglements, white for nature and death, while gray, twilight and other pale colors indicate the transition from life to death. Only here, the protagonist, a heavy-set, forty-eight-year-old Brazilian named Copetta, welcomes death and actually seeks it out. Without difficulty, he is said to have left his home, family, and possessions; to him they were merely "ein hoffnungsloses Glück" (*EB*, 9). Clearly in search of something more meaningful, he hurries to Paris, where he quickly tires of indulging in the arts, the elegant life and, as he calls them, the bestial dances. After succumbing to a severe illness, he travels to Ostende. The reader first meets him there, dressed in white, happily walking along the gray-green sea but also among the crowd of festively attired people. He is dressed in gray when he invites a woman, only identified as E., whose eyes are repeatedly described as gray, to go sailing. As they set out to sea in the graying morning, he is again dressed entirely in white. As they speed along, the light becomes ever brighter. And while she, the "old girl" in her thirties, excitedly expects an amorous adventure, he wards her off. Instead, his face is relaxed, "als ginge immer ein feierliches glückerfülltes Wort um ihn herum" (*EB*, 13). With the boat now rudderless and wave upon wave rolling in, Copetta lets himself fall back and disappears into the blue-green sea:

> Als eine hohe Wand gegen das Boot ging, hob er weit die Arme auf, legte sich wie auf ein Kissen mit dem Rücken gegen die Welle. Das Polster glitt zurück. Sie hörte, wie er etwas murmelte; sie sah noch den berauschten, verschlossenen Blick, mit dem er verschwand. (*EB*, 13)

In this scenario, nature is experienced as benevolent because Copetta is in agreement with it. Human attachments no longer have any hold on him, and he is ready to give himself up to nature. The rudderless boat is a metaphor for Copetta's having renounced autonomy (and stands in stark contrast to the Stiftsfräulein's feverish activity). The woman, who hasn't reached this stage yet, is rescued, and soon leaves for Paris, where, consistent with Döblin's notion of female destiny, she embarks on a life of prostitution. On the street, she denies herself to no one, putting herself and others at risk for disease. Later, she moves to the glamorous ballrooms, where, dressed in black silk and her eyes shining from the effects of Atropine, she performs strange and sensuous dances with her partners.[23] After a year, she returns to Ostende, no longer dressed in black but in yellow silk. She spends the day joyfully anticipating Copetta. It is again morning and light, when she jumps into a rowboat, hoping to catch up with him. Not finding him, she is overcome with fear. But she is joined by a dark figure rising from the waves. "Auf dem Kamm einer Welle schwang sich die dunkle Gestalt ins Boot" (*EB*, 16). Döblin uses the very same formulation as in the earlier story, "Das Stiftsfräulein und der Tod," suggesting that Copetta is, if not death himself, then a messenger or a helper of death. He is still in his white clothes, but strangely transformed into a mythical figure: his body is bloated, his hair encrusted with salt, seaweed hanging over his face, fine white sand and seashells pouring from his shoulders and sleeves. The scene from the previous years is repeated: once again he wards off the woman who rises in joy, looks past her, not hearing her terrified calls because of the singing of the storm. As before, he lies back in the waves with an ecstatic look. She now leaps after him and is finally embraced by his thick swollen arms. As both are united, they regain their youthful looks and are absorbed by the infinite gray-green sea.

In both stories, death is but one aspect of nature and life. Copetta and, with his help, the woman come to accept this. The Stiftsfräulein, on the other hand, remains stubborn. Döblin lifts his characters from their social settings and confronts them with the mythical forces of nature to which they must resign themselves. Death as a way out of individuation, already present in his first novel, *Jagende Rosse*, appears as a dominant theme in these stories. For example, death is similarly not resisted in "Die Helferin." In this strange and criminally tinged tale, Mike Bondi, a helper in a funeral home in New York during the previous century, causes all the sick people he visits to die peacefully within eight days. Mike Bondi is actually Bessie Bennet, a girl who died very young some eighty years earlier. Because she wanted so much to live, she was given permission to return — not to dance, as the narrator explains, but to help bring a kindly death to men.

> Die unbekannte Macht, deren Namen sie nicht nennen könne, stand da von ihrem Sessel auf und machte sie zu einer Dienerin des Todes. Sie durfte im Namen der gütigen Macht töten, was gehen wollte; die törichte Angst vor dem Sterben nehmen, sänftigen und rasch beenden. Sie sei als Helferin unter die Menschen geschickt und bringe den liebreichen Tod. (*EB*, 45)

Submitting to or embracing death is the most positive decision any of the characters in these stories make. "Die Verwandlung" is similar to "Die Segelfahrt" and "Die Helferin" in that the queen and her prince consort voluntarily renounce crown and scepter, the insignia of worldly power, and give themselves up to the sea (*EB*, 39). The initially proud and wild Miß Ilsebill in "Der Ritter Blaubart," intent on redeeming the unhappy knight through her love, finds consolation not only in resigning herself to the force of nature but also in affirming her faith in the Madonna (*EB*, 78). On the other hand, there are those who resist death, like the Stiftsfräulein. Among these are Paolo di Silva in "Der Ritter Blaubart," the dancer in "Die Tänzerin und der Leib," and Michael Fischer in "Die Ermordung einer Butterblume." They go down resisting, or in anger. Death, however, is inevitable.

The extent to which Döblin is willing to pursue this commitment to resignation and the eclipse of the autonomous individual vis-à-vis the force of nature is shown in "Der Ritter Blaubart." The fairy tale's main character, Baron Paolo di Silva, is no Bluebeard. Instead, in yet another inversion of the traditional tale, he is imbued with positive human qualities — pride, kindness, generosity, and congeniality. However, the violent encounter with a mysterious and mythical force, exposed at the end of the story as a dreadful sea monster, a Medusa, reveals once again that human autonomy and pride must be abandoned. The baron is found unconscious, without memory of what happened, wounded, frightened, and transformed. Gone are his laughter, his love of life and people; introverted and asocial, he now lives a solitary existence in the town. After a year has passed, however, he resolves to build a castle in the heath and to marry. This is a clear act of defiance, and in due time, the mythical force begins to take revenge: one wife after the other dies mysteriously. In time, the castle is destroyed and the heath on which it was built is reclaimed by the sea. In other words, the proud and self-assured Paolo di Silva has to be utterly defeated, before he too submits to a higher power. Similar to Miß Ilsebill, his last love, this power combines both nature and the Catholic Christian faith. Discovering Ilsebill's cross hanging from a birch tree, he falls to his knees and, with his forehead touching the bark, prays to the Madonna. Perhaps as an act of penance, he becomes the leader of a guerilla group in the fight against the heathen Indians in Central America. It is they who kill him treacherously. The "menschenstolzhassender Gott," who crushes the struggling human beings in "Modern" and *Der schwarze Vorhang*, reappears: nature and the Madonna are coupled and thus doubly overwhelming.

"Die Tänzerin und der Leib" is perhaps the most matter-of-fact of the stories, because the dancer's illness and death are presented as a purely clinical matter, free of metaphysical overtones. The dancer, who loses control over her well-trained body, represents another version of the struggle between free will and biological destiny that preoccupied Döblin in his earlier texts. As expected, the dancer's will is no match for her failing body, which has become her "lord." Actually, as the title already indicates, she and her body become two separate entities: "Sie führten getrennte Wirtschaft; der Leib konnte sehen, wie er sich mit den Doktoren abfand, 'Es wird schon protokolliert werden.' Damit schnitt sie der Belästigung das Wort ab" (*EB*, 20).[24] At the very end, it may be argued that she regains power briefly by destroying the body, alternately called "das dumme kranke Kindchen," "ein Stück Aas," "das träge Tier," "die Tonne das hinkende Männlein," as well as "ihr Eigentum, über das sie zu verfügen hatte" (*EB*, 19, 20). This scheme is unusual because the striving individual will is personified by a woman. However, the dancer Ella, at nineteen, is not a mature woman and never will be (unlike E. in "Die Segelfahrt"). At the same time, Ella loses control over her body at precisely the moment when she is expected to conform to her "natural calling" as a sexual object, with which the role of a dancer or artist is irreconcilable (Keck, *Avantgarde* 90–101).

Here Döblin is again subverting favorite themes in late nineteenth-century literature, music, and art: the consumptive woman as well as the child-woman. Gabriele, the musician in Thomas Mann's *Tristan* (see especially Keck, *Avantgarde* 77–89), or the courtesans Violetta in Verdi's *La Traviata* and Mimi in Puccini's *La Bohème,* come to mind. In the dancer's case, the illness remains vague, although the young woman is described very much like a consumptive patient: "Mit neunzehn Jahren befiel sie ein bleiches Siechtum, so daß ihr Gesicht abenteuerlich fahl vor dem blauschwarzen Haarknoten schimmerte" (*EB,* 18).[25] However, Ella refuses to play the role of the beautifully dying woman, whose art is further inspired and refined or whose soul is ennobled by her suffering. Ella's artistry from the beginning appears questionable. She seemed suited for the profession of a dancer owing to her peculiar temperament and her inclination to contort her limbs and make faces. Her dancing seemed to be all about controlling her body, a kind of virtuoso display. Hers was an art that, although performed through the body, emanated from the will and was completely lacking in sensuousness. "Es gelang ihr, über den üppigsten Tanz Kälte zu sprühen" (*EB,* 18). Her voice is described as "hell, ohne Buhlerei und Musik, abgehackt." In other words, she is asexual, a child-woman but without the associated appeal so common in turn-of-the-century literary and artistic representations of the type. Moreover, she was "lieblos," without empathy for her less talented colleagues. The young woman, the dancer, and her art are drawn by a narrator's cold diagnostic glance, seemingly without appreciation of the art of dancing or the artist; this perspective is sustained throughout.[26] As the story progresses, Ella's changing moods are faithfully recorded. Her overwhelming emotions are anger (at her body, the doctors, and the world of the hospital), horror and revulsion (at the doctors and patients); fear and dread leading to a childish helplessness. Then again, she takes on a distanced attitude, mocking the doctors' lack of success with her body. In contrast to some of the other stories, such as "Die Segelfahrt," "Das Stiftsfräulein und der Tod," "Die Verwandlung," and "Der Ritter Blaubart," where the emotional states are conveyed primarily through the description of bodily reactions, Döblin uses the actual terms for these emotions: *Wut, Grauen, Angst, Hohn, Haß.* As a result, the reader gains insight into the desperation of this young person, imprisoned in a failing body, in spite of the distanced narrative stance.

In time, the medical picture is transformed into a psychiatric one, when the dancer demands thread and cloth and embroiders in red the situation as she experiences it. Her embroidery shows in coarse outline the following picture of three figures:

> ein runder unförmiger Leib auf zwei Beinen, ohne Arm und Kopf, nichts als eine zweibeinige, dicke Kugel. Neben ihm ragte ein sanftmütiger großer Mann mit einer Riesenbrille, der den Leib mit einem Thermometer streichelte. Aber während er sich ernst mit dem Leib beschäftigte, machte ihm auf der andern Seite ein kleines Mädchen, das auf nackten Füßen hüpfte, eine lange Nase mit der linken Hand und stieß mit der rechten eine spitze Schere von unten in den Leib, so daß der Leib wie eine Tonne auslief in dickem Strahl. (*EB*, 21)

Far from attempting to reunite mind and body, she completes the dissociation metaphorically. But it is a last attempt to reestablish the old power relationship: "Wie einstmals . . . wollte sie ihren Willen wieder fühlen. Sie wollte einen Walzer . . . mit ihm tanzen, der ihr Herr geworden war, mit dem Leib" (*EB*, 21). Eventually, she calls for the doctor and, in his presence, kills herself by plunging the sewing scissors into her chest. The story ends with one of Döblin's striking formulations, rightfully assigning him to the Expressionists: "Ein geller Schrei stand irgendwo in der Ecke des Saales. Noch im Tode hatte die Tänzerin den kalten verächtlichen Zug um den Mund" (*EB*, 21).

"Die Ermordung einer Butterblume" is the central and most famous story of the collection. The intriguing title aside, it features a highly complex narrative structure and is generally considered the most accomplished of Döblin's early short fiction and a model of expressionist prose (Reuchlein 10–68). At first glance, Döblin's by-now familiar matter-of-fact narrative stance seems to govern this novella, too. An implicit narrator presents the protagonist, Mr. Michael Fischer, whose proper bourgeois attire (black suit, bowler hat, golden watch chain, walking stick) contrasts sharply with his odd behavior. The reader first meets him on his Sunday stroll. As he is ascending the path through the forest, he counts his steps: first forward up to a hundred, and then backward again. All the while he is vigorously swaying his hips from side to side, at times almost losing his balance. He seems self-consciously concerned about his behavior and twice turns to see if anybody is watching him, possibly his business colleagues or a lady (*EB*, 57), but resumes it whenever he is not preoccupied with something else. His friendly eyes and his "ältliches

Kindergesicht mit süßem Mündchen" (*EB*, 56) further contrast with his behavior at the office, where he regularly slaps the apprentices for being too slow in killing flies and presenting them to him arranged according to size. The impression conveyed is that of a rigid and somewhat sadistic person with an extreme need for order and control. From the beginning, however, Fischer's behavior also suggests that this control is quite tenuous, and indeed, as the story progresses, it is shown to disintegrate rapidly and completely in response to an utterly insignificant incident. Fischer furiously and groundlessly whips off the heads of common buttercups in which his walking stick gets caught. In the course of the story, Fischer displays a multiplicity of psychiatric symptoms, typical of the compulsive, the anal or repressive, the sadistic, the paranoid, and the hysterical personality.

This novella is especially intriguing, for Döblin combines his familiar objective narrative perspective with a subjective one, conveyed through the (third person) interior monologues (*erlebte Rede*) of Fischer (Marx 58). It permits the reader to follow step-by-step the protagonist's increasingly bizarre mental associations. Thus, the initial violent action is clearly linked to his bourgeois existence and connected with a certain pleasurable feeling coupled with sadism: "Warum keuchte er? Er lächelte verschämt. Vor die Blumen war er gesprungen und hatte mit dem Spazierstöckchen gemetzelt, ja mit jenen heftigen aber wohlgezielten Handbewegungen geschlagen, mit denen er seine Lehrlinge zu ohrfeigen gewohnt war . . ." (*EB*, 57). But while the apprentices could be mistreated without consequences, this is not the case with the buttercups. Fischer soon has a vision of himself and his deed of a moment ago, whereby the beheaded buttercup takes on mythical proportions. The severed head rolls into the grass and penetrates ever deeper into the ground, while from the neck of the body, the stem, white blood begins to ooze, first a little but then swelling to a stream so that Fischer has to jump to the right and the left in order to escape the slimy river. Covered in sweat, he tries to regain control, still aware that this is a matter of his imagination: "Die eigenwilligen Gedanken wollte er schon unterkriegen: Selbstbeherrschung. Diesem Mangel an Gehorsam würde er, der Chef, energisch steuern" (*EB*, 58). Regaining his self-confidence, he now imagines himself rather proudly as a murderer: "An ihn würden die Kriminalbeamten denken, an den Mörder, der schlau ins Fäustchen lachte. Herr Michael erschauerte wüst über seine eigene Tollkühnheit, er hätte sich nie für so verworfen gehalten" (*EB*, 58).

In reality, however, he is pursued by the dead buttercup and indeed by the entire forest, the smell of the flower's corpse moving right along beside him. Although overcome with dread, he at times lusts after "her," the buttercup, and the murder site. At other times, he is consumed by guilt, which leads him to anthropomorphize her: "Wenn er die Blume nur rufen könnte. Aber wie hieß sie denn? Er wußte nicht einmal, wie sie hieß. Ellen? Sie hieß vielleicht Ellen, gewiß Ellen . . ." (*EB*, 61). The preoccupation with the flower extends not only to his thoughts (conveyed by way of the interior monologues) but also to his actions. He sets up a bank account in her name and insists on a dish for her when he takes his meals, all in the hope of atoning for the murder. Then again, he wages a "guerilla war," a "secret war" against the flower, forever plotting to outwit her. In the end, he thinks he has found a way out of his quandary, and even invents a legal paragraph on guilt compensation. To this end, he brings home from the forest another buttercup and carefully nurtures it. This is supposed to free him. When the pot breaks and the landlady tells him that she discarded it along with the weed, Fischer is ecstatic. He now imagines himself released from the hold of the flower and the entire buttercup clan. "Das Recht und das Glück standen auf seiner Seite. Es war keine Frage. Er hatte den Wald übertölpelt" (*EB*, 67). This last set of associations, although the logical result of Fischer's earlier ones, is now completely at odds with any objective reality. While his initial cruelty of a year earlier was still comprehensible, his present behavior is a clear indication of a thoroughly confused subjectivity. It is not Fischer who has duped the forest, of course, but the other way around. The story ends with the protagonist disappearing into the forest, loudly laughing, never to return.

Although the portrayal of Mr. Michael Fischer's disintegration is what affects the reader most of all, a careful reading shows that this was not the author's primary concern. Fischer is obviously drawn from Döblin's psychiatric experiences and is, even if not a case study, utterly convincing. But the text contains once again a metaphysical message, as Fischer serves as an example of man's stubbornness. The power that the butchered buttercup and, eventually, the forest assume over him may at first appear as a figment of his disturbed consciousness. However, there are enough signs to indicate that there are times when this repressed little man is not merely mad but for brief moments receptive to the notion of a realm beyond his confined bourgeois existence. Thus, the destruction of the flower confronts him with the thought of the finality of death (*EB*, 61). Yet he stubbornly tries to convince himself that all was but a dream. At other times, he is overcome with dread at the thought of the weeping trees assembling in judgment over him (*EB*, 62) and acknowledges the existence of incredible things (63). He admits the need for a religion of sorts: "Jeder Mensch habe seine eigene Religion; man müsse eine persönliche Stellung zu einem unaussprechlichen Gott einnehmen. Es gäbe Dinge, die nicht jeder begreift" (*EB*, 64). At one point he breaks down weeping for the first time since his childhood: "Urplötzlich, weinte [er], daß ihm fast das Herz brach" (*EB*, 64). Ultimately, however, Mr. Michael Fischer remains "versteinert" (*EB*, 63), "der Verhärtete" (64). He chooses to struggle to regain his autonomy, only to be reabsorbed into the realm of nature, here represented by the forest, entirely uncomprehending.

Considering the array of pathological characters contained in these novellas, one must ask what Döblin intended. Since he provides neither motivations nor causes for the extreme and puzzling behavior of his characters, Döblin perplexes his readers. We thus gain no insight into these phenomena and struggle even more to locate within ourselves any empathy for the irritable characters he portrays. At a time of intensive psychiatric studies and research, Döblin's neurotic protagonists seem to be part of his literary world in the same way as Kafka's bound and caged characters are integral to his. They are part of and reflect back on everyday life, in accordance with Döblin's explanation of 1904, when he maintained that the pathological was but a heightening of the so-called normal world (*B I*, 23). Indeed, the narrative power of these tales no doubt arises from this intensification, as well as from the startling images used to convey varied mental and emotional states. The reader confronts in the pathetic and ridiculous characters, often bordering on caricatures, the anxieties, repressions, constraints, and secret desires that appeared to Döblin so characteristic of his social and historical milieu and perhaps even of the human condition generally.

However, the world of mental and emotional pathology accounts only partly for the deeply disturbing effect these stories have on the reader. Equally or more significant is the philosophical perspective. Although rooted in reality, the social world and human struggles of the narratives are for the most part not the object of these tales. Social existence is presented as meaningless and worthless: Copetta's life as a family man; the Stiftsfräulein's belated desire; the dancer Ella's longing to regain control over her body; Paolo di Silva's love of life; Ilsebill's devotion to him; Mr. Michael Fischer's bourgeois existence; and so on. Their efforts to individuate a personal destiny in the face of deterministic forces appear misguided. Döblin presents no social alternative. All that matters is the willingness to give up the illusion of self-creation and yield to reabsorption by nature. In effect, Döblin's characters must either accept or long for death.

Moreover, the characters' conduct in life bears no necessary relationship to the manner in which they leave it. For example, the queen and her prince consort, in "Die Verwandlung," are positive figures in their readiness to die, in spite of the queen's utter disregard of her royal responsibilities. Even their implied role in the killing of their child does not taint them. Copetta's self-absorption, his abandonment of his family, and his unfeeling destruction of his children's pictures and his wedding ring in no way diminish his depiction as perhaps the most positive figure of all. Inversely, but to the same narrative effect, Paolo di Silva's kindness and generosity are without value.[27]

All of this gives way to a worldview that is not only dismissive of man's psychological and social predicaments but is also amoral. Since all human strivings are viewed as futile and wrong, the distinction between good and evil becomes irrelevant. In fact, incompetence, indifference, hatred, cruelty, and violence of any kind are dominant traits in Döblin's characters, only partially alleviated by irony and humor. Characters lack mutual understanding, even when they have no quarrel with each other. They are separate and contained within themselves, windowless monads, as Johannes exclaims in *Der schwarze Vorhang* (*JR*, 160, 181).

Thus, despite Döblin's aesthetic reorientation and commitment to a more reality-based kind of writing, his fictional world remained as fatalistic as that of his earlier texts. He continued to see life as an eternal struggle and regarded man as a mere plaything of natural forces. To some extent this is understandable, confronted as he was during these years with suffering and death that no science could alleviate or prevent.[28] On the other hand, it may be argued that the aesthetic direction he endorsed — "depersonalized" or distanced writing — freed the young author from the need to exert control over his imagination. Thus, the incorporation of ugliness, cruelty, and madness, as well as the negation of the human subject, may have been part of his poetic intentions, aimed at overcoming an outdated mimetic orientation. But they were also closely connected with Döblin's worldview, which continued to see man not as the maker of his fate but as a pawn of forces beyond his control, forces demanding absolute resignation. For Kafka, too, life was a continuous and hopeless struggle against all-powerful, primarily social, forces. However, unlike Döblin's, Kafka's narrative perspective invites reader identification with the oppressed and suffering individual. In Döblin's texts, even this small comfort is absent.

Unlike Thomas Mann, Döblin never addressed the dangers posed by the prominence he assigned to the irrational and instinctual or the extreme violence permeating his writings.[29] For him, they constituted essential aspects of reality and, consequently, of literature. In the early novellas, the aberrant behavior was confined to individual characters, as we have seen. Beginning with *Die drei Sprünge des Wang-lun. Chinesischer Roman* (1915), violence became a defining feature of mass behavior.[30] Additionally, in the twenties, highly controversial ideas, such as the purification of society (*Reinigung der Gesellschaft*) and breeding eugenics (*Züchtungsgedanken*) began to appear in his fiction, essays, and "philosophical" writings. If, in the novellas, Döblin preferred mythical solutions to psychological and societal problems, the politically turbulent Weimar Republic prompted him to seek answers in the highly questionable biologism of the 1920s. Both solutions are indicative of his failure to face the urgent political and social problems of the times.[31]

Notes

[1] Prior to *Die drei Sprünge des Wang-lun* (1915) the following works appeared in *Der Sturm: Gespräche mit Kalypso. Über die Musik* (1910–11), *Der schwarze Vorhang* (1911–12), and many of the short stories which became part of *Die Ermordung einer Butterblume* (1910–12). Döblin was thus known only to a small circle of avant-garde artists and writers, who, however, were also more ready and able to recognize his innovative way of writing. (See for example, the reviews in Schuster/Bode 7–48). The only other and also the earliest publication was the one-act drama, *Lydia und Mäxchen. Tiefe Verbeugung in einem Akt* (Straßburg & Leipzig: Josef Singer, 1906).

[2] Originally published in 1883, it appeared in its 25th edition in 1895.

[3] Anthony Riley, "Nachwort," *Jagende Rosse, Der schwarze Vorhang und andere frühe Erzählwerke*, 296–300.

[4] Otto Keller defined this narrative stance as the "Zerstörung jedes festen Punktes, jeder statischen Wahrheit. Es ist der Leidensweg ins Bodenlose [. . .], ins rastlos ahasverische Dasein" (Riley, "Nachwort," *Jagende Rosse*, 299–300).

[5] There is a strong autobiographical connection between Döblin and his early protagonists in regard to his social situation, his sexual maturation, and even his questioning of language. See: Alfred Döblin, *ASLA*, 11, 15, and *SLW*, especially 167. Admittedly, Döblin's protagonist Johannes is a literary figure, but this does not, in my view, diminish the striking autobiographical parallels in the early writings and the conclusion that Döblin is working through personal problems in a rather direct manner. Despite this, Dollinger, for example, rejects autobiographical connections, examining the sadomasochistic aspects in Döblin's work solely in the context of the psychoanalytic discourse of the time.

[6] Johannes also exhibits homosexual tendencies, which, according to psychoanalytic theory, can represent a mere phase in the otherwise normal sexual maturation process. Additionally, he has masochistic fantasies that represent the obverse of his desire to inflict harm.

[7] Döblin makes this explicit: "Die Schwäche seines Gedankenwillens erfuhr er, als er vergeblich seine Begierde zu zähmen suchte" (*JR*, 130).

[8] Compare Johannes's formulations with Döblin's autobiographical reminiscences in *SLW*, 167–68.

[9] See the editorial commentary in *JR,* 306–9 and 252–80.

[10] Keck, *"Avant-garde,"* analyzes Bertha on the basis of Breuer's and Freud's hysteria studies. See especially 16–32.

[11] For Döblin's complex and shifting attitude toward Freud, see Thomas Anz 9–30.

[12] Anti-Semitism prevented him from successfully pursuing a career as a research scientist, which required a civil service appointment. (Schröter 50; Schäffner 276, note 228). It reveals the institutionalized anti-Semitic prejudice in Regensburg: the official report states that the "Israelite" Döblin was selected only because there were no other applicants. As a result, and also because Döblin married and, in the course of the next few years, became the father of three sons, he set up in 1911 a practice as a *Kassenarzt* (something akin to a Medicaid doctor) in the poor eastern section of Berlin, where he had grown up. There he remained until his forced exile in 1933. He spent the First World War as a military doctor and, beginning in the twenties, gained recognition as an avant-garde author.

[13] In addition to Schäffner, see the articles by Annette Keck, Reiner Marx, and Sabine Kyora in *Internationale Alfred-Döblin-Kolloquien Leiden 1995.*

[14] For the genesis of this text, see Alfred Döblin, *SÄPL,* 613.

[15] Both figures clearly refer to Homer's *Odyssey,* where Calypso is a nymph. Döblin's musician once refers to himself as Odysseus.

[16] For example, in the fifth conversation, the musician preaches to the fish, which he considers flesh from his flesh and blood from his blood because they ate his companions (*SÄPL,* 30). Elsewhere he is full of admiration for those who attempt to explain the variety of the world on the basis of uniform atoms (32). Most extensive is the lengthy passage: "Ich weiß, daß ich nicht wohne in diesem Körper wie in einem Hause. Zu mir gehört alles, was ich erlebe, was mir widerfährt und mit mir fährt . . . Ich kann so wenig für mich absehen von der Meereswelle, die vor mir schäumt, von dem grauen Gelb des Himmels, wie ich von meiner Hand absehen kann. [. . .] (108–9). Even his experiences with mental patients are reflected in this theoretical text (99).

[17] Döblin illustrates his deterministic worldview beautifully with the example of the fugue: "Kaum könnte ich ein besseres Gleichnis für die Freiheit des Willens finden als diese Fuge, mit ihrem Schein der Selbständigkeit in Stimme gegen Stimme, mit ihrem Getriebenwerden und Folgerichtigkeit: der Weg ist jeder Stimme vorgeschrieben, und doch geht jede eigenwillig" (*SÄPL,* 67).

[18] Since Döblin was immersed in medical research, his literary production at this time was sparse. Besides the stories, he wrote a one-act drama, *Lydia und Mäxchen. Tiefe Verbeugung in einem Akt* (1905, published 1906), which was performed the same year under the auspices of Herwarth Walden. It represents a further elaboration of the ideas in *Gespräche mit Kalypso.* And Döblin himself called it "früher, frühester Expressionismus" (*SLW,* 360).

[19] Döblin repeatedly expressed his affinity with the sick and that he felt comfortable among them. He also insisted that, besides plants, animals, and stones, he always could suffer only two kinds of people: children and the insane. And if someone should ask him to which nation he belonged, he would answer neither to the Germans nor the Jews but rather to the children and the insane (*SLW*, 92).

[20] For transcriptions of some of the protocols, see: Schäffner 276–90. Additionally, see Veronika Fuechtner's essay in this volume for a detailed analysis of Döblin's psychiatric protocols.

[21] In reality, he was much more involved with the fates of his patients, as his essay, "Eine kassenärztliche Sprechstunde" (6 January 1928) indicates. Here, he elaborates on his difficult role as physician, psychiatrist, and social worker among the working-class patients whose problems were as much the result of living and working conditions as of actual diseases (*SLW*, 98–102).

[22] *Stiftsfräulein* is a term that cannot be translated. A *Stift* was a protestant or catholic convent for unmarried, often impoverished noblewomen. The English term cannoness is misleading, as it does not contain the combination of social status and missed life that Döblin wants to convey in this story. The poet Karoline von Günderode was a *Stiftsdame*. *Stiftsfräulein* has a slightly derogatory connotation.

[23] Döblin often inserts medical details into his stories. Medicine containing Atropine enlarges the pupils. Döblin experimented with Atropine and published his results. See *EB*, 526, note to page 14.

[24] In fact, the lack of harmony or unity between Ella and her body is evident from the beginning: "Läppisch bis zu jedem Schritt, lernte sie jetzt ihre federnden Bänder, ihre zu glatten Gelenke zwingen, sie schlich sich behutsam und geduldig in die Zehen, die Knöchel, die Knie ein und die Biegung der schlanken Arme, wachte lauernd über dem Spiel des straffen Leibes" (*EB*, 18).

[25] The phrase "sie spielte weiter" follows from an earlier characterization: "[sie] wachte lauernd über dem Spiel des straffen Leibes" (*EB*, 18).

[26] This is similar to the narrator's critical and highly ironic description of the writer Detlev Spinell in Thomas Mann's "Tristan."

[27] Di Silva travels from far away to inform the father of his first mate of his son's death. He brings not only the deceased's belongings but gifts of some value.

[28] The matter-of-fact protocols are a sign of the hopelessness of the patients' conditions and also an indication of what must have appeared to the young Döblin as the medical profession's failure and inability to alleviate or cure the suffering. See Schäffner 276–90.

[29] Although the two authors are in most respects poles apart, their early writings exhibit certain parallel concerns. For Mann, as for Döblin, the irrational and instinctual played a major role, as did the fascination with and longing for death. Similarly, Mann's love for the blond and blue-eyed, contained, by his own admission, overtones of racial thinking. However, in the twenties, Thomas Mann began to see the emphasis on the irrational as a danger and in direct opposition to humanism, which he felt was essential to the survival of a civilized world. His story, "Mario und der Zauberer" (1930), his essays "Die Wiedergeburt der Anständigkeit" (1931) and

"Deutsche Ansprache. Ein Appell an die Vernunft" (1930), as well as his autobiographical text, "On Myself" (1940), are examples of his awareness.

[30] For an excellent discussion of mass violence and its relation to the futurists, see Dollenmayer, especially 17–27.

[31] There are those who see a clear resolve toward an individual political stance in Franz Biberkopf at the end of *Berlin Alexanderplatz*. See Koopmann, 109–12. Others, including this author, cannot but see a typically Döblin-like open ending. It is true, of course, that by the mid-twenties, Döblin reintroduces the human subject in his writings. However, only in *Pardon wird nicht gegeben* (1935) does Döblin deal with his indecisiveness.

Works Cited

Anz, Thomas. "Alfred Döblin und die Psychoanalyse. Ein kritischer Bericht zur Forschung." *Internationales Alfred-Döblin-Kolloquium Leiden 1995*. Bern: P. Lang, 1997. 9–30.

Dollenmayer, David. *The Berlin Novels of Alfred Döblin: "Wadzek's Battle with the Steam Turbine," "Berlin Alexanderplatz," "Men without Mercy," and "November 1918."* Berkeley: U of California P, 1988.

Dollinger, Roland. "Sadomasochismus in Alfred Döblins *Der schwarze Vorhang*." *Internationales Alfred-Döblin-Kolloquium Leipzig 1997*. Bern, New York: P. Lang, 1999. 51–65.

Hofmannsthal, Hugo. *Sämtliche Werke XXXI*. Frankfurt am Main: Fischer, 1991.

Ihering, Herbert. *Von Reinhardt bis Brecht, II*. Berlin: Aufbau-Verlag, 1961.

Keck, Annette. *"Avantgarde der Lust": Autorschaft und sexuelle Relation in Döblins früher Prosa*. Munich: Wilhelm Fink, 1995.

———. "Lektüren von Frauen. Zur De(kon)struktion literarischer Sinnbildungskonzepte im Frühwerk Alfred Döblins," *Internationales Alfred-Döblin-Kolloquium Leiden 1995*. Bern, New York: P. Lang, 1997. 71–82.

Koopmann, Helmut. *Der klassisch-moderne Roman in Deutschland: Thomas Mann, Alfred Döblin, Hermann Broch*. Berlin: Kohlhammer, 1983.

Kyora, Sabine. "Zum Paradox in Döblins frühen Erzählungen." *Internationales Alfred-Döblin-Kolloquium Leiden 1995*. Bern, New York: P. Lang, 1997. 61–70.

Mann, Thomas. "Tristan." *Gesammelte Werke VIII*. Oldenburg: S. Fischer, 1960.

Marx, Reiner. "Literatur und Zwangsneurose — Eine Gegenübertragungs-Improvisation zu Alfred Döblins früher Erzählung 'Die Ermordung einer Butterblume.'" *Internationales Alfred-Döblin-Kolloquium Leiden 1995*. Bern, New York: P. Lang, 1997. 49–60.

Mauthner, Fritz. *Beiträge zu einer Kritik der Sprache.* Vol. 1. Hildesheim: Georg Olms, 1969.

Nietzsche, Friedrich. *Also sprach Zarathustra. Kritische Studienausgabe.* Vol. 4. Ed. Giorgio Colli and Mazzino Montinari. Munich: dtv and Berlin, New York: de Gruyter.

———. *Zur Genealogie der Moral. Kritische Studienausgabe.* Vol. 5. Ed. Giorgio Colli and Mazzino Montinari. Munich: dtv and Berlin, New York: de Gruyter.

Reuchlein, Georg. "'Man lerne von der Psychiatrie.' Literatur, Psychologie und Psychopathologie in Alfred Döblins 'Berliner Programm' und 'Die Ermordung einer Butterblume.'" *Jahrbuch für Internationale Germanistik* 23 (1991): 1, 10–68.

Schäffner, Wolfgang. *Die Ordnung des Wahns: Zur Poetologie psychiatrischen Wissens bei Alfred Döblin.* Munich: Wilhelm Fink, 1995.

Schröter, Klaus. *Alfred Döblin in Selbstzeugnissen und Bilddokumenten.* Reinbek: Rowohlt, 1978.

Schuster, Ingrid, and Ingrid Bode, eds. *Alfred Döblin im Spiegel der zeitgenössichen Kritik.* Bern/Munich: Francke Verlag, 1973.

Stegemann, Helga. *Studien zu Alfred Döblins Bildlichkeit: "Die Ermordung einer Butterblume und andere Erzählungen."* Bern: P. Lang, 1978.

Sternberg, Fritz. *Der Dichter und die Ratio: Erinnerungen an Bertolt Brecht.* Göttingen: Sachse und Pohl, 1963.

Tewarson, Heidi Thomann. *Alfred Döblin: Grundlagen seiner Aesthetik und ihre Entwicklung 1900–1933.* Bern: P. Lang, 1979.

———. "Von der Frauenfrage zum Geschlechterkampf: Der Wandel der Prioritäten im Frühwerk Alfred Döblins." *The German Quarterly* 58 (1985): 208–22.

The Advent of Döblinism:
Die drei Sprünge des Wang-lun and *Wadzeks Kampf mit der Dampfturbine*

David Dollenmayer

BETWEEN 1912 and 1915 Alfred Döblin wrote his first two major novels in a sustained burst of extraordinary creative energy.[1] *Die drei Sprünge des Wang-lung* and *Wadzeks Kampf mit der Dampfturbine* encapsulate the paradoxes and polarities that characterize his oeuvre as a whole. In the catalogue of his novels, sprawling epics of mass movements in distant times and exotic places (*Wang-lun, Wallenstein, Berge Meere und Giganten, Amazonas*) alternate with works set in the urban, industrial present (*Wadzek, Berlin Alexanderplatz, Pardon wird nicht gegeben, November 1918, Hamlet oder die lange Nacht nimmt ein Ende*). In 1914 Döblin made his own *Sprung* directly from late eighteenth-century China in *Wang-lun* into early twentieth-century Berlin in *Wadzek*. Although these two works might at first appear to be poles apart, the following essay will argue that they display similarities of origin, theme, and imagery.

Upon publication in 1916, *Wang-lun* was hailed as a modern masterpiece, and reviewers compared it to cubist art (Schuster/Bode, 28–29). Two years later, *Wadzek* evoked reactions from reviewers that with few exceptions ranged from puzzled to nauseous. "Cubist" was applied to it as well — and with perhaps more justification — but the most frequent adjective in reviews of *Wadzek* is "grotesque" (Schuster/Bode, 52–58). Even as sympathetic a reader as Martin Buber, who had recommended source material on China for *Wang-lun* and to whom Döblin then sent the manuscript of *Wadzek*, was completely perplexed by it (*B I, 79*).

One thing that certainly connects the two works is Döblin's decided avant-gardism, which in 1912 received a strong impetus from Italian futurism. In March of that year, German translations of two futurist manifestos appeared in Herwarth Walden's influential journal *Der Sturm*, in whose pages Döblin had already published his early stories. The subtitle he gave the novel he began to draft in July — "chinesischer

Roman" — suggests the influence of *Mafarka le Futuriste: roman africain* (1910) by futurism's leading literary light and polemicist Filippo Tommaso Marinetti (1876–1944). Always avidly avant-garde and antibourgeois, Döblin was attracted by Marinetti's provocative aesthetics of contempt for high culture and his rhetoric of violence and misogyny: "Wir [wollen] die aggressive Bewegung, die fiebrige Schlaflosigkeit, den gymnastischen Schritt, den gefahrvollen Sprung, die Ohrfeige und den Faustschlag preisen. [. . .] Wir wollen den Krieg preisen, — diese einzige Hygiene der Welt — den Militarismus, den Patriotismus, die zerstörende Geste der Anarchisten, die schönen Gedanken, die töten, und die Verachtung des Weibes" (*Sturm,* March 1912, 828–29). This flirtation with violence and the linked disdain for women and pacifism[2] is much on display in *Mafarka le Futuriste* (1909). It begins with a lengthy depiction of the mass rape of captured "négresses" by Mafarka's mutinous troops and ends with his construction of a gigantic winged son, Gazourmah, "beau et pur de toutes les tares qui viennent de la vulve maléficiante et qui prédisposent à la décrépitude et à la mort!" (281–82).

In an open letter to Marinetti published in *Der Sturm,* Döblin admired the Italian's "Energie und Härte, Männlichkeit" in contrast to conventional contemporary fiction, "einer unter Erotismen, Hypochondrien, Schiefheiten und Quälereien berstenden Literatur" (*AzL,* 9). Like Marinetti, he despised realism's cultivation of fine psychological distinctions and primary concentration on love as a theme. Proust's *Du côté de chez Swann* and Thomas Mann's *Der Tod in Venedig,* both published in 1913, epitomize a modernism that pushes realist narrative to the limits of introspective examination of frustrated love.[3] At the same time Döblin, following in Marinetti's footsteps, was espousing a radical break with realism's authorial narrators. He calls himself a "Naturalist" (*AzL,* 13) and demands a "Fanatismus der Selbstverleugnung" and "Entselbstung" that will break the "Hegemonie des Autors." "Los vom Menschen! Mut zur kinetischen Phantasie [. . .] Tatsachenphantasie!" (18–19). These demands of the essay "An Romanautoren und ihre Kritiker: Berliner Programm" (For Novelists and Their Critics: Berlin Program), written between *Wang-lun* and *Wadzek,* are realized in the narrative practice of both, and connect them to each other.

In a "technical manifesto" of futurist literature whose German translation appeared in *Der Sturm* in October 1912, while Döblin was at work on *Wang-lun,* Marinetti had already made a similar proclamation: "Man muß das "Ich" in der Literatur zerstören, das heißt alle Psychologie" (*Sturm,* October 1912, 195). But in this same manifesto Marinetti promulgates specific stylistic dicta for futurist language: verbs only in the infinitive form, adjectives and adverbs eliminated because they introduce too much nuance, nouns in analogic pairs (not surprisingly, some examples are "Mann — Torpedoboot, Frau — Hafen, Menge — Brandung" [*Sturm*, October 1912, 194]), mathematical symbols to replace punctuation. Five months later, in March 1913, *Der Sturm* published Marinetti's supplement to the technical manifesto, which culminates in "Bataille: Poids + Odeur," a battle scene in French that actually follows these avant-garde prescriptions, consisting almost entirely of analogic noun pairs: "général îlot," "ventres arrosoirs têtes foot-ball éparpillement" (*Sturm*, 1913, 280).

Immediately following this text in the same issue, *Der Sturm* published Döblin's brilliant "Futuristische Worttechnik: Offener Brief an F. T. Marinetti" [Futuristic Word Technique: Open Letter to Marinetti] in which he digs in his heels against the Italian's reductive monomania, the "Katastrophe der fehlenden Interpunktion und der fehlenden Syntax" (*AzL*, 13). Döblin objects not just to Marinetti's stylistic prescriptions, but perhaps even more to his circumscribed subject matter. He criticizes him for equating reality with "die Welt Ihrer Automobile, Aeroplane und Maschinengewehre" (*AzL*, 10). He has fallen victim to a "lütte lütte Verwechslung: Realität ist Dinglichkeit" (*AzL*, 11). Even here in the avant-garde beginnings of his career, Döblin's inherent spirituality asserts a transcendence beyond the appearances of the real world. In his argument against Marinetti's technical rules, he even goes so far as to adduce the "Rhythmik und Verskunst" of Baudelaire and Mallarmé (but not, significantly, the practice of any other German novelists). Genuine art can also provide "Narkotika [. . .] Stimulantia." It can point "über und unter die Wirklichkeit" (*AzL*, 11).

Marinetti's insistence on his stripped-down analogies is in fact an impoverished mimesis, a "Babysprache" (Schröter, 64). Far from getting closer to reality, the text "Bataille: Poids + Odeur" is both abstract and old fashioned:

> Ihre Schlacht ist von Anfang bis Ende vollgestopft mit Bildern, Analogien, Gleichnissen. Gut, aber das sieht mir nicht sehr modern aus, ist doch rechte, biderbe, alte Literatur; ich schenke Ihnen alle Bilder, — aber heran an die Schlacht! Direkt, Marinetti! Ja, das ist bequem, den Feldherrn eine "Insel" zu nennen, die Köpfe wie Fußbälle fliegen zu lassen, die zerrissenen Bäuche wie Gießkannen sprudeln zu lassen. Spielerei! Antiquiert! Museum! Wo sind die Köpfe, was ist mit den Bäuchen!? Und Sie wollen Futurist sein? Das ist übler Ästhetizismus! Die Dinge sind einzigartig; ein Bauch ist ein Bauch und keine Gießkanne: das ist das ABC des Naturalisten, des echten direkten Künstlers. Sich die Bilder verkneifen, ist das Problem des Prosaikers. (*AzL*, 12–13)

"Man kann Ihre Schlacht noch viel besser machen" (*AzL,* 12), writes Döblin, and indeed, he was in the midst of showing how. *Die drei Sprünge des Wang-lun,* Döblin's "Chinese novel" and answer to Marinetti's "African novel," contains battle scenes that far outdo the experimental "Bataille" in their immediacy, while being composed in language far more radically new than the still conventional style — as opposed to subject matter — of *Mafarka.* Another crucial difference is that unlike Marinetti's fantasy novel, *Wang-lun* is based on a historical event, and the title figure on a historical peasant leader of the same name.

In addition to its subtitle, the "Zueignung" with which *Wang-lun* begins makes explicit its turn away from futurism. In sharp contrast to the narrative voice of the novel itself, here an authorial "I" speaks from a modern urban setting in order to declare his alienation from the technology so beloved of the futurists:

> Ich tadle das verwirrende Vibrieren nicht. Nur finde ich mich nicht zurecht.
> Ich weiß nicht, wessen Stimmen das sind, wessen Seele solch tausendtönniges Gewölbe von Resonanz braucht.
> Dieser himmlische Taubenflug der Aeroplane.
> Diese schlüpfenden Kamine unter dem Boden.
> Dieses Blitzen von Worten über hundert Meilen:
> Wem dient es? (*WL,* 7)

In the author-narrator's view, technology has failed to engender the New Man envisioned at the end of *Mafarka.* The passers-by outside his window may possess new Telefunken radios, but they are still gripped by age-old vices: greed, satiety, lewdness, brutality, ambition. He closes his window against such "Fortschritt" and identifies himself with the natural world, which has been suppressed by technology: "Ich, vom Wind gestriegelt" (*WL,* 7).

"Daß ich nicht vergesse —" (*WL,* 7), the opening fragment whose pathos is interrupted twice by the clamorous noises of the modern city invading the room where the narrator sits writing, is finally completed in a sentence that by collapsing time suggests the contemporary relevance of the novel to follow: "Im Leben dieser Erde sind zweitausend Jahre ein Jahr" (*WL,* 8). In the nominalized verbs characteristic of his style (Ribbat, 159) — "Gewinnen, Erobern" (*WL,* 8) — Döblin evokes the aggressive, triumphalist impulses of modern life celebrated in the futurist manifestos in order to demonstrate their futility by contrast to the Taoist wisdom of "ein alter Mann," Liä Dsi:

"Wir gehen und wissen nicht wohin. Wir bleiben und wissen nicht wo. Wir essen und wissen nicht warum. Das alles ist die starke Lebenskraft von Himmel und Erde: wer kann da sprechen von Gewinnen, Besitzen?"[4]

The novel, "diese[s] ohnmächtige[ ] Buch" (*WL*, 8) is thus presented as the narrator's tribute to Liä Dsi. He sits "hinter meinem Fenster" (8), which he has closed to the modern city without. The movement toward his narrative is thus from the beginning a spiritual quest, an inward withdrawal more than a historicizing recreation of an era distant in time and space.

Yet in sharp contrast to the first-person authorial voice of the "Dedication," the novel itself does indeed obliterate the "I" and all psychology. The narrator is simply the medium through which the narrative flows.[5] Nor is there anything like ratiocination on the part of the characters within the novel. The essay "An Romanautoren und ihre Kritiker," which formulates the narrative practice of the just-completed *Wang-lun* as a literary program, rejects the realist assumption of an integrated personality capable of self-analytical rationality. Novelists ought to emulate empirical psychiatry by confining themselves to "die Notierung der Abläufe, Bewegungen, — mit einem Kopfschütteln, Achselzucken für das Weitere und das 'Warum' und 'Wie'" (*AzL*, 16; Ryan, 417). The plot is driven by emotion, dialogue, and action, not by reflection.

The world of the novel is an imagined eighteenth-century China, based on Döblin's extensive background reading, with no hint of a narrator sitting in his room in twentieth-century Berlin. The meaning of words such as *Tou-ssee, Jamen,* and *Tao-tai,* for example, can only be gathered from context. Never once is there any acknowledgement of a need to explain to a European reader Chinese habits or customs, hardly ever any acknowledgement of the existence of Europe at all.[6] And yet the language is neither self-consciously "foreign" nor marshaled into the classical periods of Thomas Mann conjuring the biblical world in the *Joseph* tetralogy (1933–42), but is rather a roiling mix of extravagant expressionist lyricism, imagined Manchu ceremoniousness at the imperial court, and Berlin colloquialisms.[7]

The novel's four books chronicle a popular religious movement — led by the eponymous hero — that becomes a social rebellion against the Manchu Dynasty. The first book, entitled "Wang-lun," narrates the central character's childhood and youth as a rough-hewn practical jokester from a Shan-tung fishing village. When he witnesses the murder of an innocent Muslim by the authorities, he kills an officer in revenge and then flees to the Nan-ku mountains of Chih-li Province. There, obsessed by the recurring memory of the murder he has committed and tormented by the sufferings of his fellow outcasts, he adopts celibacy and the Taoist doctrine of wu-wei — non-resistance to fate — as a tactic against persecution by the authorities, and begins to attract followers. He sets off alone on a journey to win protection from the "Weiße Wasserlilie," a secret society of well-to-do merchants who work against the rule of the Manchus and toward the restoration of the Ming Dynasty.

For most of the second book, "Die gebrochene Melone," Wang-lun disappears from the narrative, which concentrates on the continuing growth of the sect. It now calls itself the "Wahrhaft Schwachen" (*WL*, 108) and attracts followers from all levels of society, both men and women. In Wang's absence, his friend the apostate Buddhist monk Manoh emerges as a leader and persuades the other men to abandon the principle of celibacy. They perpetrate a mass rape of the women, "ihr Gebrochenen Melonen" as Ma calls them (*WL*, 148). In contrast to Marinetti's violated "négresses," Döblin's "sisters" not only joyfully accept their rape, but begin to practice "heilige Prostitution" (*WL*, 174) — surrendering themselves to anyone — as a protective measure for the sect. Ma finds allies among disgruntled workers and peasants and even founds his own state, the "Insel der Gebrochenen Melone" (*WL*, 217) with himself as priest-king, but refuses to abandon the principle of non-resistance. Troops dispatched against him slaughter his followers and besiege Ma and a few hundred remaining sectarians. Wang-lun, returned from his journey, tries to negotiate a peaceful end to the siege. When Ma refuses to disperse his group and seems set on martyrdom and entrance into the "Westliche[s] Paradies" (*WL*, 244), Wang poisons the water supply of the city so that they will all die rather than fall into the hands of the "Henkersknechte und Blutsoldaten" (243).

In the third book, "Der Herr der gelben Erde," the narrative focus shifts again, but now to the highest level of power. In his sheltered and aestheticized existence in Peking, the Emperor Khien-lung is troubled by reports of the Wu-wei movement and its brutal suppression. He invites the Tibetan Lamaist "Papst" (*WL*, 301) or Teshu Lama, Lobsang Paldan Jische, to visit China and advise him. The Lama criticizes Khienlung for allowing the persecution of the sect and urges him to abandon the use of force. The Emperor, torn between his need to maintain Confucian civic order and his desire not to dishonor his ancestors by poorly administering his empire, seems to agree. He orders the persecution stopped, but cannot give up his prerogative to use force: "Man hätte mich längst ermordet, wenn ich auch nur eine halbe Stunde fromm in Ihrem Sinn gewesen wäre" (*WL*, 304). The narrative returns briefly to

Wang-lun. Upon hearing the gruesome details of the mass poisoning he has caused, he is devastated, withdraws to the south under an assumed name, marries, and becomes a cormorant fisherman. While "die konservativen Elemente" (*WL*, 318) at court plot the Emperor's assassination, the Teshu Lama contracts smallpox and dies without further enlightening Khien-lung. The Emperor's son succeeds in portraying the Wu-wei movement as a rebellion inspired by Tibetan lamaists and exposing China to invasion by "die langnasigen Weißen aus Indien" (*WL*, 360). Khien-lung agrees to military suppression of the sect.

The title of the fourth book, "Das westliche Paradies," anticipates its apocalyptic conclusion. As the brutal persecution resumes, the "Wahrhaft Schwachen" send emissaries to persuade Wang-lun to return as their leader. He declares that the sect will have to abandon its ideals of pacifism and take up arms (*WL*, 379), echoing the Emperor's statement to the Lama about the need for force: "Ein Wahrhaft Schwacher kann nur Selbstmörder sein" (403). Supported and financed by the Ming loyalists of the "Weiße Wasserlilie" and gaining recruits from among the poor, Wang's army carries its black banners right to the gates of the Imperial Quarter of Peking before being turned back by reinforcements. The rebel army is surrounded. Before the final onslaught of the Emperor's army, Wang is called on to pass judgment on a common robber. In a sudden revelation, he realizes that the man is exactly his age and that this could easily have been his fate. This is "sein Bruder" (*WL*, 458). He imagines returning to a criminal life himself, yet knows he cannot, because it would mean being ready to commit murder again: "Nicht morden, nicht morden!" (*WL*, 459). He orders the freeing of all prisoners, and declares, "ich will uns untergehen lassen" (*WL*, 460). He perishes along with all his followers, yet the novel ends with the suggestion that the principle of wu-wei may persist. Having lost her two children to the battle against the rebels, Hai-tang, the wife of the Emperor's victorious field commander, makes a pilgrimage to the monastery island from which Wang's friend Ma-noh had fled. The Buddhist goddess Kuan-yin appears to her, telling her to stop tearing her breast in grief: "Deine Kinder schlafen bei mir. Stille sein, nicht widerstreben, oh, nicht widerstreben." In the novel's final line, Hai-tang asks herself, "Stille sein, nicht widerstreben, kann ich es denn?" (*WL*, 480).

The preceding plot summary outlines the novel's pattern of successive build-ups and catastrophes, but it cannot do justice to its fecundity of character and incident. *Wang-lun* teems with figures, both named and anonymous: aristocrats, merchants, artisans and peasants, thieves and prostitutes, men and women. Their individual stories constantly delay and complicate the ongoing narrative. The novel begins not with Wang-lun, but with a depiction of the sectarians spreading over the countryside and winning converts. The narrative picks out the conversion stories of individual "Brüder und Schwestern":

> Da war ein frischer junger Mann aus Schan-tung, der das erste Examen mit Auszeichnung bestanden hatte. [. . .] Ein Bohnenhändler, ein rippendürrer Mann, lebte fünfzehn Jahre in kinderloser Ehe. [. . .] Tsin war ein reicher Mann vom Fuße des Tschan. [. . .] Junge Wüstlinge zusammen mit Dirnen, die sie aus den bemalten Häusern befreit hatten, wanderten herzu. [. . .] Sechs Freundinnen vom nördlichen Kaiserkanal, die man als Kinder verheiratet hatte [. . .]. (*WL,* 1–12)

Only then is Wang-lun introduced as the movement's leader, and the narrator jumps back in time to his boyhood. This mass of humanity out of which the central character emerges suggests, like the inhabitants of Berlin in *Berlin Alexanderplatz,* a kind of democracy in Döblin's fiction. His heroes are representative but in some sense also random. Others could just as easily have been central. This is the revelation that Wang himself experiences in his confrontation with the thief, his "brother,"[8] late in the novel.

This latent potentiality of all figures in *Wang-lun* to become central, their inherent equality of interest as it were, is related to the episodic structure of the novel. To be sure, the book chronicles the rise, flourishing, and eradication of the Truly Weak and their leader Wang-lun. But it is not this unidirectional line that gives the novel its dynamic. Its most basic structural principle is alternation, of which the three leaps of the title are emblematic. When they actually occur late in the fourth book, those leaps are not forward, but from side to side. Wang jumps back and forth across a stream to demonstrate to a trusted lieutenant the course of his life. His first leap was into the doctrine of non-resistance. But: "Es wird alles schlecht. Ich muß weiterspringen." The second leap is his return to anonymity as a married cormorant fisherman. Even after the Wu-wei emissaries drag him back into leadership, he has still not fully accepted the responsibility: "noch bin ich nicht da, ich kann nicht so rasch folgen" (*WL,* 465). He presents the third leap as having been inspired by his encounter with the robber. He now feels himself fully returned, "wieder zu Hause, in Tschi-li" (i.e., in spirit back with the social outcasts amongst whom he began the sect). He calls for his battle sword and declares, "hier muß gekämpft werden" (*WL,* 466). With his leaps Wang demonstrates not continuous spiritual progress toward the ideal of wu-wei, but rather spiritual ruptures and alternation.

Since the middle of the novel, when he returns with the battle sword from his mission to the "Weiße Wasserlilie," he has acknowledged the paradoxical necessity of defending the ideal of non-resistance with force. This is the paradox from which neither Wang-lun nor the Emperor can escape: any attempt to live the ideal of piety and non-resistance is suicidal. Ernst Ribbat has asserted that it is only Ma-noh and the "Gebrochene Melone" who adhere unswervingly to the principle of wu-wei (127). Yet even this is not completely accurate, for surely that principle is violated by a festival in Ma's "Insel der Gebrochenen Melone" in which a troop of imperial cavalry is massacred, Coliseum-style, as part of the festivities. Under the pressure of pursuit and persecution, neither Ma nor Wang can consistently maintain either non-violence or celibacy. The first, second, and fourth books culminate in convulsions of sex and violence, which are often obsessively linked in Döblin's works. Despite the novel's dedication to the Taoist master Liä Dsi, the presumptive ideals of non-resistance and harmony with the natural world, inherently fragile and only briefly and fleetingly achievable (Ribbat, 121), are in fact not really in evidence. The sectarians tend constantly toward ecstatic behavior rather than quiet contemplation.

Döblin's first inspiration for the novel is supposed to have been a newspaper article about a rebellion of Chinese gold miners in Siberia and its bloody suppression by Czarist troops (Muschg, 481). Walter Muschg, who edited the first post-Second World War edition of *Wang-lun,* wrote in his afterword that in the course of his background reading on China, Döblin discovered Wang-lun's eighteenth-century revolt and his interest shifted "aus der aktuellen Zeitkritik ins Historische, aus dem Politischen ins Religiöse" (482). But the novel presents neither a consistent religious vision nor an accurate understanding of Taoist polarities (Fee, 129–35). Its episodic plot dominated by figures of alternation reflects a dualism of passivity and violence to be found throughout Döblin's oeuvre.

It can be argued that indignation at injustice is as central a motivating force within the novel as is the urge toward Taoist non-resistance. Moreover, the novel's allusions to political struggles in late Wilhelmine Germany are unmistakable: the distant Emperor bent on maintaining civic and social order at all costs and willing to use the most brutal force to do so; the exploited "Bauern und Arbeiter" (*WL,* 207) who join with Ma-noh's group and ask Lenin's question, "Was soll geschehen?" (208); the impoverished salt makers whom the narrator refers to as "Gewerkschaftler" (210). In fact, the founding of the "Wahrhaft Schwachen" proceeds equally from Wang-lun's spiritual crisis after killing the officer and from his clear-eyed grasp of state violence: "Sie kommen immer wieder und nehmen etwas weg. Sie geben keinen Frieden und keine Ruhe. Sie wollen mich und euch und uns alle ausrotten und nicht leben lassen. Was wollen wir machen, liebe

Kinder?" (*WL,* 73). On the other hand, the end of the novel has been criticized for abandoning this clear-cut political conception for a "materialistische[r] Pantheismus" in which "sich [. . .] Natur und Gesellschaft zu unterschiedslosen Erscheinungsweisen vermischen" (Schröter, 57). And it is true that the final battles are more a display of pure apocalyptic violence than the depiction of a real effort to unseat the Manchus. One is fought in a lurid hail storm that levels both sectarians and soldiers into "Verfolgte":

> Chao-hoei [the Emperor's field commander] schaukelte auf seinem Schimmel, oben auf dem Hügel. Wang-lun rollte seine Walze auf der Chaussee, mahlte sein Korn. Dann riß die Schwärze des Himmels auseinander, Hagelschloßen stürzten aus dem Schlitz, tanzten auf den Schädeln. Die Wahrhaft Schwachen kämpften in dem blendenden Gewühl des Unwetters mit eisiger Gelassenheit. Keine Wunde berührte sie. Es war gleich, ob sie starben oder lebten. Das Feuer der Ilisoldaten fraß sich nicht durch, fing an zu rauchen, zu flackern. Kein stürmischer Angriff erfolgte von den Rebellen: still, weniger drängend als von ungewollter Notwendigkeit gedrängt, überwanden sie die Feinde.
>
> Als Chao-hoei sich mit seinen zertrümmerten Soldaten wandte, hingen sich die Rebellen, gezogen, an seine Spuren. Beides Verfolgte. Liefen davon, ließen die zerbrochenen Menschen, Wagen mit Stieren, muskellose Schwerter und Beile, als wäre es Jauche. (*WL,* 426)

When a group of Peking courtesans propose to Wang-lun a plot to assassinate the heads of the dynasty, he angrily throws them out. Like Ma-noh before him, he has accepted destruction with joyful fatalism: "Es ist beschlossen, vollendet, jauchzte Wang" (*WL,* 467). He repeatedly dreams in an eroticized image of being completely engulfed by the trunk and branches of a huge sycamore tree.[9] At the end, Wang sinks back into the mass. His death with a group of comrades in a burning house is by no means a climatic moment in the final battle (*WL,* 475). Attention is deflected immediately to the last stand of those still alive.

As is the case with so many of Döblin's novels, the ending of *Wang-lun* is extremely ambivalent. After the brutal "abschließenden Regierungsmaßnahmen" (*WL,* 476) against the sect, the Emperor congratulates himself that, "wenn Kung-fu-tse hier wäre, er würde nicht gründlicher vorgegangen sein als ich" (*WL,* 477). The final pages seem an attempt to counterbalance this restoration of bleak Confucian order with the conversion of Chao-hoei's wife Hai-tang to the principle of non-resistance, yet this remains a purely personal assuaging of her grief rather than a triumph of wu-wei.

A year after completing *Die drei Sprünge des Wang-lun,* Döblin composed the first draft of *Wadzeks Kampf mit der Dampfturbine* from August to December 1914, the first five months of the First World War.

In December, he volunteered for the army and served as a doctor in Lorraine and Alsace until the end of the war. The revised novel was completed by 1916 but not published until 1918. On the evidence of his surviving remarks about the novel, it is clear that Döblin thought of it as a contrasting complement to *Wang-lun*. In a 1915 letter to Martin Buber, who had reacted with perplexity to the novel, Döblin insisted on "das liebevoll komische Grundgefühl" of *Wadzek* (*B I*, 80). And thirty years later, he described its composition as an involuntary turn away "vom Schweren und Finstern" of the Chinese novel: "da schlug ich um und geriet ohne Absicht, ja eigentlich gegen meinen Willen, ins Lichte, Frische und Burleske: 'Wadzek'" (*SLW*, 291).

Whereas the *Zueignung* of *Wang-lun* announces a rejection of futurist preoccupations, the title of the new novel suggests a return to them. Indeed, that seems to have been Döblin's original intention: "ich plante die Technik des gigantischen Berlins." But in the act of writing, which Döblin always describes as involuntarily automatic, the novel "wurde ganz anders [. . .] etwas sehr Menschliches, nämlich der erste Teil davon, wie die Technik einen aus sich ausstößt, ein *komisches* Buch" (*B I*, 77). In fact however, although Franz Wadzek is an industrialist and engineer, the industrial technology of modern society is at most a vague backdrop for the psychopathology of Wadzek and his family.[10] The novel is to be sure "etwas sehr Menschliches," but not a struggle between man and machine in which man is "ejected," but rather a struggle for orientation in a hostile world, played out within a narrowly circumscribed cast of characters.

Like *Wang-lun*, *Wadzek* is divided into four books. We encounter the central character in the role of industrialist and engineer only in the first book, "Die Verschwörung," and even then only briefly. Even as the novel begins, Wadzek's competitor Jakob Rommel has already defeated him by producing a new steam turbine (Wadzek produces piston-driven machines), and also by secretly buying up shares in his company. Wadzek first tries to enlist the help of his former protégée, Gabriele (or Gaby) Wessel, who is now Rommel's mistress. She agrees to get a list of the stock certificates Rommel plans to buy in exchange for being introduced to Wadzek's daughter Herta.[11] When this plan fails, Wadzek, aided by his friend Schneemann (an engineer who works for Rommel), desperately attempts to impede his rival by intercepting and changing the text of a letter from Rommel to the agent who is purchasing shares for him.

When this attempt is also foiled, Wadzek insanely decides to barricade himself in his suburban villa in Reinickendorf along with his wife, daughter, and ally Schneemann, there to await attack by the authorities — or rather, by the whole society. This slapstick "siege" comprises the long second book, "Die Belagerung von Reinickendorf." The longer the besieged household awaits this completely illusory attack, the more Wadzek becomes entangled in his delusion. Finally he fires on supposed attackers (who are bird poachers in his front yard), is interrogated with Schneemann at the local police station, then reprimanded and released. Profoundly downcast, he returns to Berlin.

The third book, "Zu Boden geschlagen und zerschmettert," begins with a series of darkly symbolic, highly enigmatic scenes. Wadzek breaks with Schneemann because of his supposed betrayal of their cause, discovers renewed passion for his enormously fat wife Pauline, but then also renews contact with Gaby Wessel.

In the fourth book, "Man sammelt seine Glieder und geht nach Hause," after Pauline throws a disgustingly drunken costume party with two women cronies, Wadzek leaves his family and flees to America abroad an ocean liner driven by one of Rommel's steam turbines.

Unlike Martin Buber, the young Bertolt Brecht was an enthusiastic advocate of *Wadzek* and understood it as a critique of tragic heroism. He noted in his diary in 1920, "Der Held läßt sich nicht tragisieren. Man soll die Menschheit nicht antragöden. [. . .] Es läßt den Menschen schamhaft im Halbdunkel und macht nicht Proselyten" (Brecht, 48). Döblin himself tried to persuade Buber of the novel's basic comedy "der scheinbaren Tragik gegenüber" (*B I*, 80). As in the famous passage in *Berlin Alexanderplatz* in which Franz Biberkopf is contrasted to Orestes (*BA*, 98–104), Aeschylus's *Oresteia* provides the mythic prefiguration that Döblin parodies. Wadzek in his initial stance as a heroically embattled captain of industry is willing to sacrifice his daughter Herta in order to gain the advantage of Rommel. Herta herself makes the parallel explicit when she tells Gaby, "das Schicksal steht über unserem Haus. Agamemnon ist nichts gegen uns. [. . .] [Mein Vater] kommt ins Sanatorium. [. . .] du wirst ihn in der Badewanne wiedersehen" (*WK*, 40). When he returns contritely to his wife after the delusional siege in Reinickendorf, Pauline, like a latter-day Clytemnestra, "thronte heroisch über ihrer Beute" (*WK*, 228), and in the fourth book precipitates Wadzek's flight by symbolically killing him during the drunken costume party for his sacrifice of Herta: "Tot. Er ist tot! [. . .] Mein Kind hat er ausgesetzt" (295).[12]

Wadzek's struggle to live up to the heroic ideal is anticipated in the figure of his friend Schneemann. He too is an engineer and inventor. But when a powerful industrial firm steals his invention and crushes him, he curses his native city Stettin (which was also Döblin's birthplace) and settles in Berlin, where he "überhäutete sich mit Verbissenheit" (*WK*, 13). He works for Rommel and has settled into the life of a petit bourgeois with a wife and several children. His thinking is in conventional clichés: "Seine Zitate kamen aus der Tiefe und stammten aus Goethe." His politics are reactionary: "Er entdeckte in sich in Berlin eine Leidenschaft für das Militär, zu dem er wegen seiner Korpulenz nicht gekommen war." His heroic self-image survives only in dreams, in which he "wie ein alter Römer mit dem Schild im linken Arm dastand, das kurze Schwert in der rechten Faust, so den Angriff erwartend" (*WK*, 13).

In his letter to Buber, Döblin compares Wadzek to the great model for all tragicomic figures, Don Quixote, and calls Schneemann his "Comparativ" (*B I*, 80). Despite his protestations to the contrary, *Wadzek* is not comic in any conventional sense. What real humor there is in the novel is concentrated in the figure of Schneemann and his relation to Wadzek. Schneemann's function as monitory example is underlined by his name. He is a pale figure liable to melt away under the heat of adversity. Wadzek repeatedly mocks his friend's labile name, calling him "König Schneemann," "Weissmann" (*WK*, 28), and "Schneemann alias Eisbär" (220). The narrator also plays with the name, atomizing Schneemann in the act of enjoying a well-earned glass of beer into "lauter kleine biertrinkende Schneemänner" (*WK*, 120). Even Schneemann himself tries to withdraw from the Reinickendorf adventure with the words, "Der Schneeman hat ausgeschneit" (*WK*, 147). At a moment of intense fear of being drawn into Wadzek's struggle with Rommel, Schneemann even breaks into Stettin *Plattdeutsch:* "Wat glöwwst du, dat ick dun wär? Pusten wär ich dich wat! [. . .] Tauerst bedäppst du mich, dann warst mich an den Galgen trecken, du Aas!" (*WK*, 72).[13]

Wadzek's first reaction to Schneemann's exemplum of failed heroism is the desperate withdrawal to Reinickendorf. When the "siege" ends in humiliation at the police station, the shattered Wadzek recapitulates Schneemann's retreat into conventional family life in the third book. Thus Wadzek also plays out the dualism of resistance and submission that is central to *Wang-lun,* but this time against completely illusory adversaries. It is merely grotesque when Wadzek explains to a police lieutenant in Reinickendorf that "es sich [. . .] um den Kampf des einzelnen gegen das Monopolwesen, gegen das Trustsystem [handelt]." And the lieutenant is appropriately amused: "Pliemer, sehen Sie mal nach, was die Leute getrunken haben. Das Trustsystem. Es ist zum Piepen" (*WK*, 172). A scene in the novel's third book has attracted the attention of all interpreters of the novel, for although clearly symbolic, its symbolism is obscure (Links, 59–60; Elshorst, 25; Huguet, 711;

Ribbat, 177). Wadzek first calls a large wardrobe mirror in his marital bedroom "ein Loch in der Welt" (*WK,* 191) and then shatters it with his elbows. The scene marks a critical point in Wadzek's change from activity to passivity, from the pantomime of an embattled industrialist to the pantomime of a contented family man. It is important that the glass mirrors not only Wadzek, but also his "comparative" Schneemann; they stand side by side before it. Wadzek uses the mirror to compare the fallen tragic hero (himself now or Schneemann in his Stettin days) with the smug petit bourgeois: "Dies links, sehen Sie, im Spiegel, das jetzt spricht und den Mund bewegt, sind Sie — in Stettin. Sie selbst, Schneeman, nicht ich. [. . .] Ein Wink, hokuspokus, da stehen Sie, von heute, kräftig, dick, vor der Kur, nach der Kur" (*WK,* 192). When Wadzek first spits at and then shatters his own image in the mirror, he takes symbolic leave of his ideal, heroic self-image. Now he throws Schneemann out. He no longer needs him as a cautionary example, because he is about to become a Schneemann himself. Logically enough, Schneemann shortly thereafter disappears from the novel.

But the second response to Schneemann's example, Wadzek's submission to Pauline, soon proves to be as misguided as his attempt at heroism. It is nothing but an admission of defeat, the obverse of heroism, not an escape from it (although Wadzek shatters his heroic image in the mirror, he carries shards of it with him to the end of the novel). This is painfully clear as soon as the narrative focuses on Pauline Wadzek. It is difficult to think of a woman in literature more repellent than she. She is described, like some monstrous expressionist portrait, with the minute attention to physical detail called for in the Berlin Program and strictly adhered to throughout the novel:

> Frau Wadzek war einen Kopf größer als ihr Mann; sie war gewissermaßen pyramidal oder besser kegelförmig aufgebaut; während nämlich ihr Kopf mit Einschluß der Haarmassen einen normalen Umfang hatte, verschmälerten sich die Schultern, als käme nun abwärts eine graziöse feine Person, oder ein Persönchen; in der Tat schloß sich eine enge zusammengedrückte Brust an, von der Art eines eingetretenen Reifens. Darauf folgten aber erst die Brüste, die abwärts verrutscht schienen in ihren dicksten Portionen und eine beutelförmige Aufpolsterung der Vorderansicht hervorriefen. Und ihre unvermutete Anschwellung — wären diese Organe auf den Rücken verlegt, so würde man die Besitzerin als bucklig oder als Trägerin eines leidlich gefüllten Wassersacks betrachten —, diese unerwartete Anschwellung setzte sich geradlinig nach vorn und seitlich fort in Konturen, die dem Bauch der Frau Wadzek angehören mußten. [. . .] Frau Wadzek besaß ein plattes Gesicht mit etwas vorgeschobenem Kinn; den Unterkiefer streckte die Frau

gewohnheitsmäßig besonders bei Versuchen nachzudenken vor. [...] Von dem gekrümmten gebuckelten Rücken gab es einen einzigen Schwung vorn gegen Nacken und Kopf; ihm folgend stürzte der Kopf auf die Brust und baumelte da massiv. Senkrecht ergossen sich nunmehr hinterwärts die Röcke von den Hüften. (108–9)

The passage demonstrates that the objectivity of Döblin's "naturalistic" style does not preclude narrative judgment. Such judgment is simply transferred from overt narrative comment to an attitude inherent in the description of perceptual phenomena. Her exterior is here systematically dehumanized, the controlling metaphor that of a gigantic edifice. Not only is her inner life not shown; she *has* no inner life beyond her "Versuche nachzudenken." Her conversation throughout the novel consists almost entirely of hackneyed expressions of indignation, a reflection of her complete solipsism.

Gaby Wessel is Pauline's polar opposite. She is described repeatedly as beautiful and fashionable. One description of her in the novel is borrowed from the "Mode und Gesellschaft" supplement to the *Berliner Zeitung* of September 27, 1913 (*WK*, 348, note to page 31). If Pauline is solipsistic and devouring, Gaby is "sanftmütig" (*WK*, 206), defenseless to the point of masochism. She is the only character whose past is extensively narrated, which contributes to the impression that she is the only sane and normal figure in the novel. But her past consists of a series of willing submissions to sexual exploitation. Of her current relationship with Rommel, for instance, she says, "ich bin nichts Besseres als Rommels Mätresse. Das hab' ich mir gewählt" (*WK*, 10). There is no reason to think that she will be anything different for Wadzek as they head for America. She is a modern variation of the "sacred prostitutes" in *Wang-lun*, and one in a long line of prostitutes or kept women who populate Döblin's works from his very first fragmentary story "Modern" (1896) to his last novel *Hamlet oder die lange Nacht nimmt ein Ende* (1956).

Not surprisingly for a man of his time, Döblin's portrayal of women in *Wadzek* is rigidly binary. The polarity of female dominance and submission is related inversely to Wadzek's heroism and retreat into family life. Wadzek's flight with Gaby at the end of the novel is thus not really an escape from this dilemma into some positively valued synthesis, for he is still carrying metaphoric baggage in the form of a piece of the broken mirror wrapped in black paper. There are intimations that the duel for dominance has simply been transferred from Pauline to Gaby. On their way to Hamburg, she calls him "ein geborener Sklave" (*WK*, 319) and during their first unsuccessful attempt to make love, Wadzek says, "Liebe will ich nicht, ich verzichte auf Zärtlichkeit. Ich will Gehorsam"

(325). Their success at it in the final sentences is more comic than moving. Their faces are still "sich fremde [. . .] Gesichter," and having just told her to call him *du*, his final utterance is an engineer's comment on love: "Sehen Sie. Es funktioniert alles" (336).

In 1932, Döblin described his practice as a novelist thus: "Jedem meiner größeren epischen Werke geht eine geistige Fundamentierung voraus. Das epische Werk ist in einer künstlerischen Form [. . .] die Weiterführung und Konkretisierung, auch die Erprobung der bei der geistigen Vorarbeit erreichten Gedankenposition. So daß in der Regel am Schluß solchen epischen Werkes meine Gedankenposition bereits wieder überwunden und erschüttert ist. Es beginnt mit einer Sicherheit und endet mit einer neuen Frage" (*SLW*, 216). In view of this dialectical process, it should not surprise us that *Wang-lun* is followed by *Wadzek*. They share a common origin in a futurist-inspired avant-garde position and the fundamental dualism of rebellion and submission. They are also quite different, and are meant to be so. One way to express the difference between them is to say that *Wang-lun* is still readable for pleasure, while *Wadzek* is not (and probably never was). It is simply too odd and obscure a book, despite its frequent flashes of humor. Too much of it is simply grotesque without being funny.

At the end of this analysis, I would like to speculate about why this may be so. Despite Döblin's assertion that *Wang-lun* was a *Dammbruch* and simply came streaming out in eight months (*SLW*, 36), Erich Kleinschmidt's thorough notes to the *Schriften zum Leben und Werk* point out that in fact, he worked on it for ten or eleven months and wrote extensive, detailed outlines (*SLW*, 530). We know that he did wide background research (*B I*, 57–58) on Chinese society, culture, and religion. Synthesizing this material into the coherent fictional world of the novel must have required more conscious planning than Döblin liked to admit.

In the case of the first draft of *Wadzek*, on the other hand, Döblin's claim of involuntary writing may be taken more at face value: "ich schreibe stets völlig unwillkürlich, das ist keine Phrase; dies Buch ist von August bis Dezember 14 in einem Zug geschrieben" (*B I*, 80). If we can believe the report that Döblin "soll auf dem Fabrikgelände von Siemens & Halske und der AEG umfangreiche Vorstudien zu [*Wadzek*] betrieben haben" (Prangel, 33), then the novel got derailed in a much more profound way than *Wang-lun* was after its initial inspiration by the newspaper story about exploited Chinese miners in Siberia. I suggest that it may have been turmoil in Döblin's personal life that intruded and made *Wadzek* into a darkly burlesque family drama rather than a futurist-inspired struggle between man and machine.

In fact, *Wadzek* makes more use of material from Döblin's biography than any other work except *Pardon wird nicht gegeben*. Like Schneemann, Döblin came from Stettin. Like Wadzek, Döblin's father Max abandoned the family and fled to America with a lover. Like Wadzek, Döblin apparently had deeply ambivalent feelings about his wife.[14] In a brief "Autobiographische Skizze" (Autobiographical Sketch) from 1921, Döblin gives the bare-bones facts of his double career as doctor and writer, then says, "Von meiner seelischen Entwicklung kann ich nichts sagen; da ich selbst Psychoanalyse treibe, weiß ich, wie falsch jede Selbstäußerung ist. Bin mir außerdem psychisch ein Rühr-mich-nicht-an und nähere mich mir nur in der Entfernung der epischen Erzählung" (*SLW*, 37). This reticence about his own psyche of course adheres closely to the empirical psychology of the Berliner Programm. But it also protests too much.

Three years earlier, Döblin had written a more extensive autobiographical piece in which he is plagued by feelings of guilt: "gequält bin ich sehr, verfolgt. Und ich hoffe, verfolgt von mir selbst" (*SLW*, 14). Nearing forty years of age, he writes about his late sexual development, his loneliness as a medical student in Freiburg, his wish for a god-like father figure, his fear of life. The writing is an emotional confession in the first person until it takes an abrupt and unexpected turn: "Es hilft mir nicht, daß ich schreibe und schreibe. [. . .] Es soll nicht geredet werden von mir, sondern von Doktor Döblin. Dieser ziemlich kleine bewegliche Mann von deutlich jüdischem Gesichtsschnitt" (*SLW*, 16). This swerve from the first to the third person is a much more radical version of the transition from the *Zueignung* to the first book of *Wang-lun*. The essay proceeds in a new tone of distanced irony and sarcasm to tell the story of his father's abandonment of the family.

Given the chronology, it seems likely that this essay was a personal response to the January 1918 death from tuberculosis of Frieda Kunke, a young gentile nurse whom Döblin had met in 1907 while working in the Buch insane asylum.[15] She bore him a son in October 1911, but Döblin had in the meantime already become engaged to Erna Reiss, a medical student from a well-to-do Jewish family, in February of that year. They married in January 1912 (Meyer, 16–17). It is impossible to say what role family pressure played in his choice of wife. It seems certain, however, that the memory of his own father's abandonment both kept him in an unhappy marriage and led him to maintain contact with his son by Frieda Kunke.

Without claiming that *Wadzeks Kampf mit der Dampfturbine* is an autobiographical novel, I think it likely that the upheavals in Döblin's life in the years before the First World War deflected the novel from its intention of depicting the struggle of man and technology to the drama, rather conventional for his time, of a man caught in a rigidly dualistic image of women. By contrast, the tendency toward equality of significance among the numerous characters in *Die drei Sprünge des Wang-lun* extends to women as well. While the primary figures — Wang-lun, Ma-noh, the Emperor, and the Teshu Lama — are all male, numerous sub-plots feature women such as Hai-tang, women of many classes in active roles on both sides of the struggle. The theme of sexual dominance and submission is not at all prominent, and the whole question of sexuality is to a large extent resolved through celibacy on the one hand and sacred prostitution on the other. By thus avoiding the sexual pathology so prominent in his early stories and in *Wadzek*, Döblin was able to address head-on the question of the appropriate response to social injustice in *Wang-lun*. To simplify somewhat, *Wang-lun* formulates accessible problems within an exotic setting, while *Wadzek's* meaning eludes us even in the familiar setting of industrial Berlin. Not until his 1935 novel *Pardon wird nicht gegeben* did Döblin succeed in connecting his political concern for social justice with the familial crises of his childhood.

Notes

[1] Döblin had previously written the lyrical *Jagende Rosse* (1900, first published 1981) in his last year of Gymnasium and *Der schwarze Vorhang* between 1903 and its serial publication in *Der Sturm*, 1911–1913.

[2] The Austrian Berta von Suttner, author of the pacifist novel *Die Waffen nieder!*, had been awarded the Nobel Peace Prize in 1905.

[3] Döblin's hostility to Thomas Mann was life-long; his initial dislike of Proust (*SLW* 69) was later revised (*SLW*, 189).

[4] Döblin's source was apparently Liä-Dsi, *Das wahre Buch vom Quellenden Urgrund*, translated into German by R. Wilhelm (Jena: E. Diederichs, 1911). See Weyembergh-Boussart, 65 (footnote 5).

[5] There are only a very few places where the narrator calls attention to himself by anticipating coming disasters (*WL*, 87–88, 90, 100), mentioning later exaggerations of events (*WL*, 224, 366), or emphasizing his summarizing function: "Es erübrigt sich zu berichten [. . .]" (*WL*, 125).

[6] A Jesuit missionary (*WL*, 279) and an English emissary to India (295) and the "long-nosed whites" from India (360) are mentioned in passing, but these are the only — extremely periperal — references to Europe.

[7] Ribbat 160–65 provides the most detailed analysis of the novel's language.

[8] Typical of the novel's randomness and lack of closure is that Wang has an actual brother who is mentioned early in the novel (15–16) but never reappears.

[9] An obsessive image that also occurs in the story "Das Krokodil" (1917) and the science-fiction fantasy *Berge Meere und Giganten* (1924).

[10] Ribbat and others have noted the closeness of *Wadzek* to the stories collected in *Die Ermordung einer Butterblume* (1912), most of whose central characters are pathological.

[11] The novel does not make clear why Gaby demands an introduction to Herta, but earlier manuscript versions show that Döblin conceived the relationship as a homoerotic one (*WK*, 349, note to page 39).

[12] In a recent innovative approach to *Wang-lun* and *Wadzek*, Lorf looks at early twentieth-century popular reception of anthropologic information about non-European cultures. She asserts that *Wang-lun* is a mere costume drama compared to the discrepancies *Wadzek* exposes in this party scene, in which the women are costumed as Africans. This focus leads her, mistakenly I believe, to interpret this scene as central to the novel's meaning.

[13] Döblin uses dialect to comic effect at two other points in the novel (*WK*, 70, 175–77), something impossible in the imagined China of *Wang-lun*. This anticipates *Berlin Alexanderplatz*, in which *Berlinerisch* becomes the language of both characters and narrator.

[14] It is not necessary, however, to accept Ribbat's unsupported claim that "Frau Wadzek ist gewiß in manchen Eigentümlichkeiten Döblins Frau nachgezeichnet worden" (Ribbat, 174).

[15] Erich Kleinschmidt does not mention Frieda Kunke's death as a possible motivation for this essay (*SLW*, 520).

Works Cited

Brecht, Bertolt. *Tagebücher 1920–1922. Autobiographische Aufzeichnungen 1920–1954*. Frankfurt am Main: Suhrkamp, 1975.

Elshorst, Hansjörg. "Mensch und Umwelt im Werk Alfred Döblins." Diss., Munich, 1966.

Fee, Zheng. *Alfred Döblins Roman "Die drei Sprünge des Wang-lun": Eine Untersuchung zu den Quellen und zum geistigen Gehalt*. Frankfurt am Main: P. Lang, 1991.

Huguet, Louis. *L'Oeuvre d'Alfred Döblin ou la Dialectique de l'Exode, 1878–1918*. Diss. Paris-Nanterre, 1970.

Links, Roland. *Alfred Döblin: Leben und Werk*. Berlin: Volk und Wissen, 1980.

Lorf, Ira. *Maskenspiele: Wissen und kulturelle Muster in Alfred Döblins Romanen "Wadzeks Kampf mit der Dampfturbine" und "Die drei Sprünge des Wang-lun."* Bielefeld: Aisthesis Verlag, 1999.

Marinetti, Filippo Tommaso. "Die futuristische Literatur. Technisches Manifest." *Der Sturm* 133 (October 1912): 194–95.

———. *Mafarka le Futuriste: Roman Africain*. Paris: E. Sansot, 1909.

———. "Manifest des Futurismus." *Der Sturm* 104 (March 1912): 828–29.

———. "Supplement zum technischen Manifest der Futuristischen Literatur." *Der Sturm* 150/151 (March 1913): 279–80.

Meyer, Jochen. "Döblin Chronik." *Alfred Döblin, 1878–1978*. (Catalogue of an exhibition in the Deutsches Literaturarchiv im Schiller-Nationalmuseum, Marbach am Neckar). Munich: Kösel-Verlag, 1978. 10–57.

Muschg, Walter. "Nachwort des Herausgebers." In Alfred Döblin, *Die drei Sprünge des Wang-lun*. Munich: Deutscher Taschenbuch Verlag, 1989. 481–502.

Prangel, Matthias. *Alfred Döblin*. Stuttgart: Metzler, 1973.

Ribbat, Ernst. *Die Wahrheit des Lebens im frühen Werk Alfred Döblins*. Münster: Verlag Aschendorff, 1970.

Ryan, Judith. "From Futurism to 'Döblinism.'" *German Quarterly* 54 (1981): 415–26.

Schröter, Klaus. *Alfred Döblin in Selbstzeugnissen und Bilddokumenten*. Reinbek bei Hamburg: Rowohlt, 1978.

Schuster, Ingrid, and Ingrid Bode, eds. *Alfred Döblin im Spiegel der zeitgenössischen Kritik*. Bern and Munich: Francke Verlag, 1973.

Weyembergh-Boussart, Monique. *Alfred Döblin: Seine Religiosität in Persönlichkeit und Werk*. Bonn: Bouvier, 1970.

The Fall of Wallenstein, or the Collapse of Narration? The Paradox of Epic Intensity in Döblin's *Wallenstein*

Neil H. Donahue

UNLIKE MANY AUTHORS of prose fiction in the Expressionist generation, Alfred Döblin had, in addition to his training as a natural scientist and medical doctor, a penchant for theoretical reflections on his narrative craft. In fact, his essays on fiction articulate a distinct and coherent poetics for prose fiction,[1] a "prosaics," one might say, that he develops in contradistinction to Marinetti's futurism in his essay on "Futuristische Worttechnik" (1915), where he declares with aplomb and bravura: "Pflegen Sie Ihren Futurismus. Ich pflege meinen Döblinismus!" (*AzL*, 15). In essays such as "An Romanautoren und ihre Kritiker" (1913), he elaborates on this Döblinism as an extension into the modern world of an epic tradition of Naturalism, of literature as an embrace of the world, a literature that has to respond to events and developments in external reality, rather than merely to follow in the footsteps of its predecessors, or impose the author's imperious subjectivity onto the world in the manner of some Expressionists (*AzL*, 15–19).

His poetics is imbued with historical consciousness as an acute awareness of changes in the present based on knowledge of the past; the novelist needs to remain alert to the transformations in the world and find adequate means of representing them in words. The acceleration of external reality through technology (in transportation and communication, for example) has overtaken the inherited and inveterate sensibility of authors steeped in Romantic notions of empathetic projection (*Einfühlung*) that lend a psychological coloration to the world.[2] With polemical comments like "Psychologie ist ein dilettantisches Vermuten, scholastisches Gerede, spintisierender Bombast, verfehlte, verheuchelte Lyrik" (*AzL*, 16), Döblin stridently repudiates such notions in favor of a clinical, psychiatric practice of "Notierung der Abläufe, Bewegungen" (*AzL*, 16). In other words, the novelist should become a sort of detached and impartial stenographer of reality. Such a practice would demystify the poetic word and strip it of its atmospheric aura and patina of symbolic but obscure signification, as cultivated, for example, by the French Symbolists, and in Germany by Stefan George and his circle; such a contrary practice, in the experimental spirit of Expressionist prose, leads the way "aus der psychologischen Prosa" and, accordingly, puts forward in the novel "die entseelte Realität" (*AzL,* 17).

That "soulless reality" appears then in the vivid immediacy of a "Kinostil." With the early film enthusiast's view of the cinema's dispassionate objectivity and precision of perception, narrative prose reveals, for Döblin, its own kinetics, that is, the nature of its forward movement as a referential medium at the point of contact between world and word.[3] Prose no longer subdues and subordinates the world of external reality in order to frame and portray it at a politely pictorial distance; rather, narrative prose now highlights disjunctions between words, phrases, particles, clauses, and sentences, in order to throw into high relief the palpable word and the world it relates to and revels in. The omniscient narrator no longer organizes the material into a smoothly unfolding, linear narration, but juxtaposes the raw material of words as "Rapide Abläufe, Durcheinander in bloßen Stichworten. [. . .] Das Ganze darf nicht erscheinen wie gesprochen, sondern wie vorhanden" (*AzL,* 17). Like found objects, words present a separate, palpable reality as *Stil,* even as they re-present a world in fiction. Language is neither purely autonomous, a construction unto itself, nor is it purely referential, merely a window onto a fictional world: rather, language calls attention at once to itself and to its referentiality. The two impulses interfere with one another constructively to heighten, ideally, the fictional world of real words.

The narrator disappears, so to speak, behind the camera, but keeps the camera moving to call attention to the medium. Words present external reality with an immediacy undistorted by subjective, "poetic" interference. Döblin calls for "Entselbstung, Entäußerung des Autors, Depersonation" (*AzL,* 18). He aligns himself with traditions of Naturalism, but he offers an "objectivity of language" (Donahue, 130), not of pictorial description.[4] The words do not fit together to make a pictorial composition (in which one loses sight of the medium, the words); rather, a scene allows the presentation of the language that abundantly comprises that scene. With a switch or jump-cut from film as master metaphor, Döblin calls the result of this process a "steinernen Stil" because of its raw, rugged contours: the term suggests both the precision of chiseled stone, the rapid strike of applied artistic force as well as the rough density and implacability of the piled prose (in many passages "piled" almost literally for the sheer number of adjacent nouns). The term does not suggest the smooth surfaces of polished masonry; instead, the author reverses the process and uses the pen as a chisel to break words out of their traditional usages as polished by literary convention in order to open instead a quarry of verbal raw material from historical reality with all its hard edges and precipices. The novel as a quarry of language challenges the reader to move along its hard edges while looking ahead at the daunting aggregations and new formations.[5]

Through hard stylistic labor that re-forms language into new, even jarring verbal images, the author also participates directly in the world and can respond directly to its swiftly changing formations. Writing in this unusual way is a form of action, an engagement with modernity: "Die Welt ist in die Tiefe und Breite gewachsen; der alte Pegasus, von der Technik überflügelt, hat sich verblüffen lassen und in einen störrischen Esel verwandelt. Ich behaupte, jeder Spekulant, Bankier, Soldat ist ein besserer Dichter als die Mehrzahl heutiger Autoren" (*AzL*, 15). Instead of poetic flights over physical and social reality and reflection upon the world from a safe narrative distance, Döblin extols and emulates the poetic potency of those engaged directly and immediately in historical reality, here for example through finance or fighting. All three of these professions in his list of poetry-producing actors in the world, especially the soldier, merge in the figure of his wartime novel *Wallenstein* (completed 1919, published 1920) about the Thirty Years' War and its leading historical personage, Albrecht Wenzel Eusebius von Wallenstein (1583–1634).

Döblin worked on *Wallenstein* from 1916 to 1919, after a series of long prose experiments such as *Die drei Sprünge des Wang-lun* (1915) and *Wadzeks Kampf mit der Dampfturbine* (1918), as well as numerous short prose works, such as his most famous and compelling story "Die Ermordung einer Butterblume" and his critical essays, all engaged in developing for prose narrative the plasticity of form necessary to an epic of technological modernity. Yet in that framework, as part of that ongoing project, *Wallenstein* is a variation on the historical novel, set in the years 1621 to 1636 during the Thirty Years' War in the German territories; as such, the novel seems a gigantic anachronism, though imbued with the atmosphere and agony of war that surrounded him as he wrote.[6] Without the appearance of contemporaneity in his confrontation with modernity, Döblin tries to convey in *Wallenstein* the sense of war as he exploits a historical topic for its capacity to generate language. As historical fiction, but unlike earlier historical novels, *Wallenstein* is an experimental exercise in the dynamics of prose: the appearance of historical or cultural distance provides an occasion for greater verbal immediacy and proliferation. In the genre most beholden to requirements of pacing, the accumulation of detail and the forceful imperatives of plot, *Wallenstein* is, or wants to be, an epic of Expressionist intensity.

As such, *Wallenstein* is a contradiction in terms in which the tendencies toward intensity and extensity, as it were, too often remain gapingly at odds, rather than coming together to resolve that paradox, that tension in opposition, at a higher level of synthesis and insight, as they do later in Döblin's *Berlin Alexanderplatz*. Plot as a means of lending order and continuous coherence to the action of the novel here dissolves almost completely,[7] and survives only as the overall framework of political intrigue and sprawling military preparation and engagement that provides innumerable occasions for the most varied descriptions of objects and individuals, drama and dialogue, scenes and actions. Harro Müller notes aptly: "Im *Wallenstein* gibt es kein Kraftzentrum, aus dem heraus Geschichte produziert werden könnte, von einem Sinnzentrum ganz zu schweigen" (411). In particular, the titular character of Wallenstein does not provide such a center of action and meaning, as might be expected, which marks the displacement of this narrative from traditional treatments of that larger-than-life figure and releases the narrative from the centripetal gravitational pull of such a character study.[8] The figure of Wallenstein himself recedes from the foreground and gets absorbed into the overwhelming verbal fray and tumult of this non-linear, even chaotic narrative, what the late German novelist and Döblin scholar W. G. Sebald aptly called the "irritierende Gewalt dieses Romans" (Sebald, 62). The notion of history replaces plot as the organizing principle, but unlike traditional nineteenth-century historiography with its strong narrative plotting, history appears here as a sort of kaleidoscopic collage of colliding elements, a juggernaut of events and elements that intermittently lumbers and lurches forward, like the novel itself. Such a process of decentered narrative removes individual scenes or passages of description or dialogue from the necessity of ultimate integration into the larger whole, and allows them to loom large (or small) on their own with any eventual link or even allusion to later developments appearing as almost incidental, a contingency, an afterthought.

In a much later essay of 1936, "Der historische Roman und wir," published in the exile journal *Das Wort* in Moscow (edited by Bertolt Brecht, Lion Feuchtwanger, and Willi Bredel), Döblin accentuates even more fully and pointedly the different function of the historical novel:

> Der historische Roman ist erstens ein Roman und zweitens keine Historie.
> Er ist ein Roman. Warum? Er erzählt von Anfang bis zu Ende Dinge, die bestimmt in dieser Weise historisch nicht nachgewiesen werden

können, für die der Autor keine dokumentarische Unterlage besitzt. Er verleiht ihnen den Anschein einer Realität. Und schließlich arbeitet er mit Spannung, sucht unser Interesse zu erregen, uns zu erfreuen, zu erschüttern, uns anzugreifen and herauszufordern. Also er spielt auf uns wie eben ein Romanautor, überhaupt wie ein Künstler, und er entfaltet dazu die Reize seines Materials, der Sprache. Das ist also ein Roman.

Und die Historie, die der Roman nicht ist? Der Roman enthält doch genug Historie, die Autoren haben doch gewiß Bände gewälzt, der Roman verhunzt doch die Historie, er fälscht doch, unterschlägt, noch mehr als jener Biograph. (*AzL,* 171)

In strong terms, Döblin severs the novel here from any historiographical obligations in favor of the "appearance of reality" in the fiction, which does however still derive from historical research and reading, however unsystematic, and capture the atmosphere of the period; but ultimately that historical content — period, personage, background and assorted documentation — remains merely an occasion for language, for the dynamic and artful linguistic limning at length of the matter at hand.[9]

The historical novel, as understood by Döblin, renounces specific fidelity to its historical topic in order to open for itself an unlimited range, an unbounded latitude, of description that approaches what might be called historical fantasy, but stops short of, or is held back from, that leap into fantastic recreation by the raw and imposing quantity of material: he notes that "der einfache Roman von heute sich vom Märchen doch unter anderem durch eine ganz kolossale Betonung und Hypertrophie der aufgenommenen und mitgeschleppten Stoffmasse auszeichnet. Ja, wir sehen: Stoffgebiete, Räume der Realität [. . .] obwohl der Autor sich je nachdem einen gewissen Spielraum reserviert und bald mehr, bald weniger nach der Märchenseite ausweicht" (*AzL,* 175). That degree of surplus or excess in the lexical mass of the novel is central to Döblin's imaginative project. The scale of engagement with a given material anchors the text in a historical reality that is otherwise abjured, and prevents the text from acquiring the appearance of imaginative fancy as a sort of fairy-tale of illusory facticity. On the contrary, his earlier invocation of "Tatsachenphantasie!" (*AzL,* 19) suggests the necessity of historical material as a basis for the novel. Yet, nonetheless, that renunciation of strict coherency, whether historiographical or fictional in terms of plot, indeed lends to the novel, here specifically *Wallenstein,* a quality of arbitrariness that seems intended, again, to heighten the preeminence of the language, to push content into the background and the prose itself into the foreground (a contemporary called it: "Ein Kollosalgemälde für Kurzsichtige,"[10] as exemplified in the following long passage from *Wallenstein:*

Aus seinem Bau, um den herum er mit Schonung fraß, stöberte das bayrische Heer den Bastard von Mansfeld. Von da strömte ihm, wegweisend, pestilenzialischer Geruch entgegen. Eine Seuche war in dem Lager der Beidhaus ausgebrochen, hatte sich mit Werbern Furieren Streifkorps beutemachenden Tummlern blitzartig durch die Wälder und Berge verbreitet, zuckte unter Bauern und Knechte, gepanzerte Kürisser Musketenträger. Aus den Tümpeln stieg die Brut der Mücken und Stechfliegen. Unter der schilfdurchstochenen Oberfläche der Wasser, dicht am Spiegel, hingen die Millionen Larven wie herrenlose Naturtrümmer, gleichmäßig Luft saugend durch ihre kleinen Atemröhren. Dick schwoll ihr Kopf an, hob sich über den Spiegel, die Schale zitterte, knisterte, spannte sich, riß über der Schläfe, seitlich; langsam drängte sich das lange junge Gebilde durch, engangelegt Fühler Glieder Flügel, rastete, sich spreizend, auf einem Blatt der Wasserlinse, hing flügelspannend großbeinig an einer Schilfscheide. Surrte in der Dämmerung aus. Die Luft mit Zirpen und feinem hohen Singen durchadernd. Spürsame surrende Mücke mit schwankendem Ringelleib, vor sich zwischen hauchartigen Fühlern gerade ausgestemmt den langen Stechrüssel, der wie ein Spieß steif auf dem Köpfchen wuchs, vor dem Prellbock des klobigen Brustwürfels. Das trug sich tausendfach, zehntausendfach, millionenfach durch die Abendluft mit gläsernen Flügelchen. Setzte sich an den Mund, an die Stirn, auf die Hand, die ein Brot brach, an den Hals, zwischen den geschnittenen Bart des Kornetts und Rittmeisters und die venezianischen Kragen. Riß sich einer, vom Pferde springend, schweißbegossen das Wams auf, kühle Luft gegen nasse Brust gehen zu lassen, so krallte sich das kleine Flügelwesen ungesehen an die warme Haut, sog sein Tröpfchen Blut, speichelte im Biß ein Tröpfchen Gift ein. Dann konnten die Soldaten auf ihre Jagd gehen, die Leute an Torsäulen und Brunnen aufhenken, das Vieh forttreiben, gewaltig prassen-, inzwischen liefen die Fieber durch ihre Körper, Abend um Abend, verwandelten ihr Blut in einen tropischen Sumpf. Kornetts mochten brüllen, den sauren Wein dieses Jahr in Kannen schlucken, gefahrdrohend auf ihren Gäulen vor hundert Mann durch die stillen schornsteindampfenden Dörfer segeln, Leder vor der Brust, dichtmachende Papiere um den Hals, breitbackig und heiß auf den übersättigten Tieren: es vibrierte in den Knien, der Koller mußte herunter, die Waden waren schwach, vor den Augen flimmerten Regenbogen; das Frieren und Zähneklappern fing an, die Nacht lag man im Heu, im Bett, drohte heiser, als wäre nichts, und tags darauf war man schwächer, von Ritt zu Ritt gespenstischer. Und das fiel über die Obersten, die Pikeniere wie über die Huren und ihre Weibel. Die Seuche tötete nicht viele. Wen sie befiel, den machte sie schwach und noch rasender, als er schon war. Wer starb, verweste, wo er fiel. Gelb, schwach lachend ging man umeinander in der Hitze.

Bis noch das Gerücht sich verbreitete, erst im Lager bei Beidhaus, dann in Weiden, im Markte Kohlberg, es hätten sich Leute gefunden, die ein neuartiges Wesen von Krankheit zeigten. Pestbarbiere erzählten verstört von Bauern, die eine neue Krankheit in ihren Betten hätten. Die Läuse fielen das Heer an. In den geraubten Wämsern Leintüchern Betten Pelzen Schabracken wuchsen sie an den Söldnern hoch, die im Schmutz der Wälder und Straßen verkamen, machten feuchte und trockne Krätzen; bei sehr vielen geschah es unversehens, daß das tierische Gift sich in ihre Adern senkte. Sie begannen irre und fiebrig zu reden, manche zu rasen, Ausschläge bis zu Erbsengröße erhoben sich auf der zerbissenen Haut, Blutflecken sprossen in grausenerregender Weise hervor; schlafsüchtig, taub gingen sie, wo sie sich hingeflüchtet hatten, gemieden, eingesperrt, dazu verhungert zugrunde. Ohnmächtig sprachen die gelehrten Schüler des Paracelsus von den merkurialisch-schwefligen Zeichen der Seuche, von den merkurialisch-salzigen, dem Heißhunger, den Harnbeschwerden, der Wasseransammlung in den Beinen, Blutspeien, Brustgeschwulst, Melancholie. (92–94)

Here, as so often in the novel, the length of the passage interferes with the narration and obstructs plot development, but the prose opens onto the general condition of war and existence at the time, thus providing a sense of history without conveying any particular understanding of events. The evocation of disease, of plague, gains force through the non-sequitur, staccato percussions of the passage in the several series of juxtaposed nouns or adjectives without punctuation or subordination. The phrases appear in almost Cubist refraction for their own sake on the page as the immediate surface of language, occupying the visual field, without perspectival subordination to a larger pictorial composition. In reading, one has to step back as one would before an overlarge painting to find a point of imagistic integration. Here that immediacy of language and image corresponds, representatively, to the microscopic zoom of Döblin (the narrator, literary naturalist, natural scientist and during the war, military doctor), onto the "Oberfläche der Wasser, dicht am Spiegel" where there hang millions of larvae "wie herrenlose Naturtrümmer [. . .]." That latter phrase captures a paradox of Döblin's thought and writing: employing a disruptive prose style to detach scenes or objects from their context, to de-naturalize them in effect, in order to highlight them as events of language. His empiricism of language gains in dynamism designed to extend the scope and scale of the fiction on these new terms and affirm a naturalistic view of the universe that continually aims to incorporate all aspects of the world through words into the given work, at least by implication.[11] Nothing need be left out; anything could enter in.

Here, those larvae, amassed as the "rubble of nature," breathe through "Atemröhren," which calls to mind the gas masks of the First

World War in another poisonous landscape of mud and mire. The magnified description of the mosquitoes breaking free of the pupae is an ironic contrast, in its ugliness, to the familiar motif of a butterfly freeing itself, beautifully, from the chrysalis for flight; that description also anticipates the technique of New Objectivity in the visual arts, as well as later literary exercises like Robert Musil's "Das Fliegenpapier" in his *Nachlaß zu Lebzeiten* (Posthumous Papers of a Living Author, 1936), where he describes the slow, agonizing deaths of stuck flies. Further, the word "flügelspannend" is an ironically pointed rejection of the Romantic ideal of Nature as a transcendent spiritual domain, as formulated by Joseph von Eichendorff (1788–1857) in his famous poem "Mondnacht" (1837): "Und meine Seele spannte / Weit ihre Flügel aus / Flog durch die stillen Lande, / Als flöge sie nach Haus." In Döblin, mosquitoes take flight in search of blood, full of poison and disease. Döblin presents a desublimated historical reality, then and now, as swarming nature "tausendfach, zehntausendfach, millionenfach," untouched and unmoved by human concerns. Nature is anonymous: predators and prey, victors and victims alike: as the soldiers swarm "auf ihre Jagd" to plunder, pillage and destroy, so too do the mosquitoes and the lice, decimating the armies as they eat and drink and try to rest.[12] The effects of the plague compound the violence and misery of war into an Expressionist tableau of mass agonies and madness, in which short and long sentences alternate irregularly in heavy-breathing rhythms, numerous active verbs give the prose a sort of ekphrastic, dynamic stasis, almost sculptural, while sentence fragments and gruesome rhetorical amplifications seem to swirl and accumulate on the page, like paint on an apocalyptic canvas of war by Ludwig Meidner (1884–1966) or Otto Dix (1881–1969). The prose writhes, swarms, and engulfs.[13]

As a result, the historical past becomes, through the vividness and plasticity of the language, immediately present, but not at all with nostalgia or tidy, clarified hindsight as a specious "Objekt für wehmütige Dichtung" (*AzL*, 62). Rather, the past is used to provide more evidence of Döblin's naturalistic worldview, spelled out in his essay "Der Geist des naturalistischen Zeitalters" (1924). It is a secular, physical world without higher mystical, metaphysical, or theological justification, viewed in the above passage on its way to death and putrefaction. In the writing of historical narratives Döblin positions himself against the narrowing of vision that comes with distance, according to rules of pictorial perspective and historiographical practice: "die Gegenwart sieht man genau mit Einzelheiten, die Vergangenheit als Riesenblock, an dem sich nur Grobes, Allgemeines unterscheiden läßt. [. . .] Das Jetzt mikroskopiert man, die Vergangenheit sieht man mit dem Fernrohr" (*AzL*, 62). In *Wallen-*

stein in general, and vividly in the above passage, Döblin turns that telescope of historical distance around to foreshorten the past into the present in order to demonstrate the ahistorical sameness of natural existence for the "Tierart Menschen" (*AzL,* 64).[14]

Within that overriding sameness of natural existence, stripped of theological implications, variations nonetheless develop within the historical experience of a culture over time, of which he is also acutely aware: "Maßgebend für die Entwicklung, für den Wechsel der Kulturen, für den Antrieb zu neuer Variation sind besondere kraftvolle Menschen. Das sind die, in denen sich zuerst und am deutlichsten eine Variation vollzieht. Sie drängen, wie man auch historisch sieht, die Epoche im Sinne ihrer Variation weiter" (*AzL,* 65). Thus, within that framework of mankind's smallness in the natural, physical world that derives from the loss of a central and unifying belief in God and transcendence, Wallenstein emerges as an individual who embodies the early, post-medieval phase of secular, early capitalist culture, brashly engaged in warfare and profiteering as the literal enactment of Döblin's understanding of secular existence in a post-theological age: a "Dauerkrieg, permanente Eroberung der Welt, die ja grenzenlos ist" (*W,* 66).[15] Once he finally appears (on page 168 of 739!), Wallenstein is a forceful, domineering individual, an agent of worldly historical change, who is also cast in the form of some chthonic reptilian demiurge,[16] situated in a world without central meaning and coherence, which therefore ultimately escapes his full domination or control. This apparent contradiction between Döblin's naturalistic worldview and the dominant but de-centered protagonist is the paradox that informs and shapes the novel, or rather creates its curious tension in imbalance.[17]

Despite the division in the Thirty Years' War between Catholic and Protestant sides, misleading in its simplicity, Döblin loosely organizes his inchoate, churning material around the figures on the Catholic side of Ferdinand II and Wallenstein. The former is more central to the novel than Wallenstein and is invested with worldly power, but passive and reluctant to use that power or engage himself fully in the inevitable strategies and intrigues that surround him, whereas Wallenstein, an outsider, does so with alacrity and great ability; as Wolfgang Kort notes: "On the one hand, Wallenstein becomes involved in ever greater undertakings, and on the other, Ferdinand sinks into ever greater passivity" (74). But both, in their respective uses of power, figure as forces of nature, whose actions or inactions create tensions and cause movements among the powerbrokers and populations around them. Around that antipodal tension between these two figures — of pathetic passivity and prevarication in Ferdinand, and brute force, cunning, and acquisitive, resolute action in Wallenstein — the other figures of the novel revolve, moving in and out of the narrative: they appear in cameos, fuller portraits, or in involved episodes, but ultimately all are eclipsed by the discontinuous, fragmentary, massive action of the novel.[18]

Harro Müller notes that the innumerable "figures appear, disappear, reappear or never reappear at all, according to a principle of epic apposition, which simultaneously relativizes the plot as a narrative model" (292). That notion of a "principle of epic apposition" suggests that such discontinuity gathers cumulative force in the novel, but this is surely not always in evidence. Plot simply dissolves in the welter of events, isolated descriptions and characters, who have little or no psychological interiority. Often a character looms large in a scene or even a set portrait, but remains, without any further dramatic or psychological development, still essentially anonymous, despite a long name and title. The Bavarian Elector Maximilian is, however, a third main character, who is on the Catholic side but alternately at odds with Ferdinand and with Wallenstein, whereas the figure of Gustavus Adolphus, the image of whose fleets crossing over to the mainland (*W*, 489) had animated Döblin's initial interest in the period, dwindles in overall significance in the novel. The triangulation of Ferdinand and Wallenstein with another main figure of power (Maximilian or Gustavus Adolphus, among others) enhances the instability of the basic dualism in the novel in a complex interplay of attraction and repulsion, alliance and subversion, diplomacy and deception. Each new character, major or minor or fleeting, stands in relation to and extends this shifting constellation. Erwin Kobel shows how Döblin also aligns each of these main characters with natural elements (Ferdinand: earth and air; Wallenstein: earth and fire; Gustavus Adolphus: earth and water) to undergird those worldly intrigues with naturalist-philosophical materialism, though that elementalism is not regenerative. Ultimately, the masses, the armies, also figure as an entity, a character (as in the above long quotation) and a force of nature that returns matter to nature. In other words, all hover in nearness to death, the return to the elements.

In this panoramic Expressionist tableau, all characters are set against Döblin's fatalistic *Naturphilosophie* of this period, imbued with wartime pessimism. The opening scenes of feasting and hunting convey from the start that common realm of basic, if not base, animalistic appetites: "Schand und Schmach, daß einer Graf, Fürst, Erzherzog, Römischer Kaiser werden kann und der Magen wächst nicht mit; die Gurgel kann nicht mehr schlucken, als sie faßt" (*W*, 11). The Kaiser appears in this crowd as a far-from-heroic caricature: "Untersetzt, dickleibig, auf den kurzen Säulen der steif gewordenen Beine trug sich vom obersten Platz unter dem Baldachin her Kaiser Ferdinand der Andere" (*W*, 12).¹⁹ To comic effect, the sentence itself lumbers ponderously on prepositional phrases that prop up the emperor. Apart from his appetites, however, Ferdinand is not at all a strong figure. Rather he seems to represent the weakness at the core of the feudal order of the day, fearing an unmasking: "So steht es um mich, so weit bin ich; entlarvt" (*W*, 23). His insecurity, anguish and passivity show in his encounters with figures like his advisor Eggenberg, his confessor Lamormain, or, symbolically perhaps, the dwarf Jonas (*W*, 80–85).

The second book brings him into contact with Wallenstein, who appears full of initiative, thrusting himself into life — "hinter allem steckte Wallenstein" (*W*, 189) — and extending himself for the sake of military and financial gain — "Der wildgewordene Spekulant als Feldherr" (*W*, 252). In contrast to the uncertainties of Ferdinand, Wallenstein appears decisive, without reservation, sure of himself and his actions: "Bei aller Ergebenheit stahlhart trat der leidenschaftliche Wallenstein auf; er sagte nichts Neues; der Kaiser hatte auf einmal den Eindruck absoluten Entschlusses und der Macht, jeden Entschluß durchzuführen" (*W*, 223). "Hier herrschte Bestimmtheit wie im Lauf der Sonne" (*W*, 227). These pivotal scenes forge a curious bond between the two figures of power, whereby Wallenstein's charisma, vitality, and bold careerism invite the surrender of and almost magnetically attract the Holy Roman Emperor, with sexual overtones: "ein heftiges Erstaunen hatte ihn bei der zweiten Begegnung mit dem Böhmen befallen und verließ ihn nicht. [. . .] er hatte urplötzlich den Eindruck, den Faden seines Handelns zu verlieren; fühlte mit einer unklaren Freude, daß er dem Böhmen in einer Weise und mit rätselhaftem Drang vertraute, wie bisher keinem Menschen, wie vielleicht eine Frau ihrem Mann vertraute. [. . .] Ferdinand mußte den Augenblick zeichnen, in dem solch geheimnisvolles Licht in ihn fiel" (*W*, 223). Döblin repeatedly uses the image of a dragon, millipede or scorpion, appearing to Ferdinand in a dream, to capture Wallenstein's effect on the flaccid potentate: "daß es mit elektrischem Zucken ans Herz drang und stach" (*W*, 221).

From then on, however, Ferdinand's indecisiveness dilates in the midst of his worldly political and military obligations to encompass fluctuating degrees of conviction for and against Wallenstein, who repeatedly saves, with his prowess and fortune, Ferdinand's empire. By the end of Book III, the now sickly Ferdinand has slipped into a delirium of hedonistic surrender and gets "baptized" a fool by his jester with a bucket of wine. From that moment on he drifts into retreat from his role as political leader, which brings him into close alliance with the church: "Das Heilige Reich muß selbst eine große Kirche sein" (*W*, 458). But such a goal would require greater worldly fortitude and perseverance. He convenes the *Kollegialtag* and shows in his long dialogue with Lamormain that he is aware of the historical momentousness of his decision to side with either Wallenstein or the princes, the military-financial parvenu with tyrannical inclinations or the ancestral feudal powers. He vacillates and is reluctant to decide on the correct use of his power, which in effect is an abdication of his authority that marks his conscious drift away from reality, though he does dismiss Wallenstein.

As the territories stand under siege from the north he nonetheless blithely trusts in Wallenstein to save the day: "Und so leicht und beruhigend sprach der Kaiser, der sich wohlig schwer zurücklegte, daß Eggenberg den Eindruck hatte, die Sache ginge ihm nicht nah, ginge ihn nichts an" (*W*, 521). He slips into a state of heedless indifference and delusional isolation. His trajectory from the pinnacle of worldly power leads him to flee his quarters "hinaus, hinaus. Was haben sie im Kopf, das ich alles muß. Von mir bleibt nichts übrig. [. . .] Dienen! Dienen! Ich — will — nicht!" (*W*, 671). He encounters first a deranged anchorite with whom he speaks at length of spiritual matters, and then a band of robbers, and responds as if released on both levels of worldly bonds and possessions: "Da fühlte Ferdinand plötzlich die tiefe Ruhe. [. . .] Es war eine Freiheit, die ihn mit wachsender Stärke entzückte" (*W*, 675). From then on, he absents himself "auf tagelangen Ausflügen" (*W*, 695) and later in fleeing the war appears "ein vollkommener Narr" (*W*, 732). In a vivid departure from the historical record, indeed as a calculated bit of historical fantasy, Ferdinand eventually takes up with the robbers and is drawn back to the woods to keep company with a "Waldmensch," a "Tierwesen," a "Waldtier," a "Kobold," an incarnation of animality, who brings him full circle from the early scenes of feasting and hunting. However, this figure does not represent a comforting spiritual retreat into nature, but rather its irrational violence: the creature stabs Ferdinand repeatedly, throws his body into a tree and rocks it on a branch, while gazing in mute incomprehension of its deed. Nature triumphs.

In dialectical contrast, Wallenstein embraces the hard political and military realities of the day and has inspired fear in the princes, jealous of his gains in power and means. He employs those means and his men to gain more, and appears as the agent of historical change. He has the potential to break the feudal hold on the German territories and bring Germany into a phase of centralized monarchy, like France, and thus allow Germany to avoid the legacy of petty submission to authority, whose consequences extended well into his lifetime, a point of view Döblin elaborates on in his essay of 1921, "Der Dreißigjährige Krieg"

(*SPG*, 45–59). Yet the order of nature will undermine his efforts in the form of his failing health, the "Achilles heel" of gout in his foot. But unlike Ferdinand, he is not inclined to succumb to nature, and gathers his forces, personally and politically, to stand larger than life: "Da stand er, stand, in Schlesien, ein Gigant an Kraft, zahllose Kompagnien, Massen von Artillerie Munition, bezahlt aus den Steuern der gepreßten Stände, rückte sich nicht, zuckte nicht, nicht einmal vor Schande über das, was geschah. Es war bewiesen: er wollte nicht, ging eigene Wege [. . .] Auf diese erschütternde Selbständigkeit war niemand vorbereitet" (*W*, 612 and 614). As a German bearer of Renaissance individualism and secular self-reliance, Wallenstein bears the future in him, and is ignominiously assassinated. Döblin's bold sketches of the novel's main characters, though intermittent, do acquire complexity.

Dieter Mayer's study of 1972 provides the most comprehensive, systematic analysis of the novel. His later article, a condensed version of his book's argument, identifies itself as an attempt to disprove still reigning views that Döblin's novels are "wenig strukturiert" (98), hoping perhaps for the sort of consensus that has emerged about the unifying patterns, not at once apparent, that structure *Berlin Alexanderplatz*. Despite the usefulness of Mayer's book, his argument about the tight structure of *Wallenstein* seems more like a generous assumption of formal coherence than an empirically grounded assertion, and has not convinced later scholars, despite their debts to his research. Harro Müller finds the unity of the novel in its formal disorder. He cites Döblin's remark from his *Die beiden Freundinnen und ihr Giftmord* (1924) that "Die Unordnung ist [. . .] ein besseres Wissen als die Ordnung" (Müller, 293). Such a remark negates the Hegelian, historicist notion of "history as a transcendental signified" in favor of an "anti-historical, anti-humanist and post-idealist" view of history, subject to the free play, or in this novel, the wild battles, of contingency. Indeed, the desperate term "labyrinth" recurs in scholarship on the novel (Müller, 294; Kobel, 190). In effect, the novel might well be seen as structured around the tension between its unifying allegorical impulses as an abstract commentary on capitalism, on religion(s), on humanism, on historicism, on idealism, on modernity, etc. and the instability of its form, which undermines any single such unified reading, though Müller resolves this tension by turning to what he calls "anthropological discourse," a more contemporary term consonant with Döblin's views on nature, to capture the absence of any positive telos.[20] Although valuable, informative, and suggestive, such attempts to find the terms of the novel's coherence in its structure or organization, or on a higher level of abstraction in terms of *Weltanschauung*, ignore the most immediate aspect of the novel's language.

The technique of displacement characterizes, in my view, the entirety of the novel on all levels and serves the purpose of breaking down patterns that would otherwise allow what we might call a three-dimensional reading of the novel, with a depth perspective in terms of character and plot and organic coherence. The dislocations and inconsistencies encompass, for example, the novel's scenic composition (often extensively elaborated in compelling images of mass movements), the misleading section titles (the first book about Ferdinand bears the title "Maximilian von Bayern") and the displacement of Wallenstein as the central figure, the lack of sustained interiority, the sheer number of characters and portraits, the adventitious detail, and the disproportionate length of the novel. Taken together, these dislocations militate against the overall coherency of the fiction, and place style in the foreground as the end rather than the means of the work: "Der Roman wird zur Prosadichtung größten Stils" (*AzL,* 42). The content mediates the style, not the opposite. The novel purposely interferes with itself as narrative — and this is particularly apparent in what appears as a historical novel — in order to heighten its immediate presence as word formation; the disruptive narrative calls to mind always its status as verbal material, as, first and foremost, an event of language.

In "Reform des Romans" (1919), Döblin draws a comparison to painters: "denn die Maler wollen durch Ablösung von der kunstfremden Gegenständlichkeit zu der üppigsten Sinnlichkeit und Selbstherrlichkeit der Farben gelangen und der malerisch spezifischen Gestaltung" (*AzL,* 35). He returns to this analogy to conclude his definition of the new novel: "wie die Maler entwickeln, so wollen die Autoren selbständig die ureigenen Potenzen und Latenzen des Materials entwickeln. [. . .] Das Material ist es, das sie erleben, das sie treibt. [. . .] Und aus diesem lebendigen Gefühl des Materials quillt auch die Gestaltung des Wortes ganz im einzelnen, der 'Stil,' die Sätze und Satzverbindungen Formung der einzelnen" (*AzL,* 43). Indeed, the constant use of these paratactic series of appositions (of nouns, verbs, or adjectives) to add rapidity, dynamism, and accretive energy to the prose also seems to become mechanical as a too-often-repeated stylistic device, but nonetheless, it always forces *Stil* into the foreground on the page and interferes with the reader's habitual attempts to focus beyond, on the narrative developments. Those frequent parataxes constitute the key to the novel's composition, its paradoxical foreshortening of perspective at great length, and capture the cross-purposes in *Wallenstein* and in Döblin's understanding of the novel at this time, caught in the contradiction between his *Sturm* aesthetic or Expressionist impulse to revel in the verbal material for its own sake (intensity in word) and his Naturalist embrace of description (extensity in world). That interference forces at first a "microscopic" reading of the novel, rather than a "telescopic" or "macroscopic" one, which requires critical distance, rereading, and reconstruction in order to reconstitute the plot and character development, in order to regain the perspective of depth. Thus, *Wallenstein,* in form at odds with itself, forces the reader into a bifocular reception, first nearsightedly focusing on the style, and then farsightedly focusing on the characters' psychological developments as well as the political intrigues imbricated with events of war, attempting to connect and integrate them — though the author did not.

Notes

[1] Walter Sokel sets Döblin opposite Carl Einstein in order to define two poles (or antipodes) of prose fiction in the Expressionist generation, and the range of experimentation in that area.

[2] In his essay "Der Epiker, sein Stoff und die Kritik" (1921) he even coins the term "Ausführlung" (*SPG,* 340).

[3] Scherpe speaks of the "Beweglichkeit sprachlicher Mimesis am historischen Material" (229).

[4] Elsewhere I have called this experimental, avant-garde quality of his prose in the tradition of literary Naturalism an "unfettered materialism of language" (*Forms of Disruption,* 131) for its inclusiveness of words for their own sake, though without breaking entirely their referential relation to the world of objects. M. S. Jones notes the relation to the *Sturm* aesthetic: "He prefigures its methods in seeking the most intense degree of expression from the most concentrated language. But there is an essential difference between Döblin's position and what came to be official *Sturm* theory, namely his demand for a 'Kinostil.' Such a style of writing demands that the author must act as a receiving station for all surrounding reality which he then conveys in a carefully constructed work, consciously excluding all subjective reactions" (80). Jones indirectly alludes to the paradox I wish to focus on here of intensive concentration and extension, of verbal autonomy and inclusive referentiality, of diction and documentation.

[5] This distinction pinpoints the difference between Alfred Döblin's work and that of Thomas Mann, who also worked as a literary Naturalist, drawing on diverse secondary sources for their information and language, but who labored, very successfully, to hide stylistically the seams or smooth over the rough edges. Therefore, the two reside on opposite sides of a line marking the limits of the traditions of bourgeois realism, both in their techniques of composition and in the reception of their novels.

[6] In an incomplete ms. about the novel, Döblin comments on the atmosphere surrounding him at the time in Alsace and then in Berlin: "Nun, es schlugen zwar

viele Bomben in der Nachbarschaft ein, aber weder mir noch dem Manuskript geschah was. Es hat auch den langen Rücktransport neben mir im November 1918 durch ganz Deutschland mitgemacht, und lag noch in dem schlimmen Revolutionswinter 18/19 in Berlin auf meinem Schreibtisch. Vielleicht ist etwas von der furchtbaren Luft, in der das Buch entstand, Krieg, Revolution, Krankheit und Tod, in ihm" (*B I*, 533). As Kreutzer demonstrates, Wallenstein is also an analysis of the causes of war in terms of social class and financial imperatives that bring parallels to the First World War.

[7] In his "Bemerkungen zum Roman" Döblin speaks directly against the use of dramatic plotting in the novel: "Der Roman hat mit Handlung nichts zu tun" (*AzL*, 19).

[8] Döblin's fascination with the character did, however, provide the impetus for his writing: "Wie kam ich darauf, den Dreißigjährigen Krieg und Böhmen und Wallenstein auszusuchen als meinen Schauplatz und meine Figuren? Zunächst war es nur die sehr naheliegende Ähnlichkeit zwischen 1914/18 und damals: ein europäischer Krieg. Ich tastete nach Büchern. [. . .] Das ungeheure Schicksal Böhmens riß mich hin, und dieser Wallenstein, den ich so sah: als einen böhmischen Renegaten, ganz und gar kein Schillerscher 'Held' — ein moderner Industriekapitän, ein wüster Inflationsgewinnler, ein Wirtschafts- und, toller Weise auch, ein strategisches Genie, eine Figur, die nur eine Parallele Napoleons I. zuläßt" (*B I*, 533).

[9] Here, conversely, one might compare in English the novelistic biography of Wallenstein by Francis Watson, which uses narrative technique and a beautiful prose style to enhance the historical depiction of the character, while *not* repudiating scholarly or historiographical obligations. Peter Höyng examines the "Zwitterstellung" between fact and fiction in the treatments of Wallenstein by Schiller, Leopold von Ranke, and Golo Mann. Erwin Kobel also explores the comparison of Döblin's Wallenstein to that of Schiller.

[10] Moritz Goldstein. "Döblins Wallenstein-Roman: Ein Brief an den Verfasser." *Vossische Zeitung* (November 13, 1921), quoted in Scherpe (232) and in Mayer (19).

[11] Dollinger notes the "zentrale Stellung im Schaffen Döblins" (136) of this philosophy of nature and how that philosophy became a more explicit preoccupation for him in the 1920s as he continued to explore new means "dieses Totalitätsstreben mit seiner literarischen Praxis zu verknüpfen" (138). In conjunction with that view, I would like, however, to emphasize the links between Döblin's literary practice, animated by that philosophy, and traditions of literary Naturalism, from Zola in particular, with its empiricist annotation of external reality leading to passages of almost non-narrative description that verge on phenomenological inquiry into the status of an object or image, or ultimately, into language itself, which becomes the avant-garde position of the next generations. Döblin constantly pushes his prose to that limit.

[12] Dollinger's comment on *Das Ich über der Natur* also applies here: "Wir sehen hier die alte naturphilosophische Vorstellung von der wechselseitigen Erhellung von Mikro- und Makrokosmos" (143). See also Mayer, 47–85.

[13] Embedded throughout there appear sentences that by themselves embody the *Sturm* aesthetic and in their pounding rhythm and verbal starkness read like poems by August Stramm. For example, "Viele Nester leer, Sensen ohne Hände, alte Männer an den Pflügen, Krieg" (275) or "Es wird geschrien, zerbrochen, vergossen,

verwundet, erschlagen, betrogen" (312), capturing much like Stramm did for the First World War the danger and devastation of war.

[14] Müller calls Wallenstein therefore an "antihistorical and antihermeneutical novel" (*War and Novel*, 297).

[15] Leo Kreutzer, following Günter Grass, emphasizes Döblin's fascination with the economic motivation for Wallenstein's military actions (55–59).

[16] "Der Friedländer [...], ein gelber Drache aus dem böhmischen blasenwerfenden Morast aufgestiegen, bis an die Hüften mit schwarzem Schlamm bedeckt, sich zurückbiegend auf den kleinen, knolligen Hinterpfoten, den Schweif geringelt auf den Boden gepreßt, mit dem prallen, breiten Rumpf in der Luft sich wiegend, die langen Kinnladen aufgesperrt und wonnig schlangenwütig den heißen Atem stoßweise entlassend, mit Schnauben und Grunzen, das zum Erzittern brachte" (*W*, 243–44).

[17] Kobel speaks of the novel as "wiederum ein Beispiel für Döblins berüchtigte Widersprüchlichkeit" (193). Roland Links notes (77) the danger of this mix of apolitical naturalist fatalism and fascination with dominant Darwinian figures of history: the Nazis interdicted all of Döblin's writing except this one work, which could be misconstrued in terms of their own ideological purposes. Harro Müller (*War and Novel*, 296–98) contrasts the aestheticization of *Wallenstein* to the more distinct historical engagement of *November 1918*.

[18] Heidi Thomann Tewarson notes pointedly that "Die akausale Gestaltung wird im *Wallenstein* zum Problem, weil es sich hier um einen historischen Prozess handelt, der gedeutet werden will, im Gegensatz zum chinesischen Roman [*Die drei Sprünge des Wang-lun*], bei dem es um die philosophische Frage des Handelns und Nichthandelns ging. So gibt es im *Wallenstein* zu viele Episoden, die ohne Beziehung zum Ganzen stehen, ausser dass sie den Eindruck der Sinnlosigkeit des Krieges und des menschlichen Handelns verschärfen" (82). Scherpe notes that "Das Raumbild überlagert die Zeitfolge" (233).

[19] Mayer (155) sees in a phrase on this same page, "warf sich tiefer in das Gestühl" (*W*, 11), the initial leitmotif signaling the Kaiser's gradual retreat from his office and authority, from active life. Kreutzer provides a trenchant analysis of the political implications of Döblin's depiction of Ferdinand.

[20] In terms of the novel's "antihistoricism" and anthropological discourse, Müller (1997) follows the lead here of Klaus Scherpe (227; 238) in his excellent article from 1990.

Works Cited

Arnold, Armin. *Alfred Döblin*. Berlin: Morgenbuch, 1996.

Dollinger, Roland. "Alfred Döblins Naturphilosophie in den Zwanziger Jahren." In *Philosophia Naturalis: Beiträge zu einer zeitgemäßen Naturphilosophie*, edited by Thomas Arzt, Roland Dollinger, and Maria Hippius-Gräfin Dürckheim. Würzburg: Königshausen & Neumann, 1996. 135–50.

Donahue, Neil H. *Forms of Disruption: Abstraction in Modern German Prose*. Ann Arbor: University of Michigan Press, 1993.

Eichendorff, Joseph, Freiherr von. *Gedichte*. Tübingen: Niemeyer, 1996.

Eggert, Hartmut, Ulrich Profitlich, and Klaus R. Scherpe, eds. *Geschichte als Literatur: Formen und Grenzen der Representation von Vergangenheit*. Stuttgart: Metzler, 1990.

Grass, Günter. "Über meinen Lehrer Döblin." *Akzente* 14, 4 (1967): 290–309.

Hecker, Axel. *Geschichte als Fiktion: Alfred Döblins Wallenstein — Eine exemplarische Kritik des Realismus*. Würzburg: Königshausen & Neumann, 1986.

Höyng, Peter. "Kunst der Wahrheit oder Wahrheit der Kunst?" Die Figur Wallenstein bei Schiller, Ranke und Golo Mann." *Monatshefte* 82, 2 (1990): 142–56.

Jones, M. S. *Der Sturm: A Focus of Expressionism*. Columbia, SC: Camden House, 1984.

Kobel, Erwin. *Alfred Döblin: Erzählkunst im Umbruch*. Berlin and New York: de Gruyter, 1985.

Kort, Wolfgang. *Alfred Döblin*. New York: Twayne, 1974.

Kreutzer, Leo. *Alfred Döblin*. Stuttgart: Kohlhammer, 1970.

Links, Roland. *Alfred Döblin*. Berlin: Volk und Wissen Volkseigener Verlag, 1980; Munich: Beck, 1981.

Mayer, Dieter. *Alfred Döblins Wallenstein: Zur Geschichtsauffassung und zur Struktur*. Munich: Fink, 1972.

———. "Wallenstein." In *Interpretationen zu Alfred Döblin*. Ed. by Ingrid Schuster. Stuttgart: Klett, 1980: 98–117.

Müller, Harro. "'Die Welt hat einen Hauch von Verwesung': Anmerkungen zu Döblins historischem Roman *Wallenstein*." *Merkur* 39, 4 (1985): 405–13.

———. "War and Novel: Alfred Döblin's *Wallenstein* and *November 1918*." In *War, Violence and the Modern Condition*. Ed. by Bernd Hüppauf. Berlin and New York: Walter de Gruyter, 1997.

Musil, Robert. *Nachlaß zu Lebzeiten*. Reinbek: Rowohlt, 1978.

Sebald, Winfried Georg. *Der Mythus der Zerstörung im Werk Döblins*. Stuttgart: Klett, 1980.

Sokel, Walter. "Die Prosa des Expressionismus." In *Expressionismus als Literatur*. Ed. Wolfgang Rothe. Bern: Francke, 1969.

Tewarson, Heidi Thomann. *Alfred Döblin: Grundlagen seiner Ästhetik und ihre Entwicklung, 1900–1933*. Bonn and Frankfurt: Peter Lang, 1979.

Watson, Francis. *Wallenstein: Soldier under Saturn*. New York and London: D. Appleton-Century Co., 1938.

Technology and Nature:
From Döblin's *Berge Meere und Giganten* to a Philosophy of Nature

Roland Dollinger

THE RISE OF the European avant-garde movements during the first two decades of the twentieth century was closely linked to the powerful effects of technological and scientific innovations on the production of works of art.[1] Germany's rapid industrialization after its unification in 1871 not only changed the political, social, and economic map of the Empire, but also led to the development of a modernist aesthetics in all cultural spheres. The two literary avant-garde movements with which Alfred Döblin's early novels are most often associated — futurism and Expressionism — demonstrate this interplay between technology and works of art both thematically and formally.[2] The aesthetic specificity of many of Döblin's prose works is unthinkable without consideration of the impact of the technological and scientific revolutions on all areas of life.

This essay explores several texts by Döblin from the 1920s that show his growing interest in the triangular relationship between human beings, technology, and nature. In the fall of 1921 he began work on his monumental modern epos *Berge Meere und Giganten* (1924). Several months after its publication Döblin wrote an essay entitled "Bemerkungen zu 'Berge Meere und Giganten'" for *Die Neue Rundschau* (*SLW*, 49–60), one of the most prestigious literary journals of the Weimar Republic. This essay is not only the most extensive commentary that Döblin has written about his novels but it also offers us, in conjunction with his essay "Der Geist des naturalistischen Zeitalters" (1924; *SÄPL*, 168–90), some important insights into his evolving and shifting reflections on technology and nature. Although Döblin's novel and his two theoretical essays express an ambivalent attitude toward technology and nature, an ambivalence that is characterized by the polarity between the domination of and simultaneous subjection to nature, Döblin attempts to overcome this polarity in his philosophy of nature, which he presented to the public in more systematic fashion in *Das Ich über der Natur*

(1927). Through a careful reading of these texts, this essay explores Döblin's ideas about the relationships between the technological and scientific impulse of modernity, nature, and human life.

Berge Meere und Giganten

When *Berge Meere und Giganten* appeared at the beginning of the "The Golden Twenties," a period of relative economic and political stability, the literary world was stunned by both the formal radicalism and the thematic scope of Döblin's work. *Berge Meere und Giganten* was certainly the most difficult novel that Döblin had written so far. He had challenged his readers to abandon their conventional expectations about the developmental and psychological novel of the nineteenth century as early as 1913 in his famous essay "An Romanautoren und ihre Kritiker" (*SÄPL*, 119–23) but he did not realize the most radical manifestation of this so-called "Berliner Programm" until the publication of *Berge Meere und Giganten*. Exploding the chronological and spatial boundaries of the realist novel, Döblin startles the reader by moving with breathtaking speed between several continents and extending the narrated time of the novel to seven centuries. As Peter S. Fisher has written in his study *Fantasy and Politics,* Döblin was the only major novelist of the Weimar Republic who experimented with the genre of the science-fiction novel or *Zukunftsroman* (151). Unlike the majority of visionary prose written between the wars, however, Döblin's novel is not merely a reaction to the experience of political disaster following Germany's humiliating loss of the First World War, which was exploited by both right and left-wing intellectuals in their futuristic fantasies of revenge and renewal. According to Fisher, Döblin succeeded in creating a novel far more imaginative and interesting because it was "part of a larger effort to develop both a new kind of literature [. . .] and to formulate [. . .] an all-encompassing world view that revealed man's place and proper role within the universe" (151). After the publication of *Die drei Sprünge des Wang-lun* (1915) and *Wallenstein* (1920), both of which reflect Döblin's own time through the prism of the past, Döblin explored the significance of man's promethean, technological desire by turning his attention to a fictionalized future.[3] In the public library of Berlin Döblin immersed himself in atlases, geological and mineralogical literature, and books about Iceland and Greenland, all of which left their linguistic traces in his novel (Sander, *Grenzen* 77–78; "Handschrift" 64–66). At the beginning of 1922 Döblin interrupted his work as practicing physician to write most of books six and seven of *Berge Meere und Giganten* (the two central sections dealing with Iceland and Greenland). In the summer of

1922 Döblin rented an apartment near the Schlachtensee in Berlin and rewrote most of the novel, although it was not completed until the summer of 1923 (Prangel 42–43).

Berge Meere und Giganten contains a multitude of fictional characters whose motivations for their actions remain largely unexplained. No intervening authorial voice assists the reader in the process of tying together the seemingly loose ends of Döblin's many stories within the nine books of the novel. However, a close reading shows that Döblin achieves aesthetic coherence by developing the "future history" of technologically driven Western societies, and by presenting it as his grandiose vision of the heroic struggle between the ratio-technological impulse of modern man and nature. Döblin's contemporary critics were either fascinated by his extraordinary imagination and ability to give literary shape to such an abundance of material, or repelled by what they considered the pomposity of Döblin's vision of mankind's future (Sander, *Grenzen* 7–20). While it is impossible to summarize a novel whose plethora of characters and events does not offer the reader the convenience of a coherent story, some remarks about the content of *Berge Meere und* Giganten are necessary for a better understanding of its analysis.[4]

The first two books of the novel deal with the development of technology from the twentieth century to the so-called "Uralische Krieg" (*BMG*, 53) at the end of the twenty-fifth century. "Die westlichen Kontinente" (*BMG*, 11) have overcome national and racial differences through the creation of huge industrial centers — London, Brussels, Berlin, New York — where a few families share political power by controlling the technological know-how for the production of machines, weapons, and artificial food. The purpose of the ensuing devastating war against Asian countries is to deflect the subversive energies of the subjected masses onto an enemy that is outside of the rulers' sphere of influence, but the physical losses and the moral defeat of the Western Continents lead to unforeseen consequences. The third book describes the struggle for power in the area of Brandenburg between the opponents of modern technology, who regard the war and its destructive violence as a consequence of the excesses of technology, and the proponents of technology, who are bent on prolonging their political reign by controlling people through technological and scientific knowledge. The fourth book represents an intensification of this conflict between city-dwellers and so-called settlers, radical foes of the process of civilization. The fifth book brings forth new political dangers for the rulers: they are unable to stop the enemies of technology from leaving the cities and creating an anti-modern, "back-to-nature" movement. Because the settlers demand more land, the powerful elites intend to colonize Greenland after melting its ice. Both the city-dwellers, who are alienated from natural life, and the settlers, who run the risk of regressing to primitive forms of life, are unable to resist the fascination of this gigantic technological enterprise. The technological adventure of de-icing Greenland serves the purpose both of overcoming the physical weakness and decadence of the people residing within the big metropolitan centers and of reconnecting the masses of settlers with the official project of civilizing and controlling the natural environment.

Equipped with new machines, large groups of pioneers set out for Iceland in book six in order to explode the huge volcanoes on Iceland and store their natural energy with "Turmalinschleier" (*BMG,* 331). While destroying the mountains and penetrating into their inner fields of force, the explorers are overwhelmed by their proximity to the most hidden realms of nature, but they also understand that storing the sheer infinite energy of the volcanoes poses a grave threat to their existence. Five thousand men perish. Other adventurers meanwhile embark for their journey to Greenland in book seven. At first they are enchanted by the natural life that is luxuriantly growing around their ships. The fire of the volcanoes, stored in the tourmaline on their ships, causes the rapid growth of seaweed, attracts fish, birds, and other animals, and radiates an unusual light and scents that have an eroticizing effect on the conquerors. The closer they get to Greenland the greater the spiritual distance becomes between the leaders of the exploration and the political establishment at home. The unavoidable confrontation with the raging elements of nature changes their attitude toward life, and they now share sentiments toward nature very much like those of the formerly despised settlers. However, their ecstasy abruptly turns into fear once they realize the unforeseen consequences of the de-icing of Greenland. Unexplainable cyclones destroy many of their ships. Monstrous dinosaurs and other indeterminable dragon-like animals, regenerated by the effect of the volcanic energy, fly toward the continents. The leap into the future therefore dialectically ends in a pre-historic era with the creation of life that had long since perished. To protect the cities against these devastating monsters, the rulers breed human-like giants that they employ as defensive weapons across the country (book eight). Although they are effective shields against the onslaught of pre-historic life forms, these colossal beings, devoid of any human spirit, involuntarily embody technological progress in the form of regression. The masses of city-dwellers are now forced to live in underground cities where their life is reduced to the carefree existence of modern cave-men. At the same time, the rulers use their new knowledge of the transformative powers of volcanic energy to transform themselves into giants and other nonhuman species. Their god-like power to produce new forms of life confirms the dialectical process of advancing scientifically and simultaneously regressing to cultural barbarism. Finally, these rulers who have contradicted the laws of nature for centuries dissolve into the rocky wilderness around Cornwall. In the last book of the novel, old and new groups of settlers, encouraged by the prophet of love, Venaska, attempt to live a life in harmony with nature in Southern France. The survivors of the Greenland campaign, under the leadership of Kylin, join them. Although they are traumatized by their experience with the disastrous consequences of their technological hubris, they resist the temptations of a simple, bucolic life, and strive to unify technological knowledge with a new humility toward the "Urmacht" (*BMG*, 510), nature.

This cursory summary of the novel's content may give the reader an impression about the central philosophical conflict between man's desire to control nature and nature's resistance to such technologically driven enterprises. But in order to fully understand Döblin's ideas about the relationship between man and nature during the 1920s we must first turn to Döblin's essay "Bemerkungen zu Berge Meere und Giganten," where he offers some insights into the biographical and psychological origins of his novel.

"Bemerkungen zu Berge Meere und Giganten"

Critics trace the biographical origin of Döblin's novel to a family vacation at the Baltic Sea in 1921 (Sander, *Grenzen* 66–73; Müller-Salget 203–6). The cosmopolitan writer and champion of urban modernity Döblin returned to Berlin and began to see his newfound attraction for the wholeness of nature as a turning point in his career. He published his deeply personal account of this conversion-like experience of nature in 1924 as a commentary in "Bemerkungen zu Berge Meere und Giganten":

> Ich erlebte die Natur als Geheimnis. [. . .] Ich sah, ich erlebte täglich die Natur als das Weltwesen, das ist: das Schwere, das Farbige, das Licht, das Dunkel, die zahllosen Stoffe, als eine Fülle von Vorgängen, die sich lautlos mischen und durchkreuzen. [. . .] Ja, wie ist das möglich: <<Lösung>>. Was tut das Fließende, Flüssige, Warme, dem Festen, so daß es nachgibt, sich hinschmiegt. Ich weiß, daß mir oft ängstlich, körperlich ängstlich, schwindlig unter diesen Dingen wurde, — und, ich gesteh es, manchmal ist mir noch jetzt nicht wohl. (*SLW*, 51–52)

Döblin first describes his attraction to nature as a sense of loss of his self due to the constant flux of natural transformations, summarizing it with the sentence "' — Ich — bin — nicht'" (51). This overwhelming experience calls forth the defensive reaction to do "etwas Scharfes, Aktives gegen das 'Geschehen' der Natur" (52). Döblin thus conceives of a novel that would protect him against his anxiety of losing himself. He initially wants to secure the stability of his self by writing an epos dealing with the battle of modern man against nature: "Ich mußte etwas schreiben, um sie [the "things of nature"] loszuwerden" (52). In Döblin's conception of the novel we can thus see the same aggressive attitude toward nature that also characterizes the "Kampf der Natur mit der Technik" (53) throughout the novel. We may therefore read this struggle between technological man and nature in Döblin's novel as a sign of the author's own insecurity about his fascination for natural phenomena at the beginning of the 1920s.

However, neither the author nor some of his fictional characters of *Berge Meere und Giganten* remain locked in this defensive posture toward nature. After describing his efforts to keep a safe distance between himself and these disturbing natural processes, Döblin then admits to the futility of his endeavors:

> Ich war ausgezogen, um den schrecklichen mystischen Naturkomplexen auszuweichen. Und — saß mitten drin. [. . .] Die stärkste Waffe, die ich gegen diese schweren, die Brust beengenden Gedanken erhob, hatte nichts genutzt. Es ging mir selbst, wie das Thema sagt: die menschliche Kraft gegen die Naturgewalt, die Ohnmacht der menschlichen Kraft. (54)

Döblin's intent of taking up his pen in the service of civilization was not enough to block out this powerful experience of nature. Conceding defeat in this battle against nature's overwhelming impact on his psyche, Döblin assumes a new, more humble attitude toward this "furchteinflößendem Rätsel" (54). The author whose epos was supposed to prove man's superiority over nature puts down his weapon and becomes a passive medium in the service of the autonomous power of nature. The telos of his novel thus changes dramatically:

> Mein Buch war nicht mehr der gigantische Kampf der Stadtschaften, sondern Bekenntnis, ein besänftigender und feiernder Gesang auf die großen Muttergewalten. (54)

The original plan of writing a hymn about the modern metropolis is replaced by the celebration of the "Weltwesen" (54), and the intended heroic victory over nature turns into a recognition of the autonomous power of nature (Müller-Salget 207–10).

The sexual imagery in Döblin's account of his transformation is particularly striking. While he envisioned the technological battle against nature as a war conducted by men — Döblin writes of "erotischen Typen" (53) —, his recognition of the autonomy of nature leads to the glorification of the "Muttergewalten" (54). By lending nature the gender-specific attributes of a "mother," Döblin of course participates in the long history of poetic and scientific representations of nature as a feminine power that is both feared and admired by men.

Two diametrically opposed approaches to nature become evident: on the one hand, a male, technologically driven conduct of war against nature that is perceived as a female being; on the other hand, a quasi-religious celebration of nature ("Ich — betete — ," 54), perceived as a maternal power that reveals its autonomy and independence from human interference. The attempt to dominate nature is transformed into a humble relationship with what he perceives as uncontrollable female forces. Whereas the male self feels initially threatened by a primordial female power against which he tries to protect himself, images of the superiority of nature and the concomitant powerlessness of the male self dominate the rest of the essay. This unmediated alternation between the impulse to dominate nature and recognition of its independence from man also characterizes the motivations and actions of several protagonists in the novel. In the following, I will show how Döblin realizes the dialectics of technological control and male violence as manifestations of a will to power and the simultaneous passive submissiveness to nature as the structuring principle for one of his protagonists. Marduk's shifting position vis-à-vis nature and women in the third and fourth books serves as a symbol for the unresolved polarity between domination of and submission to a gendered nature that characterizes not only Döblin's comments on his novel but also the structure of *Berge Meere und Giganten*.

Marduk

At the beginning of book three, the narrator introduces the scientist Marduk as an unscrupulous politician taking advantage of the power vacuum in Berlin after the "Uralische Krieg," and establishing his reign of terror by dint of his technological knowledge. Marduk's rise to power is a good illustration of the fact that Döblin's novel is by no means an apolitical novel or an expression of his disillusionment with post-war politics.[5] On the contrary, the political content of Döblin's novel lies in the link between the political subjugation of the masses by the ruling elites and their technological domination of nature. Technology is not shown as a destructive force in itself but becomes the means by which the ruling aristocracy assumes and keeps political power by restricting access to technological knowledge. Döblin's modern epos about technology and nature thus anticipates some of Theodor W. Adorno's (1903–69) and Max Horkheimer's (1895–1973) insights into the "dialectics of reason":

> Das Wissen, das Macht ist, kennt keine Schranken, weder in der Versklavung der Kreatur noch in der Willfährigkeit gegen die Herren der Welt. [...] Technik ist das Wesen dieses Wissens. Es zielt nicht auf Begriffe und Bilder, nicht auf das Glück der Einsicht, sondern auf Methode, Ausnutzung der Arbeit anderer, Kapital. [...] Was die Menschen von der Natur lernen wollen, ist, sie anzuwenden, um sie und die Menschen vollends zu beherrschen. (Adorno 8)

In a particularly violent episode, Marduk kills his prisoners, including the mother of his friend Johannes, by confining them to an outdoor space where he experiments with the technologically induced, excessive growth of plants and trees. The unnaturally rapid growth of these organisms within the prison camp crushes the prisoners, completely absorbing and incorporating human life. The psychological meaning of Marduk's violence becomes clear if one considers what appears elsewhere in the novel as an allegory for Döblin's central theme: the representation of technology as violence against the female body of nature. Döblin depicts, for example, the exploitation of the volcanoes' energy for the purpose of melting the icy landscapes of Greenland as rape:

> Die Herren und Herrinnen der Riesenstadtschaften waren kalt und gehässig hinter der Gewalt [meaning energy] her. Wie die Räuber sich in einem fürstlichen Park verbergen und [...] die geschmückten Schönheiten auf der Wiese sich bewegen sehen, [...], und wie sie sie abschätzen, ihren Augenblick abwarten und sich auf sie stürzen, [...], so belauerten die unzähmbaren Menschen [...] das Geheimnis der Vulkane; ergriffen es, zwangen es unter sich. (*BMG*, 434)

And after the failure of the Greenland expedition, the rulers of the continents protect themselves against the terrible consequences of this mad experiment — against the onslaught of the "Urtiere" (434) — by reducing living organisms to their "Mutterstoffe" (453) and reassembling them into new, absurd forms of life. Döblin's metaphors suggest that the technological control and exploitation of nature may be understood as a violent act against the female body in general, and "Mother Earth" in particular.

The image of the scientist and engineer as rapist or murderer of "Mother Earth" was frequently used before and after the First World War in both Expressionist literature and the conservative critique of modern technology. Bernhard Kellermann's (1879–1951) Expressionist novel *Der Tunnel* (1913), for example, glorifies the engineer as a fanatic hero whose hard and numb body penetrates the earth. Ludwig Klages (1872–1956), whose essay "Mensch und Erde" ("Man and Earth," 1913) may be read as an early conservative contribution to today's ecological movement, writes about the destructiveness of Western rationality, complaining about the wounds of earth "die ihr [the earth] muttermörderisch der Geist geschlagen" (Klages, 23). And Oswald Spengler (1880–1936), the prophet of the demise of "Western Civilization" of the 1920s, writes in his *Mensch und Technik* (1931) that the history of technology is one of "unaufhaltsam fortschreitenden, verhängnisvollen Entzweiung zwischen Menschenwelt und Weltall, die Geschichte eines Empörers, der dem Schoße seiner Mutter entwachsen die Hand gegen sie erhebt"(Spengler 5).[6]

However, Döblin contrasts the technological domination of nature with a strong desire to return to a pre-modern stage. The other side of man's hubris, Döblin seems to suggest, manifests itself in a regressive behavior rejecting all technological and scientific progress. For Döblin, this anti-technological stance is merely the expression of a dangerous backward orientation, and is equally rejected:

> Neu fühlte man sich in das Gewitter ein, in den Regen, den Erdboden, die Bewegungen der Sonne und Sterne. Man näherte sich den zarten Pflanzen, den Tieren. [. . .] Zeichen von Tieren, Holzbilder Idole tauchten an vielen Gegenden auf. Man verehrte sie, stellte sich unter ihren Schutz. Stündlich war man von geheimnisvollen Kräften umgeben; Geisterglaube wurde sehr lebendig. (*BMG*, 506)

Döblin rejects this belief in natural spirits as strongly as he refutes the idea of scientific progress as panacea for a better future. Marduk's development from matricide to a leader of a group of "fanatischen Feinde der Apparate" (*BMG*, 174) is symptomatic of this unmediated and unexpected reversal. Violent aggression toward the object abruptly develops into the subject's desire for self-dissolution. Marduk's sadomasochistic relationship with a woman called Balladeuse exemplifies this dialectics of control and self-negation in his sexual life. In his "Bemerkungen," Döblin describes Marduk's death with a vocabulary that resonates with the experience of the Icelandic and Greenlandic adventurers: "Marduk wurde aufgebrochen, geschmolzen von Elina und fand zur Erde zurück" (*SLW*, 56). While a male will to power and self-preservation manifests itself through the destruction of the volcanoes and the melting down of the glaciers of Greenland, female eroticism is able to break up and melt down the male body armor. Marduk simultaneously fears and enjoys his return to nature at the hands of his lover Elina, as does the giant Delvil at the end of the novel when he dissolves into the landscape around Cornwall through the mythical mother figure Vaneska.

In his *Männerphantasien* (Male Fantasies, 1986), Klaus Theweleit associates this male fear of dissolution, a fear often accompanied by pleasure, with the destructive power of the "White Terror" after the First World War. He explains how the literature of *Freikorps* soldiers uses images of floods, breaking waves, and bursting volcanoes as metaphors for a psychologically and physically threatened male ego. The experience of warfare in the trenches, civil war, the politically chaotic situation at the beginning of the Weimar Republic, and the widespread fear of a leftist revolution all contributed to the sense of the general dissolution of traditional values and the social order. Theweleit quotes from the private correspondence of a war veteran whose language is similar to that used by Döblin in his novel:

> Der Krieg hatte die Lavadecke der erstarrten Welt zersprengt. Alle Völker der Erde waren in den Schmelztiegel der großen Umbrennung geworfen worden. (Theweleit, 300)

Ernst Jünger (1895–1998) also uses the image of the active volcano to reflect on the experience of war: "So bedeutet, an einem Kriege teilgenommen zu haben, etwas Ähnliches, wie im Bannkreis eines dieser feuerspeienden Berge gewesen zu sein" (Jünger, *Blätter* 122). Döblin's novel, one may conclude, projects onto the future battle between man and nature contemporary anxieties about the uncertain future of the Weimar Republic in the wake of a devastating war.

Only at the end of *Berge Meere und Giganten* does Döblin briefly attempt to unify what for several hundred pages have remained separate modes of life (Müller-Salget 218–21).[7] Kylin, the leader of a group of new settlers in Southern France, strives to achieve a synthesis between the rational and technological domination of nature and the equally dangerous rejection of all civilizing projects. As a former participant in both adventures, he knows of the potentially fatal consequences of an instrumental reason in the service of political interests, yet does not become a champion of man's submission to nature. What is needed according to Kylin is a balance between a reasonable application of the technological means available to men and a respectful attitude toward man's natural environment.

> Ich habe den Schmerz nicht vergessen. Wir haben die Giganten im Gedächtnis. [. . .] Wir haben auch das Feuer. Es ist uns nichts ent-

schwunden. Wir müssen dies festhalten. Diuwa, das Land nimmt uns, aber wir sind etwas in dem Lande. Es schlingt uns nicht. Wir haben keine Furcht vor der Luft und dem Boden. (*BMG*, 510)

Kylin is aware that there is a Promethean quality in man's existence that one should not simply deny. Human subjectivity and the desire to differentiate oneself from nature must instead be regarded as an expression of man's *natural* existence. Although Döblin hints at the necessity of overcoming the dichotomy between human subjectivity and a concept of nature perceived to be merely its object, he does not elaborate on this point in *Berge Meere und Giganten*. As we will see, it was not until the publication of *Das Ich über der Natur* in 1927 that Döblin returns to the problem of the position of human life within the natural universe.

Döblin's Embrace of Technological Modernity

A close analysis of Döblin's second major essay on technology of the mid-1920s reveals the extent to which he was still alternating between competing conceptions of technology in modern industrialized societies. While his novel *Berge Meere und Giganten* and the accompanying "Bemerkungen" point out the political and cultural dangers of unrestrained support for technological progress, his essay "Der Geist des naturalistischen Zeitalters" (1924) puts him into the camp of those Weimar intellectuals who defended technology against conservative cultural critics bewailing the negative spiritual effects of technology on modern life. Döblin discovers in the historical process of Germany's rapid industrialization since the mid-nineteenth century a new "Kraft" (*SÄPL*, 171) and "Impuls" (173) that does not lead to the erosion of society's spiritual values, but rather to the formation of a new mass society ("Umseelung," 173) where technology reigns supreme. Döblin argues that technology and spirit should not be seen as irreconcilable forces. On the contrary, he expects that a new spirituality of the scientific-technological age will gradually evolve. Technology signifies a "Symptom" (173) of something altogether different, the meaning of which will only become evident in the future.

Unlike his novel, Döblin's essay wholeheartedly accepts the political and cultural costs of the technologization of modern societies. He acknowledges the necessity of man's permanent conquest of the natural world and believes that there is no alternative to what he sees as its unavoidable consequences: the standardization of the metropolis; the continuing industrialization in both capitalist and socialist societies; the dissolution of the national state; the danger of imperialist wars; the eradication of gender differences in the workplace; and the socialization of human labor, a process which will lead to the creation of a more homogeneous social structure.

By accepting technological modernity as a fait accompli, Döblin's essay anticipates the heroic optimism of Ernst Jünger's vision of a technocratic society in his *Der Arbeiter* (The Worker, 1932). Both writers view the complete technological organization of modern life as the manifestation of a basic, natural human drive striving for expansion, domination, and subjugation. Both texts are above all united by a fascination with technological man — a visionary construct that is primarily characterized by its opposition to bourgeois individualism and culture as well as its ability to permeate all spheres of life. Jünger's "worker" represents a new type of human being that unconditionally accepts the triumph of technology. Jünger states in *Der Arbeiter* that

> Überall, wo der Mensch in den Bannkreis der Technik gerät, sieht er sich vor ein unausweichbares Entweder-Oder gestellt. Es gilt für ihn, entweder die eigentümlichen Mittel zu akzeptieren und ihre Sprache zu sprechen oder unterzugehen. [. . .] Die Anwendung der Mittel zieht einen ganz bestimmten Lebensstil nach sich, der sich sowohl auf die großen wie auf die kleinen Dinge des Lebens erstreckt. (166)

In his "Der Geist des naturalistischen Zeitalters" Döblin's technological discourse shares the conviction of the unavoidable rule of technology with writers such as Jünger and Spengler. Despite his acceptance of a technological future, Döblin, however, finishes his essay by asking his readers to draw the "seelischen Konsequenzen" (*SÄPL*, 190) of the scientific-technological revolution. His final sentence is puzzling, because it seems to take the essay into a different direction:

> Die Natur ist im ersten Abschnitt dieser Periode nur unbekannt und wird leidenschaftlich erforscht; später wird sie Geheimnis. Dies Geheimnis zu fühlen und auf ihre Weise auszusprechen ist die große geistige Aufgabe dieser Periode. (190)

Which secret does Döblin mean? What are the spiritual consequences of an age that according to Döblin has embarked on a secular and scientific journey? The obscurity of this last sentence demonstrates that Döblin's embrace of technology in "Das naturalistische Zeitalter" was not his final word about technology and nature. Although he leaves these questions unanswered in his essay, he returns to them three years later in his *Das Ich über der Natur*, his only philosophical book in which he tries to systematize his thoughts about the relationship between man and nature.

Döblin's Philosophy of Nature

Like the Romantic writers and philosophers of nature in the early nineteenth century, Döblin seeks the secret of nature by demonstrating that both organic and inorganic natural phenomena possess an animate quality.[8] In the introduction to *Das Ich über der Natur* Döblin writes

> Es wird von der lebenden Natur gesprochen, wie sie überall Zeichen hat. Ihre wahrhafte, bis in das sogenannte Anorganische gehende Beseeltheit wird gezeigt, und wie der Mensch, sein personales, einzelnes Ich, hier hinein verschlungen ist. (*IN*, 7)

Similar to the Romantic conception of the writer, Döblin views the modern author in *Das Ich über der Natur* as an interpreter of the (hidden) meaning of signs within nature. Döblin is convinced that the spiritual quality of nature manifests itself in its internal order, in the regularity of its structure, and its inner purpose — qualities that the modern scientist with his strictly rational and analytical approach to natural objects is unable to perceive. Assuming that the totality of nature is one living organism, Döblin points out the existence of a fundamental relationship between all beings. On the one hand, man consists of nothing but natural components and *is* according to Döblin animal, plant, water, minerals, sand, stone and much more. On the other hand, man does not conceive of himself as this natural self whose "I" is merely subjected to a superior and anonymous nature but rather as an individual, independent being who actively changes and gives shape to his world. Man is both subject and object, a paradoxical being that Döblin calls in *Unser Dasein* (1933) "Stück und Gegenstück" of nature (*UD*, 30). The existence of human beings is therefore characterized by a fundamental tension: he *is* nature and simultaneously strives to overcome the natural limitations imposed on him.

Döblin found in his philosophy of nature a discursive means to create the *effect* of a meaningful universe. In his classical study of Weimar Culture, Peter Gay ascribes to the political discourse of the 1920s a widespread "Hunger for Wholeness," a desperate need for roots and community viewed as remedies against a materialist culture and a fragmented society (70–101). While Döblin rejected both the right-wing ideal of a *völkisch* community and the communist hope for a classless society, he satisfied his own appetite for a holistic worldview with his ideas about the organic totality of nature.[9] Through the principle of individuation, human beings are simultaneously separated from and connected to a primordial being. Participating in this organic cosmos, modern man and his technological world become re-enchanted in Döblin's *Das Ich über der Natur:*

> Wird aber die Welt, ständig, augenblicklich, jetzt, real durch eine andere, ganz übermächtige Urmacht, so fühlen wir, an diesem Geheimnis sind wir beteiligt, dies hat große Wichtigkeit, jetzt erst bekommen die Dinge ein Zentrum, eine eigentümliche Sicherheit, es ist ein Anker da, dessen Tau wir vielleicht selbst in der Hand haben. (*IN,* 191)

We can now see what Döblin accomplishes with his philosophy of nature. He is able to bridge the gap between the two poles of the hostile rejection and the enthusiastic admiration of nature which was responsible for his characteristic oscillations in *Berge Meere und Giganten.* If man views himself as both subject and object, as a being that *is* nature while at the same time striving to free himself from the confines imposed on him by nature, both the desire for the aggressive control of and the pleasurable subjugation to nature become questionable attitudes. Nature no longer appears as a maternal, threatening power challenging the male self to a struggle that is fought with the means of modern technology, but as a caring mother taking the individual back to her breast (*IN,* 177).

In Döblin's philosophy of nature we are able to discern a conception of human autonomy that Evelyn Fox Keller in *Reflections on Gender and Science* (1985) calls "dynamic autonomy" (107). Keller shows in her psychoanalytically inspired analysis of the relationship between the origin of gender-specific behavior and our cultural notions of science, technology, and objectivity that the separation of the male child from his mother creates anxieties as well as desires. Through this process of separation from the primary object the desire to overcome this differentiation and simultaneously regain the original unity arises. At the same time, however, the wish to preserve one's autonomy increases, an autonomy that is threatened by the temptation to fall back upon the earlier developmental stage of dependence. During the earliest stages of childhood the processes of the separation from the mother and creation of male subjectivity lead to the increasing objectivization of the mother whom the male child begins to view as his "Other." Exaggerated and rigid notions of autonomy and masculinity are thus defense mechanisms against regressive fears *and simultaneously* the expression of regressive desires. According to Keller, this process of the creation of male autonomy and the objectivization of the mother repeats itself in the relationship between the modern scientist and his object, that is, between science and nature (75–94).

Keller's psychoanalytic approach to the history of science and technology sheds an interesting light on Döblin's texts of the 1920s. We have already seen how in Döblin's novel and his essays on technology conflicting ideas and emotions with regard to nature play a crucial role. On the one hand, these texts are characterized by the fear of an all-powerful nature with feminine connotations and loss of self, resulting in a fascination for modern technology as a manifestation of male autonomy and self-preservation. On the other hand, we can now view the rejection of modern technology and the pre-modern, primitive desire for a symbiotic relationship with nature as mirror images of the former. In his philosophy of nature, Döblin attempts to transcend this polarity through the notion of a "dynamic autonomy." As Keller's term implies, human autonomy should not be seen as static and essential, but rather as dynamic in its relationship with others and subject to constant change. The theoretical goal of Döblin's philosophical speculation is a form of knowledge that recognizes nature as a force that is independent of human existence but simultaneously acknowledges our relationship with nature. If we cease to view nature as merely an object that is radically separate from us and emphasize our similarities with nature, we may avoid both the hostility toward nature and technological delusions as well as a false veneration of nature and opposition to technological achievements.

Notes

[1] See Bürger and Poggioli, especially 131–47.

[2] For the link between Expressionism and technology see Daniels; for a discussion of Döblin's connections with Italian futurism see Scimonello and Demetz.

[3] For a discussion of the different genre designations see Klotz; more recently, Rolf Geißler has called the novel "eine Apokalypse" (157).

[4] The following summary is indebted to Klotz's "Nachwort"; for an English plot summary of the novel, see Kort (82–89).

[5] Matthias Prangel summarizes this belief when he writes that the novel signifies "einen scharfen Kontrapunkt zu Döblins politischem Engagement der ersten Nachkriegsjahre" (43).

For a more recent analysis of the novel's political aspirations see Hannelore Qual.

[6] For a survey of the relationship between technology and literature in the nineteenth and early twentieth centuries, see Segeberg. For the role of technology in the cultural criticism of Klages, Spengler, and Ernst Jünger, see Merlio.

[7] Kreutzer reads the ending of the novel as a victory of the settlers over technology (99).

[8] For a more extensive discussion of the Romantic "origins" of Döblin's philosophy of nature, see Dollinger.

[9] Kreutzer reaches a different conclusion. According to him, Döblin's identification with nature is a replacement for the failed political identification with the proletariat (81–88).

Works Cited

Bürger, Peter. *Theory of the Avant-Garde*. Trans. by Michael Shaw. Minneapolis: U of Minnesota P, 1984.

Daniels, Karlheinz. "Expressionismus und Technik." *Expressionismus als Literatur*. Ed. by Wolfgang Rothe. Bern and Munich: Francke, 1969. 171–93.

Demetz, Peter. *Worte in Freiheit: Der italienische Futurismus und die deutsche literarische Avantgarde 1912–1934*. Munich: Piper, 1990.

Dollinger, Roland. "Alfred Döblins Naturphilosophie in den Zwanziger Jahren." *Philosophia Naturalis: Beiträge zu einer zeitgemäßen Naturphilosophie*. Ed. by Thomas Arzt, Roland Dollinger, and Maria Hippius-Gräfin Dürckheim. Würzburg: Königshausen & Neumann, 1996. 135–50.

Fisher, Peter S. *Fantasy and Politics: Visions of the Future in the Weimar Republic*. Madison: U of Wisconsin P, 1991.

Gay, Peter. *Weimar Culture: The Outsider as Insider*. New York: Harper & Row, 1968.

Geißler, Rolf. "Alfred Döblins Apokalypse des Wachstums. Überlegungen zum Roman *Berge Meere und Giganten*." *Literatur für Leser* 21 (Summer 1998): 154–70.

Horkheimer, Max, and Theodor W. Adorno. *Dialektik der Aufklärung*. Frankfurt am Main: Fischer, 1969.

Jünger, Ernst. *Der Arbeiter: Herrschaft und Gestalt*. Stuttgart: Klett-Cotta, 1982.

———. *Blätter und Steine*. Hamburg: Hanseatische Verlagsanstalt, 1934.

Keller, Evelyn Fox. *Reflections on Gender and Science*. New Haven: Yale UP, 1985.

Kellermann, Bernhard. *Der Tunnel*. Frankfurt am Main: Suhrkamp, 1995.

Klages, Ludwig. *Mensch und Erde: Zehn Abhandlungen*. Stuttgart: Kröner, 1956.

Klotz, Volker. "Alfred Döblins 'Berge Meere und Giganten.'" *Berge Meere und Giganten*. Frankfurt: Büchergilde Gutenberg, 1978. 513–39.

Kort, Wolfgang. *Alfred Döblin*. New York: Twayne Publishers, 1974.

Kreutzer, Leo. *Alfred Döblin: Sein Werk bis 1933*. Stuttgart: Kohlhammer, 1970.

Merlio, Gilbert. "Kultur- und Technikkritik vor und nach dem ersten Weltkrieg." *Titan Technik: Ernst und Georg Jünger über das technische Zeitalter*. Ed. by Friedrich Strack. Würzburg: Königshausen & Neumann, 2000. 19–41.

Müller-Salget, Klaus. *Alfred Döblin: Werk und Entwicklung*. Bonn: Bouvier, 1972.

Poggioli, Renato. *The Theory of the Avant-Garde*. Trans. by Gerald Fitzgerald. Cambridge: Harvard UP, 1968.

Prangel, Matthias. *Alfred Döblin*. Stuttgart: Metzler, 1987.

Qual, Hannelore. *Natur und Utopie: Weltanschauung und Gesellschaftsbild in Alfred Döblins Roman Berge Meere und Giganten*. Munich: Iudicium, 1992.

Sander, Gabriele. "Alfred Döblins Roman *Berge Meere und Giganten* — aus der Handschrift gelesen: Eine Dokumentation unbekannter textgenetischer Materialien und neuer Quellenfunde." *Schiller-Jahrbuch* 45 (2001): 39–69.

———. *"An die Grenzen des Wirklichen und Möglichen. . . . ": Studien zu Alfred Döblins Roman Berge Meere und Giganten."* Frankfurt: Peter Lang, 1988.

Scimonello, Giovanni. "Zur Theorie und Praxis der Utopien im technischen Zeitalter. Alfred Döblins 'Berge Meere und Giganten' (1924) und F. T. Marinettis 'Mafarka il futurista' (1910)." *Reisen Entdecken Utopien: Untersuchungen zum Alteritätsdiskurs im Kontext von Kolonialismus und Kulturkritik*. Bern: Peter Lang, 1998. 69–79.

Segeberg, Harro. *Literarische Technikbilder: Studien zum Verhältnis von Technik- und Literaturgeschichte im 19. und frühen 20. Jahrhundert*. Tübingen: Max Niemeyer, 1987.

Spengler, Oswald. *Mensch und Technik*. Munich: Beck, 1931.

Theweleit, Klaus. *Männerphantasien*. Basel: Stroemfeld/Roter Stern, 1986.

"Arzt und Dichter": Döblin's Medical, Psychiatric, and Psychoanalytical Work[1]

Veronika Fuechtner

THE PHYSICIAN AND THE WRITER Döblin cannot be isolated from each other, although they are all too often studied as separate entities. Ironically, Döblin himself contributed to the perception that Döblin the doctor and Döblin the writer were two completely separate personae. In the newspaper article "Zwei Seelen in einer Brust" (Two Souls in one Body, 1928; *SLW* 103–6) the physician and the writer meet and comment on each other. Without even having met his counterpart, the physician complains that the writer's political opinions are unreliable, his books too difficult to read, and his imagination overly exuberant. The writer, on the other hand, seems more curious about the doctor, and visits him in his office in Berlin-Lichtenberg, "das merkwürdigste Milieu, das man sich denken kann" (105). But the meeting reveals that they are the exact counter parts of each other, and the writer cannot shake his increasing anxiety in the face of the doctor's "psychotherapeutischen Blick" (105). After all, he might be catching on to his psychological defects — unpleasant memories are slowly emerging. In the end the writer would prefer not to meet this "Anonymus" (106) again, to whom he was but a mere human being and ultimately just another patient. And the doctor assumes that the writer will probably make fun of him in his writing (which, of course, will not faze him, as he is quick to infer).

The intention behind this artificial separation is obviously satirical. Döblin contrasts the lone "grauer Soldat" of the working class with the narcissistic "Primadonna" (105) of the intellectual circles to depict the very different worlds he moves about in. More important, he describes two different modes of processing and representing reality, both of which are intrinsic to his writing: self-effacing analysis, psychological intuition, and shorthand descriptions on the one hand and lively fantasy, quick-witted irony, and an abundance of metaphors on the other. A closer look reveals how much these two modes have in common. The doctor and the writer find common ground in their research: the doctor loves reading the travel books that the writer uses in preparation for his works, while the writer researches the east of Berlin and writes about the people who are treated by the doctor. Both worlds and both modes are essential for Döblin's writing. This text suggests that physician and writer need to be described and understood together. The following overview of Döblin's medical, psychiatric, and psychoanalytical work shall provide a basis for understanding both.

In other autobiographical writings Döblin emphasizes that he is as much a clinician as he is a writer. In 1927 he states that he would rather abandon writing than give up his other profession, "den inhaltsvollen, anständigen, wenn auch sehr ärmlichen Beruf eines Arztes" (*SLW*, 98). In a 1946 interview, Döblin describes his medical profession as an integral part of his writing and his political thought (Bergel, 27 and 46). He claims that it allows him to explore his interest in the natural sciences and gives him access to the lives of many working-class patients. And nothing is more important, says Döblin, than the direct contact with living people, which provides the basis for his political activism. The fruitful connection of clinical theory and practice, political activism and innovative fiction came to characterize Döblin's work of the 1920s and is still perceived as the defining moment of his writing. This most visible and successful period in Döblin's writing evolved along with his medical work. In what follows, I will trace the changes in Döblin's medical career and the development of his clinical writings. Over the course of two decades Döblin moved from working as a doctor in large psychiatric institutions to consulting and treating a wide variety of patients in a small neighborhood office. The intellectual context of his writings moved from psychiatric practice to psychoanalytical thought.

Medical Studies and Psychiatric Practice — Freiburg and Berlin

At the time Döblin embarked on his medical studies, first in Berlin and then in Freiburg, the field of psychiatry was undergoing major conceptual changes. In the 1870s, psychiatry emerged as a discipline separate from neurology. It began to address the social implications of psychiatric diseases, while psychiatric care increasingly shifted to large psychiatric institutions. The conceptual focus became the isolation, management, and observation of the patient, rather than the patient's healing.[2] With Emil

Kraepelin (1856–1926) psychiatry turned away from mapping the brain for the classification of diseases, diagnostics, and pharmacology (Kiefer, 67). While still assuming a physiological basis of psychological processes, most psychiatrists analyzed these processes by studying the course of the disease and what they deemed measurable results of behavioral experiments. Diverging definitions of human experience and of attention became the crucial conceptual factors in measuring, tracking, and deducing psychological activity for psychiatrists such as Theodor Lipps, Theodor Ziehen, and Wilhelm Wundt (all of whom Döblin cited in his dissertation).

Döblin completed his dissertation on symptoms of memory loss due to Korsakoff's psychosis associated with alcoholism in 1905. His dissertation advisor was the psychiatrist Alfred Erich Hoche (1865–1943), a professed opponent of Freud's, who came from the discipline of neuropathology and subsequently developed the theory of symptom complexes, which were conceived as a secondary, more accurate diagnostic unit than the large disease classifications or small symptom elements. In 1905 this theory was just in its beginnings, and Döblin followed this trend in psychiatry by explaining psychological phenomena in psychophysical terms and by focusing on the course of the disease rather than its etiology. However, Döblin neither quoted Hoche's work in his dissertation nor did he allude to the social ramifications of alcohol abuse and the dubious social ideas that Hoche subscribed to in later publications. In 1910, for example, Hoche argued that the mental afflictions of "kultivierte Rassen" stem from their higher sense of responsibility. In his discussion of different forms of dementia he raised questions of the "soziale Brauchbarkeit" of the individual and the connection between disease, sexuality, and criminality (Binswanger, 229).[3] His notion of "geistig minderwertig" culminates in a call for the annihilation of "lebensunwertes Leben" in 1920 — long before it became a reality in National Socialist Germany (Blasius, 135).[4] In his later writings Döblin reacted to Hoche's politics. In 1939 he pointedly countered Hoche's polemics against psychoanalysis and also attacked his disciple Oswald Bumke (Anz, 23). In 1946 he published a fictionalized account of National Socialist practices of euthanasia in the psychiatric hospital Berlin-Buch, his former workplace. In this account, "Die Fahrt ins Blaue" (reprinted in Heilmann, 206–13) Döblin describes with great emotional force how the confused patients became victims of their conflicted caretakers, raising the issue of medical ethics in a postwar Germany that did not welcome such discussions.[5] Clearly, Döblin's and Hoche's politics could not have been further apart.

While Döblin's dissertation attributes the disturbances of association to changes in the brain and rejects the idea of psychological causality in accordance with Hoche's work, it also relies on a broad spectrum of other contemporary psychiatric and psychological resources from the writings of Karl Bonhöffer to those of Theodor Ziehen, whose application of physiological psychology to psychiatry and experiment parameters influenced Döblin's case study. Considering the psychiatric school Döblin was trained in, his dissertation also indicates a remarkable interest in exploring the psychological role language and personal history play in pathological conditions. Countering what he perceives as a mechanistic and solely neurologically grounded "Seelenphysik,"[6] he is looking for "das Unkörperliche im Körper" (*Gedächtnisstörungen*, 14). His dissertation investigates how memory works, how stories seem to emerge out of nothing, and how language functions in this context. He was fascinated by the idea of a link between the present and the past through the psychological existence of the past outside of our present consciousness (*Gedächtnisstörungen*, 11). Although Döblin moved away from clinical psychiatry in the years to come, he retained a strong sense of the inseparability of the physiological and the psychological and of the necessity for hands-on clinical work.

In his dissertation, Döblin creates a link between fiction and his patients' confabulations intended to bridge their memory gaps (*Gedächtnisstörungen*, 36). As other recent Döblin scholarship has shown, Döblin's dissertation is revealing in regard to his early understanding of fiction as formulated in the 1913 "Berliner Programm." Georg Reuchlin relates the psychiatric paradigm of observation (rather than explanation of psychological processes) to the anti-analytical style of narration of texts such as "Die Ermordung einer Butterblume" (written in 1904). And Roland Dollinger points out that the dissociation of memory material analyzed by Döblin parallels the dissociation of reality perception in expressionist literature (141). Döblin's dissertation can be read as a document of a specific moment of transition in psychiatry as well as an indicator of his aesthetic point of departure.

With the dissertation completed, Döblin worked successively at two large psychiatric institutions, first in Karthaus-Prüll near Regensburg (until 1906) and then in Berlin-Buch (from 1906 until 1908). In retrospect Döblin describes these years of "Einschachtelung in den Krankenhäusern" as personally and professionally deeply unsatisfying:

> Und dann war es lauter Diagnostik. Ja, was hatte ich die Jahre über in den Irrenanstalten und Krankenhäusern gelernt? Wie die Krankheiten verliefen,

welche es waren — und ob sie es wirklich waren, woran diese Leute litten. Es schmeichelte meinem Denktrieb — auch dem meiner Chefs — zu wissen, wie alles verlief. Wir wußten und damit basta. (*SLW,* 94)

According to his own account, Döblin was in charge of treating 150 women of the roughly 650 patients in Karthaus-Prüll, whom he describes as absolutely insane (*B I,* 33). His medical records from this time indicate that he was involved in observation and management rather than treatment — in some cases even questioning was not possible (Schäffner, 18). Even though Döblin refers to himself in the third person and in indirect speech in his accounts of the conversations with his patients, his appreciation of the patients' neologisms ("Sprachverwirrtheit exquisiter Art") and his featuring of what he presents as unmediated patient speech reveal the unique perspective of a budding physician-poet. One of the many patient quotations vehemently criticizes the medical profession: "Schämt Euch, Ihr wollt Ärzte sein [. . .]" (Schäffner, 17). While this quote and the related fantasy that the patients will have their day in court as witnesses against the doctors are part of the patient's delusion, its dramatic presence in the write-ups evokes the aimless circle of patient intakes, transfers, and deaths that Döblin's medical work was reduced to at that point.

Melancholia and Hysteria: Beginnings in Berlin

After his move to Berlin in 1908 Döblin began adopting a more psychological approach to psychiatry in his theoretical work. Based on the observations of two older female patients in Berlin-Buch, Döblin published "Zur perniziös verlaufenden Melancholie" (The Pernicious Course of Melancholy, 1908), in which he describes a specific case of fatal melancholia outside of Kraepelin's classifications. Döblin disagrees with the claim of neurologist Carl Wernicke that fear gradually increases in a predictable pattern in cases of melancholia. He claims instead that the two women not only went through phases of fearful anxiety before their deaths, but also through phases of deep confusion, with disturbances of their speech patterns. The latter symptoms are neither a result of an organic defect, as the autopsies show, nor are they a result of excessive affect. Therefore, Wernicke's curve of affect cannot be applied. Since a psychological factor cannot be construed for these two cases, Döblin concludes that this clinical evidence is difficult to classify. In contrast to most anamnestic literature of his time and to a greater extent than in his earlier medical records, Döblin takes great care in describing the women's facial expressions and gestures, and lets them speak for themselves. Brief moments of lucidity ("Ich weiß nicht, warum ich so viel spreche"), paranoia ("Fertig zum Abschlachten"), and the suppression of sexual desire, in Döblin's words "Versündigungsphantasien" ("Verzeihung, daß ich unten hingefaßt habe") find their way into the clinical text as direct quotes ("Zur perniziös verlaufenden Melancholie," 362 and 364). This strategy already hints at the importance that the patient's narrative would have in Döblin's later work as a therapist and also foreshadows the empathy with which he would portray fictionalized accounts of mental afflictions.

Also in 1908, Döblin discussed his work on hysteria in the "Psychiatrischer Verein zu Berlin," a forum for Berlin psychiatrists, such as Theodor Ziehen, whose work had influenced Döblin's dissertation, or Karl Abraham, who founded the Berlin Psychoanalytic Association in the same year.[7] Döblin's article "Aufmerksamkeitsstörungen bei Hysterie" (Attention Disorders in Hysteria, 1909) is based on this presentation and reads like a continuation of his search for answers to the questions raised in his previous publications: how does memory loss work, and what psychological categories beyond affect and association could account for phases of confusion and low affect? The case study describes a female patient with recurring attacks of anger that she subsequently cannot recall. The patient stubbornly declines to acknowledge her illness and instead complains about unrelated minor physical symptoms. Focusing on the psychological rather than the physiological, Döblin describes the patient's family history not as a history of hereditary but of relational problems. Döblin draws a connection between his patient's visions and her more or less conscious fears evolving around her sterility, and suspects that this is the real "illness" she is trying to hide with such vehemence ("Aufmerksamkeitsstörungen," 476). He goes on to outline the repression of unwelcome feelings and the ensuing shift and reattachment of her emotions to a potentially less threatening complex — her attacks. Drawing upon Sigmund Freud's *Zur Psychopathologie des Alltagslebens* (1901), he determines this process in his patient to be pathological in contrast to the normally occurring amount of repression and shift of affect. Quoting Pierre Janet's psychological work, Döblin describes a psychological energy that is pathologically withdrawn from normal social interactions and instead released in the attacks. Distancing himself from the neurologists Carl Wernicke and Josef Breuer, he claims that this psychological energy describes neither a physical nor a neurological entity. It captures the degree of attentiveness ("Aufmerksamkeitswerth") as it relates to the affect, the senses, and the imagination. He concludes that the idea of psychological energies is a necessary complement of the prevalent association theory ("Associationslehre"). By isolating the category of attention and emancipating it from affect and association, Döblin indeed moves away from psychological association theory as set forth by Ziehen or Münsterberg or Wilhelm Wundt's theory of apperception ("Apperceptionslehre"). In his view, the focus on attention as a measurable psychological energy could lead to a whole new psychological curve.

> Indem affectgetragene Vorstellungen und Hallucinationen sich ungehindert der Aufmerksamkeit bemächtigen können, wird ein ganz unübersehbarer discontinuierlicher Ablauf geschaffen, mit vielen Gipfeln. ("Aufmerksamkeitsstörungen," 482)

As a contemporary psychiatric review pointed out, Döblin coined the term "Dysergasie" for the malfunctioning of psychological energy, for its unregulated distribution ("Energasie," on the other hand, indicates the normally coordinated function and expression of this energy) (Ilberg, 604).

More than twenty years later, Döblin commented on his findings in "Aufmerksamkeitsstörungen bei Hysterie." Summarizing that this specific case of hysteria was based on changes in the dynamics and energies of the soul, he cryptically states that Freud's work represented nothing miraculous to him personally (*SLW*, 93). While this quote has been frequently cited as evidence for a complete dismissal of Freud, it more accurately suggests (especially in light of his later involvement with the Berlin Psychoanalytic Institute) that Döblin himself and other clinicians and theorists were already working with concepts akin to those of Freud before they were labeled Freudian. By 1909 Döblin had clearly moved away from clinical psychiatry and was experimenting with a more psychological perspective.

In 1910 Döblin took up once more the topic of confabulations and problems of categorization and published "Zur Wahnbildung im Senium" (Delusions in Old Age). In this comparison of two cases of senile psychosis, Döblin claims that senile psychosis has as little to do with old age as "Jugendirresein" with young age. Age factors and psychotic factors need to be carefully diagnosed on a case-to-case basis. Emphasizing the nosological over the psychological interest, and closely engaging with Kraepelin's work, Döblin points out the organic character of psychosis and hereditary factors, while at the same time further applying his theory of psychological energies. He renews his critique of the prevailing ideas of affect, differentiates between different types of feelings ("Unlustgefühl," "Unsicherheitsgefühl," and "Unglücksgefühl"), and elaborates on the connection between "Auffassung" (defined as the totality of all associative efforts) and "Empfindung" (sensory perceptions defined as energetic entities). The instance of "Auffassung" channels the development of these energies and produces "Richtungsvorstellungen." Psychosis takes advantage of physical frailties (for example the smell of old age) and incorporates them into its expression (as the paranoiac idea of a vapor produced by enemies). However, in one of the cases, the paranoiac ideas also have a psychologically protective and redeeming function ("Schutz- und Lustfaktor"). In his usual manner Döblin leaves much room for the patients' picturesque complaints, the "altweiberhafte Unterhaltungskonfabulation": acid powders, ringworms, and mean nurses take center stage in dramatic first-person narratives.

The Experience of the First World War and the Berlin Psychoanalytic Institute

Döblin's renewed emphasis on the organic in his article "Wahnbildung im Senium" mirrors his temporary turn to internal medicine. He had left the psychiatric clinic of Berlin-Buch for the department of internal medicine of the hospital Am Urban in Berlin-Kreuzberg before publishing the article.[8] Increasingly frustrated with the limits of psychiatric treatment, Döblin decided to seek psychological answers in the physical realm. Not in the brain — he elaborates in retrospect — but in the glands and the metabolism (*SLW*, 93). Over the course of a brief and very productive period he published a series of articles on topics such as bone weakness, blood sugar, and body temperature.[9] In 1911 he opened his own practice for low-income patients, first on Bluecherstrasse 18, near the hospital Am Urban, and in 1913 in Berlin-Lichtenberg, where he continued to treat psychiatric cases. In his short newspaper essay "Die Nerven" (1914) Döblin returns to the topic of hysteria, mentioning Freud explicitly, and for the first time points out the significance of psychotherapy in its treatment: "[. . .] die Psychotherapie hat in ihre Rechte zu treten" (*KS-1*, 156). Döblin started treating patients with psychoanalytical methods in the same year (Anz, 18). Moreover, his war experience as a military doctor in Saargemünd and Hagenau and his indirect experience of the battle of Verdun further intensified his interest in psychoanalysis (Meyer, 20). The primitive and brutal treatment of war neurotics during and after the First World War led many other doctors to reevaluate their approach to the treatment of trauma, and the clinical study of war neurosis became the theoretical stepping-stone for the concept of the ego in psychoanalytical theory.[10]

Upon his return to Berlin at the beginning of 1919, Döblin set up a practice as a psychiatrist and general practitioner. Following a period of war-related instability and the tragic death of his sister Meta, Döblin found himself in a moment of personal crisis.[11] His rapprochement to psychoanalysis was certainly sparked by his medical work and his theoretical interest in psychological theory, but there must have been personal reasons that prompted him to seek psychoanalytical counseling.[12] According to Minder, Döblin underwent a training analysis with the psychoanalyst Ernst Simmel in 1919 (162).[13] Next to Karl Abraham and Hanns Sachs, Simmel was one of the leading figures of the Berlin Psychoanalytic Institute, and Döblin's encounter with him marks the beginning of his involvement with the Institute, its clinical practice, its theory, and its politics.

By the 1920s Karl Abraham's informal psychoanalytic reading group, which dated from 1908, had developed into the Berlin Psychoanalytic Institute with its own clinic. This mecca of progressive psychoanalytical thought counted psychoanalysts such as Erich Fromm, Wilhelm Reich, and Melanie Klein among its ranks. The emphasis on the political and social implications of psychoanalysis, the application of psychoanalysis to fields such as law, pedagogy, and medicine, the desire to reach beyond the traditional bourgeois clientele, as well as the strategy to popularize psychoanalysis through the media were some of the traits that made the Berlin Institute unique in its time. The Institute's work was perceived as part of a larger social and cultural network, and included writers like Arnold Zweig, Hermann Graf Keyserling, and Stefan Zweig. Other prominent figures of the Weimar Republic like Helene Stöcker, at the forefront of the Women's Movement, or Magnus Hirschfeld, the founder of modern sexology, were also connected to the Institute. The Institute even collaborated with the UFA film studio and expressionist film director G. W. Pabst to bring the story of a successful psychoanalytical therapy to the big screen: the feature film "Geheimnisse einer Seele" (Secrets of a Soul) premiered in 1926.[14]

At the end of 1921 Döblin declared that he was "doing" psychoanalysis — a statement that left open whether he was approaching it as a patient or as a doctor. According to the psychoanalyst Heinrich Meng, Döblin conducted psychoanalytical therapies in the clinic of the Berlin Institute (Meng, 65). The clinic provided free treatment to low-income patients and the institute regularly trained outside doctors in specially designed courses to familiarize them with psychoanalytical treatment.[15] In 1923 Döblin described the work conditions at the clinic, where cases ranging from neurasthenia to paralysis were treated in several sessions per week over the course of half a year. He publicly praises the work of the clinic as absolutely necessary to fight "die Misere der neurologischen Behandlung Geringbemittelter," and points out the inefficiency of insurance-approved traditional treatments (*KS-2*, 272). As a "Kassenarzt," a provider within the public insurance network, Döblin could function as a mediator between the medical establishment and psychoanalysis, as the latter was not yet subsidized by public health insurance. In strikingly similar fashion to Ernst Simmel, who viewed the psychoanalytical liberation of the individual as beneficial to society as a whole, Döblin describes psychoanalysis as an inner sewer system: "Die Psychoanalyse ist eine seelische Drainage, innere Kanalisation; wie denkt man Menschen zu sanieren, die ihren inneren Unrat nicht loswerden?" (*KS-2*, 272). Without this kind of sewer system the massive social pressure at the bottom of daily life in the city of Berlin could rise up in uncontrollable ways.[16] Döblin also took an interest in Simmel's pet project, the "Psychoanalytische Klinik Schloß Tegel," the first psychoanalytical clinic in the world, where primarily neurotics and addicts were treated and where Freud stayed as a guest on his trips to Berlin. Döblin participated in the opening ceremonies in April 1927.[17] His involvement with the Berlin group of the "Allgemeine Gesellschaft für Psychotherapie," where he was a board member along with the psychoanalyst Karen Horney and the psychiatrist Arthur Kronfeld (the founding father of psychosomatics), further demonstrates his mediating role between psychoanalysis and medicine (Kittel, 58). The psychoanalyst Werner Kemper recalls a heated discussion on psychoanalytical theory with Simmel, Döblin, and Kamm at the "Romanisches Café" (according to a contemporary Berlin travel guide a hot spot for "Irrenärzte und das Künstlervölkchen" and appropriately nicknamed "Café Größenwahn" (Szamatari, 114).[18] Although Döblin is not listed as a member of the institute in any available records, he was perceived as part of the younger, more politicized circles, and participated in institute events such as the 1922 Berlin convention of the International Psychoanalytic Association. In 1926, he gave a warm and poetic keynote address for the institute's celebration of Sigmund Freud's seventieth birthday.[19] He traces Freud's development from neurology to psychoanalysis (mirroring his own path) and portrays Freud as a pathbreaking benefactor of humanity. Döblin's enthusiastic lobbying for Freud as a member of the awarding committee of the 1930 Goethe Prize of the City of Frankfurt played a key role in turning the vote in favor of Freud. In the committee minutes, Döblin describes how he overcame his initial reluctance towards psychoanalysis, and presents himself as a "Psycho-Analytiker."[20] He expresses the hope that the emerging science of psychoanalysis become the means of a major enterprise: creating a new man capable of freeing himself of the current social and mental misery.

Socialism, Psychoanalysis, and Medical Practice

By the 1920s Döblin began to emphasize the inseparability between his medical practice and its social, political, and ethical dimension, and often described how his patients brought their living conditions into his doctor's office (*SLW*, 95). Like many proletarian doctors, "Arbeiterärzte," of the time, Döblin became a member of the organization of socialist doctors, "Verein Sozialistischer Ärzte," a forum for discussions on medicine, psychoanalysis, and socialism. The VSÄ was the brainchild of Ignaz Zadek, Ernst Simmel, and Karl Kollwitz, the husband of Käthe Kollwitz. Other members included Georg Benjamin (Walter Benjamin's brother), the sexologist Magnus Hirschfeld, and his collaborators Max Hodann and Arthur Kronfeld.[21] Döblin took great interest in the work of Hirschfeld's Institute for Sexual Research and knew Hirschfeld and Hodann socially. Alongside Kronfeld, he became one of the VSÄ's representatives to the Berlin chamber of doctors in 1930.[22] Moreover, he wrote for the official organ of the VSÄ, *Der sozialistische Arzt* (co-edited by Simmel), for example in defense of the dramatist and fellow "Arbeiterarzt" Friedrich Wolf and his controversial play about abortion, *Cyankali § 218* (1929).[23]

Döblin's patient records from the years 1923 to 1926 give a vivid picture of the way in which his new affiliations also impacted his medical practice.[24] His patients, who came to consult him in his office at Frankfurter Allee 340 in the working-class neighborhood of Lichtenberg, often were factory workers, postal workers, or railroad workers. Many of them had been sent by their employee health insurance in order to ensure that they were fit to return to work. The insurance questionnaires suggest that psychological disturbances were often suspected to be the effects of simulation and exaggeration. The patient records indicate that Döblin tended to justify sick-leaves to his patients' employers or health insurance carriers. He describes this particular form of "Medizin [. . .] der Arbeiterklasse" in terms of a solidarity with his proletarian patients that would be envied by private patients (*SPG*, 242). In this context Döblin's practice of granting sick leaves for psychological reasons takes on a socio-political dimension. The violence of psychological life, "die Gewalt des psychischen Lebens," was as existential to Döblin as any aspect of physical life — in his medical work as well as in his writings (*KS-2*, 262).

In his function as psychiatrist and general practitioner Döblin treated patients for a large variety of symptoms and diseases. The railway worker Karl D. came in for a common cold. Wally D. fell from a factory staircase and still was able to get up by herself, as Döblin remarks empathetically.

Louise B. paid frequent visits in the company of her husband Albert — he was treated for a stomach ulcer while she was treated for menopausal disturbances. Friedrich A. had trouble sleeping and Helene M. came to talk about her father's suicide. Alma S., who had been buried alive, came to see him as well as Max B., who is labeled by Döblin as "alter Psychotiker." Erwin H., a one-time visitor, was simply diagnosed with "Onanie."[25]

Even more than five years after the war, Döblin was still treating a considerable number of cases of war neurosis and was therefore directly involved with one of the main theoretical and clinical concerns of the Berlin Psychoanalytic Institute. The descriptions of war trauma in these patient records along with the routine questions regarding war neurotics in the health insurance questionnaires depict just how much mid-twenties Berlin was still suffering from the psychological consequences of the First World War. In his article "Das kranke Volk" (The Sick People) Döblin describes the daily life of the war neurotic as a never-ending continuation of the war. His constant confrontation with the neurotic "Kriegsgang" led to his conclusion that there is an irreparable and potentially explosive process of attrition within the lower classes.

Döblin usually treated neurotic patients in a series of meetings once or twice a week — some of them over the course of several years. In the short vignette "Eine kassenärztliche Sprechstunde" (Visiting Hours of a Public Insurance Doctor, 1928) (*SLW*, 98–102) Döblin points out the importance that listening has for his medical work. He observes that his patients might complain about physical pain, but really want to tell him something else about their lives and about themselves (*SLW*, 100). For Döblin, the role of a doctor is inherently connected with the role of a therapist, and he perceives within himself a great sensitivity and ability to analyze the unconscious.[26] These qualities are also featured in a publicity photograph taken for the press: Döblin sits at his office desk, hunched forward with a concentrated expression, facing his wife, Erna Döblin, who poses as his patient. Instead of sitting on the opposite side of the desk indicating the usual hierarchy of doctor and patient, she is sitting right next to him on the same side of the desk, indicating a more equal relationship. Although Döblin's desk is covered with books and a large array of intimidating medical instruments and medications, Döblin is turning away from this display of medical knowledge and faces his supposed patient. Regardless of whether this staged setup corresponded to his daily practice or not, the image conveys the manner in which Döblin wanted to be perceived as a doctor. It immediately captures the doctor and patient conversing on equal terms, thus embodying the central feature of his approach to medical practice.[27] For Döblin this constitutes one of the attractions of psychoanalysis:

Bei jeder Seelenarbeit aber von Arzt und Patient heißt es, mit offenen Karten spielen. Man spricht deutsch, nicht einseitig lateinisch, und in jedem Sinne hat man miteinander deutsch zu sprechen. Das ist etwas Demokratisches. (*KS-3*, 52)

Döblin's notes of a conversation in 1921 offer a glimpse into his therapeutic work. At first he takes notes on the physical well-being of his patient and diagnoses a deterioration of her condition and back aches. He goes on to describe her dreams. Then he moves on to taking down observations on her childhood: her love for her older brother and the beatings she received for her stubbornness.[28] He concludes with a comparison that his patient draws between him and another man: the excitement, the heart palpitations that she feels, "wenn sie zur Stunde kommt," are exactly the same as in her meetings with "K." In these notes, Döblin departs from a diagnosis of physical symptoms, progressing instead to an interpretation of dreams and the reflection of childhood events, and ending with a situation of transference. This succession corresponds very much to a typical setting in a psychoanalytically oriented therapy — then and now.

Döblin's development from psychiatry to psychoanalysis and from institutional medicine to social medicine can also be traced in his writing. Instead of writing strictly clinical papers for an audience of medical experts, Döblin turned to writing newspaper articles for a mass audience about medical or psychoanalytical topics and their political dimension. In the 1920s his essayistic and fictional writing became more and more a forum for his clinical and psychological conceptions. The psychopolitical dimension of his work as a proletarian doctor and therapist influenced his particular literary psychology and impacted his most highly acclaimed fictional works.

In his writings Döblin displays familiarity with psychoanalytical journals such as *Imago*, refers to questions of psychoanalytical theory and practice such as the issue of lay analysis, which was hotly debated especially at the Berlin Psychoanalytic Institute, and reviews a broad spectrum of psychoanalytical literature ranging from Sigmund Freud's *Beyond the Pleasure Principle* to Melanie Klein's *The Psychoanalysis of Children*.[29]

Not only in his institutional affiliations, but also in his writings, Döblin understands himself as a mediator between medicine and psychoanalysis. For Döblin, psychoanalysis is a promising new discipline, "wissenschaftlich gestaltete Beichte und Seelenchirurgie" that needs to be taken seriously by the medical profession and science (*KS-2*, 274). However psychoanalysts also need to take medicine more seriously, stick to "Klinik, Klinik, Klinik" instead of getting caught up in hypertheoretical and unintelligible "Pseudophilosophie" (*KS-2*, 273). Citing Freud's metaphor that psychoanalysis and medicine are digging at the opposite sides of a tunnel, he urges both sides to collaborate and enrich each other in order to meet in the middle. However, Döblin had his own vision of what psychoanalysis meant. His not always consistent self-perception as psychoanalyst, psychologist, or psychiatrist and his sympathy for the contemporary "wild analyst" Georg Groddeck, suggest that he could hardly be called an orthodox Freudian.[30] Despite his admiration for Freud's work, he took the liberty to criticize what he perceived as dogmatism within the psychoanalytical movement and compared Freud's position with the autocratic manner of Louis XIV (*KS-2*, 262). Beyond all dogma, his papers contain notes on Freudian, Jungian, and Adlerian psychoanalysis, and he discusses and integrates a wide range of psychoanalytical theory into his psychological model.

Die beiden Freundinnen und ihr Giftmord: Psychoanalysis and Fiction

The 1924 amalgam between case study and fiction *Die beiden Freundinnen und ihr Giftmord* exemplifies Döblin's integration of clinical, psychoanalytical, and fictional language. It was based on the Klein-Nebbe murder case, which took place in the Wagnerstrasse in Berlin-Lichtenberg — the immediate neighborhood of Döblin's apartment and doctor's office. The story is quickly told: Two unhappily married young women, Elli and Grete, share their stories of abuse, fall in love with each other, and plot to kill their husbands; and in the case of Link, Elli's husband, they succeed. In his fictionalized account, Döblin employs Freud's topographical model simultaneously with Adler's physiological model of the soul. On the one hand, he employs Freudian terminology of the conscious and the unconscious and metaphors such as submerged thoughts to illustrate the mechanism of repression (*BF,* 29).[31] On the other hand, he operates with Adler's notion of organ inferiority ("Organminderwertigkeit") and the inferiority complex ("Minderwertigkeitsgefühl") and uses metaphors of the soul as a body (*BF,* 48).[32] Even though Döblin roots feelings of inferiority or psychological infantilism in organ inferiority, he never ceases to emphasize the circumstantial and social explanations for the psychological conflicts he presents: his protagonists' actions are determined as much by Oedipal reenactment as by their bodies.

Döblin's foldout appendix to *Die beiden Freundinnen und ihr Giftmord,* titled "Räumliche Darstellung der Seelenveränderung," is a truly fascinating and unique visual representation of his psychological model.[33] Döblin's sketches emphasize the spatial and dynamic character of psychological processes and invite comparison to Freud's rendering of the soul in his 1923 *Das Ich und das Es* — which was reviewed by Döblin.[34] Like Freud, Döblin depicts the soul as a circle. But while Freud's circle still evokes the shape of a brain, Döblin insists on an abstract representation of the soul, and disconnects his model from nerve endings and frontal lobes. Instead of general instances of the soul (such as the id) every soul circle includes smaller circles that represent different psychological complexes at play within the soul, for instance, hate or homosexuality (*BF,* 110). The idea of a super-ego, which Döblin also emphasized in other writings and which Freud only conceived years later, is already clearly present in Döblin's model in complexes such as "Elternliebe." Like Freud, Döblin built gradual levels of consciousness into his model. The closer a psychological complex rises to the surface of the soul, the more conscious it becomes. The bigger it grows, the more dominant and pathological its manifestation. Döblin's psychological complexes stand in dynamic relation to each other. They can feed each other (e.g., the perversion of the violent husband Link feeds his "Grundverstimmung"), or they can produce separate entities (e.g., Grete's "Gefühlsmasse" and sexuality together produce her homosexuality). In contrast to other contemporary models of the soul, Döblin's model has the relationships between the protagonists built in (e.g., Elli's homosexuality is directed toward her lover's soul, while her hate is directed toward her husband's soul). Instead of representing the mechanisms of trauma and repression, which infuse Döblin's narration, his visual model focuses on the development of the crisis, the measurability, and the dramatic effect of mental energy and its social dynamics. While Freud's effort is directed towards establishing a generally viable model of the soul that is applicable to any other instance, Döblin's effort lies in representing and emphasizing the specifics of this one particular case. Even though Döblin is clearly influenced by the visual traditions he quotes (Freud, and in the case of his handwriting analysis, Ludwig Klages), his images resist the scientific claim perpetuated by the tradition of visual representations in the fields of psychiatry and criminology. According to Döblin, his representation does not claim theoretical truth. It is grounded in the history of our imagination of the soul, the "Seelenvorstellungen." Rather than writing science with representations of the invisible, he chooses to write fiction.[35]

From "Sadismus" to "Grundverstimmung" Döblin uses a wide range of terms from psychoanalysis and psychiatry to describe the inner life of his protagonists in *Die beiden Freundinnen und ihr Giftmord*. He suggests that these terms should not be understood as units of the soul, but as clinical units or units of perception ("Beobachtungseinheiten"), which resonate with his psychiatric background (*BF,* 111). But at the same time his stated purpose is to pair clinical terms with non-clinical terms, rather than to adhere to a purely clinical vocabulary. In this instance the illusion of an objective observer is given up, and the result is a highly subjective narration, a fiction, rather than a clinical psychology. Döblin's redefinition of the clinical enables him to broaden his clinical vocabulary and to add his own literary imagery, lending it the same weight and respectability. The term "Gefühlsmasse" seems to encompass Grete's evasiveness, her whining, and her overly emotional personality all at once. Link's "Grundverstimmung" resembles the psychoanalytical diagnosis "depressive Grundverstimmung," but goes beyond the clinical concept, since Döblin suggests very matter-of-factly that Link actually dies from it. As in his earlier clinical case studies, Döblin gives ample room to direct speech — in this case literal quotes from the women's love letters. This time, Döblin's careful editing of the women's voices reinvents the "Volksmund": simple proverbs become psychological metaphors and daily routines mirror complicated psychological processes. Considering the fact that the psychiatric tradition Döblin was trained in is based on the assumption of neutral observation, on the presumably objective description of what is visible, Döblin's fusion of observation with a subjective literary stance seems provocative. His move to what could be called "clinical fiction" is one of many examples of his development from Freiburg psychiatry towards Berlin psychoanalysis.

According to Döblin, the soul stands in close symbiotic relation to its surroundings and thus no being can be described and understood individually:

> Die Menschen stehen mit anderen und auch mit anderen Wesen in Symbiose. Dies ist schon eine Realität: die Symbiose mit den anderen und auch mit den Wohnungen, Häusern, Straßen und Plätzen. (*BF,* 114)

With the assumption of an inherent connection between soul and milieu, individual and societal drives within the soul become indistinguishable. An "Elterninstinkt" is both a specifically bourgeois impulse and an expression of an individual attachment — an expression of biology and society at once, as well as of Döblin's own version of the super-ego. The individual soul becomes the ground where societal impulses clash (*BF,* 81). "Seelenmasse" is more than a descriptive term — it is an instruction to read the soul in connection with its surroundings, in terms of a soul politics.[36] In describing a psychological process like alienation from the self, Döblin's text also evokes its societal dimension, in this case the Marxist understanding of alienation (*BF,* 20). The fact that Döblin takes great care in positioning *Die beiden Freundinnen und ihr Giftmord* as well as *Berlin Alexanderplatz* within a (sub-) proletarian environment, and describes the psychological violence as part of a structural societal problem supports this reading.

Döblin's psychological model emerges in the context of a highly politicized psychoanalytical scene specific to Berlin, which was the point of departure for pioneers of political psychology such as Wilhelm Reich and Ernst Simmel. It attempts a fusion of psychoanalytical thought with social theory that evokes comparisons with the project of the Institute for Social Research in Frankfurt and prefigures important debates such as the role of the masses and the public. The idea of the mutually determining relationship between human beings and historical processes that Döblin championed in his 1930 "Wissen und Verändern" is already present in the epilogue of *Die beiden Freundinnen und ihr Giftmord*.[37] For Döblin there was no individual psychological self-actualization, but a historical process that actualizes itself in the human mind.[38] Later, however, Döblin worried about a psychological analysis that could reduce the individual to a marionette of its environment. While acknowledging the fact of human dependency on societal circumstances, he grounds his psychological model in "Wissen und Verändern" in the idea of an untouchable core of human agency. Reclaiming the power that the individual human being has over the course of the world, he cites the psychoanalyst C. G. Jung and his concept of archetypes, genetically encoded ideas, and images that are shared by all people in their collective unconscious (*WuV*, 153).

Berlin Psychoanalysis and the Collective Soul

Döblin takes on a perspective specific to the Berlin psychoanalytical context when in his birthday speech for Freud he addresses the critical question of why Freud did not translate his insights into a theory of societal change or practical political work. Döblin answers the question by portraying Freud as a mistrustful pessimist. However, he sees himself as part of a force that will fight back against the materialist remnants of a past age with a politicized enlightening version of psychoanalysis (*KS-3*, 55). Freud's destruction of the idea of an isolated self becomes the point of departure for an investigation into its societal dimensions and for Döblin's credo: "Wo ich bin, sind mehrere versammelt" ("Blick auf die Naturwissenschaft" [View of the Sciences, 1925], 1138).

The political dimension of Döblin's psychological model is also prominent in his depiction of war neurosis. Simmel was convinced that the impetus for and vehemence of radical political activism in the Weimar Republic was connected with the psychological consequences of the war.

This idea was shared by Döblin, who in *Die beiden Freundinnen und ihr Giftmord* presents radical political activism as an expression of a genuinely military state of mind. In his article "Zur Psychoanalyse der Kriegsneurosen" (The Psychology of War Neurosis, 1919) Simmel describes the specific state of mind of a war neurotic. According to Simmel, the war neurotic has experienced a dramatic weakening of his personality complex in the military (the term personality complex can be read as a predecessor for the concept of the ego).[39] Simmel points out the special vulnerability of the masses — they are lowest in military rank, more exposed to humiliation, and less equipped to avert and treat a neurosis. Familiar with the treatment of war neurotics, Döblin picked up on Simmel's idea of a diseased people in his 1921 *Frankfurter Zeitung* article "Das kranke Volk."[40] Like Simmel, Döblin emphasizes the fundamental threat that war neurosis poses, especially for the lower classes, and compares it to other contagious diseases like tuberculosis. Döblin also views war neurosis as a problem rooted in and enforced by capitalist economy. Both operate with the idea of a collective soul, for Simmel the "Volksseele," for Döblin the "Seelenmasse."[41] Both see a problem in what they perceive as a change of morals in postwar society: as Simmel calls it, "der entfesselte Geschlechtstrieb," and as Döblin calls it, "die Neigung zu Exzessen." This badly directed surplus of energy becomes a prime example of the psychological consequences of the war. In a 1919 article for the Vossische Zeitung titled "Psychoanalyse der Massen," Simmel describes how the war has lifted morality from the border between the conscious and the unconscious and thus unleashed uninhibited primal drives that will govern the people (*Psychoanalyse*, 37).

Döblin pursues this idea in *Die beiden Freundinnen und ihr Giftmord* and in *Berlin Alexanderplatz*. The war continues at home and perverts the private space. Both male protagonists in *Die beiden Freundinnen und ihr Giftmord* are war veterans. They either dominate or crave to be dominated in order to experience intimacy. Döblin is going a step further by tying the violence and sadism of the two war veterans to a specific fragility of the masculine soul. In notes titled "Civilisation und Kultur" Döblin mentions the blurring of gender distinctions by "Vermännlichung" in the context of central societal developments of the 1910s.[42] This societal masculinization and the effects of the war led to an administered mode of pent-up violence that is ready to break out at any moment within the individual as well as on the social level. Simmel's profiles of war neurotics, weakened egos seeking approval in violent acts, their personality splits, their flight from reality and their militant political activism populate Döblin's fiction. In this context *Berlin Alexanderplatz* reads very much like a narrative of a pathological individual and collective unconscious. Franz Biberkopf's description evokes the clinical picture of a war neurotic, whose only true language is the language of violence. The world around him is still at war, the borders between the unconscious and the conscious have broken down, and the violence underlying the daily life of Berlin may break out at any moment. The notion that the soul has become a battlefield infuses Döblin's fiction of the 1920s.

With a knowledge of Döblin's medical work in these years, many more of his writings can be interpreted in light of the theoretical context of Berlin psychoanalysis. Döblin's readings of the work of Theodor Reik and Franz Alexander have yet to be explored. Alexander's 1923 talk "Der biologische Sinn psychischer Vorgänge" (The Biological Meaning of Psychological Processes), which Döblin reviewed, stands in close affinity with Döblin's conceptions of human drives, regression, biology, nature, and the soul as he elaborates them in "Buddho und die Natur" (1921) and *Das Ich über der Natur* (1926). Döblin never subscribed to just one theory; he cultivated his own original approach to psychiatry and psychoanalysis, and his literary imagination is obviously informed by his medical work and clinical conceptions. Döblin was acutely aware of the pathology his narration represents, and wrote from a standpoint of political psychology.

After the success of *Berlin Alexanderplatz* Döblin temporarily gave up his license as a "Kassenarzt." To his great chagrin he was never able to practice again. Due to his membership in the Verein Sozialistischer Ärzte, his efforts to regain his license before fleeing Germany remained fruitless and his countries of exile, France and the US, did not recognize his German medical training (Lüth, 43). He lost the profession that had ensured his access to people and their stories and had allowed him to integrate his political and poetic ambitions on a different level.[43] The relationship between Döblin the physician and Döblin the writer needs to be fully explored. Our understanding of Döblin's writing can only benefit from an integration of his two lives.

Notes

[1] *SLW*, 92 ("Arzt und Dichter"). Parts of this article are based on material from my dissertation and another article that focuses on Döblin's relationship to the Berlin Psychoanalytic Institute. My research for this article and my prior projects would not have been possible without grants from the University of Chicago, the American Psychoanalytic Association, and the Deutsches Literaturarchiv Marbach. I also owe

thanks for the generous intellectual support from my dissertation committee and many other scholars and friends, especially Sander L. Gilman, the members of the Berlin circle of historians of psychoanalysis, and the Internationale Alfred-Döblin-Gesellschaft.

[2] See Feger and Gilman, *Seeing the Insane*.

[3] Hoche points out the increased criminal potential of the demented, introduces the category of "moralisches Irresein," and goes to great length to distinguish mental diseases from "gewöhnliche moralische Verkommenheit." See also *Deutsche Zeitschrift für Nervenheilkunde* (1910), 196.

[4] In 1920 Hoche published, together with the legal expert Karl Binding, "Die Freigabe der Vernichtung lebensunwerten Lebens. Ihr Mass und ihre Form," which describes the mentally ill as "Ballastexistenzen." In his 1935 autobiography, Hoche alludes to his earlier experiments with executed inmates ("allerfrischestes Untersuchungsmaterial") and gloats about the "übles Schicksal" that one of his enemies under the "rotes Regime" has now suffered. Despite his marriage to a Jewish woman, he also tells a thinly veiled anti-Semitic anecdote ("Der kleine Kolb"): Hoche, *Jahresringe*, 229, 236 and 222. For a complete and differentiated account of Hoche's life and work see Müller-Seidel.

[5] According to Döblin himself, his article was only reluctantly published, after months of waiting. See Heilmann, 206–13.

[6] With this term Döblin refers especially to Gustav Theodor Fechner's "Psychophysik." The bibliography of his dissertation lists Fechner, and in 1923 he predicts a Fechner renaissance. However, the term also has ties to the antique tradition of biologically grounded psychology going as far back as Thales and Hippocrates. See Dessoir, 3.

[7] Döblin, "Über einen Fall von Dämmerzuständen 1.2. 1908." Döblin also participated in a discussion of the talk "Die Wassermannsche Reaktion bei der progressiven Paralyse und paralyseähnlichen Erkrankungen" by Max Leopold Edel on 19 December 1908. Among the discussants was the psychiatrist Hugo Liepmann (1863–1925), whose contributions bridged psychology and psychiatry. Another member of the association was Otto Juliusburger, a psychiatrist with psychoanalytical interest, whose expert statement on the Klein-Nebbe case is featured by Döblin in *Die beiden Freundinnen und ihr Giftmord*. See Feger, 265 and 295.

[8] Döblin was officially elected as "Assistenzarzt für die I. Innere Abteilung des Krankenhauses am Urban" on 23 November 1908. Akten des Städtischen Krankenhauses am Urban betreffend die Protokolle aus den Sitzungen der Krankenhaus Deputation Band III, Nr. 123, Fach 23, Blatt 27. I owe Dr. Thomas Müller, Freie Universität Berlin, many thanks for this information.

[9] Both Lüth and Huguet give short diverging bibliographies of the clinical works.

[10] Many psychoanalysts who later became part of the Berlin Institute experienced the First World War as military doctors. Their opposition to radical physical treatment of shell shocked patients such as the Kaufmann method, a brutal electric shock treatment, and their experimentation with and promotion of the psychoanalytical method gave the psychoanalytical movement a major boost. Ernst Simmel and Karl Abraham give vivid accounts of the psychiatric treatments that Döblin must have encountered during his military service and draw new theoretical conclusions in

regard to shell shock. See Brecht, 28, Abraham, 76, and Simmel, *War Neuroses,* 7–8. See also *Zur Psychoanalyse der Kriegsneurosen.*

[11] Huguet, *Alfred Döblin.* Still in 1920 he writes in a letter to Efraim Frisch about his fragile psychological state: "Ich bin nicht in Ordnung, bin seit über einem Monat aus meinem Nervengleichgewicht" (*B I*, 114).

[12] "Von meiner seelischen Entwicklung kann ich nichts sagen; da ich selbst Psychoanalyse treibe, weiß ich wie falsch jede Selbstäußerung ist." Alfred Döblin, "Autobiographische Skizze," *Autobiographische Schriften,* 21.

[13] See the biographical essay on Ernst Simmel in Simmel, *Psychoanalyse,* 9–12. The fact that Döblin was involved with psychoanalysis on a rather personal level at the onset of the 1920s is supported by a notebook entry Döblin made in 1921. There he describes one of his own dreams from the night of April 19th. He dreams that he has to redo the final school exam in order to choose a proper profession this spring. After his exam he is standing in his black suit in the school courtyard and realizes that he has already taken the exam. He spends the rest of the dream trying to convince his teachers that he already is a medical doctor. While this dream reflects insecurities about his own social status and professional recognition, as well as the importance Döblin places on his medical profession, it also hints at a different mode of self-analysis that Döblin adapted in consequence of his involvement with psychoanalysis.

[14] See Ries, Gast, and Lacoste.

[15] In 1920 Karl Abraham gave a six-week introductory lecture course on psychoanalysis, Ernst Simmel gave three lectures on war neuroses, and Karen Horney held four talks on the practical use of psychoanalysis exclusively for doctors. See *Psychoanalytisches Institut,* 31.

[16] Ernst Simmel writes about the clinic: "Es war ein gewagtes Unternehmen, in einer Zeit wirtschaftlichen Zusammenbruchs ein Institut ins Leben zu rufen, das den Versuch unternehmen sollte, die psychoanalytische Behandlung gerade denen zugänglich zu machen, die an ihrer Neurose ganz besonders schwer infolge der gleichzeitig bestehenden wirtschaftlichen Not litten oder gerade infolge ihrer neurotischen Gehemmtheit ganz besonders der materiellen Verelendung preisgegeben waren." *Psychoanalytisches Institut,* 8.

[17] Döblin signed the guest book. Signature in "Chronik des Sanatoriums Schloß Tegel Psychoanalytische Klinik. Eröffnet am 10. April 1927. An der Eröffnung nahm teil: Dr. Alfred Döblin." Courtesy of Ludger M. Hermanns, Berlin, who made this entry available to me from his private archive.

[18] "Ich erinnere mich eines Abends, richtiger einer Nacht, wo wir uns dort zu viert mit Simmel, Kamm und Döblin (der, obwohl nicht eigentlicher Analytiker, doch lebhaften Anteil an unserem Arbeitsgebiet nahm) über die neue uns damals alle bewegende Lehre vom bedingten Reflex stritten. Hier packte die im Institut bei der Diskussion der Großen nicht recht zu Wort gekommene jüngere Generation meist erst richtig aus." Kemper, 269.

[19] The Berlin Psychoanalytic Institute had organized a big official event in the luxury hotel Esplanade that included other well-known writers such as Lou-Andreas Salomé and Stefan Zweig.

[20] "Die Dinge sind noch nicht genügend geklärt, wir müssen mit altem Herkommen brechen, um zu neuen Menschen zu kommen. [...] Ich bin ja selbst Psycho-Analytiker. Ich habe intensiv ablehnend die Gesichtspunkte verfolgt, allmählich ist mir das Problem aufgegangen. Ich habe mich gesträubt, diese neuen Gedanken aufzunehmen. Diesen Prozeß, den wir einzeln erleben, den werden ganze Wissenschaften nacherleben müssen." Plänkers, 254–331. See also Schievelbusch, 77–93.

[21] "Magnus Hirschfeld." *Der Sozialistische Arzt* 3, no. 4 (April 1928): 47–48. Döblin knew Hirschfeld personally and described him as a trial expert in his 1924 book *Die beiden Freundinnen und ihr Giftmord*. Max Hodann (nicknamed "Hoden-Maxe") was acquainted with Brecht and Döblin, and the psychiatrist Arthur Kronfeld had published his poetry in the expressionist magazine *Der Sturm* (which also counted Döblin among its frequent collaborators; see Kittel, 8 and 10). Kindler describes an evening with Hodann, Brecht, and Döblin (Kindler, 81–82). In exile in Sweden, Hodann continued to be part of Brecht's circle (Ruprecht, 62). My dissertation deals extensively with the connections between Döblin and the Institute for Sexual Research.

[22] In regard to Döblin's involvement in the VSÄ see *Der Sozialistische Arzt* 3, no. 11 (November 1931). Döblin became a substitute representative for the VSÄ as part of a joint list of leftist doctor organisations, the "Freigewerkschaftliche Liste."

[23] *KS-3*, 259–61. *Cyankali* was the most popular play on German stages in 1929. On 19 January 1931 Wolf was arrested on grounds of violating the abortion law (§ 218) and released after international protests (among others by Bertolt Brecht, Arnold Zweig, and Ernst Toller). He subsequently mounted a major publicity campaign against § 218 and for the release of his doctor colleague, Else Jacobowitz.

[24] They are preserved at the Deutsches Literaturarchiv Marbach under A. Döblin, Patientenbücher aus der Arztpraxis.

[25] Some of his patients were potentially dangerous. The patient files contain a note in which the transferring doctor describes a violent attack by one of the patients. The doctor could only liberate himself after a long struggle and complains about his broken watch chain. The note is dated 21 January 1926 and was written by Dr. Keuler. Alfred Döblin, "Verschiedenes," Deutsches Literaturarchiv Marbach.

[26] "... große sensible Aufnahmebereitschaft, unerhörte Fähigkeit analytischen Eindringens, namentlich in der Richtung des Seelisch-Unbewußten." Döblin, "Ich unterhalte mich mit meinen Eltern und Lehrern." In a contemporary account Döblin comes across as a sympathetic and caring doctor. The publisher Helmut Kindler recalls visiting Döblin's doctor's office under the pretense of a sprained leg. Döblin prescribed an ointment and asked how many days Kindler would like to take off. He added, smiling, that he himself used to hate school. Kindler, 79.

[27] Döblin's oldest son, Bodo Kunke, remembers that the desk was standing in the middle of the office. The desk and the huge amount of books seemed to dominate the room. There was no couch in the room. Bodo Kunke, interview by author, 21 August 1999.

[28] "Die Liebe zu ihrem ältesten Bruder, d[ie] fürchterlichen Schläge, d[ie] sie für ihren Trotz von klein auf gekriegt." Alfred Döblin, "Notizbuch" (25 pages, date on the cover end of 1921), Literaturarchiv Marbach.

[29] See especially Döblin, "Metapsychologie und Biologie." In his 1923 article "Praxis der Psychoanalyse" Döblin first opposes lay analysis, voicing medical concerns: "Es

erübrigt sich, auf die Hilflosigkeit des Nichtmediziners (oft auch des Nichtpsychiaters) vor vielen Symptomen hinzuweisen, die in den Behandlungen auftreten können und auftreten, mit denen der Laie natürlich nichts anfangen kann, weil er sie nicht erkennt" (*KS-2*, 272). By 1926 he had changed his mind, citing Freud's "Die Frage der Laienanalyse": "Man kann Freud ganz darin beistimmen, daß auch Laien, Nichtmediziner, analysieren sollen." Döblin, "Die Seele vor dem Arzt und Philosophen," *Vossische Zeitung*, 28 November 1926. (This line is not reprinted in *KS-3*.) In regard to the discussion of lay analysis at the Berlin Institute, see Schröter.

[30] George Groddeck (1866–1934) was the founding father of psychosomatic medicine in Germany. Described as a great analyst by Freud himself, he taught and practiced his clinical methods at the Sanatorium Groddeck in Baden-Baden (1900–34). Among other works he published the psychoanalytical novel *Der Seelensucher* (1921) and *Das Buch vom Es* (1923).

[31] "Ganz unterirdisch begleitete ihn noch ein anderes Gefühl." The Freudian topographical model is omnipresent in Döblin's terminology of the soul and its components: "Seelengebiet," "Seelenzone," and "Seelenmasse." See *BF*, 15, 42, 52 and 112.

[32] "Es war einmal Selbstpeitschung, Unterwerfung, Kasteiung, Buße für die eigene Minderwertigkeit und Schlechtigkeit. Es war auch ein Heilungsversuch dieses Minderwertigkeitsgefühls: durch Beseitigung des Mehrwertigen." According to Adler, biological weakness in an organ or organ system results in weakness in the corresponding nerve apparatus. This biological condition can either lead to compensation (by another organ or capacity) and an ultimately normal life, or larger psychological problems. See Adler, *Praxis und Theorie der Individualpsychologie*, 216. See also Adler, *Die Theorie der Organminderwertigkeit*, and Gilman, *Making the Body Beautiful*, 263–65. Within one passage Döblin can move back and forth between this dynamic and spatial soul model that obeys the laws of mechanics to a physiological representation of the soul. The metaphor of a dynamic balance is followed by the metaphor of the soul as a body and then by the metaphor of a submerged wish: "Das feine Spiel der statischen Kräfte war gestört; der Mechanismus mühte sich wieder, sich einzustellen, verlangte Rückkehr zum alten sicheren Zustand. [. . .] Sie war in einem Reinigungsprozeß begriffen; um einen eingedrungenen Infektionsstoff sammelten sich die Eitermassen an. Es war schon der unterirdische Wille zu einer Tat in ihr gediehen" (*BF*, 55).

[33] This appendix was unfortunately only included with the original edition.

[34] Freud, *Das Ich und das Es*, 252 (reviewed in *KS-2*, 263–66). In later years Freud's model included the instance of the super-ego. See Freud, *Neue Folge der Vorlesungen zur Einführung in die Psychoanalyse*, 85. The comparison of Döblin's sketches with other psychoanalytic models sheds more light on Döblin's intentions. By 1935, Carl Gustav Jung also conceived of the psyche as a circle. His circle consisted of many layers, from sensation as the top layer to the collective and personal unconscious as the core layers. See Jung, *The Tavistock Lectures*, 44. Already in 1919 Adler attempted a detailed graphic representation of the soul (a complicated interplay between different axes of inferiority feelings, fears, weaknesses, and dangers), but unlike Döblin restricted this attempt to the neurotic soul. In fact, Adler claimed that abstract representation is more appropriate for the neurotic than for the healthy soul, and links the symbolic with the neurotic. See Adler, *Über den nervösen Charakter*.

[35] His images are conceived as a rapprochement rather than a representation, an attempt to describe a specific situation rather than a generally valid scientific model. In the description accompanying his representation, Döblin explains that his images should capture the development of the case ("Hauptpunkte der Entwicklung"). This emphasis on the fictional element of his representation is enforced by the way he justifies his choice of a spatial model of the soul: "Hier liegt der Hauptakzent nicht auf der theoretischen Wahrheit, sondern auf der Anschaulichkeit, der Möglichkeit, leicht wenigstens das Wichtigste zu sagen" (*BF*, 111).

[36] Another example of this strategy is Döblin's analysis of Elli's handwriting, in which he diagnoses a petit-bourgeois attitude as a psychological trait. See *BF*, Appendix.

[37] The Institute for Social Research was founded in 1924 as part of the Frankfurt University. By the early thirties Max Horkheimer was its director, and the larger circle of the institute included Friedrich Pollock, Leo Löwenthal, Theodor W. Adorno, Walter Benjamin, Erich Fromm, and later, in exile, Herbert Marcuse. The Frankfurt Psychoanalytical Institute was founded in 1929 and was housed in the same building. For further information in regard to the history of the Institute for Social Research in connection with the Frankfurt Institute for Psychoanalysis, see Schievelbusch, Brecht, and Wiggershaus.

[38] "Und da ist es nicht der Mensch, der sich darstellt und entwickelt, sondern eine breitere oder engere Weltmasse" (*BF*, 117).

[39] In his introduction to the volume Freud calls this specific state the "kriegerisches Ich," who becomes a "Doppelgänger" and threatens to kill the "Friedens-Ich" in the neurotic conflict. In contrast to Simmel, Abraham emphasizes the sexual etiology of the neurotic conflict also for the cases of war neurosis. See *Zur Psychoanalyse der Kriegsneurosen*, 5.

[40] Döblin's title "Das kranke Volk" is a direct quote from Simmel's article "Psychoanalyse der Massen" and demonstrates their intellectual closeness. See Simmel, *Psychoanalyse*, 41.

[41] However, Döblin's "Seelenmasse" also encompasses inorganic matter and contains a spiritual dimension, which distinguishes it from contemporary psychoanalytical conceptions.

[42] "Verwischung der Geschlechtscharaktern durch Vermännlichung." The notes probably originate from the time between 1919 and 1922. Alfred Döblin, "Civilisation und Kultur," Deutsches Literaturarchiv Marbach.

[43] "Als Erwerbsquelle wählte ich die Medizin, in der Absicht, an die Naturwissenschaften und die Biologie heranzukommen, denn nichts ist so wichtig, als der direkte Kontakt mit den lebenden Menschen. Ich bin so auch zugleich sozial und auf meine Weise politisch tätig gewesen" (Bergel, 27).

Works Cited

Abraham, Karl. "Zur Psychoanalyse der Kriegsneurosen." *Gesammelte Schriften.* Vol. 1. Ed. by Johannes Cremerius. Frankfurt am Main: Fischer Taschenbuch Verlag, 1982. 69–77.

Adler, Alfred. *Praxis und Theorie der Individualpsychologie.* Darmstadt: Wissenschaftliche Buchgesellschaft, 1965.

———. "Die Theorie der Organminderwertigkeit und ihre Bedeutung für Philosophie und Psychologie." *Heilen und Bilden: Ein Buch der Erziehungskunst für Ärzte und Pädagogen.* Ed. by Alfred Adler and Carl Furtmüller. Munich: Verlag von J. F. Bergmann, 1928.

———. *Über den nervösen Charakter.* Munich and Wiesbaden: Verlag von J. F. Bergmann, 1943.

Alexander, Franz. "Der biologische Sinn psychischer Vorgänge." *Imago* 9 (1923): 35–57.

Anz, Thomas. "Alfred Döblin und die Psychoanalyse. Ein kritischer Bericht zur Forschung." *Internationales Alfred-Döblin-Kolloquium Leiden 1995.* Ed. by Gabriele Sander. Bern: Peter Lang, 1997. 9–30.

Bergel, Violante. "Gespräch mit Alfred Döblin." *Standpunkt* 1, no. 11 (1946): 27 and 46.

Binswanger, Otto, et al., eds. *Lehrbuch der Psychiatrie.* 4th edition. Jena: Verlag von Gustav Fischer, 1915.

Blasius, Dirk. *Einfache Seelenstörung: Geschichte der deutschen Psychiatrie 1800–1945.* Frankfurt am Main: Fischer, 1994.

Brecht, Karen, Hermanns Ludger, et al., eds. *"Hier geht das Leben auf eine sehr merkwürdige Weise weiter . . .": Zur Geschichte der Psychoanalyse in Deutschland.* Hamburg: Verlag Michael Kellner, 1985.

Dessoir, Max. *Geschichte der Neueren Deutschen Psychologie.* Berlin: Carl Duncker, 1902.

Dollinger, Roland. "Korsakoff's Syndrome and Modern German Literature: Alfred Döblin's Medical Dissertation." *Studies in Twentieth Century Literature* 22, no. 1 (1998): 129–50.

Feger, Gabriele. "Die Geschichte des Psychiatrischen Vereins zu Berlin." Diss. Freie Universität Berlin, 1982.

Freud, Sigmund. *Das Ich und das Es. Gesammelte Werke* XIII. Frankfurt: Fischer, 1999. 235–90.

———. *Neue Folge der Vorlesungen zur Einführung in die Psychoanalyse. Gesammelte Werke* XV. Frankfurt: Fischer, 1999.

Fuechtner, Veronika. "Alfred Döblin and the Berlin Psychoanalytic Institute." Diss. University of Chicago, 2002.

———. "Östlich um den Alexanderplatz: Psychoanalyse im Blick von Alfred Döblin." *Mit ohne Freud*. Ed. by Regine Lockot and Heike Bernhardt. Gießen: Psycho-Sozial Verlag, 2000. 30–50.

Gast, Lilli. "Einleitungsvortrag zur Filmvorführung 'Geheimnisse einer Seele.'" In *Spaltungen in der Geschichte der Psychoanalyse*. Ed. by Ludger M. Hermanns. Tübingen: edition diskord, 1995. 272–78.

Gilman, Sander L. *Making the Body Beautiful*. Princeton UP, 1999.

———. *Seeing the Insane*. Lincoln: University of Nebraska Press, 1996.

Heilmann, Hans-Dieter. "Alfred Döblin: Die Fahrt ins Blaue." *Aktion T 4: 1939–45; Die "Euthanasie"-Zentrale in der Tiergartenstrasse 4 1939–1944*. Ed. by Götz Aly. Berlin: Edition Hentrich, 1989. 206–13.

Hoche, Alfred Erich. *Christus der Jüngling*. Freiburg i.B.: Urban-Verlag, 1930.

———. *Die Geisteskranken in der Dichtung*. Munich: J. F. Lehmanns Verlag, 1939.

———. *Jahresringe*. Munich: J. F. Lehmanns Verlag, 1935.

Huguet, Louis. *Alfred Döblin: Elements de biographie*. Diss. Paris 1968.

———. *Bibliographie Alfred Döblin*. Berlin: Aufbau-Verlag, 1972.

Ilberg, G. "Alfred Döblin: Aufmerksamkeitsstörungen bei Hysterie." *Neurologisches Centralblatt* 28, no. 11 (1 June 1909): 604.

Jung, C. G. *Tavistock Lectures (1935). Collected Works* XVIII. Trans. by R. F. C. Hull. Princeton, NJ: Princeton UP, 1976. 5–182.

Kemper, Werner. "Werner W. Kemper." *Psychotherapie in Selbstdarstellungen*. Ed. by Ludwig J. Pongratz. Berlin, Stuttgart, Vienna: Huber, 1973. 260–345.

Kiefer, Mathias. *Zur Entwicklung des Seelenbegriffes in der deutschen Psychiatrie*. Essen: Verlag Die blaue Eule, 1996.

Kindler, Helmut. *Zum Abschied ein Fest*. Munich: Kindler, 1991.

Kittel, Ingo-Wolf. *Arthur Kronfeld 1886–1941*. Konstanz: Bibliothek der Universität Konstanz, 1988.

Kunke, Bodo. Interview by the author. 21 August 1999.

Lacoste, Patrick. *L'étrange cas du professeur M. Psychanalyse à l'écran*. Paris: Éditions Gallimard, 1990.

Leibfried, Stephan, and Florian Tennstedt. *Berufsverbote und Sozialpolitik 1933*. Bremen: Universität Bremen, 1980.

Lüth, Paul. *Alfred Döblin als Arzt und Patient*. Stuttgart: Hippokrates Verlag, 1985.

Maaß, Ingrid. *Regression und Individuation: Alfred Döblins Naturphilosophie und späte Romane vor dem Hintergrund einer Affinität zu Freuds Metapsychologie*. Frankfurt am Main: Peter Lang, 1997.

"Magnus Hirschfeld." *Der Sozialistische Arzt* 3, no. 4 (April 1928): 47–8.

Meng, Heinrich. *Leben als Begegnung*. Stuttgart: Hippokrates Verlag, 1971.

Meyer, Jochen, ed. *Alfred Döblin. 1878–1978*. 4th edition. Marbach am Neckar: Deutsche Schillergesellschaft, 1998.

Minder, Robert. *Dichter in der Gesellschaft*. Frankfurt am Main: Insel Verlag, 1966.

Müller-Seidel, Walter. *Alfred Erich Hoche: Lebensgeschichte im Spannungsfeld von Psychiatrie, Strafrecht und Literatur*. Bayerische Akademie der Wissenschaften, Sitzungsberichte. Vol. 5. Munich: Verlag der Bayerischen Akademie der Wissenschaften, 1999.

Plänkers, Thomas. "Die Verleihung des Frankfurter Goethe-Preises an Sigmund Freud im Jahre 1930." *Psychoanalyse in Frankfurt am Main: Zerstörte Anfänge, Wiederannäherungen, Entwicklungen*. Tübingen: edition diskord, 1996. 254–331.

Psychoanalytisches Institut and Deutsche Psychoanalytische Vereinigung, ed. *Zehn Jahre Berliner Psychoanalytisches Institut 1920–1930*. Meisenheim: Verlag Anton Hain, 1970.

Reuchlein, Georg. "'Man lerne von der Psychiatrie.' Literatur, Psychologie und Psychopathologie in Alfred Döblins 'Berliner Programm' und 'Ermordung einer Butterblume.'" *Jahrbuch für Germanistik* 23, no. 1 (1991): 10–68.

Ries, Paul. "'Geheimnisse einer Seele': Wessen Film und wessen Psychoanalyse?" *Jahrbuch der Psychoanalyse* 39 (1997): 46–80.

Ruprecht, Thomas M., and Christian Jenssen, eds. *Äskulap oder Mars? Ärzte gegen den Krieg*. Bremen: Donat Verlag, 1991.

Schäffner, Wolfgang. "Psychiatrisches Schreiben um 1900." *Jahrbuch der deutschen Schillergesellschaft* 35 (1991): 12–29.

Schievelbusch, Wolfgang. *Intellektuellendämmerung*. Frankfurt: Insel Verlag, 1982.

Schröter, Michael. "Zur Frühgeschichte der Laienanalyse." *Psyche* 50, no. 12 (1996): 1127–75.

Simmel, Ernst. *Psychoanalyse und ihre Anwendungen: Ausgewählte Schriften*. Ed. by Ludger M. Hermanns and Ulrich Schultz-Venrath. Frankfurt: Fischer, 1993.

———. "War Neuroses and 'Psychic Trauma' (1918)." *The Weimar Republic Sourcebook*. Ed. by Anton Kaes, Martin Jay, and Edward Dimendberger. Berkeley: U of California P, 1995. 7–8. Translation from *Kriegs-Neurosen und Psychisches Trauma*. Munich/Leipzig: Otto Nemnich, 1918.

Szamatari, Eugen. *Das Buch von Berlin: Was nicht im Baedecker steht*. Munich: Piper, 1927.

Wiggershaus, Rolf. *Die Frankfurter Schule*. Munich: dtv, 1988.

Zur Psychoanalyse der Kriegsneurosen. Internationale Psychoanalytische Bibliothek Vol.1. Leipzig and Vienna: Internationaler Psychoanalytischer Verlag, 1919.

Works by Alfred Döblin

(Not listed in the general bibliography.)

Döblin, Alfred. "Aufmerksamkeitsstörungen bei Hysterie." *Archiv für Psychiatrie und Nervenkrankheiten* (1909): 464–88.

———. "Blick auf die Naturwissenschaft." *Die Neue Rundschau* 34, no. 2 (1923): 1132–38.

———. "Buddho und die Natur." *Die Neue Rundschau* 32, no. 2 (1921): 1192–1200.

———. "Bürgel und Reik, Astronom und Psycholog." *Der Querschnitt* 12, no. 12 (December 1932): 914. Reprinted in *KS-3*, 320–22.

———. "Das Ewig-Weibliche meldet sich." *Literaturblatt der Frankfurter Zeitung* 65, no. 17 (24 April 1932): 11. Reprinted in *KS-3*, 297–300.

———. "Das kranke Volk." *Frankfurter Zeitung*, 7 May 1921 (Evening Edition).

———. "Dichtung und Seelsorge." *Blätter für evangelische Geisteskultur* 4, no. 7/8 (1928): 306–8.

———. [Linke Poot]. "Ehebilder. Aus Erfahrungen eines Arztes." *Frankfurter Zeitung*, 14 July 1922.

———. "Eine neue Psychologie von Mann und Weib." *KS-2*, 178–82.

———. *Gedächtnisstörungen bei der Korsakoffschen Psychose*. Inaugural-Dissertation zur Erlangung der medizinischen Doktorwürde, Medizinische Fakultät der Albert-Ludwig-Universität zu Freiburg i.B., 1905.

———. "Gegen die Kulturreaktion! Gegen den Abtreibungparagraphen! Für Friedrich Wolf!" *Der Sozialistische Arzt* 7, no. 3 (March 1931). Reprinted in *KS-3*, 259–61.

———. "Gegenstände, die zu unzüchtigem Gebrauch bestimmt sind." *Aktionsgemeinschaft für geistige Freiheit*, 20 November 1928.

———. "Ich unterhalte mich mit meinen Eltern und Lehrern (5. Fortsetzung)." *Frankfurter Zeitung*, 21 July 1928.

———. "Kassenärzte und Kassenpatienten." *Der Querschnitt* 9, no. 5 (May 1929): 313. Reprinted in *SPG*, 240–44.

———. "Metapsychologie und Biologie." *Die neue Rundschau* 33, no. 2 (1922): 1222–32. Reprinted in *KS-2*, 182–93.

———. "Die Nerven." *KS-1*, 151–56.

———. "Praxis der Psychoanalyse." *Vossische Zeitung*, 28 June 1923. Reprinted in *KS-2*, 270–74.

———. "Protokoll eines Plädoyers für Sigmund Freud." 24 April 1930. *KS-3*, 221–27.

———. "Psychoanalyse von heute." *Vossische Zeitung*, 10 June 1923. Reprinted in *KS-1*, 261–66.

D. [Alfred Döblin]. "Psychoanalytische Literatur." *Literaturblatt. Beilage zur Frankfurter Zeitung*, 28 August 1927.

———. "Die Seele vor dem Arzt und Philosophen." *Vossische Zeitung*, 28 November 1926. Reprinted in *KS-3*, 75–80.

———. "Sigmund Freud. Zum 70. Geburtstage." *Vossische Zeitung*, 5 May 1926. Reprinted in *KS-3*, 44–55.

———. "Soll man die Psychoanalyse verbieten?" *Berliner Tageblatt*, 5 May 1925. Reprinted in *KS-3*, 14–16.

———. "Die Spannung in Berlin." *Prager Tagblatt*, 30 October 1923, reprinted in *KS-2*, 320–23.

———. "Zur perniziös verlaufenden Melancholie." *Allgemeine Zeitschrift für Psychiatrie und psych.-gerichtliche Medizin* 65, no. 3 (1908): 362 and 364.

———. "Zur Wahnbildung im Senium." *Archiv für Psychiatrie und Nervenkrankheiten* 46, no. 3 (March 1910): 1043–61.

Döblin's Berlin:
The Story of Franz Biberkopf

Gabriele Sander

BEFORE THE PUBLICATION of *Berlin Alexanderplatz* in 1929, Döblin had been criticized by the literary establishment on various occasions for his penchant for historical, mythological, and exotic material and for stubbornly avoiding the immediate present in his novels. In early 1927, the author was still defending his working method, which rested on the principle of "künstlerische Transformation" (*SLW,* 80). As he wrote, the last thing he wanted to do was subject the "beobachtetes Material" of his environment to a literary reworking: "Ich kann viel besser schreiben — und zwar viel sicherer und realer — über das, was in China und Indien vorgeht, als das, was in Berlin vorgeht" (*SLW,* 79). At the same time, Döblin certainly knew the expectations of the reading public, which is revealed by the ironic observation in the third draft of the *Berlin Alexanderplatz* prologue: "[. . .] das ist endlich mal von dem Autor ein gutes soziales Buch. Das tut uns bitter not, [. . .] und der Autor hat endlich einmal seine Pflicht erfüllt und sich von seinen überspannten Ideen losgemacht, die ja letzten Endes faules bourgeoises Zeug sind" (*BA,* 819–20).

Shortly before Döblin began his new novel, he soberly assessed his success as an author. His frustration at the disappointing response to his previous works — the Indian epic *Manas* (1927) and the natural-philosophical text *Das Ich über der Natur* (1927) — and at the attendant commercial misfortune is clearly reflected in the tone of resignation struck in his self-portrait "Arzt und Dichter," published on October 28, 1927:

> Es ist, um einfach und relativ ernst zu sein, so, daß ich nach meilenlanger medizinischer Vorbereitung, nach jahrzehntelanger literarischer Arbeit weder ärztlich noch literarisch existenzfähig bin.
> [. . .] ich werde, wenn die Umstände mich drängen, eher, lieber und von Herzen die Schriftstellerei in einer geistig refraktären und verschmockten Zeit aufgeben, als den inhaltsvollen, anständigen, wenn auch sehr ärmlichen Beruf eines Arztes. (*SLW,* 96, 98)

Whether Döblin seriously considered giving up writing at this point, as the closing passage suggests, is questionable. In any case, it is certain that he was looking for a solution to his economic and artistic crisis. The way out of this crisis opened up as he began work on *Berlin Alexanderplatz* in the fall of 1927; writing the novel became at the same time a way home, a return to the roots of his writing. By way of detours, Döblin found his way to the theme of his life: the metropolis Berlin.

The search for adequate subject matter led him to his immediate environment. More than any other author, he seemed predestined for the literary representation of the eastern districts of Berlin, a milieu with which this passionate flaneur and medically trained observer of the "little people" was intimately familiar. The concrete impetus for the new novelistic project cannot be established; however, the choice of the city theme might have been influenced by the popularity of Berlin as a motif in contemporaneous art. The much-discussed premiere of Walter Ruttmann's documentary montage film *Berlin — Die Sinfonie der Großstadt* (Berlin — Symphony of the Metropolis) on September 23, 1927 could have served as an impulse during this "incubation period" toward the literary reworking of the Berlin theme. Another source of inspiration must have been the photo volume by Mario von Bucovich. It appeared in 1928 under the title *Berlin*, with a preface by Döblin (*KS-3*, 153–59), at a time when he was probably already involved in his own Berlin project. There are striking correspondences of motif and atmosphere between individual photos and localities from *Berlin Alexanderplatz*. The film and the photo volume could thus have conveyed visual stimuli and, as it were, added fuel to Döblin's fire — as did the publication of the German translation of James Joyce's novel *Ulysses* in October, 1927.

Although there is no record of an initial spark, it is plausible that it derived from the memory of an experience Döblin had had four years earlier, and which he had portrayed in the essay *Östlich um den Alexanderplatz* (Eastward Around the Alexanderplatz, 1923):

> Da agiert auf dem Hof mit drolliger Theatralik ein schäbiger jüngerer Mann herum und singt — singt, ja was? Heil dir im Siegerkranz. Mit allen Strophen; ich höre es zum ersten Male seit 1918 und glaube es nicht. Die Leute kichern, einige sind betreten; der brüllt weiter. (*KS-2*, 299)

In this essay, Döblin presented a literary portrait of the *Scheunenviertel*, the area near the Alexanderplatz where the Eastern European Jews lived, which was near his home and medical practice and which would later play an important role in the first book of *Berlin Alexanderplatz*. (The incident with the young singer also figures in the first section of the novel.) Again and again Döblin circled the area around the Alexanderplatz, which he experienced and described as a social focal point. And so he placed at the end of another article, "Eine unbekannte Strahlenart" (1925), in which he describes a series of criminal cases heard at the youth office, a brief sketch of the young offenders' milieu that similarly anticipates the later novel:

> Nach zwei Stunden spaziere ich selbst nach dem Alexanderplatz, die aufgebuddelte Straße entlang. An der Ecke von Wertheim stehen die Obstwagen. Einer schreit Hosenträger aus. [...] Hier herum passiert all das Malheur. Wie lustig und naiv es dabei hier ist. Nur "in den Herzen" brennt allerlei, wie eben im Gericht, bei der Tat, nach der Tat, bei der Untersuchung, bei der Strafe. Und das sieht man nicht mit Augen. Es ist eine Strahlenart, die die Physik nicht kennt. (*KS-3*, 19)

The date when Döblin first began writing *Berlin Alexanderplatz* cannot be precisely determined, but all the evidence points to October 1927. On April 8, 1928, Döblin wrote about the topic and style of his new "Berliner Roman" in his autobiographical essay "Zwei Seelen in einer Brust" (1928; *SLW*, 105). During the summer he began the systematic revision of the manuscript, from which he presented two excerpts in August 1928, on the occasion of his fiftieth birthday. In the following months, he pushed ahead rapidly with writing the novel; it carried on into the winter of 1928–29. Döblin then had a typescript of the finished manuscript made in the spring of 1929, which he once again thoroughly revised. The process of making corrections lasted into late summer and extended into the printing phase. After negotiations over publishing the novel in a Berlin newspaper had failed (*SLW*, 464), the left-liberal *Frankfurter Zeitung* took over the preprinting and presented the work to its readers in twenty-nine installments from September 8 to October 11. Then, at the beginning of October 1929, the book *Berlin Alexanderplatz* came out in a printing of 10,000 copies.

According to Döblin's own statements, the explanatory subtitle *Die Geschichte vom Franz Biberkopf* was added at publisher Samuel Fischer's request.[1] It was, however, also in accordance with the author's intention, for the double title signals both the hierarchical relationship and the tension between a city-epic and a gruesome criminal ballad. An omniscient narrator repeatedly interferes in the telling of the story of Franz Biberkopf, the "ehemaligen Zement- und Transportarbeiter" (*BA*, 11). Ironically distanced, the narrator comments on what is narrated with an air of knowing superiority: "Ich habe ihn hergerufen zu keinem Spiel, sondern zum Erleben seines schweren, wahren und aufhellenden Daseins" (*BA*, 47). The didactic impetus already dominates the prologue, which prepares the reader for the drastic cure prescribed for the main character, and anticipates its meaning and goal: "Wir sehen am Schluß den Mann wieder am Alexanderplatz stehen, sehr verändert, ramponiert, aber doch zurechtgebogen" (*BA*, 11). This formulation, reminiscent of the "reconstruction" of Galy Gay in Brecht's drama *Mann ist Mann* (1926),[2] refers unmistakably to the exemplary meaning of a social outsider's existence: "wir könnten Schritt um Schritt dasselbe getan haben wie er" (*BA*, 217).

Döblin begins each chapter with a brief overview (akin to the epic titles used in Brecht's "epic drama"), which points to "eine überlegene Erzählregie" (Bayerdörfer, "Döblin," 162). They describe the period of time from Biberkopf's release from the Tegel prison to his symbolic rebirth after the death of the "old" Biberkopf.[3] The protagonist is cast as a man who is good-natured and naive, but also compulsive and susceptible to excesses of violence and alcohol, a man who, because of his psychic as well as his political-ideological instability, cannot manage to realize his good intentions and establish a middle-class existence. He now experiences the urban reality from which he has been cut off for four years as an alarming pandemonium, as a chaotic, hostile place, which he believes he must counter with the attitude of a warring conqueror. He refuses the assistance offered from various sides, believing only in his own strength. Although he finds it agreeable when two friendly Jews take him into their home shortly after his release and encourage him "mit Geschichtenerzählen" (*BA*, 63), he closes himself to the wisdom they impart. Biberkopf's lack of human insight prevents the development of friendships and leads to repeated disappointment. His relationship to women is characterized by latent aggressiveness, but also by the traumatic fear of repeating the killing of his girlfriend Ida, which had put him in Tegel in the first place, convicted of manslaughter. After Biberkopf has tried several occupations and, lacking perseverance, suffered several setbacks, he becomes an alcoholic and ends up in criminal circles. He enters into a strange love-hate relationship with the career criminal Reinhold, who, in the midst of a theft, pushes Franz from the car and thereby leaves him crippled. Even this experience does not cause Franz to change his ways. On the contrary, he becomes a professional fence and pimp. During this time, he falls in love with the childlike woman Emilie Parsunke, a prostitute working for him, whom he calls Mieze. He boastingly introduces his beloved to Reinhold. In her naiveté, Mieze goes on an outing with Reinhold, who then murders her. It is this murder, after which Biberkopf suffers a nervous breakdown and is committed to the Berlin-Buch psychiatric ward, that finally brings about his transformation. In the face of death, he recognizes "seine Irrtümer, seinen Hochmut und seine Unwissenheit" and is "zerbrochen" (*BA*, 411), in order to make room for the new Biberkopf, who now carries the two first names Franz Karl. In an open final tableau — perceived by the reading public at that time as unsatisfactory[4] — a purified, self-critical, and alert Biberkopf appears as a "Hilfsportier" (*BA*, 452) on the Alexanderplatz. Through death's teachings, he is prepared for life's struggles.

Franz Biberkopf's fable of initiation forms the core of the work.[5] To lend this story as much contemporary appeal and authenticity as possible, Döblin collected, both before and while writing, numerous current newspaper clippings of the most divergent political opinions and integrated them into his text, literally with scissors and glue (Stenzel, 39–44). Döblin weaves the central theme of the Biberkopf story into a dense fabric of contemporary discourses and intertextual allusions. Over long stretches of text, the digressive montage elements (including literary quotations and parodies, newspaper announcements, weather reports, and collages of popular songs and advertisements) press the main plot into the background and abolish its chronology in favor of simultaneous polyphony. An especially large amount of space is occupied by biblical and mythological montages that implicitly comment upon and transcend the story's events: for example, the Agamemnon myth, the paraphrased stories of Job and Isaac, and quotations from the Apocalypse, which are repeated like a leitmotif.

This bold montage technique was criticized by many contemporary reviewers, and in some cases it met with a complete lack of understanding. The work nonetheless established Döblin's reputation as one of the most significant and innovative authors of his generation. The extraordinarily lively journalistic response to the book — over 100 reviews were published in German and foreign periodicals — quickly made *Berlin Alexanderplatz* a bestseller. Further editions soon followed, and by 1933 50,000 copies had been printed. Between 1931 and 1936, the novel appeared in nine languages, including Dutch, English, Italian, Spanish, French, and Russian.

The arts sections of the most renowned newspapers celebrated the novel as the outstanding literary event of 1929 and counted it among the milestones of German novels. Satisfaction, pride, and a certain local patriotism over Döblin's urban novel were evident, above all, in the discussions by Berlin newspapers. On November 2, 1929 the prominent critic Herbert Ihering even suggested Döblin's name for a Nobel Prize.

Berlin Alexanderplatz became a political issue primarily as a result of the controversy instigated by orthodox Marxists. While a few right-wing papers took issue with the representation of a criminal milieu, it was left to the reviewers of communist periodicals to engage in ideological mudslinging against Döblin. They accused him of having betrayed the goals of the proletarian class struggle by centering his counter-revolutionary novel on a politically ignorant worker-type, who lacked any trace of class-consciousness. The periodical *Die Linkskurve*, the voice of the "Proletarian Revolutionary Writers Association,"[6] became the site of a war of words. Döblin reacted to a polemical article by its co-editor, the poet Johannes R. Becher (1891–1958) with a rebuttal entitled "Katastrophe in einer Linkskurve" (*SPG*, 247–53), in which he caustically ridiculed the "Milchbrei der Phrasen des Kommunistenhäuptlings Becher" and his "geschriebenen Quarkkäse" (252). The periodical's next issue included yet another installment of the polemic, entitled "Herr Döblin verunglückt in einer 'Linkskurve,'" by Otto Biha, to which Döblin did not respond. The ideologically motivated attacks did not hinder the triumphant progress of the novel, whose unique quality was now undisputed. As a modern classic, it became not only a model for younger authors, but also the standard for judging subsequent Berlin novels. Until today, literary criticism frequently measures contemporary novels about the metropolis against *Berlin Alexanderplatz;* even discussions of prose texts set in reunified Berlin seldom lack a comparative allusion to Döblin's masterpiece. Despite the title's broad familiarity,[7] however, it remains doubtful whether the understanding of the text and its author has become any more sound. This, at least, is the concern of research on Döblin that began in the mid-fifties and since then has become — in regard to *Berlin Alexanderplatz* — highly specialized.[8]

Döblin's masterful play with literary traditions and topoi opens doors in numerous directions for interpreters of the novel and offers many possible connections: to biblical and mythological characters, for example, and to models from literary history. The wealth of topical and metaphorical constellations, of discourses and linguistic styles, matches the great number of interpretive approaches that focus on the novel's linguistic and narrative traditions. Thus, for example, the allusions to the parable of Everyman and the links to medieval miracle plays, as well as the Dance of Death, are of great interest to scholars. They demonstrate Döblin's recourse to the model of street ballads revived by Frank Wedekind (1864–1918), Walter Mehring (1896–1981), Brecht, and others. Others are concerned with the relation between Biberkopf's story and the classical *Bil-*

dungsroman, or novel of development — an interpretive line that extends from the critic Walter Benjamin (1892–1940) to the present day.

Berlin Alexanderplatz exceeds all of Döblin's earlier works in its commanding use of the intellectual and cultural heritage and of borrowed linguistic and textual material on both the macro- and micro-structural levels. He is much more open, but also more aggressive, in his treatment of literary traditions than in earlier works. He now includes sizeable passages of "lower" kinds of texts — which he had, until now, limited to his journalistic articles. Through its extraordinary breadth of literary references, *Berlin Alexanderplatz* becomes a text constructed from texts. Admittedly, this could also be said of the earlier novels such as *Die drei Sprünge des Wang-lun, Wallenstein,* or *Berge Meere und Giganten*, because of their numerous underlying source texts. In these works, however, Döblin still chose, for the most part, a cryptic way of citing things, that is, a method of seamlessly melding together and transforming the pre-texts.[9] But in *Berlin Alexanderplatz,* the author lets his readers participate, as it were, in the process of constructing the montage. He achieves this by revealing the manner in which the citations are incorporated into the text. As a result, that which is foreign always appears as foreign and no longer as the text's adopted own. Döblin thereby stages the world as a cacophony of voices, as a dense network of texts communicating with one another. The reproduced linguistic material enters into dialogue simultaneously with itself and with the reader; it produces a practically endless fabric of words and sounds that can be continued at will.

Because of the density of quotations and other forms of allusion to earlier canonical and popular works, one can speak in this polyphonic novel of a work of "intensiver Intertextualität" (Pfister, 29). The intertextual character is intensified, on the one hand, through the "Autorreflexivität,"[10] and on the other, through the fact that the texts quoted or referred to are often situated in semantic and ideological tension with one another. Not only does Döblin make use of diverse methods of textual integration, he also presents a spectrum of functional possibilities of meaning. The manuscript collection (kept in the German Literature Archive in Marbach), reveals three different models: Döblin integrated some of the passages from other texts directly into the manuscript by quoting them either from memory or from a draft. In many cases, however, he chose the additive form of the so-called insert, on which he copied down the passages borrowed from another source. He then gave the location of the quoted material within the manuscript with letters or numeric symbols. An intensification of this procedure is the collage of textual excerpts — based more or less on the model of Dada artists —

that is, pasting newspaper clippings directly into the manuscript, as mentioned above.

Even his earliest writings indicate that Döblin was aware that every work draws from the repository of literary tradition and also inscribes itself within literary history. In a draft for a speech from early 1933 called "Blick auf die heutige deutsche Literatur," Döblin demands of the author and artist that he must be "vor allen Dingen im Besitz des bestehenden, vorliegenden Materials," because "Literatur zeugt Literatur." He explained this striking formula with the following words: "das übergebene, überlieferte Material der Literatur etc. sind die eigentlichen Produktionsmittel für die Gestaltung der Bewußtseinsinhalte" (*SÄPL,* 284–85). With this statement, Döblin does not negate the originality and autonomy of the written artwork. Rather, he is cognizant of the fact that writing takes place by accessing the stores of cultural knowledge and collective memory. On various occasions, he describes this with the term "Erbschaft." In his major philosophical work *Unser Dasein* (1933), he connects this to the term "Resonanz":

> Und durcheinander kommen [...] im Kunstwerk allerlei Zeitepochen zum Wort und zeigen sich vorhanden und noch lebendig. [...] Durch die Erbschaft werden sehr viele Dinge aufbewahrt, und so weich und so vielseitig ist die lebende Substanz des Erzeugers, daß ganz Entlegenes, auch Zeitfernes, in ihm schwingt, resoniert und resonieren kann. (*UD,* 253)

When Döblin refers, explicitly or implicitly, playfully or seriously, to existing textual material in almost all of his prose works, he is fully aware of operating within a tradition and conscious of the historical and connotative dimension of language. He wrote as early as 1910 in *Gespräche mit Kalypso. Über die Musik,* that the word triggers within the person "einen umschriebenen, wenig veränderlichen Erinnerungsverband" (*SÄPL,* 61), and is thereby the bearer of super-individual or collective experiences. An author as creative as he was obsessive, Döblin was not only familiar with "das Getriebensein von Gestaltungen" (*SÄPL,* 144);[11] he also knew about the productive power inherent in language: "man glaubt zu schreiben und man wird geschrieben [...]" (160).

Döblin recognized the importance of linguistic tradition and repeatedly acknowledged his indebtedness to particular literary models, specifically, the epic tradition derived from Homer and proceeding through Dante, Cervantes, Dostoevsky, and de Coster. At the same time, he knew that the artist can "nicht mehr zu Cervantes fliehen, ohne von den Motten gefressen zu werden" (*SÄPL,* 119). His concept of modernism not only forbade him to simply appropriate tested ways of writing; it required artistic experimentation and, at times, the radical destruction of recognizably outdated forms. For Döblin the "epische Kunstwerk" was "keine feste Form, sie ist wie das Drama ständig zu entwickeln, und zwar durchweg im Widerstand gegen die Tradition und ihre Vetreter" (*SÄPL,* 225).

The intertextual references and especially the literary paraphrases in *Berlin Alexanderplatz* can thus be seen as a field of tension between "Materialkontinuität" and "Tempoverschiebung" (*SLW,* 284). One discerns, on the level of content, two poles in the text montages. On the one hand, there is the affirmative reference, for instance, to biblical pretexts like the stories of Isaac and Job, or the insertion of documentary texts taken from legal or medical files. On the other hand, there is the radical deconstruction, for example, of pop songs and advertising texts, but also of texts that belong to the literary canon. In this regard, the reworking of texts "gegen den Strich des Originals" (Pfister, 29) deserves particular attention. This appears in those sections of *Berlin Alexanderplatz* that can be understood as literary parodies in the broadest sense. The novel's diverse means of intertextual play become evident in the juxtaposition of passages that refer implicitly to their literary pretexts with those that carry clear intertextual signals.

Since Döblin placed a criminal, a murderer, in the center of his novel, it seems only natural to refer to other authors who also made criminals the protagonists of their works. This pattern of interpretation can already be found in contemporary discussions, in which Biberkopf was perceived, for instance, as a Woyzeck figure or a Dostoevsky type (Sander, 156). As more recent literature shows, the claim that certain Dostoevsky novels and characters serve as a model for *Berlin Alexanderplatz* has become a fixed element in the discussion. In his recent postscript to the S. Fischer special edition of the novel (1999), the writer Dieter Forte (1935–) compares Döblin's work with Dostoevsky's *The Idiot* (1868), discerning obvious "Parallelen im Handlungsgerüst der beiden Romane":

> Im Formalen die gleiche übersteigerte Sprache, die gleiche labyrinthische Erzählweise, im Inhaltlichen der gleiche Großstadthintergrund einer sinnlos funktionierenden Gesellschaft. So wie Franz Biberkopf, aus dem Gefängnis entlassen in einem Wirbel von Eindrücken mit der Straßenbahn in die Stadt Berlin fährt, fährt Fürst Myschkin, aus einem Sanatorium kommend, mit dem Zug in einem Wirbel von Eindrücken nach Petersburg. (488)

Forte tries to bring to light further analogies — for example, between Rogozhin and Reinhold, who both embody the principles of evil and amorality. Both attempt to murder the friends to whom they are bound in love-hate relationships, and both ultimately become the murderer of their friends' respective lovers, that is of Nastasia Filipovna and of Mieze. While Biberkopf is admitted to the madhouse, Prince Myshkin returns to the sanatorium.

Indeed, Dostoevsky's importance for Döblin's writing is beyond dispute and has repeatedly been a topic of study.[12] But despite all superficial proximity, there is no way to prove conclusively that Döblin based his *Geschichte vom Franz Biberkopf* consciously on *The Idiot,* or that this work served as a model for him. According to his own statements, during his youth *The Idiot* was his "liebstes Buch," which — despite his fascination — he never read completely. Since then, he writes, he has held it "noch [. . .] gelegentlich in den Händen," "die und die Seite gelesen"; but "er [sc. *Der Idiot*] konnte mir nicht helfen." "[. . .] fast die Hälfte des Buches," Döblin writes in 1922, "kenne ich möglicherweise heute noch nicht" (*SLW,* 41–42).

Forte's claim, which silently assumes Döblin's intimate knowledge of the novel, is at least original to the extent that other studies usually refer only to *Crime and Punishment* (1866). They refer to the conspicuous "affinity" between Mieze, who is really Emilie (Parsunke) but would rather be called "Sonya," and the childlike and selfless prostitute Sonya Marmeladova, who is supposed to have been the model for the former. A facial feature, Mieze's "russische Backenknochen" (*BA,* 257), is always taken as an intertextual signal. Kirstin Breitenfellner dedicates an entire chapter of her book *Lavaters Schatten* (Lavater's Shadow, 1999) to this reference. Like Forte, she deals with similarities in character formation, but she also emphasizes the important differences. She thus comes to the conclusion that one can understand *Berlin Alexanderplatz* "auch als einen Gegenentwurf zu *Schuld und Sühne,* der zeigen will, daß man einem Franz Biberkopf nicht so leicht helfen, ihn nicht so leicht bekehren oder bessern kann wie einen intellektuellen, reflektierten Raskolnikow, daß einen Franz Biberkopf das gute Beispiel und die selbstlose Liebe nicht erlösen kann" (159–60).

It remains to be seen whether the recognition of such references to world literature further our understanding of the text. In any case, detecting such character models is not imperative. This also applies to the connection established by Yoshihito Ogasawara to Goethe's *Werther* (1774) as well as to Gottfried Keller's Bildungsroman *Der grüne Heinrich* (1854–55), which is based upon a few descriptive details (133). In her first encounter with Franz, Mieze wears a "weißes leichtes Kleidchen," in which she looks "wie ein Schulmädchen." Franz is immediately "entzückt" and experiences her appearance as a "Wunder" (*BA*, 256–57). Döblin's presentation of Mieze draws undeniably on the classical topos of an idealized femininity and its various formulations and trivializations. It is still an open question whether Döblin, in his description of Mieze, was in fact thinking of Goethe's Lotte, who also wears a simple white dress in her first appearance, or of a similar scene from Gottfried Keller's novel. More important than this superficial intertextual reference for the interpretation of this scene in *Berlin Alexanderplatz* is its ironic-critical play with the motif of innocence. The recourse to this literary set piece and cliché of femininity is intended to expose masculine projections, that is, to uncover Biberkopf's problematic relationship to women, which wavers between violent rejection of femininity and taking refuge in the childlike woman.

The examples cited up to this point have dealt with more or less hidden intertextual references, based upon motif analogies between individual narrative sequences in *Berlin Alexanderplatz* and certain classical works of literary prose. In other scenes, though, Döblin engages quite openly with his literary predecessors and, in several instances, even calls them by name. The spectrum here extends from canonical works of world literature to texts from popular culture, in which case Döblin does not shrink even from silliness and atrocious puns when paraphrasing the texts of advertisements and popular songs. As the following examples will show, these often parodistic and playful references follow a common aim. Intertextuality is used in the novel not only for the portrayal of characters and milieu, but is also made to function as a critique of language and ideology. Döblin utilizes the intertextual references to make the modern reader conscious of the threat of linguistic manipulation, to expose empty phrases and false pathos, and for the "Auseinandersetzung mit dem Heroismus des Abendlandes" (Keller, 205), that is, to confront both the concept of the hero of classical tragedy and the Prussian-soldierly ideal of masculinity. The privileged instrument for the satirical destruction of the sublime and the heroic is parody, which corresponded to Döblin's proclivity "sich über die ernstesten Sachen lustig [zu machen]" (*SPG*, 134) and opened up great opportunities for him to apply his natural Berlin wit.

In particular, the numerous quotations from German soldiers' songs provide stimuli for reflecting critically on masculine heroism. When, right at the beginning, Biberkopf unreflectively bellows a few stanzas from Max Schneckenburger's (1819–49) song *Die Wacht am Rhein* (1840), and particularly the words "[k]riegerisch fest und markig" (*BA*, 18), he is characterized as being susceptible to patriotic-chauvinistic slogans. The repetition of individual song lines continues like a leitmotif up through the novel's final section, tracing Biberkopf's political and private biography.

The protagonist appears from the first moment on as an insecure, threatened, and manipulable personality, who, like the paranoid title figure in the novel *Wadzeks Kampf mit der Dampfturbine*, oscillates between heroic self-overestimation, inferiority complexes, and self-pity. In characteristic fashion, Biberkopf enters Berlin as a conqueror after his release from the "mighty fortress" of the prison. Accompanied acoustically by war songs, he marches through Berlin "wie einer von der Garde" (*BA*, 160), driven by the desire for order and peace and quiet (95). This soldierly-heroic attitude becomes particularly clear in a chapter from the sixth book with the heading "Vorwärts, Schritt gefaßt, Trommelgerassel und Bataillone" (291). It begins with a reminiscence of Biberkopf's war experiences, which indeed traumatized him, but did not make him attentive to the false ethos of comradeship and the empty patriotic phrases suggestively conveyed by the soldiers' songs. His memories forge a thematic bridge to the following montage of marching songs by Ludwig Uhland (1787–1862) and Alexander Cosmar, the rhythm of which seems to reassure him:

> Da marschiert Franz Biberkopf durch die Straßen, mit festem Schritt, links rechts, links rechts, keine Müdigkeit vorschützen, keine Kneipe, nichts saufen, wir wollen sehen, eine Kugel kam geflogen, das wollen wir sehen, krieg ich sie, liege ich, links rechts, links rechts. Trommelgerassel und Bataillone. Endlich atmet er auf.
>
> Es geht durch Berlin. Wenn die Soldaten durch die Stadt marschieren, eiwarum, eidarum, ei bloß wegen dem Tschingdarada bumdara, ei bloß wegen dem Tschingdarada dada. (*BA*, 291–92)

Even in Biberkopf's erotic adventures, a warlike attitude characterized by latent violence reappears again and again. We can already see this in a chapter of the first book with the richly suggestive title: "Sieg auf der ganzen Linie! Franz Biberkopf kauft ein Kalbsfilet" (*BA*, 37). After her initial resistance, Ida's sister Minna gives in to Franz's sexual advances; he experiences the encounter as a triumph of his masculinity — especially after his previous bouts of impotence. This feeling of elation is followed by an ironic commentary conveyed by a song collage: "Er krabbelte hoch, lachte und drehte sich vor Glück, vor Wonne, vor Seligkeit. Was blasen die Trompeten, Husaren heraus, halleluja! Franz Biberkopf ist wieder da!" (*BA*, 40). Here the narrator resumes the earlier trumpet motif, which is taken from Ernst Moritz Arndt's (1769–1860) *Lied vom Feldmarschall* (1813) and also turns up in Wilhelm Hauff's (1802–27) melancholic *Reiters Morgengesang* (1824), cited multiple times as a leitmotif later in the story. In general, this scene assembles a whole series of image and song citations from the sphere of the military and war, which function as a critical accompanying text and cast Biberkopf's relationship to women in a specific light.

In addition to the protagonist's emotional affinity to the soldiers' song, there is his complementary susceptibility to sentimental pop songs and — because of his predilection for excessive consumption of alcohol — to drinking songs and sayings. The many love songs taken from contemporaneous operettas and variety shows are, for the most part, reproduced in parodistically distanced form and situated in contexts that unmask the texts' kitschy insincerity and triteness. When Biberkopf approaches a prostitute in the Elsasser Street, the text comments on this encounter with the phonetic corruption of a refrain from Walter Kollo's (1878–1940) operetta *Der Juxbaron* (1916): "Wenn ein Mädchen einen Hörrn hat, den sie liebt und den sie görn hat" (*BA*, 35). The same stylistic device also appears in the repeated leitmotif citations from Uhland's innocent, sentimental poem "Der gute Kamerad" (1809). The narrator reproduces the soldiers' song, made popular by Franz Silcher's musical arrangement, with the same form and pronunciation as Biberkopf's "tapfer und satt" rendition in a bar:

> "Ich hatt einen Kameraden, einen bessern gibt es nicht. Die Trommel schlug zum Streiheite, er ging an meiner Seiheite in gleichem Schritt und Tritt. In gleichem Schritt und Tritt." Pause. Er singt die zweite Strophe: "Eine Kugel kam geflogen, gilt sie mir, oder gilt sie dir; sie hat ihn weggerihissen, er liegt zu meinen Fühüßen, als wärs ein Stück von mir. Als wärs ein Stück von mir." Und laut den letzten Vers: "Will mir die Hand noch reichen, dieweil ich eben lad. Kann dir die Hand nicht geheben, bleib du im ewgen Leheben, mein guter Kameherad, mein — guter Kameherad." (*BA*, 91)

In another example, the substitution of one word is enough to give the saccharine sentimentality of the pre-text a somewhat sour taste. The line "zwei rote Rosen, ein zarter Kuß," taken from the popular song by Walter Kollo and Kurt Robitschek (1890–1950), becomes in the novel "zwei rote Rosen, ein kalter Kuß" (*BA*, 220). The setting is a jealous scene between Cilly and Reinhold, which will be discussed below.

Of course, the narrator also occasionally reproduces individual song lines in their original, authentic form. This is primarily the case when the lines are already humorous and reveal an ironic or macabre undertone, as in the following chanson:

> Ich reiß mir eine Wimper aus und stech dich damit tot. Dann nehm ich einen Lippenstift und mach dich damit rot. Und wenn du dann noch

böse bist, weiß ich nur einen Rat: ich bestelle mir ein Spiegelei und bespritz dich mit Spinat. (*BA*, 235–36)

In many cases, the narrator tries to outdo the platitudes of pop songs and operetta texts by adding puns or alienating features. From time to time, the context lends a note of indecency to harmless folk and children's songs, as, for instance, in the scene from the opening section of the novel, when Biberkopf follows a prostitute up to her room:

Das schwammige Weib lachte aus vollem Hals. Sie knöpfte sich oben die Bluse auf. Es waren zwei Königskinder, die hatten einander so lieb. Wenn der Hund mit der Wurst übern Rinnstein springt. Sie griff ihn, drückte ihn an sich. Putt, putt, putt, mein Hühnchen, putt, putt, putt, mein Hahn. (*BA*, 33–34)

By no means does Döblin's parody of trivial texts limit itself to the purpose of uncovering ideological attitudes and false feelings, exposing meaningless shells of language as such, or caricaturing antiquated forms of expression. Exposing the characteristic kitsch, for example, of poems such as E. Fischer's "Es geht sich besser zu zweien" (Things Are Better as a Pair) is certainly an amusing game for the author, but also an easy one (*BA*, 97). Such citations are meant for the reader's enjoyment. Döblin simply cut the religious, edifying poem from the Sunday paper *Der Friedensbote* and pasted it into the manuscript, deleting two stanzas.

The quotations from canonical literary texts play a decisive role in the destruction of the heroic and the solemn. The text repeatedly measures the dramatic fall from the heights of "classical" pathos to the banality of everyday life, and it utilizes this discrepancy for comic effect. This follows a definite semantic pattern, in which a formulation from a text of high literary culture is transferred onto a concrete, everyday situation and confronted with it for satirical purposes. A dialogic variation of this kind of play is the contrasting montage of citations from both high and low literature. Thus, the narrator at one point follows a weather forecast that predicts the "Erwärmung der Temperatur" with an advertisement that makes use of Mignon's famous Italy poem from Goethe's Bildungsroman *Wilhelm Meisters Lehrjahre* (Wilhelm Meister's Apprenticeship, 1795–96):

Und wer den neuen NSU-6-Zylinder selbst lenkt, ist begeistert. Dahin, dahin laß mich mit dir, du mein Geliebter, ziehn. (*BA*, 160)

The automobile advertisement is taken up again in a later passage, where it forms part of a parodistic series of citations. It is directly followed by the formulation, "Na, dann ist alles im Lot, lachte Franz," to which the narrator adds the ironic, critical commentary:

Doch mit des Geschickes Mächten ist kein ewiger Bund zu flechten. Und das Schicksal schreitet schnell. Tragen Sie, wenn Sie am Schreiten behindert sind, Leisers Schuh. Leiser ist das größte Schuhhaus am Platze. Und wenn Sie nicht schreiten wollen, fahren Sie: NSU ladet Sie zu einer Probefahrt im Sechszylinder ein. Grade an diesem Donnerstag ging Franz Biberkopf mal wieder allein durch die Prenzlauer Straße [. . .]. (*BA*, 193)

Here the verb "schreiten," to stride, produces a kind of textual chain reaction: the paraphrased citation from Friedrich Schiller's *Lied von der Glocke* (1800) brings about the association of two highly trivial slogans from the world of contemporary advertising. In the following example, the situational context similarly indicates the narrator's reference to a classical text sequence. This time the connecting link is an object. When Cilly realizes that Reinhold is deceiving her, in her rage, she plots a bloody revenge: "Sie trägt schon frei nach Schiller den Dolch im Gewande. Es ist zwar nur ein Küchenmesser, aber dem Reinhold will sie eins für seine Gemeinheiten geben, wohin ist egal" (*BA*, 220). When it is transferred onto a drama of jealousy within a group of pimps and prostitutes, the motif of tyrannicide from Schiller's ballad *Die Bürgschaft* (1798) becomes a joke. The text exposes the noble pathos of the original for what it is — for Döblin it evidently retains only the status of a work of art from a pre-modern past.

It is well known that, from his youth on, Döblin was a great admirer of Heinrich von Kleist (1777–1811). He held *Penthesilea* (1808) in especially high regard — probably because of his obsessive fondness for the battle of the sexes — describing the drama as "Kleists mächtigste und ureigenste Dichtung" and as an "abgründiges Werk" (*KS-2*, 215). On the other hand, he was quite critical of Kleist's anti-Napoleonic hate songs *Germania und ihre Kinder* (1803). And, in light of the nationalist-chauvinist appropriation of certain Kleist dramas in productions of the 1920s, he also began to have reservations about *Der Prinz von Homburg* (1809–11), the favorite play of Kaiser Wilhelm II.[13] Nonetheless, Döblin uses Kleist for similar parodistic purposes as he did the much more canonical Goethe and Schiller. In a chapter of the second book entitled "Lina besorgt es den schwulen Buben" (*BA*, 70), Biberkopf's friend Lina is outraged at his trafficking in newspapers aimed at sexual enlightenment. When she sees that the publication caters to homosexuals and lesbians, she is transformed into a "Mänade" (*BA*, 75). This mythological exaggeration prepares the reader for the "Vorstoß à la Prinz von Homburg" (*BA*, 77) that Lina undertakes shortly thereafter.[14] The depiction of her pressing into the "war zone" at Biberkopf's side is preceded by a montage of diverse texts that clearly cohere, however, to the theme of love and homosexuality. After the episode of the anonymous

"Glatzkopf," whose love for a "hübschen Jungen" (*BA*, 75) becomes his undoing, there is a transitional passage of associatively linked advertising texts, followed by a parody of a highly trivial novel by Selli Engler. This work, entitled *Erkenntnis*, deals with a lesbian relationship. Döblin caricatures the author's style in the manner of the famous and prolific author of numerous nineteenth-century novels, Hedwig Courths-Mahler (1867–1950) by inserting bracketed commentary. He increases his ridicule through the transcription of punctuation marks, which pile up so much at the end that the actual text disappears beneath them:

> Sie aber rührte sich nicht, Komma, zog nicht die Decke fester über sich, Punkt. [. . .] Ihre glänzenden Augen irrten flackernd im Dunkeln umher, und ihre Lippen bebten, Doppelpunkt, Gänsefüßchen, Lore, Gedankenstrich, Gedankenstrich, Lore, Gedankenstrich, Gänsefüßchen, Gänsebeinchen, Gänseleber mit Zwiebel. (*BA*, 76–77)

The "culinary" endpoint functions as a kind of self-parody of Döblin's parodistic methodology and thus as an expression of "Autorreflexivität" (Pfister, 27). This can also be found, for example, in the Max Rüst episode, in which the narrator casts a brief glance into the life of a fourteen-year-old boy by drafting his future obituary (*BA*, 54).

Back to Franz and Lina: after the digression into the area of popular literature, the next chapter section resumes the main plot by describing an argument between the two, after which Lina reluctantly joins Biberkopf in selling the papers. In no time, however, Lina changes her mind, and here, the narrative moves to the next literary parody. In the portrayal of Lina's furious attack on Biberkopf for selling what to her were scandalous magazines, the narrator falls back on "Sprach- und Bildelemente [. . .], die mit der Vorstellungswelt der handelnden Personen nicht das geringste zu tun haben" (Ribbat, 192). When Lina's march in the direction of the "Kampffront" is described in grotesque exaggeration as "selbständige[r] Vorstoß à la Prinz von Homburg" (*BA*, 77), it produces a "komischer Kontrast" that could hardly be any greater. The "Heroentum des klassisch-höfischen Idealismus" (Ribbat, 192) is placed in relation to a purely emotional "Kampfhandlung" (*BA*, 77), motivated by an ignorant, intolerant, uneducated Polish girl. As in the Schiller example, this technique produces an enormous contrast between the ideal and the banal. The fact that Döblin chose a Kleist play for this purpose might appear "relativ beliebig" (Ribbat, 193), since he could have made use of any similar text of classical literature. Clearly, Döblin's primary concern here was to reveal the distance between modern man and his language and the conflicts and pathos of classical tragedy. The citations from *Der Prinz von Homburg* therefore take on an exemplary function.

This also applies, mutatis mutandis, to the scene in which a flashback depicts Biberkopf's fatal attack on Ida with the help of paraphrases from Aeschylus' *Oresteia*. Even the heading signals that we are once again dealing with the theme of heroism: "Ausmaße dieses Franz Biberkopf. Er kann es mit alten Helden aufnehmen" (*BA*, 98). The reference to the mythological pre-text occurs despite the narrator's ironic note that one can conduct a "zeitgemäße Betrachtung" of the homicide based on its conformity to physical laws "gänzlich ohne Erinnyen." "Man kann Stück für Stück verfolgen, was Franz tat und Ida erlitt" (*BA*, 100). The conscious rejection of the tragic model and the reduction of the event to its facticity cast the violent act as the result of a scientifically comprehensible causal chain with fatal effects. The blows Biberkopf delivers to his victim lead to the "Verlust der Vertikalen bei Ida, Übergang in die Horizontale"; the narrator's conclusion states, "Es gibt nichts Unbekanntes in der Gleichung" (*BA*, 100). Rather than grant the murderer any exonerating moral or psychological motives, and rather than place him in a proud line of innocent, yet guilty tragic heroes, the text depicts him as a brutal, uncontrolled, and unscrupulous sexual offender. This portrayal effects a radical demystification and demythologization of the classical hero. The stylistic device is the contrasting montage of quotations from the *Oresteia* and scientific "formulas," namely Newton's first and second laws. The two modes of observation are indeed juxtaposed in sharp dichotomy, yet both are equally subject to the narrator's derision. From the very beginning, the scattered references to mythological figures and ideas, as well as the selective citations from classical Greek drama, of texts from the "Zeit unserer Urgroßmütter," are placed under the sign of "veränderte Zeiten" (*BA*, 98). In this way, the text calls into question their paradigmatic status for modern man. Because he lacks any understanding of guilt at this point, Biberkopf appears as Orestes' antithesis; he forms the greatest possible opposition to the scrupulous, highly reflective hero of classical drama. The manuscript reads, "So unterscheidet sich deutlich und sichtbar Franz, ein einfacher Berliner von Art, von dem alten Orestes." The narrator intensifies this contrast through commentary in contemporary jargon: for instance, when he refers to the Furies and their dogs as an "unsympathische Menagerie" and classifies their effect as a "Vorbereitung für die Klapsmühle" (*BA*, 98). Nevertheless, the point is not simply to mock an "antike Vorstellung" (*BA*, 98) but rather to demonstrate great historical differences in the perception and moral judgment of an act of murder, to demonstrate the unbridgeable distance between worldviews. The topoi of the hero and of fate, as they are passed down in classical Greek tragedy, appear completely foreign and devoid of meaning.[15] Just how far the murderer Biberkopf is removed from the scrupulous, matricidal Orestes comes to the fore in the concluding passage of the flashback to Biberkopf's bloody deed:

> Der sie getötet hat, geht herum, lebt, blüht, säuft, frißt, verspritzt seinen Samen, verbreitet weiter Leben. Sogar Idas Schwester ist ihm nicht entgangen. Mal wird es auch ihn erwischen. [. . .] Aber es hat noch gute Weile damit. (*BA*, 102)

In fact, quite a bit of time will pass before Biberkopf's "earthly path" comes to an end. In the face of death, the Furies will seize hold of him too, just as they did Orestes, until he finally understands his guilt and regrets his evil deeds. The numerous intertextual references to biblical and mythological figures have long since given the reader insight into the main character's incorrect actions and deficits, and thanks to the ironic-didactic narrative commentary, the reader is always several steps ahead of the "Enthüllungsprozeß" (*BA*, 453). Biberkopf himself, however, still requires the instruction of a "dunkle Macht" called "Tod," who enlightens him "über seine Irrtümer, seinen Hochmut und seine Unwissenheit" (*BA*, 411). Following his purification, or more precisely, his rebirth, Franz Karl Biberkopf seems immunized against the seductive power of warlike rhythms. Thus, a song variation with an entirely new sound reads, "Lieb Vaterland, kannst ruhig sein, ich hab die Augen auf und fall sobald nicht rein" (*BA*, 454). Rather than approach the world in a conquering march, the protagonist opts for a slower, more careful stride at the side of his fellow man. The acceptance of personal responsibility and guilt is accompanied by the departure from his earlier belief in fate and his false understanding of heroism.

Of course, Biberkopf's new existence as a porter, that is, as an attentive, controlling watchman, does not mean that he rejects the aggressive principle of life. The montage of verses from various march songs that continues into the epilogue makes this clear in a suggestive way. In this montage, the "Grundmelodie der Schlacht des Lebens" continues to assert its validity (Bayerdörfer, "Der Wissende," 159) On the formal level, the concluding song citation simultaneously maintains intertextuality as the dominant structuring principle and the novel's central mode of expression.

— *Translated by Brian Tucker*

Notes

[1] See *SLW*, 312.

[2] See Schuhmann 97–104.

[3] The prison is located in Tegel, to the north of the city.

[4] For contemporaneous responses to the novel and its final sequence, see Sander 137–64.

[5] See Stauffacher's postscript to *BA*, 844–45.

[6] This group was founded on October 19, 1928; it was the successor of "Gruppe 1925," to which Döblin had belonged for a while.

[7] Rainer Werner Fassbinder's opulent 1980 television production of *Berlin Alexanderplatz* definitely contributed to this popularity.

[8] A thorough survey of the various editions and the research history can be found in Sander, 164–220.

[9] For this notion of transforming pre-texts, see Lachmann, *Gedächtnis* and "Intertextualität."

[10] According to Pfister, this is the case when an author reflects on "intertextuelle Bedingtheit und Bezogenheit seines Textes in diesem selbst [. . .], d.h. die Intertextualität nicht nur markiert, sondern sie thematisiert, ihre Voraussetzungen und Leistungen rechtfertigt und problematisiert" (27).

[11] Even in his last notes he described himself as a "demütiger Diener meiner Eingebungen und Gesichte" (*SLW*, 477).

[12] For a discussion of this influence see Weyembergh-Boussart.

[13] See *KS-2*, 222; for the reception of Kleist in Döblin's work, see Ribbat, especially 189.

[14] The "Vorstoß à la Prinz von Homburg" is the result of the prince's spontaneous action in battle.

[15] Compare also Biberkopf's remark in a bar: "Ich bin Gegner des Fatums. Ich bin kein Grieche, ich bin Berliner" (*BA*, 56).

Works Cited

Bayerdörfer, Hans-Peter. "Alfred Döblin: *Berlin Alexanderplatz*." *Romane des 20. Jahrhunderts*. Vol. 1. Stuttgart: Reclam, 1993. 158–94.

———. "Der Wissende und die Gewalt. Alfred Döblins Theorie des epischen Werkes und der Schluß von *Berlin Alexanderplatz*." *Materialien zu Alfred Döblin "Berlin Alexanderplatz."* Ed. by Matthias Prangel. Frankfurt am Main: Suhrkamp, 1975. 150–85.

Breitenfellner, Kirstin. *Lavaters Schatten: Physiognomie und Charakter bei Ganghofer, Fontane und Döblin*. Dresden: Dresden UP, 1999.

Keller, Otto. *Döblins Montageroman als Epos der Moderne*. Munich: Fink, 1980.

Lachmann, Renate. *Gedächtnis und Literatur: Intertextualität in der russischen Moderne*. Frankfurt am Main: Suhrkamp, 1990.

Lachmann, Renate, and Schamma Schahadat. "Intertextualität." *Literaturwissenschaft: Ein Grundkurs*. Ed. by Jörn Helmut Brackert and Jörn Stückrath. Reinbek: Rowohlt, 1995. 677–86.

Ogasawara, Yoshihito. *"Literatur zeugt Literatur": Intertextuelle, motiv- und kulturgeschichtliche Studien zu Alfred Döblins Poetik und dem Roman Berlin Alexanderplatz*. Frankfurt am Main: Lang, 1996.

Pfister, Manfred. "Konzepte der Intertextualität." *Intertextualität: Formen, Funktionen, anglistische Fallstudien*. Ed. by Ulrich Broich and Manfred Pfister. Tübingen: Niemeyer, 1985. 1–30.

Ribbat, Ernst. "'Ein roher Hund ist der Mensch, wenn er dichtet.' Zur Kleist-Rezeption im Werk Alfred Döblins." *Internationales Alfred-Döblin-Kolloquium Marbach 1984–Berlin 1985*. Ed. by Werner Stauffacher. Bern: Lang, 1988. 185–95.

Sander, Gabriele. *Erläuterungen und Dokumente: Alfred Döblin. "Berlin Alexanderplatz."* Stuttgart: Reclam, 1998.

Schuhmann, Klaus. "Zertrümmerung der Person: Galy Gay (Brecht) und Franz Biberkopf (Döblin) im Vergleich." *Internationales Alfred-Döblin-Kolloquium Leipzig 1997*. Ed. by Ira Lorf and Gabriele Sander. Bern: Lang, 1999. 97–104.

Stenzel, Jürgen. "Mit Kleister und Schere. Zur Handschrift von *Berlin Alexanderplatz*." *text + kritik* 13/14: Alfred Döblin (1972): 39–44.

Weyembergh-Boussart, Monique. "A. Döblin et F. M. Dostoievski: influence et analogie." *Revue des langues vivantes* 35 (1969): 505–30.

Döblin's Engagement with the New Media: Film, Radio and Photography

Erich Kleinschmidt

Early Encounters with Film

D ÖBLIN WAS AN INQUISITIVE AUTHOR, who strolled through Berlin, the center of his life, with open eyes and ears, as one for whom everything became fit material for his writing. Innovations and especially all things technical fascinated him: "eine surrende Dynamomaschine in einem Keller, an dem ich vorbeigehe, wühlt mich auf; ich gehe beschenkt 'wie im Traum,' es ist ein Anruf, meine Kraft ist wieder da" (*SLW*, 39). Not surprisingly, the technological innovation of Lumière's cinematograph caught his attention. Döblin was one of the first to visit the cinemas then opening in Berlin,[1] and promptly wrote about the "Theater der kleinen Leute" (Theater of the Little People, 1909) (*KS-1*, 71–73). However, his interest was aroused less by the new medium of moving pictures and more by the locales in which they were shown, the "Kientopps," as they were colloquially called in Berlin.[2]

Döblin was captivated by the audience and the atmosphere, where "ein Monstrum von Publikum, [. . .] eine Masse, [. . .] dieses weiße Auge mit seinem stieren Blick zusammenbannt" (*KS-1*, 72). He remarked on the audience's primal needs, its simple greedy voyeurism, its desire to be "gerührt, erregt, entsetzt [. . .]; mit Gelächter losplatzen" (*KS-1*, 71). "Kientopp" did not aspire to art and its lofty experience, but catered to the "schaurige Lust am Schauen von Greuel, Kampf und Tod."[3] Film in its early years was characterized by its appeal to bare emotions, above all the "höchst Verwunderlichen und durchaus Gräßlichen" (*KS-1*, 71). Indeed, the first films were shown in amusement parks, panoptica, varietés, and flea markets. In time, cinemas were established in various other places, such as "in verräucherten Stuben, Ställen, unbrauchbaren Läden," and finally in "großen Sälen, weiten Theatern" (*KS-1*, 71).

Unlike the theater, with its regular performance time, cinemas served an audience that liked to take advantage of the continuous showings, depending on the occasion, time available, or the schedule of the day. This fact of not being bound to a certain time constituted the market value of the new medium and also became symptomatic for the changing attitude of urban modernity. The conditions varied considerably, however, from country to country. In Germany, the movie theaters were rather modest places and offered continuous showings. In Great Britain cinemas were elegant showplaces that offered their shows at fixed times just like the theaters. Thus, the contention that the audience of early cinema was primarily proletarian is not altogether true. Other social groups with leisure time, from sales clerks, to ladies out shopping, to educated *flaneurs*, frequented the cinema as a place where one could spend one's time pleasantly (Altenloh). The Viennese cultural critic Raoul Auernheimer therefore called the cinema an "Automatenbüffet des Geistes," "jederzeit willig, den Appetit des Passanten zu befriedigen" (*Hätte ich das Kino*, 23). Moreover, the cinema was relatively inexpensive, which made it accessible to the less affluent than were the expensive theaters.

"Proletarian" as a category for early cinema, therefore, refers not so much to the sociological reality as to an aesthetic disqualification. The film offerings were considered by educated people, including Döblin, as being on the level of mass literature or even trashy literature, a view Döblin stated explicitly. He particularly appreciated the fact that at the end of the show "das Kinema — schweigt" (*KS-1*, 73). It was not to be taken seriously as an art form, but could be appreciated as a new urban form of entertainment of considerable attractiveness.

After 1910 the search for artistic functions of the new medium began in the form of the "cinema debate,"[4] in which Döblin did not participate. Due to the "scenic" mode of action, the intent was to set off the film from drama and stage performance. Whereas the theater thrived on dialogue, on words, the film was silent.[5] Theoretically the narrative element plays no role in the film. The fact that, in addition to the piano accompaniment, a narrator commented on the silent action of the film during the showing,[6] was a provisional aid without systematic effects.

Since Döblin at that time considered himself a genuine and practicing epic writer, it is understandable that he could gain very little from film and cinema poetologically. He therefore also did not participate in the debate on film as a serious art medium. Even the first German art film, *Der Student von Prag*, based on a script by Hans Heinz Ewers in collaboration with Paul Wegener, did not resonate with Döblin, although the much-lauded first performance on August 22, 1913 in Berlin was a social event.

He showed little interest in the many "cinema pieces," written by noted younger authors beginning in 1913 in a kind of creative push. The same is true with regard to the epochal, legendary *Kinobuch* initiated by Kurt Pinthus,[7] which featured an impressive sixteen Expressionist avant-garde authors (among them Franz Blei, Max Brod, Albert Ehrenstein, Walter Hasenclever, Else Lasker-Schüler, Heinrich Lautensack, Ludwig Rubiner, Paul Zech). In this instance, too, Döblin revealed himself as an author over and beyond current trends and tendencies. He went his own way with regard to the cinema.

In the spring of 1913 (March/April) Döblin published his manifesto "An Romanautoren und ihre Kritiker. Berliner Programm" in Herwarth Walden's *Der Sturm* (*SLW*, 123–27), the leading Expressionist journal. In this essay, Döblin proclaimed his fundamental poetological principles for the new novel, his "Döblinismus" (*SLW*, 119). Döblin mentions cinema, but uses it only metaphorically in his definition of "Döblinismus." The cinema does not serve him to find guidelines for his epic writing since he considered the reality of contemporary cinema to be simplistic and destructive for the novel.[8] Only the experience of the cinema show appears useful for his concept of the new epic novel.

Döblin used the term "Kinostil" to describe his innovative model of the novel, but this does not mean that he actually adapted filmic techniques to literature. Döblin meant by this merely that literary representation must describe the sequence of the "Fülle der Gesichte ... in höchster Gedrängtheit und Präzision" (*SÄPL*, 121). The goal of such narration is to attain a kind of perception that lets the text appear not "wie gesprochen, sondern wie vorhanden" (*SÄPL*, 122). For Döblin, the "cinematic style" is therefore based not on writing with a "film" technique,[9] whose real possibilities were in any case not very well developed in 1913. Döblin was interested in the distanced representation of the world by the moving images of film. In his view, the manner of presentation of film did not require a narrator to order reality, as in the traditional novel. The images narrate themselves without the mediation or authority of an author.

Döblin did not recognize the fact that script, direction, and camera technique also generate a narrative authorship for the film, because he was not interested in the realities of filmmaking. He saw in the film merely the pure surface medium without a recognizable "depth structure" capable of creating causality. This is what mattered to him, because he wanted to subject the author to a "Fanatismus der Entäußerung" (*SÄPL*, 122).[10] The epic writer does not act as a creative intervening "I," but rather he dissolves in his objects of representation: "ich bin nicht ich, sondern die Straße, die Laternen, dies und dies Ereignis, weiter nichts" (*SÄPL*, 122).

The "cinema style," which Döblin also called "den steinernen Stil" (*SÄPL*, 122), aimed at a narration that no longer required a perceiving author and his subjectivity. The epic text is the result of an objectified apperception that functions like a camera and accordingly does not judge what is being captured. Street and lamp make their own images.

The cinema thus served Döblin only as a conceptual garment for an epic theory of recording reality that is in its core based on science and medicine. The "Berlin program" makes this very clear. The new novel should orient itself on the model of positivistic and descriptive psychiatry. "Man lerne von der Psychiatrie, der einzigen Wissenschaft, die sich mit dem seelischen ganzen Menschen befaßt; sie [. . .] beschränkt sich auf die Notierung der Abläufe, Bewegungen — mit einem Kopfschütteln, Achselzucken für das Weitere und das 'Warum' und das 'Wie'" (*SÄPL*, 121–22) This is what film does — it merely records and does not explain. The characteristic function of the traditional narrator, however, is to explain, establish connections, and show cause and effect. Döblin sets against this his new concept of the novel, which justifies narrative movements without explanation, impressionistically ("Moment um Moment aus sich rechtfertigt," *SÄPL*, 125), and records them in such a way that storytelling has an effect similar to that of an unwinding film.[11]

Döblin's theoretical demands as set forth in the "Berlin program" were realized in his great China novel *Die drei Sprünge des Wang-lun* (completed in May 1913, but not on the market until 1916). In this novel, he put into practice his theory of the unmediated depiction of reality through causally unconnected events. Contemporary critics failed to recognize Döblin's singular use of film and cinema, since the reference medium used by Döblin was too new and its potential not yet understood. The fact that it was more than just the basis for the metaphorical formula of "Kinostil" is not explicitly stated in his poetological writings, but appears in rudimentary form in his notion of a kind of writing that goes beyond "the great novel" in short forms.

Elements of this are present in the "Zueignung" to *Wang-lun*, an introductory preface of one and a half pages beginning with the phrase, "Daß ich nicht vergesse," where Döblin lets the overwhelming simultaneity of the impressions of the metropolis Berlin run like a film. The optical and acoustic perceptions confuse the author and the narrator who comments: "Ich tadle das verwirrende Vibrieren nicht. Nur ich finde mich nicht zurecht" (*WL*, 7). Döblin's experience of the metropolis Berlin was similar to that of Franz Kafka around the same time, when after his visit to the Prague cinema, he commented: "Bin ganz leer und sinnlos, die vorüberfahrende Elektrische hat mehr lebendigen Sinn."[12]

Döblin's second attempt at "filmic" writing, in which he attempted to put into practice his program uncompromisingly, remained unpublished for unknown reasons. It is a short text found among his posthumous papers under the generic title "Roman."[13] An extremely dense, phantasmagoric text, no longer concerned with reality, it presents a "sprachliche Realität" of the highest "Plastik, Konzentration und Intensität" (*SÄPL,* 119), in order that the narrated, reported material can be "seen." In brief sentences and often only key words such as "Die Lustseuche," Döblin created an non-narrative sequence of scenes of the life and collapse of a city on the sea, a text that one may consider a genuine "Sprachfilm." The formal experiment, Döblin's endeavor to distance himself from the contemporary, futuristic style of Marinetti (1876–1944), represents the most far-reaching attempt to create an early "filmic" writing style in German as well as international avant-garde literary modernism.

Döblin's Experimentation with Film

Döblin began his own productive work in film rather casually after the First World War, in the fall of 1920.[14] He wrote the filmscript "Die geweihten Töchter" (The Consecrated Daughters, 1924),[15] his attempt to connect to an evolving, more sophisticated, and intellectual film aesthetics. Here Yvan Goll's (1891–1950) insight articulated in the same year may have played a role: "Basis für alle kommende Kunst ist das Kino. Niemand wird mehr ohne die neue Bewegung auskommen [. . .]" (137). Against the background of his own poetics of the novel, Döblin now tested the possibility of transferring it to film, without concerning himself all too much with the reality of the cinema.[16]

He articulated this demand in a "Vorbemerkung" to the filmscript, which emphasizes his desire to use "noch wenig oder gar nicht versuchte Mittel," in order to elevate the action of the film to a "geistig höhere Stufe" (*DHF,* 325). Döblin's filmic goal was to attain "völliges optisches Denken und Phantasieren," independent of the means of expression of the actors and solely with "den eigenen Mitteln der optischen Phantasie" (*DHF,* 325). This included the almost total renunciation of subtitles or word insertions, which were routinely used in "literary" silent film.

The plan for more or less intensive chains of images resulted in a conception of film corresponding to Arnold Zweig's "Theoretische Grundlegung des Films in Thesen" (Theses on the Theoretical Foundation of Film, 1922): "Schicksalsgestaltung, die in wortlos anschaubaren Szenen ein Leben oder einen Handlungsablauf so anordnet, daß aus dem Zusammentreten der bewegten Menschen und der belebten Natur ein Sinnbild für die Verlassenheit oder Erhabenheit, für das Geleitet- oder Preisgegebensein des Menschen auf der Erde sich darbietet."[17] Zweig considered the typical example for this to be Paul Wegener's *Golem* film, which was first shown in Berlin on October 29, 1920. It is possible that Döblin's own work on a five-act film was inspired and influenced by these "Bilder aus einer alten Chronik" in "fünf Kapiteln."[18]

The subject of the filmscript "Die geweihten Töchter" is an abstruse story whose content was based on Döblin's one-act play "Comteß Mizzi" of 1908, which was not published in his lifetime (first published in *DHF*, 32–61). According to his idea, the world should be liberated from the constraints of diabolical sensuality through "geweihte Töchter" who dedicate themselves to a "sacred prostitution." A count uses his daughter Mizzi to this end, which leads to complications, because she falls in love and thus fails in the task of prostitution. The end of the story culminates in an apocalyptic fire that consumes all the protagonists. On the one hand, Döblin seemed to be adapting his script to the sensationalistic and voyeuristic desires of the public, and on the other insisting on a topic that was ideologically important to him, since "sacred prostitution" also plays an important role in other of his early works, especially *Wang-lun*.

 The tension between his own original ideas and existing filmic conventions, which is also reflected in the script,[19] characterizes Döblin's limited relation to film (Prodolliet; Melcher). He perceived it as a medium of increasing cultural importance, in which one must therefore participate. His decision, however, was not without problems. There were deficits in the choice of subject and form. Döblin was not really able to free himself from the original dramatic form in favor of a strictly filmic conception. This criticism, however, holds true only for the extant script. The film was never made, but it is possible that a more convincing filmic rendition might have been achieved. The filming of Georg Kaiser's (1878–1945) Expressionist drama *Von Morgens bis Mitternacht* (From Morning to Midnight, 1916) by Karl-Heinz Martin, made in 1920, but never shown in Germany, illustrates what an ingenious film adaptation of a drama could achieve.

Döblin lacked the connections that might have made publication of his script possible, and might have drawn the attention of filmmakers. Only in 1930 did the *Literarische Welt* show an interest in the "Geweihten Töchter" "wegen der merkwürdigen bildhaften Assoziationstechnik Döblins — Symbole der Ketten, der Flammen, der Tiere, der Blumen — , die in ihrer irrationalen Lockerung, schon wie eine Vorstufe zu der Technik des *Alexanderplatz* anmutet."[20] This point of view seems to confirm the generally accepted thesis that Döblin's great Berlin novel was based on a "filmic" writing style. However, this overlooks the fact that the script of the "Geweihten Töchter" remained caught in a traditional epic conception and style and could not reflect the standard of a "bewegte Dichtung" as set forth in film theory (Goll, 138).

The "film author" Döblin judged his attempts in the new medium quite sharply himself, and in 1922 expressed himself very critically about the possible artistic qualities of film on the occasion of a survey of "German writers on film." According to Döblin, film takes language away from the writer and destroys the imagination, because film forces it to a single, "optical" level (*KS-2*, here 124). He criticized the technical possibilities of a potential "Kunstprodukt" film, which in his view were deficient and could not be a "Produkt der Kunst": "das Filmmaterial ist nicht kunstfähig" (*KS-2*, 125).

If one takes this appraisal seriously, then one can hardly assert that Döblin was influenced by film in his work as epic writer. On the contrary, film should have learned from literature. But Döblin did not even suggest that that was feasible; instead he suggested painting as a productive reference for "Filmmanuskriptproduzenten," because painting too operated with the "zweidimensionalen Fläche" (*KS-2*, 126). Such an approach reduced film to a static pictoriality. Since film essentially consists of moving sequences of images, Döblin's conception missed the essential point, and cannot be considered a knowledgeable assessment regarding the infusion of cinema into the "Rayon der Literatur" (*KS-3*, 131).[21]

The often-repeated allusion to Döblin's "filmic writing style" must therefore be refuted. It originated with contemporary critics of *Berlin Alexanderplatz* and has been repeated ever since. An example is Herbert Ihering's review from 1929: "[. . .] alles ordnet sich zu einem funkelnden, zuckenden Bildstreifen, zu dem Wortfilm 'Berlin Alexanderplatz,'" (Schuster/Bode, 227).[22] Constant repetition does not make this thesis any more pertinent, if it claims to serve as more than a mere metaphor for the genuinely literary style of Döblin's "ultra-kinematographischer" achievement, which explodes "das Potential des Mediums Film [. . .] Die filmische Schreibweise Döblins [. . .] überfordert [. . .] schlichtweg den Film" (Hurst, 264). Different media are not simply translatable or transferable from one to the other (Kittler, 355). A novel does not function as a "film."[23]

Döblin's reserved relation to film changed around 1930, along with his changing conception of literature. In place of a rather elitist conception of art, Döblin now wanted to reach a broader, mass audience: "Senkung des Gesamtniveaus der Literatur. Aus dem Bildungskäfig, in dem unsere heutige Literatur steckt, in dem sie von breiten Volksmassen nur als

Attribut der feinen Leute angesehen wird, muß sie heraus" (*SÄPL,* 270). The mass medium of film opened new possibilities here that a "changed author" must use, as Döblin said in the interview, "Nur der veränderte Autor kann den Film verändern" ("Only the changed author can change film," 1930; *KS-3,* 230–32). Accordingly, Döblin used the projection of slides and film (modeled on Erwin Piscator's stage directions) as commentaries to directly address the audience in addition to the spoken text for his drama *Die Ehe* (1929/1931, first performance Munich, October 20, 1930).[24] The intent of the projections was to assist the spectator in interpreting the plot (Ditschek, 204–8).

In addition to his ideological reorientation aiming for a literature (and art) more accessible to the masses, the advent of sound in film played an important role in changing Döblin's attitude toward film. By adding language, so important to Döblin, to film, the word could even assume function beyond literature: "Worte werden Freskocharakter bekommen müssen, sie werden tiefer sein müssen als bisher, fester stehen müssen" (*KS-3,* 231–32). By this Döblin meant not so much orality and the atmosphere of language (Scheunemann, 86–94), as he did the emphasis on language as a productive force capable of creating associations. The sound film provided the new medium with a common linguistic space that silent film lacked.

In the context of a poetics for Weimar cinema (Kappelhoff, 313–14), Döblin distinguished between textual and filmic expertise. What mattered to him was "eine wirklich intensive Gemeinschaftsarbeit" between the literary author and a "Filmschaffenden" (*KS-3,* 231). This included the insistence on writers' say in film projects, because language in film has "eine andere Größe und eine andere Valeur als in Büchern und auf dem Theater" (*KS-3,* 231). But the advice and competence of the filmmaker were also desirable, in order to open "neue Vorhänge" (*KS-3,* 231) for the author.

Döblin collaborated with Hans Wilhelm on the filmscript for *Berlin Alexanderplatz.*[25] The division of labor cannot be ascertained; Wilhelm was probably responsible for the sequence of scenes, especially since Döblin's script did not fulfill his theoretical demands for words capable of producing powerful images.[26] The spoken word plays a role for the particular quality of this sound film, insofar as one of the first-rate theater directors of the Weimar Republic, Karl-Heinz Martin, was entrusted with the rehearsing of the dialogue. Directed by Phil Jutzi and with an excellent cast, including the actor Heinrich George as Biberkopf, *Berlin Alexanderplatz* was one of the more ambitious achievements of German film history before 1933.

The contemporary reviews (partly reprinted in Belach/Bock, 224–36) ranged from reserved to negative with regard to the film's relationship to the novel.[27] Siegfried Kracauer, for example, noted the "Kompromiß zwischen den filmischen Möglichkeiten des Romans und den Forderungen der Branche" und lamented that an opportunity had been wasted "einen Film zu schaffen, der Zustände episch vermittelt."[28] Thus the cinematic version of *Berlin Alexanderplatz* remained without significance for the intellectual and aesthetic connection between literature and film. It also did not make Döblin into a "film author," noted for his achievements in this area.

Döblin himself saw the filming less as a compromise with his book than as an extension of it. In an interview for the first showing (October 8, 1931), he emphasized the additional atmospheric achievement through photography, acoustical authenticity, and music in the film.[29] This corresponds to Döblin's original intention to glue a newspaper text into the manuscript of *Berlin Alexanderplatz*. The text that is missing in the final version deals with the "Detail im Film" allowing for an "ästhetischen Genuß für das Auge" (*BA*, 787) without distracting from the plot. A dimension of "surplus value," made possible by film, comes into view here.

Despite his involvement with the medium film on the occasion of the production of *Berlin Alexanderplatz*, Döblin did not start any other film projects before emigrating from Germany on February 28, 1933. Only under the depressing conditions of his exile in France did he turn to another film project, called "Natascha macht Schluß" (first printed in *DHF*, 365–404). It featured a tragic/grotesque subject and an ironic commentary on Döblin's own fate of emigration seen through a fictional subject. Thematically as well as stylistically the concept was similar to that of his first novel completed in Paris *Babylonische Wandrung* (1934). Döblin did not get beyond a fragmentary drafting of the filmscript. It is a minor work prompted by circumstances, but which did not chart new territory in terms of either theme or film technique. The draft filled the productive gap before the beginning of the *Amazonas* trilogy that initiated a new phase of Döblin's epic writing during his exile.

The Second World War and the occupation of France forced Döblin to continue his flight and brought him to safety in Hollywood and into contact, albeit involuntary, with the big Hollywood studios, which provided him along with other German exile authors with a one-year employment contract in order to make possible their admittance to the United States. Döblin thus ended up at Metro-Goldwyn-Mayer (from October 1940 to October 1941) together with Walter Mehring, Alfred Polgar, John Kafka, and Jan Lustig. Their superior was Georg(e) Froeschel who had been the former chief editor of the publisher Ullstein in Berlin, had emigrated to the United States in 1936, and had worked for MGM since 1939.

Döblin felt out of place, because he misunderstood the situation and function of a film writer in Hollywood and thus rejected it. He did not understand the production needs of the studios, and felt his drafts to be useless because they were rejected: "Wir schrieben viel, [. . .] aber es gelang uns nichts" (*SLW*, 371). But he continued to contribute ideas for scenes (Froeschel, 14), which ended, with the help of George Froeschel, in the final versions of two successful films that were released in 1942, *Mrs. Miniver* (directed by William Wyler, based on the novel by Jan Struther) and *Random Harvest* (directed by Marvin LeRoy, based on a novel by James Hilton) (Kleinschmidt, "Nachwort," 664).

In addition he wrote a first version of "Die Enteisung Grönlands" (The De-icing of Greenland) (first printed in *DHF*, 405–17) based on his great utopian novel *Berge Meere und Giganten* (1924), which was beyond the possibilities of film adaptation — and not just within the American context. Matters stood differently with the scenario "Bergromance" (first printed in *DHF*, 418–33), featuring a wild battle of the sexes, and the fairly complete film draft "Staatsanwalt Fregus" (Prosecutor Fregus) (first printed in *DHF*, 492–534) set in the criminal drug milieu of a Southern state. Although he borrowed motifs from his previous work, Döblin appears here as a skillful script writer, whose basic ideas were still too complicated but would have been usable if reworked as filmscripts usually are. But he never had the chance to rework the scripts, since his limited contract was not renewed, in spite of Thomas Mann's advocacy. Right from the beginning MGM did not intend to continue his contract. The employment offers were the result of a political decision made to enable Döblin's flight from Europe. Hollywood was not interested in epic writers, especially not self-willed ones like Döblin.

Döblin wrote little about his experience in Hollywood. This work was of secondary importance for him anyway, because aside from the script writing, which he disliked, he continued working on his own literary texts. These included (until January 1941) the autobiographical report about his flight, "Robinson in Frankreich" (published in an expanded version in 1949 under the title *Schicksalsreise*), and the second volume of his most extensive work, *November 1918* (published 1948–50). Film had no place either practically or poetologically in his writing.

Döblin's film works were attempts to handle a medium that was not his own. It offered him some formal stimulation, but never assumed a significance of its own. That may be an astonishing statement considering

Döblin's openness to technical innovation, his intellectual flexibility, and his powers of observation. Film and cinema remained a small part of the world of experience from which he drew stimuli for his creative written work. Film stood entirely in the service of his literary praxis and theoretical reflection. Döblin determined the parameters of the influence and did not immerse himself in the unique sphere of the new medium. He is therefore neither a film theoretician nor an author who was poetologically influenced by film. The cinematic quality that is ascribed to Döblin's writing style is based on his own conception of the novel as a "new epic art form." He did not borrow this conception but developed it independently, based on what he recognized as the changed conditions of language and narration that de-emphasized the importance of the author. His new conception opened up for him a mode of writing that may remind us of cinematic modes of narration but did not derive from them.

Radio Theory and Radio Works

The other new medium that appeared at the beginning of the 1920s, radio,[30] fascinated Döblin from the start, including its technical aspects. He was even active as a radio hobbyist.[31] However, he considered the aesthetic possibilities of the radio secondary to those of film. Never would "das Radio [. . .] ganz mit dem Film konkurrieren können — der laufende Bildstreifen ist dem Radio, dem Hörstreifen, weit überlegen" (*KS-3*, 146; "Hörstreifen" refers to the soundtracks of the newly invented sound movies, used sometimes by radio stations instead of records). Instead he saw the radio's significance as a mass medium for the dissemination of information ("Verbreitung der Bildungsbasis," *KS-3*, 146).[32] Beginning in the second half of the 1920s, Döblin participated as "Radioaktive(r)" (*SÄPL*, 260) in radio broadcasts and also created his own, though rather insignificant, contributions for the "Funkstunde."[33] This involvement qualified him, aside from his position as writer and the membership in the Prussian Academy of Art, to take part in the Kassel conference "Literatur und Rundfunk" (Literature and Radio; September 30 to October 1, 1929), organized by the National Radio (Reichsrundfunkgesellschaft) and the academy, where he gave the keynote lecture on the conference theme (*SÄPL*, 251–61).

He extolled the advantages of the new medium due to its ability to reach a much greater public than the print media. Among the areas for which the radio was most suited he mentioned music, followed by news and journalistic contributions.[34] The "fast unglückliche Rolle der Literatur im Rundfunk" took third place (*SÄPL*, 254). However, this was true only for a literary practice that had not yet adapted itself to the new medium. A changed literature that emphasized the spoken rather than the printed word could certainly become effective in the new medium. Döblin considered essays and lyric poetry the ideal genres for the radio, but thought that dramatic writings and prose fiction texts were less well suited. For an effective presentation of drama the optical aspect, the total stage experience relating text and acting, was lacking. In addition, he saw theater as a community-building collective experience, whereas radio, despite its mass audience, appeared to him as an individual listening activity.

Döblin's reservations about radio drama are not lacking in irony. At the same time that he gave his Kassel lecture, a radio version of his experimental drama *Lusitania* of 1919 was broadcast on Leipzig radio on October 18, 1929. It was produced by Hans Peter Schmiedel, and adapted by Döblin himself (see the documentation in *DHF*, 549; Melcher, 186–88). Döblin never commented on the quality of his one-act play broadcast. *Lusitania* had been written before the invention of the radio and was untouched by the public discussions about the radio play in 1924/25 (Stoppe); its largely surreal plot was astonishingly close to the principles of the literary radio play after 1945.

The experimental nature of Döblin's stage play anticipated what a real radio play could do with the medium. This case underscores Döblin's creative independence, who did not necessarily find his solutions through the experience of existing media, but developed them on his own. He anticipated something aesthetically that was realized only later. His forward-looking ideas not withstanding, the pioneering Döblin was an "untimely" author.

In his lecture "Literatur und Rundfunk," Döblin considered radio's possibilities for the modern novel as even more limited than for the drama. For the modern novel that "jedenfalls in [. . .] heutige[r] Form für den Rundfunk [. . .] zu hundert Prozent ausfalle" is "ein Buchroman und für ihn ist der mündliche Vortrag ein Fehler." The author of *Berlin Alexanderplatz* insisted on the principle of rapid reading "über die Seiten" (*SÄPL*, 259), which alone allows for the "Breite, Ausdehnung und [. . .] Fluß" of epic works (*SÄPL*, 258). Listening simply takes too long, Döblin observed. In addition, he viewed the "tönende Sprache" as interfering with the reader's imagination, "das geistig sinnliche Mitphantasieren" and the resulting "notwendige Selbsthypnose" under the direction of the author (*SÄPL*, 259).

All these assessments, which did not go unopposed at the conference, referred to the printed novel (Hay, 131–37; 211–14). A future epic novel, a real *Rundfunkepik,* capable of making use of the characteristic features of the new medium could, in Döblin's view, adjust to the specific conditions of the radio, such as, "Hörbarkeit, Kürze, Prägnanz, Einfachheit" (*SÄPL,* 261). Developing these possibilities would lead to the creation of "wirklichen Hörspielen," which would, on the one hand, break down the barriers between lyrical, dramatic, and epic genre conventions[35] and, on the other hand, allow for the integration of music and sounds. In his critique as well as his theory of radio, Döblin proposed a model for the "Eintritt von Literatur in den Rundfunk" (*SÄPL,* 261).

Speaking on the radio was uncomfortable for Döblin, because the audience was too anonymous for him, "ein Monstrum und besteht aus hunderttausend Einzelwesen" (*SÄPL,* 260). In contrast to other radio theoreticians of the time who, like Brecht, asserted the collective character of radio, which fosters connections and interaction, Döblin saw the radio as "eine typische Erscheinung der Vereinsamung, der Isolation" (*KS-3,* 202). Radio "kennt kein Kollektivum," so that the speaker in front of the microphone has no contact with his audience and is bound "in dieses schauerliche Schweigen jenseits des Mikrophons" (*KS-3,* 203).

Despite such views, which also relate his subjective experience of radio, Döblin was one of the authors who contributed to the history of radio during the Weimar Republic. The radio play *Die Geschichte vom Franz Biberkopf,* based on the novel *Berlin Alexanderplatz* and preserved as a sound recording, is one of the pioneering achievements of an early "radio epic," and clearly exceeded the prevailing standards for radio play production. The decision to make a radio play resulted from Döblin's contemplation of writing a drama based on the work, which he quickly decided would be an unsuitable vehicle for transmitting Biberkopf's "melody of fate": "Es konnte nur ein Rundfunk-Hörspiel oder ein Film werden" (*DHF,* 657).

Despite the congruence on the level of the plot, the radio project is not simply a broadcast version of the novel, but a genuine literary radio piece suited for the medium. The genesis of the radio play is difficult to trace, since there is both an extant script version (*DHF,* 273–317) and a broadcast version that is shortened by about a fifth and preserved only acoustically. Döblin wrote the original text in 1930. The broadcast version, which left out parts of the complex performance structure, was made initially in collaboration with Alfred Braun, the designated director for the broadcast, and then with the actual director Max Bing. Even in its shortened version, the radio play was still far more ambitious than what was considered possible at the time.

The cuts in the script concerned not only obvious political passages but also the mythical and allegorical Job scenes, clearly suggesting the need to sacrifice the novel's complexities. The broadcast version is tighter and more coherent. In general, Döblin's specifically epic collage elements ("voices") were taken out in favor of as clear a structure as possible. This made the text more listener-friendly and sharpened the didactic intent. The multi-layered theme of sacrifice in the novel was reduced in favor of an easy-to-follow story.

Contemporary radio listeners never heard the *Geschichte vom Franz Biberkopf*. An original broadcast date of September 30, 1930 from 8:35 to 10:15 P.M. was said to have been scheduled, but, as we have come to know in the meantime, it was postponed and then entirely cancelled (see the documentation in *DHF,* 559 and 648). Political considerations after the spectacular Reichstag election of September 14, 1930, when the National Socialists gained control of the parliament, obviously played a role, but Döblin's conceptual objections to the cuts seemed to have been important as well (*DHF,* 649). The phonograph recording came about as a result of this cancellation. It was meant to preserve the performance, which featured top actors as speakers (above all Heinrich George as Biberkopf and Hilde Körber as Mieze) for a later broadcast date.

Döblin's attempt at radio literature, which would have given him significant publicity befitting his desire to break out of the "Bildungskäfig" of printed literature (*SÄPL,* 270) thus was practically without consequence. What could have made radio history was preserved in the archive only by good fortune. Not until August 11, 1963 did the newly produced "first broadcast" of the radio play take place on East Berlin radio,[36] based on a transcription of the old phonograph records by Wolfgang Weyrauch. The first West German broadcast, on Norddeutscher Rundfunk, followed soon after on September 15, 1963 . In the 1960s and 70s the old recording of 1930, preserved in the German Radio Archive, was broadcast several times. Its aesthetic effect seems diminished in the face of the rich postwar history of the literary radio play in Germany. What was a pioneering experimental attempt in 1930 lost its impact when taken out of its historical context and in view of the evolution of the genre.

The significance of Döblin's radio play lay in its attempt to mix epic and dramatic elements and creatively to integrate sounds and music in a coherent fashion. Real and surreal elements met. All scenes were cut without transitions, which, in conjunction with the speaking style, gave the whole play an atmosphere of acceleration and agitation. It was the metropolis Berlin that made its appearance on the radio. The piece used a technique of representation that assumed that the listener had a flexible imagination and the capacity to absorb many impressions at once. Döblin thus demanded from the radio listener what he expected from the reader of a novel. In this way Döblin lifted the radio play to the level of his own epic praxis of literature. The spoken texts, which only suggested the Berlin dialect but in no way exactly imitated it, touched only tangentially on the novel. Döblin wrote the radio play as a new text and only programmatic passages, such as the ending, with its discussion about the place of the individual within the collective, was taken from *Berlin Alexanderplatz*. The independent status that Döblin gave the radio play shows him to have been one of the most important authors in the early history of the genre.

Döblin renewed his contact with radio at the outbreak of the Second World War, when between September 1939 and May 1940 he worked for the French "Haut-Commissariat de l'Information" under the direction of Jean Giraudoux. He wrote a memorandum "Hinweise und Vorschläge für die Propaganda nach Deutschland hinein" (Remarks and Suggestions for the Propaganda into Germany) (*SPG*, 404–16) in which audio media (radio, loudspeakers, phonograph records) play a role (Schäffner, 127–40). Drafts by Döblin for "Disques pour le front," that were produced at the time but have since been destroyed, are preserved in his unpublished papers (*SPG*, 416–18). These activities again show him to be conversant with the new media, although they contain intellectual excesses that cannot be overlooked.

After his return from exile, Döblin once again worked on radio essays for the Südwestfunk in Baden-Baden between 1946 and 1952. In particular, he had a regular fifteen-minute radio program under the title "Kritik der Zeit." Held in a casual style, it dealt with current events as well as with literary, philosophical, and social topics.[37] For an analysis of Döblin's perception of the postwar world, these contributions are not uninteresting, but they are unproductive for an explicit engagement with the medium of radio. Döblin was no longer theoretically concerned with the possibilities of radio; he also did not take notice of the beginnings of a new radio play tradition.

Photography

Photography did not interest Döblin in the context of his literary work. Just as with film, he acknowledged it as a part of the modern environment deserving of attention, but he did not make use of it. There is only one text in which he elaborated his views on photography. He wrote the foreword "Von Gesichtern, Bildern und ihrer Wahrheit" (Faces, Images and their Truth, 1929) (*KS-3*, 203–13) to a book of photographs titled *Antlitz der Zeit: Sechzig Aufnahmen deutscher Menschen des 20. Jahrhunderts* (Portrait of our Time: Sixty Photographs of German People of the

Twentieth Century, 1929) by the noted photographer August Sander (1876–1964). It was a selection of photographs from a large documentary project, which Sander brought out in advance. Nothing is known about Döblin's relations with Sander.

Döblin approached the topic of photography from a rather personal point of view. He was at the time concerned with the "Abflachung," the "Verwischung persönlicher und privater Unterschiede" of the human face as a result of two forces: death and the class system of modern society (*KS-3*, 204). Döblin had used for comparison the pictures of death from another book entitled *Das letzte Gesicht* (The Last Face), also published in 1929.[38] They contrast with the images of living people, which in Sander's rendering conveyed the person's occupational and social position rather than his or her individuality. This generalization appealed to Döblin, especially with regard to the prototypical character of Franz Biberkopf in *Berlin Alexanderplatz*, and formed the link to the "collective" face of the dead. It was the transition from an individual identity to a collective one that intrigued Döblin. He felt an affinity with Sander because as author, he was similarly intent on achieving an "alienating" change of perspective: "Plötzlich werden wir uns selber Fremde und haben etwas über uns gelernt" (*KS-3*, 209).

Döblin distinguished Sander's work from that of the group of "aesthetic" and merely "realist" photographers whom he found uninteresting. He saw in Sander and his photographs an epistemological project: "Die Bilder [. . .] sind Worte dieses Philosophen" Sander, who is writing "eine Art Kulturgeschichte, besser Soziologie, der letzten dreißig Jahre" (*KS-3*, 211). This is inspiring to Döblin because the images prompt him to tell stories: "sie laden dazu ein, sie sind ein Material für Autoren" (*KS-3*, 213). The images were comparable to newspaper notices, which had long served Döblin as seeds for his associative storytelling. Sander's photographs increased Döblin's curiosity in this new medium, the usual form of which, photojournalism, had been of little interest to him.

Photography, like film, was essentially foreign territory for Döblin (as was painting).[39] Both media could be integrated within his epic writing practice only in a very limited way. The new media enriched the material foundation of his writing, but they did not change it substantially. Döblin's literary modernity and the pioneering nature of his writing did not result from borrowings from the new media. Rather, they derived from the author's lifelong commitment to language as a productive force.

— Translated by Detlev Koepke

Notes

[1] For 1910, 139 cinema theaters are listed. See *Hätte ich das Kino!* 18.

[2] "Kientopp" (after 1905), out of which arose the word "Kino" (around 1910), which until about 1920 was treated as masculine (der Kino). See H. Paul, *Deutsches Wörterbuch*, 458.

[3] Walter Serner, "Kino und Schaulust" (1913), in Anton Kaes, ed., *Kino-Debatte*, 53–58, here 54.

[4] See Kroebner. Specifically on Döblin (with the older literature), see also Andrea Melcher.

[5] See Kurt Pinthus, *Das Kinobuch* (1914): "The essential aspect of the theater is denied to the cinema: the dialogue, the word" (20).

[6] See, for example, Kurt Pinthus, who saw the cinematic version of a novel by Otto Pietsch, *Das Abenteuer der Lady Glane*, with a narrator: "the background of the pathetic piano tinkling was drowned out by the voice of a narrator [. . .] commenting on the action." *Das Kinobuch*, 9.

[7] The first edition appeared at the end of 1913. In a new edition of 1963, the editor Kurt Pinthus reports on its creation in a new introduction.

[8] See Döblin, "Bemerkungen zum Roman" (1917), where he laments the "Leseunfähigkeit des Publikums," which results in a simplification of the novel. The simplified novel is seen as a negative sign of the times ("das völlige Debakel des Romans"). The fault for this is attributed above all to the newspapers, which aim at a rapid, superficial reading style: "In die gleiche Kerbe wie die Zeitung schlägt der Film" (*SÄPL*, 124).

[9] On the relationship between a literary "cinema style" and the early cinema, see Harro Segeberg on Döblin 211ff.

[10] See also *SÄPL*, 123: "Entselbstung, Entäußerung des Autors, Depersonation." See Erich Kleinschmidt, "Depersonale Poetik."

[11] In this regard one cannot speak of Döblin as having a "filmic" writing style in the customary sense, by which is meant a process of perception and representation that creates aesthetically. See Mirjana Stancic and Thomas Wägenbaur.

[12] See Franz Kafka, *Tagebücher*, November 20, 1913, 95.

[13] Döblin's text was first published in Erich Kleinschmidt, "Roman im 'Kinostil,'" 574–86.

[14] See Döblin to Albert Ehrenstein October 14, 1920: "einen — Film habe ich zu meiner Unterhaltung geschrieben [. . .]." *B I*, 116.

[15] Partial first publication in *Das Dreieck* 1 (1924), 22–24; complete in *DHF*, 325–64.

[16] See Karl C. Führer, especially 741–66.

[17] Reprinted in Pick, *Schriftsteller und Film*, 12.

[18] Paul Wegener, *Der Golem wie er in die Welt kam. Eine Geschichte in fünf Kapiteln* (1921). The only "expressionistic" film that Döblin explicitly remembers later is Robert Wiene's *Caligari* of 1919. See *KdZ*, 120.

[19] On the situation around 1920, see also Jürgen Kasten, regarding the "film poet" Carl Mayer, the creator of the *Caligari* script.

[20] *Die Literarische Welt* 39 (1930): 4.

[21] A casually positive reference to cinema is found in a theater review by Döblin from 1923, "'Kreislers Eckfenster': Zur Überwindung des Dramas" (*KS-2*, 236–38). This is a matter of a technical stage innovation, the "Kreisler stage," with the possibility of rapid scene changes: "Es ist das Überkino," says Döblin, because there exists the possibility of a "erzählende(n) Kinodrama(s)," so that "die Literatur nicht das Kino, sondern das Kino die Literatur geschlagen hat" (238).

[22] This was critically dismantled by Hurst, 256ff. A traditional argument, in contrast, for a "filmic" writing style is made by Melcher, 81ff. See also Wägenbaur, 128ff.

[23] See Christian Jürgens.

[24] Printed version (deviating somewhat from the stage version) in *DHF*, 172–261.

[25] On Hans Wilhelm, see Roden.

[26] On the filming see Eggo Müller, 91–115.

[27] See, for example, Hans Siemsen: "Aus Döblins herrlichem Alexanderplatz-Roman [. . .] kann man keinen Tonfilm machen. Er hätte nur der Anlaß zu einem Tonfilm sein können. [. . .] Von Döblins Dichtung gibt der Film so gut wie nichts" (reprinted in Belach/Bock, 235).

[28] Kracauer, "Literarische Filme," 859.

[29] "Gespräch mit Alfred Döblin." *Licht Bild Bühne*, 1931, No. 240: "Die Photographie — die unverändert die Atmosphäre, das Lokalkolorit des Alexander-Viertels spiegelt, zweitens die Sprache, die Franz Biberkopf unmittelbar sprechen läßt und daher akustisch echter als jeder Roman sein kann, und dann drittens die Begleitmusik, die besonders wirksam das ewig Gleitende in diesem Biberkopfschicksal unterstützt und ausdrücken kann." The passages are reprinted in the edition of *BAD*, 787.

[30] On the subject of radio during the Weimar Republic, see Führer, 766–80; on research on radio, see Harro Zimmermann, 9–27.

[31] In 1928 Döblin wrote in "Ein Brief — kein Interview — über den Rundfunk": "ich war eine ganze Zeit passionierter Bastler" (*KS-3*, 146). Döblin also had his picture taken in front of the technical installations of a film studio. See *Alfred Döblin 1878–1978*, catalogue of the Marbach exhibition, ed. by Jochen Meyer (Munich: Kösel Verlag, 1978), 253, photo no. 128.

[32] On Döblin as a theoretician of the radio see Matthias Prangel, 221–29.

[33] Louis Huguet, *Bibliographie Alfred Döblin*, No. 942, 953–54, 958, 961, 963–64, 968, 977–78. The five extant contributions are reprinted in *KdZ*, 329–74. For a complete listing of Döblin's radio appearances, see Melcher, 199–201 (30 items).

[34] Döblin's ideas for more topical and political programs are sketched out in his response to a survey in 1928, "Zur Ausgestaltung des Programms": "rein mit dem Mikrophon in die Aktualität des täglichen Lebens" (*KS-3* III, 148).

[35] Removing genre boundaries corresponds to Döblin's general poetics in 1930. See for example his programmatic statements in "Der Bau des epischen Werks" (1929): "im Epischen auch lyrisch, dramatisch und reflexiv sein" (*SÄPL*, 227).

[36] Reprinted in Schwitzke, "Sprich, damit ich dich sehe," Vol. 2, 21–58.

[37] The contributions are published in *KdZ*, 26–292 (between October 8, 1946 and September 3, 1950). For commentary on these texts, see Geißler and Birkert.

[38] Edited by Emil Schaeffer with an introduction by Egon Friedell. Zurich: Orell Füssli, 1929.

[39] See his famous, scandalizing talk in the Berlin Sezession exhibit (April 11, 1931), where Döblin, as a representative of all authors, attested to the artists present that paintings, their paintings in particular, no longer spoke to him: "Wenn ich ihre Bilder sehe, spricht das nicht zu mir" (*KdZ*, 371).

Works Cited

Altenloh, Emilie. "Zur Soziologie des Kino. Die Kino-Unternehmung und die sozialen Schichten ihrer Besucher." Diss. phil. Jena 1914.

Berlin Alexanderplatz: Drehbuch von Alfred Döblin und Hans Wilhelm zu Phil Jutzis Film von 1931. Mit einem einführenden Essay von Fritz Rudolph Fries und Materialien zum Film von Yvonne Rebhahn. Munich: edition text + kritik, 1996.

Birkert, Alexandra. "'Kritik der Zeit' (1946–51). Anmerkungen zum 'Neuen Aufklärungsfeldzug' Alfred Döblins im Südwestfunk Baden-Baden." *Internationale Alfred-Döblin-Kolloquien Marbach 1984–Berlin 1985*. Ed. by Werner Stauffacher. Bern: Peter Lang, 1988. 79–92.

Ditschek, Eduard. *Politisches Engagement und Medienexperiment: Theater und Film der russischen und deutschen Avantgarde der zwanziger Jahre*. Tübingen: Narr, 1989.

Fraenkel, Heinrich. *Unsterblicher Film: Die große Chronik: Von der Laterna Magica bis zum Tonfilm*. Munich: Kindler, 1956.

Froeschel, George. "Döblin in Hollywood." *Die Zeit*, No. 24 (June 15, 1962): 14.

Führer, Karl C. "Auf dem Weg zur 'Massenkultur'? Kino und Rundfunk in der Weimarer Republik." *Historische Zeitschrift* 262 (1996): 739–81.

Geissler, Rudolf. "Zusammenbruch und Neubeginn. Zu den Rundfunkkommentaren von Thomas Mann (1940–1945) und Alfred Döblin (1946–1952)." *Literatur für Leser* 19 (1966): 1–16.

Goll, Yvan. "Das Kinodrama" (1920). *Kino-Debatte: Literatur und Film 1909–1929*. Ed. by Anton Kaes. Tübingen: Niemeyer, 1978. 136–39.

Hätte ich das Kino! Die Schriftsteller und der Stummfilm. Exhibition of the Deutsche Literaturarchiv in Marbach (April 24–October 31, 1976). Catalogue by Ludwig Greve, Margot Pehle, and Heidi Westhoff. Munich: Kösel, 1976.

Huguet, Louis. *Bibliographie Alfred Döblin*. Berlin and Weimar: Aufbau-Verlag, 1972.

Hurst, Matthias. *Erzählsituationen in Literatur und Film: ein Modell zur vergleichenden Analyse von literarischen Texten und filmischen Adaptionen.* Tübingen: Niemeyer, 1996.

Jürgens, Christian. "Das 'Man' ohne Eigenschaften oder: Fluchtlinien der Aufschreibesysteme." *Die Perfektionierung des Scheins: Das Kino der Weimarer Republik im Kontext der Künste. Mediengeschichte des Films.* Vol. 3. Ed. by Harro Segeberg. Munich: Fink, 2000. 275–98.

Kafka, Franz. *Tagebücher.* Ed. by Hans-Gerd Koch, Michael Müller, and Malcolm Pasley. Frankfurt am Main: Fischer, 1990.

Kappelhoff, Hermann. "Jenseits der Wahrnehmung — Das Denken der Bilder." *Die Perfektionierung des Scheins: Das Kino der Weimarer Republik im Kontext der Künste. Mediengeschichte des Films.* Vol.3. Ed. by Harro Segeberg. Munich: Fink, 2000. 299–318.

Kasten, Jürgen. "Literatur im Zeitalter des Kinos I. Zur Theorie und Geschichte des Drehbuchs im Stummfilm." *Die Perfektionierung des Scheins: Das Kino der Weimarer Republik im Kontext der Künste. Mediengeschichte des Films.* Vol.3. Ed. by Harro Segeberg. Munich: Fink, 2000. 241–74.

Kino-Debatte: Texte zum Verhältnis von Literatur und Film 1909–1929. Ed. by Anton Kaes. Tübingen: Niemeyer, 1978.

Kittler, Friedrich. *Aufschreibesysteme 1800–1900.* Munich: Fink, 1985.

Kleinschmidt, Erich. "Depersonale Poetik. Dispositionen des Erzählens bei Alfred Döblin." *Jahrbuch der deutschen Schillergesellschaft* 26 (1982): 383–401.

———. "Roman im 'Kinostil.' Ein unbekannter Romanentwurf Alfred Döblins." *Deutsche Vierteljahrsschrift* 63 (1989): 574–86.

Koebner, Thomas. "Der Film als neue Kunst. Reaktionen der literarischen Intelligenz. Zur Theorie des Stummfilms." *Literaturwissenschaft — Medienwissenschaft.* Ed. by Helmut Kreuzer. Heidelberg: Quelle und Meyer, 1977. 1–31.

Kracauer, Siegfried. "Literarische Filme." *Die Neue Rundschau* 42 (1931): 859–61.

Melcher, Andrea. *Vom Schriftsteller zum Sprachsteller? Alfred Döblins Auseinandersetzung mit Film und Rundfunk (1909–1932).* Frankfurt am Main: Peter Lang, 1996.

Müller, Eggo. "Adaption als Medienreflexion. Das Drehbuch zu Phil Jutzis 'Berlin Alexanderplatz' von Alfred Döblin und Hans Wilhelm." *Das Drehbuch: Geschichte, Theorie, Praxis.* Ed. by Alexander Schwarz. Munich: Schaudig, Bauer, Ledig: 1992. 91–115.

Paul, Hermann. *Deutsches Wörterbuch.* 9th edition. Tübingen: Niemeyer, 1992.

Pick, Erika. *Schriftsteller und Film: Dokumentation und Bibliographie.* Berlin: Akademie der Künste der Deutschen Demokratischen Republik, 1979.

Pinthus, Kurt. *Das Kinobuch: Kinodramen.* Leipzig: Kurt Wolff, 1914.

Prangel, Matthias. "Die rundfunktheoretischen Ansichten Alfred Döblins." *Literatur und Rundfunk 1923–1933*. Ed. by Gerhard Hay. Hildesheim: Gerstenberg, 1975. 221–29.

Prodolliet, Ernest. *Das Abenteuer Kino: Der Film im Schaffen von Hugo von Hofmannsthal, Thomas Mann und Alfred Döblin*. Freiburg, Switzerland: Universitätsverlag Freiburg Schweiz 1990.

Roden, Johanna W. "Hans Wilhelm." *Deutsche Exilliteratur seit 1933*. Vol.1. *Kalifornien*. Ed. by John M. Spalek and Joseph Strelka. Bern: Francke, 1976. 827–32.

Sander, August. *Antlitz der Zeit: 60 Aufnahmen deutscher Menschen des 20. Jahrhunderts*. Munich: Kurt Wolff, 1929.

Schäffner, Wolfgang. "Logistik der Dichtung. Döblins kriegs- und medientechnische Erprobung der Literatur im Commissariat à l'information." *Internationales Alfred-Döblin-Kolloquium Paris 1993*. Ed. by Michel Grunewald. Bern: Peter Lang, 1995. 127–40.

Scheunemann, Dietrich. "'Collecting Shells' in the Age of Technological Reproduction. On Storytelling, Writing and the Film." *Orality, Literacy, and Modern Media*. Ed. Dietrich Scheunemann. Columbia, SC: Camden House, 1996. 79–94.

Schuster, Ingrid, and Ingrid Bode, eds. *Alfred Döblin im Spiegel der zeitgenössischen Kritik*. Bern and Munich: Francke, 1973.

Schwitzke, Heinz. *"Sprich, damit ich dich sehe." Vol. 2: Frühe Hörspiele*. Munich: List, 1962.

Segeberg, Harro. "Literarische Kinoästhetik. Aspekte der Kino-Debatte." *Die Modellierung des Kinofilms: Zur Geschichte des Kinoprogramms zwischen Kurzfilm und Langfilm 1905/6–1918* [Vol.2 of *Mediengeschichte des Films*]. Ed. by Corinna Müller and Harro Segeberg. Munich: Fink, 1998. 193–219.

Serner, Walter. "Kino und Schaulust" (1913). *Kino-Debatte: Texte zum Verhältnis von Literatur und Film 1909–1929*. Ed. by Anton Kaes. Tübingen: Niemeyer, 1978. 53–58.

Soppe, August. *Der Streit um das Hörspiel 1924/25: Entstehungsbedingungen eines Genres*. Berlin: Spiess, 1978.

Stancic, Mirjana. *Filmska poetika u ranim pripovijetkama Alfreda Döblina* [The "Filmic Style" in the Early Stories of Alfred Döblin]. Zagreb: Nakl. Zavod MaticeHrvatske, 1994.

Wägenbaur, Thomas. "'Schreiben wie Film.' Joyce, Döblin und die Anfänge interaktiver Literatur im Hypertext." *Macht, Text, Geschichte: Lektüren am Rande der Akademie*. Ed. by Markus Heilmann and Thomas Wägenbaur. Würzburg: Königshausen & Neumann, 1997. 128–42.

Wegener, Paul. *Der Golem wie er in die Welt kam: Eine Geschichte in fünf Kapiteln*. Berlin: Scherl, 1921.

Zimmermann, Harro. "Radio — Modernisierung der Sinne. Forschungsperspektiven zwischen Literatur- und Kulturwissenschaft (am Beispiel der zwanziger Jahre)." *Zeitschrift für Literaturwissenschaft und Linguistik* 28 (1998): 9–27.

Döblin's Political Writings during the Weimar Republic

Wulf Koepke

DÖBLIN'S INTENSE INVOLVEMENT in a wide range of social and political issues during the years from 1918 to 1933 is documented by a wealth of contributions to journals, newspapers, and radio programs. He wrote autobiographical sketches, eyewitness accounts of social and cultural events, commentaries on his works, theater and book reviews, essays on literature and aesthetics, and articles on matters of public health. But above all, Döblin voiced his opinions in political commentaries, very personal and often rambling, and always with an unmistakable sarcastic and witty tone, that he called "Glossen." It is this humorous, satirical perspective that typified both Döblin's own political attitude and that of other intellectuals during these years, among them Kurt Tucholsky (1890–1935) and Erich Kästner (1899–1974). One might say that Döblin, while coming from the tradition of the *feuilleton* and staying close to the witty and deflating style favored by Berlin writers and cabarets, invented his own genre, the "Glosse." It typically mixed firsthand accounts of current happenings with very personal reflections and associations. This associative style switched back and forth between cultural events and street scenes, between comments on the government and the economy, and always sprinkled this discursive mixture with moral reflections. However, while the writer clearly upheld basic values such as honesty, responsibility, and solidarity, and chastised hypocrisy, greed, and selfishness, it is not always possible to pin him down to a clearly defined political position within the context of Weimar politics. He remained an unpredictable free spirit. Many of his contemporaries and a good number of later critics rebuked him for his non-partisanship (Müller-Salget, 249–59, Sebald). The political dimension of Döblin's writings still awaits a detailed analysis in order to assess its place in the context of his entire oeuvre and its relation to the political thinking of other Weimar writers.

The First World War had been a watershed for most German intellectuals with regard to their attitudes toward society and politics. They realized that they could no longer afford the luxury of withdrawing into the ivory tower, to ignore the events of the day and leave politics to the politicians. They had to get involved socially and politically. The loud patriotism of 1914 had been a first spontaneous and unconsidered expression of political engagement. Döblin shared in this widespread chauvinism in his embarrassing article "Reims" of December 1914 (*SPG,* 17–25), in which he defended the destruction of the cathedral of Reims by the German army. However, a more sober reflection followed, together with a serious questioning of authority inspired by his increasing pacifism. Döblin witnessed the German defeat, the revolution, and the resulting anarchy in the Alsatian town of Hagenau, from where his military hospital was repatriated to Berlin after the Armistice in November 1918. His account "Revolutionstage im Elsaß" (Revolutionary Days in the Alsace) ends with the statement: "Ich muß mich erst zurechtfinden" (*SPG,* 71).

Back in Berlin, Döblin tried to make sense of the many strident voices of the time of the "revolution" of November 1918, which did not look like a revolution to him. He joined the USPD, the Independent Social Democratic Party of Germany, the pacifist left wing of the social democrats, without being totally convinced of its course. The USPD tried to establish a position between the reformist SPD and the newly founded revolutionary KPD, the Communist Party of Germany, led by Karl Liebknecht and Rosa Luxemburg. When the USPD dissolved in 1921, Döblin joined the SPD, again without much conviction and without becoming an active member. His true political position can perhaps be best defined as anarchist (Belhalfaoui, 127–28).

His disorientation after returning from Alsace is evident in the "Glossen" written for *Die Neue Rundschau* between 1919 and 1921, and then occasionally in the *Frankfurter Zeitung,* under the pseudonym of "Linke Poot," which literally means "left paw." Döblin published the *Neue Rundschau* articles as a collection, titled *Der deutsche Maskenball* (The German Masked Ball, 1922), which is also the title of one of the contributions. Two chapter headings illustrate Döblin's attitude at this time: "Kannibalisches" and "Überfließend von Ekel" (Overflowing with Disgust). "Linke Poot" sees a world of senseless killing and cruelty in which human beings have turned into cannibals. Other dominant themes are the ongoing starvation and the black market in the wake of the First World War, prostitution, the failure of the churches to provide help and guidance, the general demoralization, the cruelty of the victorious Allies, the ridiculous research being carried out by the Prussian Academy of Sciences, the lack of meaning in modern art. The hope for social renewal that Döblin had in 1918 is soon dashed. Instead of the first German democratic republic, he sees a state more akin to the old feudal and authoritarian order, a "kaiserliche deutsche Republik" (*WuV*, 24). The new government is incapable of reorganizing the social structures or overcoming the outdated attitudes of the old imperial Germany. Döblin the observer is overwhelmed by the aimless mob and the masses of people in the big city that make humane existence impossible. Law and order have been destroyed, and the people do whatever it takes to survive. And yet the semblance of the old order stubbornly persists, especially in the form of hypocrisy. "Linke Poot" is not impressed by the cultural achievements of the day; he sees little true innovation and much pretense. The overall impression is of a grotesque carnival. The Germans are unable to come to grips with their defeat, while the victorious Allies are incapable of committing to a new and just world order. A future war is already in the making.

Between 1921 and 1924 Döblin contributed over eighty reviews on the Berlin theater scene to the liberal *Prager Tagblatt*. The motive was primarily economic, as the galloping inflation forced him to look for extra income in a more stable currency outside Germany. Very much in the style of "Linke Poot," these lively, witty, and satirical reviews were also cutting and disrespectful even of famous names. Döblin frequently combined theater and book reviews, interspersing them with personal observations and political remarks. Döblin's assertion, "Ein Kerl muß eine Meinung haben" (A Guy Must Have an Opinion), accurately expresses his spontaneous and often hastily formed opinions (*KS-2*, 374–6).

In order to illustrate Döblin's method, two texts will be discussed more closely. "Europäische Krise, Gesang, Film" (*KS-2*, 66–70) appeared on 28 April 1922 in the *Prager Tagblatt*. It starts with a very subjective look back on the past theater season. For Döblin, three memorable 1922 productions of earlier plays stand out: *Wenn wir Toten erwachen* (When We Dead Awaken, 1899), Henrik Ibsen's last play; *Die Mütter* (The Mothers, 1896), by Georg Hirschfeld; and *Der Meister* (The Master, 1904) by Hermann Bahr, the latter mostly because of the great performance of Eugen Klöpfer. The plays all deal with Döblin's main concern: the opposition between "real life" on the one hand and business and fatalistic passivity on the other. Döblin then goes on to a performance of the "Englischen Sänger," an a capella group who sing ancient music. From there he jumps to a gala matinee of the movie *Hanneles Himmelfahrt* (Hannele's Ascent to Heaven), based on Gerhart Hauptmann's play of 1893. This provides the occasion for a discussion of cinema. For Döblin, movies are much more important than theater, since many more people see them. He does not mind the occasional tastelessness and enjoys the action on the screen. "Im ganzen: der Film ist auf gutem Wege, nicht das gebildete Publikum" (*KS-2,* 70). The educated audience that considers film barbaric and low-class is wrong in their prejudice: the movies reflect the realities of modern life, even if they do not belong among the "Kulturprodukte." In this manner, Döblin takes his readers from one extreme to the other and tries, above all, to shock and question the values and prejudices of the educated classes, whose taste, he feels, is hopelessly antiquated.

The second review, "Patriotik, Bürger Schippel, Berliner Allerlei" (Patriotism, Citizen Schippel, Berlin Medley), dated 7 March 1923 satirizes German patriotism on the occasion of a performance of Schiller's *Wilhelm Tell* (1804) in which the actor portraying the protagonist seems so passive and soft that it is not convincing when he shoots his arrow. The actor "weiß das bestimmt nur aus der Lektüre des Schauspiels *Wilhelm Tell*" (*KS-2,* 220-23). If he had not read Schiller, he would not know that he was supposed to kill. Döblin enjoys the satire of Carl Sternheim's comedy *Bürger Schippel* (1913), as it shows the transformation of the revolutionary proletarian into a bourgeois. And although the people in the audience enjoy it too, they do not seem to understand that they are seeing a mirror of themselves: "Es fühlt sich keiner getroffen" (*KS-2,* 221). But the real force of Döblin's sarcasm is directed against the performance of Eberhard König's patriotic "Festspiel" in verse, *Stein* (1909), about the Prussian minister Baron von Stein, who along with Hardenberg and Altenstein instituted the reforms of 1807; it was performed somewhere in the Berlin suburbs. Such productions were part of the lively culture of Berlin, but unfortunately, for Döblin, most of the performance was not very enjoyable, especially since it seemed to correspond to the political trend of reactionary patriotism. For Döblin, the seemingly non-political entertainment industry was part of a right-wing escapism that sought refuge from the pressing social and political problems during the early years of the Weimar Republic. In these reviews, Döblin offers a very personal perspective on Berlin's cultural events, conveying some of the atmosphere of postwar life in the city along with his own worldview and social criticism — all of this in witty and sharp language, with an underlying sarcasm that is nevertheless ready to respect true achievements.

Döblin became active in the new writers' organization, the "Schutzverband Deutscher Schriftsteller" (SDS). In 1920, he was elected a member of its committee, and in 1924 he became its president. Together with his fellow writers, he fought against censorship and for freedom of speech and of the press, which was often attacked in the 1920s under the pretense of "pornography."

The anti-Semitic riots of 1923 in the Scheunenviertel, the Jewish quarter of Berlin, led Döblin to become more concerned with the fate of his co-religionists. He refused an offer by Zionist organizations to visit Palestine, but in 1924 traveled to Poland in search of the "genuine Jews," as he called the unassimilated Eastern European Jews. This gave him first-hand experience of traditional Jewish life, as documented in his *Reise in Polen* (1925). At the same time, a visit to the St. Mary's Church in Cracow left a deep religious impression on him that would reemerge during the Second World War.

In 1925, Döblin joined a group of socialist and liberal writers organized by Rudolf Leonhard, the so-called "Gruppe 1925." Among its members were Johannes R. Becher, Ernst Bloch, Georg Kaiser, Hermann Kasack, Oskar Loerke, Walter Mehring, and Bertolt Brecht. Their discussions in the apartment of Marxist philosopher Fritz Sternberg gave Döblin a deeper insight into the tenets of Marxism. Döblin, together with Brecht and Arnolt Bronnen, participated in a number of theater events that turned out to be scandals. In 1926, the "Gruppe 1925" and like-minded writers fought unsuccessfully against the promulgation of the "Gesetz zur Bewahrung der Jugend vor Schund- und Schmutzschriften," in short the "Schund- und Schmutzgesetz," a law that was invoked against what the official censors perceived to be the damaging influence of pornography in literature and art on Germany's youth.

In 1928, Döblin was elected a member of the Section for Literature in the Prussian Academy of the Arts. The section was politically polarized, and Döblin's election succeeded against the votes of right-wing writers Erwin Guido Kolbenheyer (1878–1962), Josef Ponten (1883–1940), and Wilhelm Schäfer (1868–1952). During the following years, numerous conflicts occurred within the section, prompted by the sharply divergent political views of the writers and their conception of the nature and social functions of German literature. Right-wing nationalism stood against the cosmopolitanism of the liberal and left-leaning writers. The conflicts finally led to the resignation of Kolbenheyer and his group and the election of Heinrich Mann as the chairman of the section in 1931. In February 1933, the section was once more reorganized, now in accordance with the dictates of the National Socialist regime. During his membership in the academy, Döblin tried to foster a closer cooperation between it and the Germanistische Seminar of the University of Berlin, represented by Julius Petersen. Also during these years, Döblin gave many readings from his works, appearing in many localities, including radio stations and department stores.

The publication of *Berlin Alexanderplatz* in 1929 made Döblin instantly famous and brought him to the limelight at a time when the Weimar Republic showed many signs of falling apart, and the worldwide economic depression began to be felt in Germany. The political and economic crisis brought to light a latent disorientation of society in general, and of liberal intellectuals in particular. It was felt especially among the students, who saw few professional prospects, had lost their faith in the democratic system, and were groping for help and orientation in their political views. There was a loud cry for action among the young, but nobody seemed to know which way to go. In this situation the parties representing the two political extremes, the Communists and the National Socialists, offered the most attractive alternatives, whereas the Social Democrats and the liberal groups were unable to come up with the necessary solutions. However, a number of intellectuals raised their voices. On July 5, 1930, the journal *Das Tage-Buch* printed an open letter from a student in Bonn by the name of Gustav René Hocke, asking Döblin for advice and orientation.

Döblin's answer grew into a series of letters, which appeared in 1931 in book form under the title *Wissen und Verändern! Offene Briefe an einen jungen Menschen*. It was a programmatic statement of Döblin's social and political beliefs, and is symptomatic for the position of liberal intellectuals during the last years of the Weimar Republic. It confronts one of the crucial questions for the young generation: what should be their views about Marxism and the Socialist parties? Surprisingly, an equally important question was conspicuously ignored: what was to be done about the rise of National Socialism? After all, the Nazis had scored a stunning victory in the Reichstag elections of September 1930, which condemned the government to rule by emergency decrees without a working parliamentary majority.

It is also surprising to see that Döblin dismissed capitalism as a possible alternative. But in his view, capitalism led to poverty and degradation. Therefore, socialism was the only path toward a more humane and democratic social system. However, the Russian experiment, while infinitely better than Western capitalism, had resulted in "Kollektivismus mit Staatskapitalismus" (*WuV*, 140). Class struggle never results in real socialism. Döblin's position was to affirm "die urkommunistische der menschlichen individuellen Freiheit, der spontanen Solidarität und Verbindung der Menschen" (*WuV*, 142). Human individual freedom, spontaneous solidarity, and cooperation among people remained the basis for his political ideas, which did not follow Marxist and Leninist party doctrines and strategies. Instead, Döblin's political ideas share certain similarities with those of Peter Kropotkin (1842–1921), whose "communist anarchism" also emphasizes human individualism, mutual help, and solidarity. Döblin remarks that his answers and ideas are meant for the "geistige Menschen," a term that corresponds loosely but not exactly to the word "intellectual." These "geistige Menschen," although hard to define in sociological terms, were considered a separate social group in the discourse of the 1920s. Döblin's emphasis on the "geistige Menschen" and their beliefs shows an affinity to Karl Mannheim's (1893–1947) "sociology of knowledge," which Mannheim expounded in his book *Ideologie und Utopie* (1929). Mannheim insisted on the freedom of the "geistige Menschen" from party politics and prescribed ideologies, and maintained that intellectuals were "freischwebend," free-floating, that is, not belonging to any specific social class or political party. Döblin's statement that the "Zugang zum Volk wird in Deutschland durch die Parteien versperrt" (*WuV*, 144) expressed his rejection of party politics and class warfare. Economic interests and party ideologies prevented dialogue between the people and the intellectuals. Döblin distinguished between the workers and their leaders or theoreticians. The workers have the right instincts, but they are easily misled. Döblin's goal is a humanistic, non-ideological socialism. It can be argued that he pursued this political goal all his life, even after his conversion to Catholicism.

Döblin also commented on what he viewed as the moral and political degradation of the German "Bürgertum." This German bourgeoisie or middle class had been unable to maintain its liberty against the absolutist princes because it followed Martin Luther's commandment to be obedient to one's worldly rulers. The "Bürger" turned into an obedient subject. Therefore, the intellectual could not now find his place among the middle class, which had betrayed its own ideals of liberty and justice. The only possible place for the intellectual is at the side of the working class, which has assumed the struggle for the ideals that the bourgeoisie has forsaken. The focus of Döblin's argument is to find the correct place for intellectuals within the socialist movement.

Döblin also polemicizes in *Wissen und Verändern!* against Marxist materialism. He argues against Marxism's reduction of human beings and their history into purely economic terms, and confronts the Marxist view of history with his own kind of "dialektischen Naturismus" (*WuV*, 211). For Döblin the scientist, the basis of human life is the interaction with nature, both animate and inanimate, and correspondingly, the interaction of mind and body. Ideas are by no means a mere superstructure of material conditions, as Marx proposes. On the contrary, ideas are the prime movers of human history, and thus knowledge and the clarity of ideas are the precondition for any solution to the seeming impasse of the time.

In addition, Döblin claims in *Wissen und Verändern* that the theoreticians of the working class movement are wrong. On the one hand, they are too much influenced by bourgeois thinking, and on the other, are given to too many utopian dreams. Döblin characterizes the two main parties, the SPD and the KPD, as deviations from the true idea of socialism. The "reformist" SPD is already largely assimilated into the bourgeoisie, whereas the revolutionary and dictatorial KPD insists on radical change of society, leading to the dictatorship of the proletariat. The ideas of Marx can be helpful, as they are opposed to the policies of the socialist parties, but it is also necessary to go beyond Marx. It is the responsibility of the "geistige Menschen" to rise above the existing class divisions and their ideologies, and to work out and communicate the ideas of a true humanism based on solidarity, peace, justice, and the end of the exploitation of labor. At the end of *Wissen und Verändern*, Döblin tells Hocke to consider these political ideas: "Seien Sie ohne Sorge, dann wissen Sie auch bald, was Sie zu tun haben" (231). What Döblin means is: find your own way and think it through.

Wissen und Verändern! was widely reviewed (Schuster/Bode, 267–304). As the majority of the reviewers noted, it was definitely not a blueprint for action, and maybe not even helpful advice. At best, it emphasized a humane socialism characterized by voluntary association instead of the coercive power of states and political parties. Typically, Döblin's ideas led to a discussion group that met in his home, and not to a political movement. This group disbanded in 1933. It is revealing that in 1938–39 Döblin became part of another group of disenchanted communists that held its meetings in Paris, including Willi Münzenberg, Arthur Koestler, and Manès Sperber. Although this group, along with its journal, *Die Zukunft* (The Future), was swept away by the events of the Second World War, its experiences and worldview were recorded in important texts. This political background has to be kept in mind for the evaluation of the novel *November 1918* and also for Döblin's Christian confessions.

Döblin repeatedly warned of the dangers and the power deriving from German feudalism and its political and military organizations in texts ranging from *Der deutsche Maskenball* to *November 1918*. However, the name "Hitler" and "National Socialism" do not appear in *Wissen und Verändern!* Apparently, even after September 1930, Döblin considered the Nazis a short-lived phenomenon, soon to be forgotten after the end of the economic depression. *Wissen und Verändern!* is symptomatic for the final years of the Weimar Republic, both in its desperate and utopian outlook, and its lack of perspective on the need for immediate concrete political action and change. Döblin, like others, was considering the wider perspective without being aware that the Weimar Republic was on the point of coming to a catastrophic end. He did not immediately recognize the significance of Hitler's rise to power or the consequences for his own life. In February 1933, when Döblin was warned that it was high time to escape from Germany, he was completely unprepared for his life in exile.

During the years 1919 to 1933, Döblin maintained his presence on the literary scene in Berlin. He represented the type of the urban writer who got involved in all facets of life, who was open to new ideas and developments, who liked controversy and debate, and whose writings encompassed a wide variety of genres. It would be one-sided and wrong to consider Döblin only a novelist. His essayistic and other writings are mostly responses to problems of the day and were meant to make a difference in political and cultural life. His political and social views were expressed in *Wissen und Verändern!* and elaborated further in *Unser Dasein*. This book, published in Germany in spring 1933, moves from a philosophy of nature to a conception of anthropology and human history, with a special emphasis on the fate of the Jewish people, and provides the underpinnings for Döblin's political and social attitudes. These attitudes are reflected in the epic narratives of *Amazonas* and *November 1918;* even in exile they retained their utopian character, while trying to come to grips with the tragic failure of the Weimar Republic and the impossibility of realizing a humanistic form of socialism. But Döblin's vision of voluntary solidarity seems to have been too idealistic for the political realities of the 1930s and the foreseeable future.

Works Cited

Beyer, Manfred. "Vorwort." Alfred Döblin. *Ein Kerl muß eine Meinung haben: Berichte und Kritiken 1921–1924.* Munich: dtv, 1981. 5–14.

Belhalfaoui, Barbara. "Alfred Döblin und die Sozialdemokratie." *Internationale Alfred-Döblin-Kolloquien Marbach a.N. 1984–Berlin 1985.* Ed. by Werner Stauffacher. Bern: Peter Lang, 1988. 127–42.

Koepke, Wulf. "Alfred Döblins Überparteilichkeit. Zur Publizistik in den letzten Jahren der Weimarer Republik. *Weimars Ende: Prognosen und Diagnosen in der deutschen Literatur und politischen Publizistik 1930–1933.* Ed. by Thomas Koebner. Frankfurt: Suhrkamp, 1982. 318–29.

Links, Roland. "*Der deutsche Maskenball* von Linke Poot." *Mare Balticum 1999.* 96–100.

Müller-Salget, Klaus. *Alfred Döblin: Werk und Entwicklung.* 2nd rev. ed. Bonn: Bouvier, 1988.

Riley, Anthony W. "*Berlin, im Dezember* (1926). Ein unbekannter Artikel Alfred Döblins." *Internationales Alfred-Döblin-Kolloquium Leipzig 1997.* Ed. by Ira Lorf and Gabriele Sander. Bern: Peter Lang, 1999. 83–96.

Schuster, Ingrid, and Ingrid Bode, eds. *Alfred Döblin im Spiegel der zeitgenössischen Kritik.* Bern/Munich: Francke, 1973.

Sebald, Winfried G. "Alfred Döblin oder die politische Unzuverlässigkeit des bürgerlichen Literaten." *Internationale Alfred-Döblin-Kolloquien Basel 1980– New York 1981–Freiburg i.Br. 1983.* Ed. by Werner Stauffacher. Bern: Peter Lang, 1986. 133–9.

Vanoothuyse, Michel. "*Linke Poot.* Le débuts de Weimar et les intellectuels." *Études allemandes* 6 (1993): 215–28.

Döblin, the Critic of Western Civilization: The *Amazon* Trilogy

Helmut F. Pfanner

IN AN AUTOBIOGRAPHICAL TEXT titled "Epilog" (*SLW*, 304–21), written and published in 1948, Döblin comments extensively on the genesis of his tripartite novel now commonly known as the *Amazon* trilogy. The author remembers the days he spent in the Bibliothèque Nationale in Paris during the mid-1930s looking at maps of South America and studying the historical accounts of this southern portion of the Western Hemisphere. The reader cannot overlook the spontaneity with which the author approached his subject; he had hardly any prior knowledge, but soon began asking some serious questions.

> Eines zog das andere nach sich. Ich las von den indianischen Ureinwohnern, stieg in ihre Geschichte und las, wie die Weißen hier eindrangen. Wo war ich hingeraten? Wieder das alte Lied, hymnische Feier der Natur, Preis der Wunder und Herrlichkeiten dieser Welt? Also wieder eine Sackgasse? (*SLW*, 315)

While phrases like "Wieder das alte Lied?" and "wieder eine Sackgasse?" recall some of Döblin's earlier works, such as *Berge Meere und Giganten*, which had received little more than "eine Art Achtungserfolg" (*SLW*, 311), the passage as a whole seems to question the author's achievements at a time when he was living with his family in exile in France, and the world he knew was threatened by political usurpers in Germany. Döblin added several more paragraphs to the passage above in order to justify not only his choice of a topic that was both geographically and historically remote — and thus might appear as an escape from reality — but also to state its social and political relevance. By mentioning the missionary Bishop Las Casas, who during the final chapters of the first part of the trilogy emerges as a positive counterforce to the murderous and greedy European conquerors of South America, and by calling the entire first book a "Vorspiel" to what still was to come, the author stresses the structural significance of the last two books and the thematic unity of the entire opus. Döblin summarizes the three parts as an attempt to fulfill three goals: (1) "diesem Flußmeer zu geben, was des Flußmeeres war, auch die Menschen zu zeichnen, und die Weißen nicht aufkommen zu lassen," (2) to portray "den großen Menschheitsversuch, die Jesuitenrepublik am Paraná," and (3) "die furchtbare, trostlose, brütende Verlorenheit, die nachbleibt, zu zeichnen" (*SLW*, 315–16). The accuracy of this assessment will become apparent in my close reading of the trilogy and in my interpretation of it as a thematically consistent expression of Döblin's criticism of Western civilization.

Due to Döblin's epic style of narration, the reader may not immediately see the connection between the various plots and subplots of the three parts of the trilogy. In the first part, titled *Das Land ohne Tod* (*LoT*), with no, or at the most, only minimal auctorial interference, the author depicts a broad tapestry of the conditions in the Amazon region before the arrival of the Europeans, and he relates the stories of several conquering expeditions. In addition to the Amazon, the neighboring areas now belonging to Venezuela, Peru, Bolivia, and Ecuador make up the geographical background to this volume. The second part, titled *Der blaue Tiger* (*DbT*), is by far the most extensive one of the three volumes. It gives a vivid account of the foundation, development, and demise of the Jesuit missions in a section of land that today is shared by Argentina, Paraguay, and Uruguay. Here too the narration frequently shifts between plots and subplots, which — in addition to the multi-faceted story of the Jesuit missions itself — include the sea voyage of the first Jesuits to South America and their experiences in Piratininga (later renamed Sao Paolo) and the skirmishes between the attacking Paolists and the defending missions.[1] Also included are the professional and private activities of Church officials outside the missions, as well as scenes at the royal courts in Spain and Portugal, and at the Vatican. In the third part, titled *Der neue Urwald,* the main action does not even take place in South America, but in Central Europe, specifically Poland, Germany, and France, and it is only in the latter portion, subtitled "Abgesang," (*DnU*, 121–76), in which the narrator returns to parts of Guyana and, bordering on it, a mountainous portion of Northern Brazil. In this part, several characters vie for the position of principal protagonist until a Polish playboy named Jagna assumes this role; he reemerges in "Abgesang" under the new name Vivien, which is then changed once again to Kungereku by the Indians at the very end of this book. What complicates the reader's understanding of this trilogy even further than its many plots and subplots is the narrator's frequent changes of perspective in the form of "erlebte Rede" (interior monologue) and Döblin's overall distancing of himself from the changing scenes of narration.

Readers not used to Döblin's epic style will do well to remember that it is not a single plot, or even a combination of several plots, that form the structural unity of this novel. The key to our understanding of the trilogy lies in its many thematic parallels and correspondences, occurring in both diachronic and synchronic patterns. They all relate to the main themes of the trilogy and provide a lucid reflection of the author's pessimistic view of Western civilization. However, "Western" in this context is no mere synonym for "European" or "North American"; rather it stands for any progressive phase of social and technological development anywhere on Earth in which people fall out of harmony with nature. Therefore, in Döblin's view, the people of the so-called "primitive" cultures are no less prone to the adverse effects of life devoid of harmony with nature than the people of technologically advanced societies. One of the most distinguishing marks of the *Amazon* trilogy is that it reflects the dangers of progressing civilizations at various stages of development, from the South American cultures of a bygone era to those of contemporary Europe. In Döblin's perspective then, the civilizing development was also underway in South America at the time of arrival of the conquistadores, though it had not yet reached the crisis stage that he saw in what is commonly referred to as the "West."

If one considers the more or less chronological sequence of the three parts of the novel, it may come as no surprise that the trilogy depicts a progressive separation of human beings from their original harmony with nature. The circle from beginning to end ends, at least in theory, in the first and the fifth chapters of *Der neue Urwald,* in which the Polish equivalent of the German Faust, Jan von Twardowski, a figure from the Middle Ages, comes back to the present. He calls upon the great European thinkers and scientists of the Renaissance, above all Copernicus, Galilei, and Giordano Bruno, and asks them to recant their ideas that have led to the inventions and discoveries of modern times. While Copernicus and Galilei, in line with their historically compromised characters, quickly accept their guilt and hide their faces in shame, it takes some persuasion on Twardowski's part to make Bruno admit his guilt. But finally the Italian theologian, who had defended his belief on the funeral pyre, cannot deny the negative consequences of his historical insistence on truth in a world infected with dogmatism and superstition; and he comes to lament his part in having precipitated humanity's misguided course of development:

> Es ist eine geschändete Menschheit. Wir haben alles umsonst getan. Sie sitzen tiefer in Schande als in unserer Zeit. Wir haben ihnen alles gege-

ben, was wir sahen und fühlten. Und dies haben sie daraus gemacht, dies ist daraus geworden: die Möglichkeit, sich an kein Gesetz zu halten, alles zu verklären, was ihrer Bosheit einfällt, sich gegen jedes Gefühl abzuhärten. Wo gibt es eine Gemeinheit, vor der sie zurückschrecken, welche Lüge schleudern sie nicht unter die Menschen. Ja, das geschieht, und ich hab es gesehen und gehört. (*DnU,* 116)

Bruno ends his expression of regret with a call for the destruction of the modern world, but he also expresses hope for humanity's redemption on the individual level, that is, in the experience of suffering — thus becoming a clear spokesperson for the author. His appeal for social and moral reform comes to a climax in words that he utters in a sharp hissing voice: "Die Zeit wird reif. Rettet die Menschheit vor dem Untergang! O geschändete Welt! O herrliche Erde" (*DnU,* 118). To be sure, Bruno's spark of hope does not carry over to Twardowski, who condemns the former for his adverse part in history. However, the last word in the two men's debate is reserved for Bruno at the end of the ghostly conversation in the cathedral of Cracow, as he appeals to humankind for a change in its further course of development. This historical dialectic, as expressed in the discussion between two figures — individual human egotism versus life in harmony with innocent nature — forms the common denominator of the three parts of the novel, and combines all its apparently diffuse sections.

On the one side of the dialectic, there are characters in all three parts of the novel who demonstrate a strong greed for wealth and power. This greed drives the European conquerors to cross the Atlantic Ocean and search for new land, and to decimate and enslave the native Indian population. Yet the narrator claims that the white conquerors' cruel and brutal methods are not much different from those soldiers who fight the wars in Europe, wars that are the cause of European princes' need for gold and other riches from the New World. The Europeans' hunger for wealth continues on an even larger scale during the time that is depicted in *Der blaue Tiger,* in which the narrator focuses upon the new settlers in the emerging cities along South America's east coast and in its hinterland. Not only self-elected "kings" such as Nicolaus Riubuni but wild gangs under nameless leaders rob and attack both the native Indian population and the prosperous Jesuit missions. Finally, in *Der neue Urwald* the narrator focuses upon a few individuals who in their personal relationships typify the more general situation of the modern human masses. Two young Germans, who carry the non-descriptive names Posten and Klinkert, and their Polish counterpart Jagna, demonstrate extremely selfish behavior, and their egotism in both professional and personal matters has become symptomatic for modern civilized man.

Döblin thus tells the reader that the basis of people's social and political behavior has remained the same during the past three hundred years, and that the whites' mistreatment of the Indians in *Das Land ohne Tod* continues in the battle of the sexes in *Der neue Urwald*. In each case people use others as objects. How the same motive has become characteristic of human behavior at historically different times is also expressed in linguistic terms: the captain named Puerto who has vowed to make it his daily task to kill a dozen Indian natives justifies his action by calling his victims "Unkraut" (*LoT*, 220), thus echoing Nazi propaganda for the treatment of Jews and gypsies during the time Döblin was writing the novel. The reader can see another parallel to the persecution of political and racial minorities during the Third Reich when Jagna sees his female victims "nicht als Damen, Fräulein, sondern als Sachen, Tiere" and when he chases after women, bis "das Wild gestellt ist" (*DnU*, 38). The three parts of the trilogy are connected by the many cases of human beings subjugating other human beings. One incident occurs in the second part of the trilogy, when the self-proclaimed king Riubuni uses slaves to carry him in a carriage in an effort to set himself apart from the natives, "da jetzt sogar die Wilden schon beritten waren" (*DbT*, 186). Ironically, his power comes to an end when he is killed by another Paolist. A similar rupture of a chain of power occurs in the third part, when Jagna uses and betrays Marianne, a married woman, after she has been deserted by her husband. Since Marianne sees no other way out of her emotional dilemma but suicide, Jagna must also bear the responsibility for her death; he further adds to his guilt when he kills her husband, although there is a certain element of self-defense (*DnU*, 51).

In sharp contrast to the greed and cruelty of the above-mentioned individuals, and representing the other side of the dialectic, the trilogy is also inhabited by others who live in peace and harmony with their surroundings. For instance, when the first white men appear among a tribe of Indians in *Das Land ohne Tod* and fall sick from drinking the water that the Indians poisoned through their method of catching fish, the Indians nurse the whites back to health. To the Native Americans it is incomprehensible why the whites, as soon as they are well, shoot their guards and disappear without leaving a token of gratitude (*LoT*, 18–26). Also, when the Indians kill animals, it is not out of greed. Seeing them as their ancestors, they depend on them as means of survival (*LoT*, 240). In *Der blaue Tiger* entire Indian tribes align themselves with the Jesuits, for they see in them their protectors from persecution by the Paolists.

The Indians' peaceful example has such a strong influence on the Jesuits that one of them, named Mariana, becomes so enchanted by their nature rituals that he too paints his face and participates in their dances (*DbT*, 91–100). By the same token, his superior, named Emanuel, finds it hard to resist the feminine charm of an Indian woman called Maladonata and is thus lured by nature (164–66). Also feeling the positive attraction of nature, the prisoners who escaped a *bagno* in French Guyana are taken in by a remote tribe of Indians, where they receive food and shelter and the care of the medicine man (*DnU*, 160).[2] The Indians' greatest fear is the Blue Tiger, a mythological animal that symbolizes war and conquest by outsiders. Periodically the Blue Tiger brings disaster into the world and destroys the humans' habitat. Therefore, when the Indians witness the destructive ways of the whites, they first perceive them not as people but as metaphysical beings, thinking that the Blue Tiger has returned to Earth. The Indians' initial respect, which later is changed to fear, is increased by the fact that some of the whites ride on horses, a practice that the Indians have never seen before.

It is interesting to note that Döblin has reserved the tiger metaphor for the title of the second part of the trilogy, in which Indian culture plays a much smaller role than in the first part. He thereby underlines the connection between the progress of European culture in South America and the natives' justified fear of the whites. By the same means he also buttresses the thematic bridge between the three parts by making the destructive force of war and human competition the dominant literary motif of the entire novel. Nevertheless, the tiger metaphor is spun throughout the three parts. In *Das Land ohne Tod* the whites are said to be "wilde Tiger" (58);[3] in *Der blaue Tiger* Pater Montoya refers to the white city dwellers as "Tiger und Löwen," when he asks rhetorically why the Indians, referred to as a "Lammherde," are supposed to fear them (235, also 381); and in *Der neue Urwald* the same metaphor is contained in the words of an old Indian man: "Am Himmel unter dem Lager des Großen Vaters liegt der blaue Tiger. Wenn die Erde schlecht wird, gerät der Große Vater in Zorn, schickt den blauen Tiger auf die Erde und läßt zerstören" (170, also 176).

In accordance with the polarity of Döblin's cultural dialectic, the metaphor of the Blue Tiger has its antipode in the metaphor of the water spirit Sukuruja. This mythological figure plays a dominant role in the first part of the trilogy, where it represents the glorification of innocent nature in opposition to the destructive force of human beings. Interrupting his story of a matriarchal society, the narrator inserts two short sentences, set off as a single paragraph: "Sukuruja, die große Mutter des Wassers, stieg in den Fluß. Der Fluß schwoll und streckte sich stolz und glücklich" (*LoT,* 72). The spirit of Sukuruja ominously reemerges with the appearance of the white men (*LoT,* 83–84), and it takes on the form of a snake moving between the trees of the jungle as the power of the whites increases (262–63, also 280 and 281) until it disappears again, at least temporarily, in the waters of the Amazon at the end of *Das Land ohne Tod.*

Although the second part of the trilogy is longer than either of the other two, there is less mention of Sukuruja; it relates the story of the gradual transformation of virgin land into the blossoming colonies of the European missionaries. However, when the young Jesuit Mariana adopts Indian ways, he succumbs to the call of the water spirit and drowns in the rapids of the River Parañá (*DbT,* 103–4). Sukuruja is also mentioned during the final chapters of *Der blaue Tiger,* where the water spirit keeps the Indians connected closely to nature (325 and 337). In *Der neue Urwald* the water spirit is not mentioned as long as the action takes place in Europe, but it reappears and dominates the third part's closing chapter, following the disappearance of the European fugitives in the unmapped jungle of the border region between French Guyana and Brazil (*DnU,* 181–82).

All through the novel it is water that attracts people in their attempt to escape the negative forces of civilization. Following the course of the great Amazon River in an easterly direction, the Indian tribes attempt to escape the adverse consequences of historical development by seeking the "Land without Death." This place, ironically, turns out to be the sea (a significant symbol in Döblin's work), where the search comes to an end, and where the wandering Indians finally join their ancestors in their permanent home. The message is clear: the "Land without Death" cannot be found on earth because it exists only in the state of death itself, wherein there is no more death.

This lesson also must be learned by the Europeans, whose political and social struggles constitute a constant "Kampf gegen den Tod" (*LoT,* 86). No wonder then that the whites too, in their search for eternal life, come into such close contact with water: in order to reach the Western Hemisphere, they must cross the Atlantic Ocean; and after their landing on the north coast of South America, they follow the course of the rivers in their search of the "Südmeer" and of the Amazon River's estuary. Consequently, Orellana and his companions disappear from history on their adventurous trip along the Amazon (*LoT,* 84), and one of the German mercenaries in the service of Spain, Nicolaus Federmann, drowns near the coast of Venezuela before he can realize his plan of returning to Europe (196). As previously mentioned, the young Jesuit drowns when he tries to cross the River Paraña (*DbT,* 104); and although the escapees from the Guyana *bagno* lose their lives in the unmapped region between Guyana and Brazil, they are summoned by the spirit of the Amazon River (*DnU,* 173). However, what distinguishes the disappearance of the white invaders from the death of the natives is that the whites are generally not missed by anyone: " [. . .] die Nachricht vom Tode des Kaplans rührte keinen" (*LoT,* 99), while the dead natives live on in the dances and the memories of their survivors (266).

At this point it is necessary to note that the polarity in Döblin's novel is not just one of Europeans versus Native Americans. To be sure, both groups belong to almost diametrically opposed stages of human development: one characterized by harmony with their fellow man and nature, the other by brutality toward others and attempts to dominate nature. But the Indians too are prone to disunity, which Döblin sees as a major cause of historical degeneration. This becomes evident early on in the first part of the trilogy, where the disunity of the Indian tribes is seen as being responsible for their political vulnerability (*LoT,* 34–35 and 57). Similarly, in the second part, Indian tribes let themselves be used by the Paolists to fight against other tribes (*DbT,* 178). In the third part, finally, the Indians are horrified by the European idea of social justice. They suggest that, rather than the poor killing the rich, it should be the other way around because they see the poor as disturbers of the peace who lack authority. This is argued in full awareness of the disunity among the whites in Europe, a disunity that accompanies them into the new land, filling the Indians with fear and foreboding (*DnU,* 169). The most obvious indication of the Indians' danger of going in the direction of the whites is in their relationship of the sexes: after the warrior women have overthrown their male dominators at the beginning of *Das Land ohne Tod,* their political system soon develops into a female tyranny over men (278–79). The force of Döblin's observation is not diminished by the fact that, in his description of the matriarchy of the Amazons, the author, with his customary disregard for historical facts, attributes the source of the name "Amazons" to the river rather than to its etymologically correct source in Greek mythology. A future synthesis of the rights of the two sexes seems to be suggested by the image of men and women fighting together against their common enemies.

On the other hand, not all the Europeans are depicted as negative counter-poles to the innocence of many of the Indians. The best example of a positive European in Döblin's narrative is of course Las Casas, the Spanish missionary bishop, whose figure emerges in stark contrast to the greedy conquistadores in *Das Land ohne Tod.* The clergyman is respected by the Indians as a defender of human rights as much as he is belittled by the members of his own ethnic group. The bishop even brings about a change of heart in the previously mentioned captain, Puerto, who has vowed to kill a dozen Indians each day. Following Las Casas's reasoning and request, Puerto renounces his horrific vow and even feels remorse before his death (*LoT,* 247). In an inner vision, Las Casas sees himself before the king of his native country, Spain, accusing him of having forsaken his responsibility as a Christian ruler by letting his vassals tyrannize the native populations of the Western Hemisphere (*LoT,* 234). Later, no longer dreaming, Las Casas reports his observations of the atrocities committed by the Europeans in New Spain to his superiors in Europe, but finds no understanding and is ridiculed for being senile and "kindisch" (*LoT,* 253). Speaking as the author's mouthpiece, and as such anticipating the immoral acts depicted in the third part of the trilogy, Las Casas renounces his task as a missionary to the Indians: "Wenn ich könnte und noch jung wäre, würde ich diese Länder hier verlassen und würde in die wilden Länder gehen, nach Europa, und versuchen das Christentum zu predigen. Aber ich bin alt und hoffnungslos" (*LoT,* 241). It is certainly also an expression of Döblin's sympathetic view of the Spanish missionary when he lets him die in harmony with nature, embraced by the water spirit Sukuruja, in obvious deviation from historical fact since the real Las Casas died only after his return to Europe.

But even the greedy and bloodthirsty conquistadores, when they are seen as individuals, are no negative absolutes on Döblin's polar scale of civilized history. He repeatedly makes this point when he states that even the most cruel conquerors were no worse than the others. For example, his judgment of Ambrosius Alfinger, a German mercenary in the service of the Spanish king, is that he was "nicht schlechter als die andern" (*LoT,* 94); this comes shortly after we have learned that Alfinger ordered his dogs to devour a group of Indian prisoners and to have seventy more Indians beheaded in order to intimidate the population of a village into handing over its gold treasures. With the same modification of judgment, the narrator says of another notorious conqueror, the Spaniard Ximenes von Quesada, "Er war nicht schlechter oder besser als andere. Was ihn trieb, wußte er sowenig wie die andern" (*LoT,* 104). These words also express Döblin's assessment of the complete senselessness of the Europeans' hunt for wealth and power, a thought pervading all three parts of the trilogy and reaching its climactic expression in *Der neue Urwald,* when its protagonist Jagna renounces his life as a European playboy and joins a group of prisoners sent to the French Guyana *bagno.*

Closely connected to the question about the logic or insanity of the Western striving for wealth and power is the notion of its implied guilt. Most of the invaders of South America give no thought to the unethical basis of their actions, or they simply try to justify their human misdeeds with their loyalty to the Spanish — or in the case of the Paolists, the Portuguese — crown (e.g., *LoT,* 96 and 242). The fact that such reasoning itself does not fully reflect reality is contained in Las Casas's words to a group of Spanish soldiers: "Wir sind von der Krone nicht hergeschickt worden, und der Heilige Vater von Rom hat das Land nicht darum der Krone Spaniens zugesprochen, damit wir hier die Sintflut spielen und das Lebende ausrotten" (*LoT,* 236). However, even if there were some truth to their attempted excuse, the invaders would be hard pressed to find the answers to the questions posed by the Indian leader Zippa to a group of murderous Europeans:

> Warum bleibt ihr nicht zu Hause, sät und erntet? Warum zerstört ihr unser Land? [. . .] Euer Papst und der König leben jenseits des Meeres. Niemand hat sie hier gesehen. Sie kennen unser Land nicht. Wie kann der Papst dem König ein Land schenken, das er nicht kennt und das ihm nicht gehört, und wie kann der König solch Geschenk annehmen? (*LoT,* 138)

The whites have no answer to these questions, or their attempted response only reflects their imperialistic and militaristic thinking: "Wenn er [der Zippa] eine Anwort haben will, so soll er Leute ausstatten, wie der König uns ausgestattet hat, und soll ihnen befehlen, über das Meer zu fahren. Sie werden die Antwort erhalten" (*LoT,* 139). In Döblin's view, the question of guilt falls back on the conscience of each individual. This realization pervades the stream-of-consciousness lamentation of Captain Puerto shortly before his death, a death which he accepts as a just punishment for his misdeeds and with the knowledge that his life, like that of the Indians, has been a futile search for the "Land without Death":

> Jach, liebe Mutter, hast mich geboren und bin ein Lump gewesen und hab dich verlassen, jach, liebe Mutter, ich dank dir, daß ich lebe. Jach lieber Vater, hast mich gezeugt, Räuber werden lassen, Lump, hab dich verflucht und verrucht. Dank, lieber Vater, ich dank dir. (*LoT,* 248)

Puerto's acceptance of his wretched life and death anticipates the existential questioning of the prisoners on their way to the *bagno* in French Guyana toward the end of the third part of the trilogy, where the above quotation reoccurs with a slight variation (*DnU,* 141). In each situation the characters take stock of their lives in a manner very similar to that of the vagabond poet François Villon, who before his untimely death lamented the adverse circumstances of his wretched life.[4] Since the narrator speaks these words in the form of stream-of-consciousness without quotation marks, the reader of *Der neue Urwald* does not know if they apply to all the prisoners standing on the ship's deck or to Jagna alone, who has joined the group voluntarily. Certainly for Jagna, to whom the words relate most directly, death in the jungle comes as a form of purification from his immoral life. For him too, the "Land without Death" is found through restored harmony with nature in death, which, despite its apparent senselessness, gains meaning on the individual level as it did for Puerto and Zippa.

Such reasoning relates closely to Döblin's view of institutional religion, which is another important aspect of this novel's critique of Western civilization. When Bishop Las Casas states that it is not God but Satan who entices the Europeans to conquer land in the Western Hemisphere (*LoT*, 243), he expresses Döblin's thinking, who has no sympathy for the missionary zeal of the Europeans. Döblin's critique of religion as promoted by the church is frequently very specific. Although the conquistadores see themselves as "Kämpfer für die heilige Kirche" (*LoT*, 91) and proclaim a "Gott im fernen Himmel," it is said of them that "Millionen Priester konnten sie nicht veranlassen, seine Gebote zu befolgen" (96). Ironically, however, in the second part of the trilogy it is the converted Indians who take the Christian rules seriously and make them the basis for their daily practices: "Die Väter hatten ihnen gesagt, was Sünde ist. Was man ihnen sagte, hielten sie fest, Wort für Wort" (*DbT*, 230). Conversely, the hypocrisy of the whites is apparent on many levels, making Döblin's critical perspective obvious. It reaches a climax with Bishop Felix, who lives with his mistress, using his castrated servant Alfio as a front for the woman's husband and the father of their child (*DbT*, 253). In the third part of the trilogy, which takes place primarily in Central Europe, Catholic celibacy rules are broken routinely by several of the principal characters.

However, it is important to note that Döblin's position throughout the novel, while certainly very critical of organized religion and Western religious hypocrisy, does not come across as irreligious or anti-Christian. As one of the work's most positive figures, Las Casas is clearly a practitioner of true Christian values, as evidenced by the statement of one of his superiors in Europe: "Es kommt [ihm] nicht auf das Christentum, sondern auf das Wohlergehen der Wilden an" (*LoT*, 254). Las Casas's way of thinking and acting at the end of *Der blaue Tiger* is also shown to be correct, and this is reconfirmed when the narrator states: "Es geschah alles, was der alte Las Casas vorausgefühlt hatte. Das Christentum suchte sich vor seinen Anhängern zu den Dunklen zu retten. So weit war es mit den Weißen gekommen" (*DbT,* 217).

It is in this context that one must see the history of the Jesuit missions, to whose foundation and development Döblin devotes so much space in the second part of the *Amazon* trilogy. At first it seems that with the arrival of the Jesuit Fathers a new spirit is entering the Christianization of South America, a spirit that is in sharp contrast to the imperialistic goals of most of the earlier missionaries. The Jesuits become a thorn in the side of the Paolists and their collaborating slave traders even before they set foot on land, when they dare to search for their stolen luggage on the Paolists' ship. The Fathers' questions about the strictly guarded camps of the Indians arouse the suspicion of the traders and businessmen of Piratininga, the settlement that is later renamed Sao Paolo. As a result of their inquiries, the Jesuits are closely watched by the Paolists on their westward move. The Paolists see the Jesuits as a direct threat to their interests, especially when it becomes clear to them that the Jesuits, in contrast to earlier Europeans, manage to earn the trust of the natives, great numbers of whom then seek their protection.

However, the Jesuits' situation is eventually seen in a new light by their senior leader, Emanuel, when he starts to doubt the purpose of their undertaking. While talking to one of the other Fathers, Cataldino, Emanuel expresses fear that their notable successes in the founding and managing of the thriving missions will arouse the envy of the Paolists and thus ultimately cause their own downfall: "O glaub mir, Cataldino, wir sind auf einem falschen Weg. Wir sollen nur herumgehen und lehren" (*DbT,* 149). The Jesuit leader is the first to experience the truth of his warning, when he is killed by the self-proclaimed king Riubuni in an attack on his mission (*DbT,* 192). Nevertheless, the Jesuit missions continue to grow in strength and number, especially because of the great loyalty of the Indians, who equate them to the Biblical Jerusalem (*DbT,* 190). With the precision of a Greek tragedy, the Jesuits' doom comes at the moment of their greatest strength, that is, when they equip themselves against the Paolists' attacks with arsenals of weapons. This brings to a climax the greed and envy of the powers of the world and church along the eastern coast of the continent. The narrator summarizes the Fathers' mixture of naive self-confidence and ill-conceived hubris: "Sie verwandelten sich. Der Rausch eines neuen Daseins drang in sie. Dagegen hatten sie ihre Arche nicht abgedichtet. Die neuen Väter schlugen die Augen auf und sahen, was sie hatten. Sie regierten. Und es tat wohl zu regieren" (323–24). The same mixture of political and religious skepticism is expressed a few pages later in the chapter entitled "Die christliche Republik im Glanz" (The Christian Republic in Splendor): "Der Ruf der christlichen Republik hatte sich verbreitet, man sprach mit Angst, mit Begeisterung von dem Kommunismus, den die Jesuväter im Neuen Indien durchgeführt hatten, das mischte sich mit aufrührerischen Reden, die spanische Krone fühlte sich nicht wohl" (*DbT,* 326). The fatal blow to the Jesuit missions in South America is dealt in Europe: in a treaty between Spain and Portugal the majority of the land occupied by the Jesuits in the Western Hemisphere falls under the jurisdiction of Portugal, and both Jesuits and Indians are ordered to leave their missions.

In the last few chapters of *Der blaue Tiger,* Döblin tells of the departure of the expelled Jesuits from South America and their martyrdom in a Portuguese prison, showing the reader how their noble beginning is followed by shameful defeat. However, as political victims, the Jesuit missionaries of South America also take on a new position within the author's polarity between spiritual harmony with nature and worldly greed for wealth and power. Döblin closes the second part of the trilogy by comparing the imprisoned Fathers with the depraved and lecherous young Portuguese king and the corrupted Prime Minister Pombal. Therefore, on the scale of the author's ideological polarity, the Jesuits are ultimately restored to a more positive position when compared to the evil excesses of the other representatives of Western civilization.

Since Döblin never visited South America, any discussion of his critique of Western civilization in the novel must take issue with his treatment of history. Werner Stauffacher, as the editor of the novel's critical edition, has pointed out Döblin's very free adaptation of historical events in the novel. Döblin does not include dates, nor does he adhere to the historical chronology (*DnU,* 251–56). The *Zeittafel* or chronology provided by the editor begins with Columbus's discovery of America in 1492 and ends with the abolishment of the Jesuit order by Pope Clemens XIV in 1772. It furnishes the reader with the succession of events that form the historical background of the various plots and subplots of the trilogy. In one of the most blatant — though clearly intended — deviations from the historical facts, Döblin lets Bishop Las Casas die among the Indians in the New World rather than after his return to Spain, as the *Zeittafel* indicates (*DnU,* 253). In view of such deviations from history it may be justified to ask if the *Amazon* trilogy can even be classified as a "historical" novel. The answer is positive only if one accepts the author's definition of this literary genre and allows for two kinds of "historical" novels.

Döblin was aware of the criticism being leveled at the authors of historical novels at a time when this genre was blossoming among writers in exile as well as in what has since been labeled Germany's "inner emigration." He discusses the question extensively in an essay titled

"Der historische Roman und wir," where he draws a clear line between the traditional historical novel and his own (*SÄPL,* 291–316). For the former kind he gives the novels of Felix Dahn (1834–1912) and Gustav Freytag (1816–95) as examples, thus naming two German writers of the nineteenth century who in their works tried to represent historical situations as accurately as possible. In clear contrast, he and some of his colleagues in exile tried to use a historical background primarily to shed light on contemporary social and political concerns.

According to Döblin, every good novelist bases his works on "real" situations, and therefore every good novel is to some degree "historical." What in Döblin's opinion distinguishes his novels from those of the more traditional writers is that he uses a historical pretext only to carry into it "das Feuer einer heutigen Zeit" (*SÄPL,* 312). In this sense some of his novels written before his exile were "historical," especially *Wallenstein,* in which the author used the turmoil of the Thirty Years' War in order to depict the inhumanity of war from a twentieth-century perspective. Similarly, Döblin wrote the *Amazon* trilogy to show the evil consequences of a development that is based on human greed and loss of harmony with nature. Unlike the historian, however, who would have tried to recreate the past as objectively as possible, the "historical novelist" Döblin made no secret of his ideological position. In his theoretical essay he called his aim "die Parteilichkeit des Tätigen," meaning that he distances himself from "der Sphäre der Gewalt, der Menschenverachtung und der Grausamkeit. [. . .] das Schreckliche ist nicht um seiner selbst willen aufzusuchen, sondern als abscheulich und entartet zu zeichnen" (316). Clearly, Döblin's demand for the writer's partisanship had special relevance during the time in which he wrote both the essay and the *Amazon* trilogy.

There are many parallels between the cases of cruelty and immorality depicted in the *Amazon* trilogy and the persecution of various categories of people considered biologically inferior in Nazi Germany. The killing and enslaving of the Indians by the conquistadores in *Das Land ohne Tod* — Döblin devotes much space to the stories of the two Germans among them, Alfinger and Federmann — reminds the reader of the "ethnic cleansing" and imprisonment of undesirable people as carried out by the Gestapo and the concentration camp guards under Hitler. The lawlessness and opportunistic circumvention of established rules by the Paolists and colonial authorities in *Der blaue Tiger* reflect the similar situation in the Third Reich. The immoral practices of the various protagonists in *Der neue Urwald* — again it is not coincidental that most of the action takes place in Germany and that the perpetrators are several Germans and one Pole — have their parallel in the general deterioration of human coexistence in Central Europe during the 1930s. In his satirical portrayal of Nazi ideology, Döblin has a student speak in the racist language of the Third Reich: "Die Nation ist die größte aller Realitäten. Sie muß sich gegen die heutige Masse wenden. Die Herrschaft der Besten wird die Realität von morgen sein und die Diktatur der Untermenschen ablösen" (*DnU*, 70).[5]

With keen foresight into the future of twentieth-century Europe, Döblin also saw his depiction of the conquest and flight of the masses in South America as events still to come after his completion of this novel in 1937. In a direct parallel to the reported foundation of the Jesuit republic in the second part of the trilogy, Döblin joined the Jews' search for new land through his interest in the territorialist movement or *Neulandbewegung* in the early thirties;[6] and just as the Jesuit settlements were doomed to failure due to internal and external circumstances, Döblin eventually became very critical of the *Neulandbewegung*, and distanced himself from it.[7] Even the narrator's repeated claim that the cruelty and greed of the conquistadores were motivated and spurred on by their inferior positions and by their lack of social acceptance in Europe (e.g. *LoT*, 108 and 106) has its parallel in the psychological make-up of several Nazi leaders as failures in professional life and social misfits.

The most direct references to National Socialism occur in the third part of the trilogy, which also chronologically comes closest to making this historical novel a topical one. If one replaces in the following quotation the words "ein König oder ein Feldhauptmann" with "Hitler," the reader gets a description of the political situation of the 1930s in Germany: "Und würde jetzt ein König oder ein Feldhauptmann das Zeichen geben, so würden sie wieder zusammenlaufen, zu Krieg und Abenteuer, Raub und Mord, und sich in Schiffe werfen, um zu vernichten und vernichtet zu werden" (*DnU*, 63). One may also hear an echo of speeches by fascist politicians like Hitler, Mussolini, and Goebbels in this utterance by one of the protagonists of *Der neue Urwald*:

> Nation war die Sache der Könige, jetzt sind wir die Könige. Unsere Sache ist aber die Technik und Industrie, nichts anderes, und wir sind im Begriff, die Welt umzustürzen. Das Ziel ist, die Barrikaden, die die Arbeiter, Geldsäcke und Gefühlsbolde gegen den Ansturm der Technik errichtet haben, niederzulegen. (*DnU*, 71–72)

In an almost direct reference to the social ideology of National Socialism, the narrator states: "Man sprach an den Biertischen in großen Tönen von dem Männerrecht, das die Staaten errichtet haben, wollte Ahnentafeln wieder einführen" (*DnU*, 131); and: "Auf den Straßen marschierten die neuen Sbirren. Ihr Gesang und Marschschritt scholl herauf" (136). Also, the mention of the chaotic political situation at the end of the Weimar Republic, referred to as die "Totgeburt von Weimar" (*DnU*, 57–58), is a clear reminder of a slogan used by Nazi politicians to undermine the credibility of the democratic system. This is clearly mirrored in the sentence: "Die Parteien, die sich bekämpften, waren von der robustesten niedergeworfen, die sich dann in der allgemeinen Verwirrung, unter dem Jubel vieler Leute [. . .] als Staat proklamierte" (*DnU*, 128).

There is no doubt that for Döblin the thought of his homeland was constantly present as he wrote the *Amazon* trilogy. It is this thought, as reflected in the many thematic parallels with the contemporary German situation in the three parts of the novel, that is responsible for the work's stylistic and thematic unity. A close linguistic analysis would show that the narrative tone is the same throughout the three parts and that there are many perceptible linguistic echoes. For the description of the jungle in South America, for example, the author employs almost the same list of nouns as for the description of the social jungle in Central Europe: "Es kam der Wald, Dornen, Käfer, Würmer, Skorpione, Hitze, Nässe, Hunger, Durst, Erschöpfung. [. . .] aus dem Sumpf und dem schwankenden Boden gerieten sie in das Dickicht, die Dornenbüsche und das Lianengestrüpp" (*LoT*, 108). And: "Es kamen die Dornen, Käfer, Würmer, Skorpione, Hitze, Kälte, Nässe, Hunger, Durst. Die Bäume standen furchtbar dicht, aus dem Wald gerieten sie in Sumpf, aus dem Sumpf in das Dickicht und Dornengestrüpp" (*DnU*, 7). In the first passage Döblin describes a real jungle, in the second one the metaphorical jungle of a highly civilized but morally degenerate Europe. Great natural disasters, such as erupting volcanoes and tidal waves, occur in all three parts as metaphors for the volatile political circumstances of Europe and for the unending flood of lawless adventurers and desperadoes pouring into South America.[8] Copernicus and Giordano Bruno are mentioned in connection with the author's narration about the great changes in Western civilization in *Der blaue Tiger* (317–18); and the same historical characters become the key figures in *Der neue Urwald* (2–20 and 110–20). The third part also contains another account of the main conquerors of South America whose stories occupy large sections of the first part, as well as a reminder of the failure of the Jesuit republic, which is focused on in the second part (*DnU*, 143). Although more of these direct correspondences between the three parts could be listed, it is important to remember that the most unifying feature of the trilogy lies in its consistent criticism of Western civilization as Döblin saw it: a society governed by egotism, greed for possessions, exploitation of the weak and poor, internal competition, arrogant striving for honor and power, excessive pleasure hunting, religious fanaticism and hypocrisy, the reification of human relations, and the loss of the individual's harmony with nature.

At this point it is useful to take a look at an article Döblin wrote soon after his completion of the *Amazon* trilogy, which contains the philosophical basis of the work in a nutshell. The article is entitled "Prometheus und das Primitive" and first appeared in 1938 in *Maß und Wert*, the exile journal edited by Thomas Mann and Konrad Falke (*SPG*, 346–67). The article's title reflects the same polarity that governs the narration in the trilogy: Prometheus standing for the human desire to rule and to discover, and the "primitive" referring to the original harmony of humankind with nature. Since the beginning of history, according to Döblin, humans have been torn between two opposing forces: on the one side the striving for new territory in both physical and spiritual terms, and on the other side the attempt to regain lost ties to nature. Since neither of the two forces occurs without a trace of the other, each gain by one side causes an increase in the desire for the other, and both sides share the hope of arriving at a synthesis, a goal that no human being ever seems to be able to achieve. Döblin lists the original sin of Adam and Eve, symbolized by their eating the forbidden fruit, and Prometheus's robbing the fire from the gods as examples of mythological transgressions in the one direction (away from nature), and the irrational veneration of the golden calf by the Israelites and the rebellion of the early Christians against the rational system of the Roman state as examples of mankind's going in the opposite direction (toward nature and primitivism). The battle between the two forces reached a stage of crisis during the sixteenth century as a result of the Protestant Reformation's secularization of medieval religious values and the Renaissance's placement of the human individual in the center of the universe. Never before, says Döblin, has the Promethean force in humans gone to such an extreme as during the past three hundred years, because people have become "nihilistisch vereist" and "Züchtung, Spezialisierung, Versachlichung des Menschen wird stolz und überlegt betrieben" (*SPG*, 362).

It is apparent that Döblin's article expresses thoughts that were shared by other critics of modern civilization, such as Max Horkheimer (1895–1973) and other members of the Frankfurt School, who criticized political and economic capitalism, by Arthur Koestler (1905–83) with his criticism of materialistic communism, and by Oskar Maria Graf (1894–1967) with his cultural criticism of both capitalism and communism. What distinguishes Döblin from these critics is his radical attack against modern civilization from a social-political as well as a moral-religious perspective.

As we know from Döblin's own report about the genesis of the *Amazon* trilogy, he was in the midst of reading Kierkegaard's *Either — Or* (1843), from which he was distracted as he became fascinated with the maps and ethnographic histories of South America. While this diversion eventually inspired him to write the *Amazon* trilogy, Kierkegaard's religious polarity of materialism versus spiritualism left its mark both on his novel and the related essay.

This brings us to the question of the novel's textual sources. As Werner Stauffacher has suggested, Döblin's knowledge of the history of the Jesuit republic in South America had gained from the satirical chapter in Voltaire's *Candide* (1753) titled "Comment Candide et Cacambo furent reçus chez les Jésuites du Paraguay" ("How Candide and Cacambo were received by the Jesuits of Paraguay"). However, for the actual historical facts the author consulted a number of other books, also listed by Stauffacher,[9] specifically: Theodor Koch-Grünberg's *Indianermärchen aus Südamerika* (1927), Alfred Métraux's *La réligion des Tupinamba et ses rapports avec celle des autres tribus Tupi-Guarani* (The Religion of the Tupinamba and Their Relation to that of Other Tupi-Guarani Tribes, 1928), R. P. François-Xavier de Charlevoix's *Histoire du Paraguay* (1758), and Christoph Gottlieb von Murr's *Geschichte der Jesuiten in Portugal unter der Staatsverwaltung des Marquis von Pombal* (History of the Jesuits in Portugal under the Administration of the Marquis of Pombal, 1909). Stauffacher's edition contains a detailed analysis of Döblin's use of sources, and points out his deviations from historical facts and chronology (208–17), deviations which in themselves also reflect Döblin's criticism of Western civilization.

Döblin's *Amazon* trilogy was first published in two volumes in 1937–38 by Querido Verlag, a German exile publisher in the Netherlands. The first volume carried the title *Die Fahrt ins Land ohne Tod: Roman* (Journey to the Land without Death: Novel) and corresponds to *Das Land ohne Tod*. The second volume, titled *Der blaue Tiger: Roman*, contained both *Der blaue Tiger* and *Der neue Urwald*, the latter constituting books 6 and 7 of volume two. Only when the work was republished for the first time after the war was the second volume separated into two, with books 6 and 7 of the originally-published second part receiving the title of the present third volume *Der neue Urwald*, and the title of the first volume being slightly altered: *Das Land ohne Tod*. Because of the special circumstances of this edition — there was no clearly stated cross-reference between the three parts of the trilogy and the general resistance to the reception of exile literature in post-war Germany — the work did not find many readers.

An unfortunate event twisted the reception of the trilogy when the *Ausgewählte Werke* began to appear in the early 1960s. Walter Muschg's one-volume edition of 1963, which was the first edition of the trilogy to use the title *Amazonas*, did not only make numerous editorial alterations, it omitted the entire third part, *Der neue Urwald*. Although this was remedied by a reprint of *Der neue Urwald* by the Gerstenberg Verlag in Hildesheim, and by Manfred Beyer's East German edition of *Amazonas*, it offered a truncated text to most readers until Werner Stauffacher's new edition in *Ausgewählte Werke* appeared in 1988.

Although the trilogy had a limited readership in 1937 and 1938, it was critically acclaimed. The most significant review came from Hermann Kesten (1900–1996). Ferdinand Lion (1883–1965), in the journal *Maß und Wert*, compared Döblin with Thomas Mann, which caused Mann to react angrily. There is a remarkable review by Jorge Luis Borges (1899–1986), who compared Döblin's novel to Flaubert's *Salammbô* (1863). The few reviews of the postwar edition dwelt mainly on the religious issues as a prologue to Döblin's conversion; so did Walter Muschg in his afterword to his 1963 edition, whereas Manfred Beyer in his afterword to his 1973 East German edition (831–52) gave ample background information, as did the studies by Sperber, Erhardt, and Brüggen.

The present analysis has shown the three parts of the *Amazon* trilogy to be closely connected by their strong criticism of Western civilization and the fact that this criticism is not limited to any nation or geographical region. Although Europeans and North Americans have perhaps erred the most in their betrayal of humankind's original harmony with nature, Döblin portrayed similar developments at various stages in the "primitive" cultures of South American Indians, and showed how Western people can regain their harmony with original nature, the "Urnatur." It is Döblin's depiction of the evils of modern civilization, along with their consistently epic style, that give the three parts of his *Amazon* trilogy their coherence; and as long as these evils — possessiveness and greed, the struggle for power, military and economic wars, the persecution of minorities, religious hypocrisy, opportunistic thinking, and moral corruption — continue to be widespread social and political phenomena, Döblin's novel will not lose its relevance.

Notes

[1] Döblin used the terms "Paolisten" (Portuguese "Paulistas") and "Mamelus" (Portuguese "Mamelucos") interchangeably in referring to the first Portuguese settlers of São Paolo, who eventually mixed with the Indians and colonized the Brazilian hinterland. See, for example, *DbT,* 177.

[2] Döblin used the Germanized version "Bagno" of the term *bagno* (Italian for "bathroom"), or French "bagne"; this denotes a penal colony, as established at various French cities during the eighteenth century and still in existence in Cayenne (French Guayana) until 1854.

[3] Other examples of this metaphor in *Das Land ohne Tod* occur on pages 126, 146, 210, 278, 281.

[4] For this comparison, I am indebted to Heidi Thomann Tewarson.

[5] Döblin is here engaged in a critique of Nazi language similar to that of Victor Klemperer in his systematic study *LTI. Notizbuch eines Philologen,* first published in 1947 by the Aufbau-Verlag, Berlin. (*LTI* stands for Lingua Tertii Imperii = Language of the Third Reich).

[6] For further details on Döblin's political engagement in his writings, see Klaus Müller-Salget, "Döblin and Judaism," 243.

[7] See Döblin's essays "Der neue Territorialismus" and "Von Führern und Schimmelpilzen," ("Of Leaders and Mould Fungus") in *SjF* 342–43 and 351–55.

[8] See for instance *LoT,* 149 and 267; *DbT,* 214; and *DnU,* 141.

[9] Stauffacher follows George Bernard Sperber's *Wegweiser im "Amazonas": Studien zur Rezeption, zu den Quellen und zur Textkritik der Südamerika-Trilogie Alfred Döblins* (Munich: Tuduv-Verlagsgesellschaft, 1975) (*DnU,* 208).

Works Cited

Alfred Döblin 1878–1978: Eine Ausstellung des Deutschen Literaturarchivs im Schiller-Nationalmuseum Marbach am Neckar. Exhibit and Catalogue by Jochen Meyer in collaboration with Ute Doster. Munich: Kösel, 1978.

Alfred Döblin im Spiegel der zeitgenössischen Kritik. Ed. by Ingrid Schuster and Ingrid Bode in collaboration with the Deutsches Literaturarchiv Marbach am Neckar. Bern and Munich: Francke, 1973.

Arnold, Armin. *Alfred Döblin.* Berlin: Morgenbuch Verlag, 1996.

Auer, Manfred. *Das Exil vor der Vertreibung: Motivkontinuität und Quellenproblematik im späten Werk Alfred Döblins.* Bonn: Bouvier, 1978.

Brüggen, Hubert. *Land ohne Tod: Eine Untersuchung zur inneren Struktur der "Amazonas-Trilogie" Alfred Döblins.* Frankfurt am Main, Bern, New York, Paris: Peter Lang, 1987.

Bürger, Jan. "'Ich war ein Berliner.' Mehr als vierzig Jahre verbrachte Alfred Döblin östlich des Alexanderplatzes — jetzt wirft eine neue Ausgabe seiner Briefe Licht auf das Leben des Roman-Revolutionärs und Kassenarztes." *Literaturen*, 2 (2001), No. 7/8: 124–27.

Charlevoix, R. P. Pierre François-Xavier de. *L'histoire du Paraguay*. 3 vols. Paris: Ganeau et. al., 1756.

Dollinger, Roland. *Totalität und Totalitarismus im Exilwerk Döblins*. Würzburg: Königshausen & Neumann, 1994.

Erhardt, Jacob. *Alfred Döblins Amazonas-Trilogie*. Deutsches Exil 1933–45, vol. 3. Worms: Georg Heintz, 1974.

Flaubert, Gustave. *Salammbô*. Trans. from French. New York: The Modern Library, 1929; 1st ed. Paris: H. Lévy, 1863.

Graf, Oskar Maria. "Der Moralist als Wurzel der Diktatur: Eine geistesgeschichtliche Betrachtung." Oskar Maria Graf, *Reden und Aufsätze aus dem Exil*. Ed. by Helmut F. Pfanner. Munich: Süddeutscher Verlag, 1989. 241–344.

Grass, Günther. *Über meinen Lehrer Döblin und andere Vorträge*. LCB-Editionen 1. Berlin: Literarisches Colloquium, 1968.

Horkheimer, Max, and Theodor W. Adorno. *Dialektik der Aufklärung: Philosophische Fragmente*. Frankfurt am Main: Fischer, 1971.

Kesten, Hermann. Review of Döblin's *Die Fahrt ins Land ohne Tod*. *Das Neue Tagebuch*, 22 May 1937.

Kierkegaard, Søren Aabye. *Entweder — Oder: Ein Lebensfragment*. Ed. by Viktor Eremita. Trans. from Danish by O. Gleiss. Dresden: L. Ungelenk, 1927; 1st. ed. Copenhagen, 1843.

Kiesel, Helmuth. *Literarische Trauerarbeit: Das Exil- und Spätwerk Alfred Döblins*. Tübingen: Niemeyer, 1986.

Klemperer, Victor. *LTI [Lingua Tertii imperii]: Notizbuch eines Philologen*. Berlin: Aufbau, 1949.

Kobel, Erwin. *Alfred Döblin: Erzählkunst im Umbruch*. Berlin, New York: Walter de Gruyter, 1985.

Koch-Grünberg, Theodor. *Indianermärchen aus Südamerika*. Jena: Diederichs, 1927.

Koestler, Arthur. *The Yogi and the Commissar: And Other Essays*. New York: Macmillan, 1945.

Links, Roland. *Alfred Döblin*. Berlin: Volk und Wissen, 1980.

Mann, Thomas. *Tagebücher 1937–39*. Ed. by Peter de Mendelssohn. Frankfurt am Main: Fischer, 1980.

Métraux, Alfred. *La religion des Tupinamba et ses rapports avec celle des autres tribus Tupi-Guarani*. Paris: Leroux, 1928.

Müller-Salget, Klaus. *Alfred Döblin: Werk und Entwicklung.* Bonner Arbeiten zur deutschen Literatur, 12. Bonn: Bouvier, 1972.

Murr, Christoph Gottlieb von. *Geschichte der Jesuiten in Portugal unter der Staatsverwaltung des Marquis von Pombal.* Ed. by Christoph Gottlieb von Murr. New improved ed. by J. B. Hafkemeyer. Freiburg im Breisgau, 1909.

Pfanner, Helmut F. "Alfred Döblin, Thomas Mann, and Hitler's Rise to Power." In *Approaching a New Millenium: Lessons from the Past, Prospects for the Future.* Proceedings of the 7th Conference of the International Society for the Study of European Ideas (ISSEI), 14–18 August 2000, University of Bergen, Norway.

———. "Der entfesselte Prometheus oder die Eroberung Südamerikas aus der Sicht Alfred Döblins." *Geschichte und Gegenwart* 17, No. 4 (December 1998): 219–29.

Sperber, George Bernard. *Wegweiser im "Amazonas": Studien zur Rezeption, zu den Quellen und zur Textkritik der Südamerika-Trilogie Alfred Döblins.* Tuduv Studien, Sprach- u. Literaturwissenschaften. Munich: Tuduv, 1975.

Voltaire, François Marie Arouet de (M. le Docteur Ralph). *Candide, Ou l'Optimism.* London, 1759.

Weyembergh-Boussart, Monique. *Alfred Döblin: Seine Religiosität in Persönlichkeit und Werk.* Abhandlungen zur Kunst-, Musik- und Literaturwissenschaft, 76. Bonn: Bouvier, 1970.

Wichert, Adalbert. *Alfred Döblins historisches Denken: Zur Poetik des modernen Geschichtsromans.* Germanistische Abhandlungen, 48. Stuttgart: Metzler, 1978.

Döblin's *November 1918*

Helmuth Kiesel

HOW DID HITLER COME ABOUT? This question pre-occupied German authors in exile to the exclusion of nearly all others, and spurred ever-new attempts at answers. To a great extent, Döblin's exile work is likewise determined by this question. All the novels he wrote after his flight from Berlin are, to a certain extent, reflections on the history of National Socialist rule, and have the Third Reich as their vanishing point, so to speak. *Babylonische Wandrung oder Hochmut kommt vor dem Fall* (published 1934–35), a wide-ranging survey of the history of violence, ends with the echoes of the marching steps of soldiers. *Pardon wird nicht gegeben* (1934–35) recapitulates the political-social development between 1895 and 1930, thus ending with the world economic crisis that paved the way for the rise of National Socialism. The *Amazon* trilogy (1937–38) portrays the murderous conquest of South America by Europeans and the destructive tendencies within European "civilization"; performing a remarkable leap across two centuries, it too ends with the time when National Socialism came to power. The voluminous "Erzählwerk" *November 1918*, finally, is a multi-layered account of the events in which Döblin saw the actual origins of National Socialist rule: the disastrous First World War and the subsequent "German revolution" of 1918/19, which was crushed by the combined efforts of the Social Democratic national government, the general staff, the army, and the *Freikorps*. Döblin saw the National Socialists' coming to power and their accompanying brutal acts of violence as the culmination and conclusion of the ill-fated German revolution. The question of what made Hitler's rule possible — a question posed by Döblin also in his speech at the Pablo Rey Playhouse in Santa Monica in August 1943, on the occasion of his sixty-fifth birthday — thus focused on the revolution of 1918/19, often referred to as the "November revolution." It became the topic of Döblin's most extensive narrative work, the current edition of which spans 1,950 pages.

The first volume as originally conceived, *Bürger und Soldaten 1918*, was the only part of the novel to be published before the Second World War, appearing with Querido in Amsterdam in 1939. Between 1948 and

1950 the novel was published as a trilogy, consisting of *Verratenes Volk, Heimkehr der Fronttruppen,* and *Karl und Rosa;* the bulk of *Bürger und Soldaten 1918* was excluded by the French censors because it is critical of the historical events in Alsace in November 1918 and the French treatment of Germany after the First World War. Only excerpts from the volume were incorporated into the postwar edition. It was not until 1978 that the entire work became available to the public in three parts in four volumes.¹ As in other cases, Döblin preferred to call this work an "Erzählwerk" rather than a "Roman," in order to emphasize its epic character; however, the designation "Roman" has some justification as well.

The completion of the novel required almost six years. Döblin began with the first part toward the end of 1937, while still in Paris; it was completed in early 1939 and published by Querido in Amsterdam in October 1939. He had just managed to complete the manuscript for the second part before he was forced to flee Paris in May 1940 to escape the invading German troops; the manuscript accompanied him on his traumatic flight through southern France and, by way of Spain and Portugal, to America. In Hollywood, where he took an apartment in November 1940, he first reworked the second part. In February 1942, he began work on the third part, which was completed in May 1943.

The long and adventure-filled process of writing this work affected its contents as well as its style. Changes in the meaning of the work were above all a result of Döblin's conversion to the Catholic faith, which had long been in the making, but was accelerated by the uncertainties of his flight and completed and sealed by his baptism in the Blessed Sacrament Church of Hollywood. This conversion process is twice reflected in the *November* trilogy — the protagonists Friedrich Becker and Rosa Luxemburg undergo a process of transformation and Christianization. The style or mode of representation was likewise impacted by his flight to America, inasmuch as Döblin was cut off in Hollywood from the historical sources he had previously consulted. For the first two parts of the *November* trilogy, Döblin had conducted intensive studies of the relevant literature at the Bibliothèque Nationale in Paris; in Hollywood, lacking an equivalent library, he was forced to ask Hermann Kesten to undertake a few investigations in New York and supply him with the most important information regarding the "Spartacus" uprising (*B I,* 270). The fact that the last part of the trilogy, which took shape in Hollywood, lacks the multi-faceted character of the first and second parts may have to do with this corresponding lack of access to appropriate historical documentation and accounts. However, it should also be noted that in Hollywood Döblin found what he called "vorzügliche amerikanische Bücher" about Woodrow Wilson (*B I*, 271) from which he drew his inspiration for the impressive passages about the "großen Vernünftigen" from Princeton (*N-II/2*, 85–95, 437–86).

The *November* trilogy is of course not the work of a historian, who would have endeavored to present as objective a picture as possible of the revolution, using as many sources as possible. What Döblin sought were documents suited to render his picture of the revolution multifaceted and vivid. His historical-political verdict on the revolution was already firmly established before he began writing. It derived from personal observations and ongoing debates about revolutionary developments during the Weimar Republic.

Döblin had enlisted as an army doctor and was stationed on the heavily contested German-French front (Saargemünd, Hagenau) beginning in 1915 and remaining there until the armistice. It was thus in Hagenau that he experienced the start of the revolution; it spread rapidly throughout Germany, sparked by the sailors' uprising in Kiel on November 3, 1918, and led to the abdication of the Kaiser and the proclamation of the Republic on November 9. From Hagenau, Döblin returned by hospital train to Berlin around November 18, and from then on, he observed the course of the revolution closely with his own eyes — wandering among the little people, as he put it in his article "Die Vertreibung der Gespenster" (*SPG*, 71–83). Remarks in letters and essays from the time of the revolution, which lasted through the winter of 1918–19, indicated that Döblin sympathized with the revolution in principle and considered not only the democratization of Germany but also a change in property relationships to be necessary. At the same time, he had doubts about the spiritual foundations of the revolution and was disappointed by the paucity of revolutionary will among the masses and by the incapability of the leading men surrounding Liebknecht and Luxemburg. The main thesis of the novel's account of the revolution had already taken shape for Döblin as it was happening or in any case shortly thereafter: the revolution was not only betrayed ("verraten") by the Social Democratic politicians of law and order Ebert and Noske, but also badly played ("verspielt") by the Spartacist communist revolutionaries. In *Berlin Alexanderplatz* (1929) too, workers are shown to complain that they were betrayed "von den Bonzen," that is, by the Social Democratic government in 1918/19 (*BA*, 86).

Döblin's utilization of documents for his portrayal of the revolution may be described as tendentious. This is true not only with regard to his selection of the cited documents, but also his portrayals, his commentaries, and his speculative elaborations of documentary materials. Döblin considered his use of such methods thoroughly legitimate. He had written on the subject of historiography on numerous occasions in the 1920s and 1930s. In an essay of 1936, "Der historische Roman und wir," he came to the conclusion that every kind of historiography was to a great degree constructed and written from a certain perspective, such that the "Wahrheitsideal" or "Objektivitätsideal" of scientific historiography must be considered "wahnhaft" (*SÄPL,* 291–316). In contrast to a historiography that adheres closely to more or less arbitrarily preserved data, he preferred a freer poetic representation, for two reasons: first, because he believed that a poetically enriched and restructured representation of history approached real history and its driving forces more closely than scientific historiography, which deals only with handed-down material; and second, because he believed that every writing of history pursued certain intentions, and that these are not only better followed in the form of the historical novel, but also easier to recognize and assess. In keeping with these sentiments, Döblin wrote in the same essay "Mit Geschichte will man was," and named the "Parteilichkeit des Tätigen" as the force that gives quality and meaning to the writing of history (*SÄPL,* 302 and 314).

The formulation "Parteilichkeit des Tätigen" suggests a Marxist background, and although Döblin took a very critical position toward Marxism — particularly in its contemporary form — this may not be entirely false; for Döblin, criticism of Marxism was not the same as the rejection of all of its impulses. However, one must also think of Döblin's fascination with Nietzsche, who profiled three distinct types of history in his epochal work "Vom Nutzen und Nachteil der Historie für das Leben" (The Use and Abuse of History, 1874): the "monumentalische," which holds the great deeds and figures of the past before the eyes of the active, striving agents of history as a source of encouragement and as models for emulation (258); the "antiquarische," which gives those who wish to preserve and honor the past (258) a feeling of well-being and contentment (265–66); and the "kritische," which helps those who suffer and are in need of liberation to destroy and dispense with the past through a process in which they drag the past to judgment, examine it with exactitude, and finally render a verdict on it (269). Two of these three modes of engagement with the past can be found in Döblin's novel: the story of the failed German revolution is critically scrutinized and condemned by Döblin as the prelude to the National Socialist ascent to power and reign of terror; several outstanding figures who in Döblin's opinion had at least pursued the right path are portrayed as "monumentalisch" (Rosa Luxemburg, for example, but above all Woodrow Wilson). These two modes of considering history have their corresponding narrative modes: the critical perspective is rendered in a satirical style, bordering at times on caricature; the monumental is presented in a dramatic style that, in the case of Wilson, takes on a virtually hagiographic tone.

In addition, Döblin sought to show the history of the German revolution in its totality: in its entire social breadth, political intricacy, and ethical complexity. This was to be accomplished by rendering it as a multitude of mutually competing, affirming, or critical histories reflecting as many actualities and eventualities as possible. Overall, the novel brings together more than fifty sub-plots or chains of events of varying importance and length.

Döblin was not able to maintain this bold narrative approach, however. While the first part is characterized by ever-changing settings and a perplexing number of contrasting snapshots, this technique is considerably reduced in the second part and done away with entirely in the third. That this simplification was the consequence of a conscious change in the conception of the work is suggested by a letter, dated March 15, 1940, in which Döblin speaks of "fesselnde formale Probleme" with regard to the nearly-finished second part, as well as by a comparison of the manuscript, typescript, and printed version (*B I,* 240). Here it can be seen that the second part was made more lucid through subsequent rearrangements of parts, and that it was restructured with a view to the third part. This might be seen as the regrettable abandonment of an ambitious artistic form, and indeed, it does entail certain sacrifices. The feeling of simultaneity and diverse perspectives was lost as was the sense of anonymous revolutionary events resulting from an almost incomprehensible number of variously motivated individual occurrences. However, it must also be admitted that fidelity to the earlier narrative mode would have made *November 1918* even more impenetrable and difficult to read.

The first part, entitled *Bürger und Soldaten 1918,* deals with the time period from November 10–22, 1918 and offers accounts of many episodes from the end of the war and the simultaneous outbreak of the revolution in Alsace: screaming soldiers and squadrons of sailors with red flags, the formation of citizens and soldiers councils, the disempowerment of military commanders and civil authorities, the dissolution of households, and various revolutionary takeovers. At the same time, the first Social Democratic chancellor, Friedrich Ebert, issues calls for "Ruhe und Ordnung." A multitude of personages surface briefly to contribute their parts in the ongoing events and then disappear; only a few reappear again later to illustrate how the revolution affected the people. Major figures from the historical events of 1918/19 are mentioned or shown in political action. The central figures of the fictional events — the seriously wounded Lieutenant Friedrich Becker, the likewise wounded Lieutenant Johannes Maus, and the erotically enticing nurse Hilde — receive more attention, and take on clear contours.

The central figure of the novel is Friedrich Becker, a doctor of classical philology who went to war as a reserve lieutenant with patriotic convictions and an aesthete's readiness to die; he suffered a spinal cord injury during an attack, and now, suffering intensely, sees the world and life very differently. His thoughts dwell upon the many war dead and the misguided life he had led until he was wounded. He considers such misguidedness typical for his generation, and thus counts it among the preconditions of the war. During the long journey home in the hospital train from the Alsatian city of Hagenau to Berlin, Becker lapses into hallucinatory or visionary states during which the medieval Alsatian mystic Johannes Tauler (1300–1361) appears to him and prepares him for the excruciating journey that will lead him to a religious existence and to Christianity. Döblin's Tauler also contains aspects of Kierkegaard (Kiesel, 438–40), whose works Döblin had read before Tauler's. In tracing Becker's development, he makes use of Kierkegaard's differentiation between aesthetic, ethical, and religious existence: having reached the ethical stage as a result of his injury, Becker devotes himself during the journey to Berlin to the study of two works that had a formative influence on his pre-war thinking: the famous first chorus from Sophocles' *Antigone*, which takes as its theme the greatness of man (*N-I*, 166), and Richard Wagner's opera *Tristan und Isolde* (168), which is — in Nietzsche's words — filled with "Sehnsucht nach den Geheimnissen der Nacht und des Todes" (Nietzsche, I, 479). In this way, Becker takes leave of the haughty humanism and thoughtless aestheticism of his pre-war existence, and professes his commitment to an ethically responsible life.

A relatively large portion of the first part (and of the first volume of the second part, up to Hilde's move from Strasbourg to Berlin) is devoted to a number of stories set in Alsace that illustrate revolutionary events from various angles. Among these is the story of the soldier René, who returns from the war to the ostentatious world of civil society and is quickly swallowed up in a life- and love-starved war widow's salon; while this story is but a brief episode, it offers a sharp contrast to that of the protagonist Becker, who never loses sight of the intentions with which he returns from the war. Finally, at the end of the first part, the poet Stauffer is introduced, whose story takes on a significance of its own and serves as an example of a "private" revolution. Stauffer too is an example of the aestheticism of pre-war society, which must be overcome through ethical reflection. In connection with Stauffer, Döblin provides an ironic, even satirical portrait of the "Rat der geistigen Arbeiter," a group of intellectuals who met in Berlin at the outbreak of the revolution to issue manifestoes on how to renew the world. These "gewaltige Dinge," Döblin remarks ironically, before relating the proposals, their grandiose ideas, which "[stellten] die vierzehn Punkte Wilsons [. . .] spielend in den Schatten" (*N-I*, 297). This portrayal makes it clear that no serious contribution for the reformation of German society could be expected from this group; they do not constitute a political force.

The second part is subdivided into two volumes that appeared under the titles *Verratenes Volk* (Volume 2, now *N-II/1*) and *Heimkehr der Fronttruppen* (Volume 3, now *N-II/2*). It covers the period from November 22 to December 14, during which everything was in turmoil. On November 9, the Republic was declared not once but twice in Berlin: first as the "German Republic" by the Social Democrat Philipp Scheidemann, speaking from a window of the Reichstag, and again as the "free, socialist republic of Germany" by Karl Liebknecht, one of the leaders of the radical socialist Spartacist party, from the balcony of the royal palace. As Döblin shows through glimpses into various milieus, it is now thoroughly unclear which of these claims predominates, and various political groupings attempt to advance their own programs. The first chancellor of the republic, the Social Democrat Friedrich Ebert, presiding over the council of the people's delegates (Rat der Volksbeauftragten) makes it his goal to establish "Ruhe und Ordnung." To this effect, he collaborates with the general staff of the army, which has opened its headquarters in Kassel in an effort to undermine the Spartacist revolution, and in any case is prepared to lend Ebert its support to forestall further revolutionary developments. The two Spartacist leaders, Karl Liebknecht and Rosa Luxemburg, acting with the support of Lenin's emissary Karl Radek, intensify their agitation for the continuation of the revolution to bring about political and social change — not merely democracy but socialism. On several occasions, explosive situations arise in which the council of the people's delegates is in danger of losing control over the assembled masses, but the incendiary words — the revolutionary "Parolen" — are never proclaimed (*N-II/2*, 66). Radek looks on, disappointed and angered, as Liebknecht, filled with "Bedenken" (*N-II/2*, 359) permits Ebert to crush the revolution with the help of the army. At the same time, Wilson arrives in Paris and is received as potential savior of Europe, but experiences one disappointment after the other in the course of the tedious peace negotiations. He returns to America a broken man, having failed in the "erste[n] große[n] Versuch, den Völkern Frieden zu bringen, ohne sie zu unterjochen" (*N-II/2*, 476). One of the last chapter titles in the second part reads, "Der große Vernünftige verläßt sein Amt" (*N-II/2*, 478).

The major figures of the fictional events are likewise affected by the turmoil of these weeks between November 22 and December 14; they too are beset by confusion and indecisiveness. Becker and his comrade in arms Maus vainly attempt to reach a clear position with respect to the revolution; Maus in particular vacillates between revolutionary and counterrevolutionary zeal. Nurse Hilde, who had returned to her family in Strasbourg, is forced to come to terms with her free-spirited past and decides to travel to Berlin in order to seek out Becker and Maus and to return to work in an army hospital. Combining features of the Mona Lisa and the Madonna in — to borrow Rilke's term — the figure of a "Madonna Lisa,"[2] she is largely confusing (*N-II/2*, 21–3; *N-III*, 174–78). Becker is at first afraid of her erotic power and embarrassed by her religious contemplations; nevertheless, she becomes Becker's first guide on his path to a Christian life. This path leads Becker deeper and deeper into spiritual tumult and physical suffering — and at last to the "Tor des Grauens und der Verzweiflung" (*N-II/2*, 169), of which Tauler had warned him, and behind which encounters and conversations with the devil await. The latter appears three times and in three different guises: first as an intellectually provocative and erotically attractive man (*N-II/2*, 200–210), that is to say, as the embodiment of a negative inner voice and of repressed drives; then as an intimidating lion (217–26), that is, as a symbol of the will to power, which is also the topic of the second conversation; and finally as a rat (243–54), and that is to say, as a figure of destructive intellectualism and negative animalism in humans. The common theme of these three encounters with the devil is the question about the origin of evil in the world and whom man might turn to for guidance and spiritual support. In the end, Becker is so overcome with doubt that he tries to hang himself — but he is saved, because the knot comes untied. His attempted suicide subsequently proves to be the turning point: he is now ready for the message of Christianity. He begins by reading the Bible, and quickly comes upon the beatification passage in the Sermon on the Mount (Matthew 5). He recognizes it as the spiritual orientation that he has been lacking, and resolves to follow uncompromisingly its teachings, which he formulates as responsibility before God for mankind and the course of the world, truthfulness, peacefulness, and solidarity. He is now ready for the Lord's Prayer, and while he recites it, his mother places on his desk the crucifix that he had received at his confirmation — thereby restoring a center of orientation, or "Mittelpunkt," to Becker's world (*N-II/2*, 333). The "private" revolution of the poet Stauffer is likewise hastened along: Stauffer's efforts to reappraise his ethically irresponsible past are recounted in detail; it is time, as he asserts, "die Fundamente seiner Existenz [zu] prüfen" (*N-II/2*, 151). Everything is in flux, which initially appears to be positive, in spite of the confusion; but it is also clear that these unstable circumstances cannot last.

It can be said that the second part of *November 1918* speaks, politically, for the necessity and possibility of a new international order, and ethically, for the choice of conscience over weapons. This choice is required not only of the political leaders such as Ebert and Liebknecht, but also of private citizens such as Becker and Maus and of the members of the Imkers, a working-class family deeply impacted by the hardships resulting from the war economy. The Imkers must decide whether to continue to accept the exploitation of their labor or to stand up and join the revolution. Here, even more than in the first part of the trilogy, Döblin's intent was to portray the German revolution in its full breadth and in full awareness of its limitations (Althen, 81–203). He aimed to portray all of the powers involved, the revolutionary soldiers and the increasingly radical Spartacists, the calculating republican government and the old power elites, and the various classes within the population, with their distinctly different positions in regard to the unfolding events. All of these groups opposed each other and limited each other's powers; but their overall sphere of influence was reduced by the repressive policies of the victorious Allies.

This attempt to present social-political circumstances in their totality has its linguistic counterpart in the polyphony of the work, in which a great many human experiences and illusions, complaints and hopes, needs and desires are given expression, and various discourses — humanist, socialist, pacifist, terrorist, religious, mystical — cross paths with each other and compete for attention (Dollinger, 178). This polyphony, with its disparate stylistic modes, nevertheless succeeds not only in displaying the plethora of forces and views competing with each other during the revolutionary period; it is also representative of a time that has come apart at the seams, in which any agreement about even the most basic values seems out of reach. Germany finds itself, as a mocking observer comments, "im Stadium des freien Sprechens und Durcheinanderredens," and there it will remain; in the land of poets and thinkers, no one wants to be carried away from words to deeds (*N-II/2*, 268).

The German revolution, to which Thomas Mann assigned the characteristically German quality of "Gutmütigkeit" (*Essays III*, 358), passed from its initial rapid success of November 9 into a period of unproductive debates and actions that had at most a symbolic character. As a result, it took on what contemporary and later historians have called a certain "Operettenhaftigkeit" (Rosenberg, 44) or even "Lächerlichkeit" (Haffner, 120). Döblin likewise perceived a burlesque streak, and he makes his views known in the novel — as he had previously done in his critical "Linke Poot" commentaries of 1919–21. He presents many events in a comic light, exaggerating them to the point of grotesqueness or accompanying them with mocking or cynically unmasking commentary (*N-II/2*, 262–72). Thus *November 1918* was once dubbed an "Epik des Hohnes" (Mayer, 124). It should not be overlooked, however, that this mockery to which Döblin subjected the failed German revolution was the expression of a pain stimulated again and again during the time he was writing by the bloody triumphs of National Socialism. At the same time, Döblin's position with respect to the revolution was ambivalent. Despite the good he saw in the revolution, which he considered necessary, it was at the same time condemnable in light of its unavoidable victims. For Döblin, a historical moment such as the Spartacist uprising of January 5–6, 1919, when a decisive word from Liebknecht or Luxemburg might have sufficed to spark the revolution, was in ethical terms a moment of insoluble aporia: he who fails to step in on the side of the revolution seals his own guilt. Consequently, the "Vermittlungskommission" charged with mediating between the revolutionaries and the government is referred to as a "Hinrichtungskommission" (*N-III*, 447) and its work condemned as a crime against the people and against world peace (318). However, he also seals his own guilt who, like an absolute ruler or field marshal, sacrifices human life in the interest of the revolution. Accordingly, in the aftermath of the failed January uprising, Rosa Luxemburg accuses Karl Liebknecht of having driven the workers to their deaths like a tsar or Napoleon, and says that he must now take responsibility for his actions (*N-III*, 513).

The third part of the *November* trilogy, in which Döblin's ambivalence vis-à-vis the revolution is most clearly manifest, bears the title *Karl und Rosa* and covers the period from mid-December 1918 to January 15, 1919. At the initiative of Liebknecht and Luxemburg, the Berlin revolution takes on new momentum and repeatedly endangers the Social Democratic government. The major political figures are introduced and characterized, necessitating at times a glance back to the time before

November 9, 1918. Thus the beginning finds Luxemburg still imprisoned in Breslau, where she had been sent due to her antiwar protests. She is mourning her friend Hans Diefenbach, killed in France, and lapses into a "Haftpsychose" (*N-III*, 31), in which she — like Becker during his return from the war — begins to hallucinate, undertaking extensive journeys and conducting debates about the condition of the world with her dead friend — and later with Satan. Döblin's portrayal of Luxemburg as highly pathological goes far beyond anything contained in her prison letters and notes, which Döblin had read. However, his intention was not to denounce Luxemburg as a neurotic or hysteric; rather, he wanted to demonstrate that the war and revolution must inevitably have detrimental consequences for people with the social consciousness and ethical standards of a Rosa Luxemburg. Her pathological grief is nothing more than a consistent ethical reaction to deeply unethical social and political circumstances. These circumstances also include details Luxemburg learns about the Leninist revolution in Russia: that the constitutional assembly had been dissolved under the threat of violence; that democracy was abandoned in favor of dictatorship; that mass executions became the order of the day (*N-III*, 20–29; 63–69; 91–92).[3] Lenin's revolution is called a counter-revolution (*N-III*, 25) (not only an unusually harsh judgment, but also an unusually clear one for a time in which most intellectuals saw Soviet communism as the path to salvation).

Rosa Luxemburg's portrayal is followed by that of Karl Liebknecht, Friedrich Ebert, and Gustav Noske. Liebknecht, like Rosa Luxemburg, is the subject of a highly nuanced rendering extending over several chapters — as a humanist and idealist, as a sufferer and mourner, and as a revolutionary leader who looks to Lenin for guidance, but lacks the latter's unscrupulousness, and is thus unable to lead the revolution to success. Ebert appears initially as a spiritually corrupt but tactically experienced party functionary whose bonhomie conceals the fact that he is — in Döblin's portrayal — a stupid politician of "law and order" still devoted to the idea of state authority and fully prepared to let blood spill in order to stem the flood of the revolution and keep power in his hands. Gustav Noske, the Social Democratic people's representative for the Army and Navy is shown as the "Bluthund" (*N-III*, 309) that he himself professed to be, ready to lead government troops and the reactionary Freikorps to Berlin in order to put down the Spartacist uprising and liquidate the revolution. While Luxemburg and Liebknecht are depicted with respect and sympathy, the portraits of Ebert and Noske contain a satirical streak and even tend toward caricature. Döblin's treatment of Ebert is one-sided, as it attends very little to the difficulties he faced in dealing with domestic and foreign affairs, his desire for peace, and his success in preventing both a civil war and an intervention of the victorious powers. To be sure, Ebert's legacy, like that of the revolution and its outcome, continues to be the subject of controversy, depending to a significant degree on the historian's political standpoint. Sebastian Haffner's 1969 account of the German revolution and the "Revolutionverhinderer" Ebert is nearly identical to that of Döblin (90–93). Heinrich August Winkler, on the other hand, arrives at a more positive estimation of Ebert's politics. While Haffner, like Döblin, speaks of a "verratenen Revolution" and charges Ebert with this betrayal, Winkler writes of a "gebremsten" revolution and refrains from the use of any incriminating or disparaging vocabulary (33–68).

Interwoven with the portrayals of the major historical political players and the portrayal of revolutionary events are the stories of the fictional Becker and Stauffer. The poet Stauffer, debating the question of whether or not to become engaged in the political struggles, decides to rehabilitate his private life and distance himself from politics. Stauffer, the prototype of the German intellectual, having grown up in what Thomas Mann called the "machtgeschützten Innerlichkeit" (*Essays IV*, 65) of the Wilhelminian Empire, remains predisposed and willing to leave politics to others; he neither understands nor accepts the need for a new approach to political questions. Becker has recovered to the point where he can once again take up his teaching career. He begins his class with the study of Sophocles' *Antigone,* which he uses to spark debate about the difference between state and divine mandates and about the relationship between the state and the individual (*N-III*, 187–202). At the suggestion of his students, Heinrich von Kleist's drama *Prinz Friedrich von Homburg* is brought into the discussion as well (*N-III*, 221–26). As would be expected, Becker argues for the primacy of divine principles and calls individuals to resist state mandates that contradict divine commandments. The interpretation of *Antigone* that takes shape through Becker's teaching is most certainly directed against the well-known analysis of the philosopher Hegel who upheld the predominance of the state over the individual. Hegel's philosophy in general had, in the eyes of many, exerted a pernicious influence on German history with its glorification of state power. For Döblin, Antigone, as a passive heroine, as a woman and a sufferer, is the diametrical opposite of the idolized aggressive, masculine hero; as a person of religious and ethical convictions, she stands in opposition to the absolute dominance of state interests and mandates; as a mourner with a firm belief in the afterlife, she rejects the monistic reduction of man to earthly existence, because this reduction, according to Döblin, implies a radical devaluation of man.

Antigone becomes a *Leitfigur* for Becker. But it is not only he who walks "auf den Spuren der Antigone," as the chapter is titled (*N-III*, 425); Rosa Luxemburg, the mourner, lives in the spirit of Antigone as well. And both must learn what it means to model themselves after Antigone.

In the last third of the third part, the revolutionary events and Becker's story become interwoven. Between late 1918 and early 1919, the political climate shifts, as the Spartacist agitation intensifies. On January 5 and 6, 1919, previously unseen numbers of Spartacists come together, ready for revolution, and wait for hours for a cue or a call to action; but the leaders are unable to reach a decision, and the masses disperse. In their place, government troops and Freikorps led by Noske arrive to crush the uprising. Many revolutionaries are shot or brutally killed. By January 12, the January or Spartacist uprising is suppressed; on January 15, Liebknecht and Luxemburg are gruesomely murdered. At this point, even Becker finds his way into the fighting in spite of his pacifist views, compelled to take part out of solidarity with the besieged rebels; after the failure of the uprising, he is sentenced to prison for his participation. Becker's comrade in arms, Maus, also reappears. Having conveniently shed his earlier sympathies for the revolutionary goals, he is now fighting as an officer of the Freikorps. In this role, he happens upon the wounded Becker, but refuses to help him, leaving him to be mistreated and arrested. The revolution is thus shown to divide men and drive them into different and opposing camps.

Döblin relates the murder of Liebknecht and Luxemburg by a liquidation commando in great detail (*N-III*, 585–93). The atmosphere of hatred, the rabble-rousing propaganda, and the meanness and brutality of the myrmidons are presented in unsparing fashion. The whole episode is an aesthetic depiction of violence that is hard to bear, but is required by the nefariousness of this deeply consequential and brutal murder; anything else would have been a palliation. Equally difficult to bear are Luxemburg's visions of the devil during the last days of her life, as she attempts to come to terms with the problem of evil and the impossibility of improving the world. The contents of these hallucinations correspond to the tragic pessimism found in a number of Luxemburg's statements about the totalitarian development of Lenin's revolution (*N-III*, 256–58). Nonetheless, the portrayal of these pathological or hallucinatory sentiments gives them an alienating quality.

Historically speaking, the murder of the two revolutionaries ended the revolution in Berlin, and because the murderers were dealt with extraordinarily mildly, an unrelenting series of political murders by forces on the right followed (Hannover-Drück, 116–26). From this point on, Döblin only hints at the historical developments that followed: the resurgence of reactionary political forces and the simultaneous spread of a cold pragmatism. Becker, sentenced to three years in prison, is at a loss in this violently pacified but hopeless society; he develops sectarian leanings, becomes an evangelist, and finds himself once again cast into doubt. His end — like that of Rosa Luxemburg — takes the form of a fight with the devil. Or, put another way, it is psychomachy in the manner of late classical or medieval epics and dramas: as a battle between good and evil within the soul of a man, and at the same time a battle between good and evil spirits for his soul. This psychomachy obviously collides with conventional conceptions of modern literature, and particularly with the principle of realism.

Of course, Döblin had long since abandoned the principle of realism. In his fundamentally important poetological essay "Der Bau des epischen Werks" of 1928/29 (*SÄPL*, 215–45), Döblin holds that a novel should not merely encompass reality in all its fullness, but should also break through that reality in the direction of existential human situations; in other words, reality should be made transparent in order to reveal basic patterns and the hidden meaning of human life and of history. This, Döblin believed, could be achieved through the use of old myths, legends, and fairy tales, and religious traditions. Consequently, in *Berlin Alexanderplatz* and subsequent novels, mythological and religious representations and symbolism take on considerable importance, both in terms of structural function and metaphorical meaning. This applies to *November 1918* as well, where historical actions of men are seen repeatedly through the models of mythological figures and events or placed within the context of Judeo-Christian religious teachings and their paradigmatic events. This "Hunger nach dem Mythos," which Theodore Ziolkowski has called the "Mythophilie" of modern German literature (170), represented a search for answers about the meaning of life and history, that, while corresponding to historical facts, were illuminating in a more transcendent way. However, Döblin's fondness for embedding contemporary historical events in Judeo-Christian religious teachings was much less characteristic of the times and therefore had an alienating effect on many readers.

A complete list of the mythological and quasi-mythological figures invoked in the *November* trilogy cannot be given here. The majority are taken from Greek mythology, but others come from the legends of Christian saints (St. George, St. Anthony), from the world of the German legends (Eckhart, Tristan and Isolde), and from modern literature (Don Quixote, Michael Kohlhaas). A particularly important figure, whose employment also reveals the sophistication with which Döblin interprets his sources, is Laocoon. He is introduced on three occasions: first by the narrator in reference to President Wilson, in order to make it clear that this was a politician worthy of great admiration, who failed due to overpowering circumstances (*N-II/2*, 306); then by Liebknecht, who draws a comparison between himself and Laocoon, which, however, proves to be false, because his failure was not only due to circumstances but also to his timidity (*N-III*, 326); and finally by the protagonist of the fictional events, the scholar of classical literature Becker, who uses the comparison to Laocoon to expose man's fundamental limitations due to his inner disposition and external circumstances (*N-III*, 644). Thus the mythological references are applied to very different cases.

Four mythological or quasi-mythological motifs take on particular importance: first, the legend of Tristan and Isolde in Wagner's rendering, reflecting the aesthetic and morbid pre-war tendencies of Friedrich Becker (*N-I*, 168; *N-III*, 640); second, the myth of Antigone, which Becker shows to be pertinent in his teaching after the war (*N-III*, 187–202) and which appears once again in the fate of Rosa Luxemburg (*N-III*, 16); third, the mythically presented story of the voyage of the Puritans on the *Mayflower* to American shores (*N-II/2*, 11), which is seen as the attempt to change humankind's sinful history and establish a true Christian spirit on earth. It is this historical, or rather mythic, background that gives President Wilson's European peace mission its religious aura. Finally, the story of the Russian Revolution (*N-III*, 20–26), which for many contemporaries had already attained mythological status and was intended to reveal the wretchedness of the German revolution. In all four cases, this recourse to mythological or quasi-mythological motifs serves to define character and plot. Döblin uses mythology to provide insight into his perspective of the ill-fated German revolution. Characteristically, he achieves his end by using not one but a multitude of myths or even mythologies that function in various ways — to affirm, criticize, complement, or qualify each other. Thus Rosa Luxemburg is not just a new Antigone, but also the bride of the rebellious Satan, modeled after Milton's *Paradise Lost* (*N-III*, 298–304; 576–80), while Wilson is the successor not only of the Pilgrim fathers, but also of Laocoon and of Don Quixote.

Döblin's vision of Judeo-Christian salvation appears as early as in the first volume of *November 1918*, before his conversion to Catholicism. There, after describing the victory celebrations and festivities at the end of the First World War, Döblin writes that in the black cloud still blanketing Europe, the face of the eternal had appeared, and that the eternal one had looked sadly at all that had happened in the last four years, and it had all slipped away (*N-I*, 208). Later, his nemesis Satan emerges in

Luxemburg's and Becker's hallucinations: Satan, who, by pointing out the deficiencies in the world, pushes Luxemburg to rebel (*N-III*, 298–304) and visits Becker in various guises in order to entice him away from the path of salvation (*N-II/2*, 200–210). As in the Baroque morality plays, man in Döblin's novel is positioned between God and Satan, and human history appears as a religious story between heaven and earth. Accordingly, the November revolution becomes much more than just an episode of German or European history. As an integral part of the Christian history of salvation, it reveals the political weaknesses of the protagonists, the misguided course of history, and man's lapse into evil.

In conclusion, we can say that Döblin wanted to portray the German revolution not only in its multifaceted historical breadth, but also in the context of Western mythology and the history of salvation. He sought to accomplish this by presenting not merely the social or worldly totality but an encompassing totality of being and meaning, emblematic — according to Georg Lukács in his *Theorie des Romans* (1920) — of the ancient epics. This encompassing presentation seemed impossible in the modern novel, which was "Ausdruck der transzendentalen Obdachlosigkeit" (32) even if, as Lukács conceded, the "Gesinnung zur Totalität" (47) was still present. To some extent, Döblin had already pursued such a totality in *Berlin Alexanderplatz;* but in that work the meanings of the figures and motifs suggesting a cosmic totality remained vague and metaphorical. In *November 1918*, and particularly in the sections written after his conversion to Catholicism, he went a step further and plainly put forward the notions of salvation and a cosmic totality governed by religious principles. This explains Döblin's audacious manipulation of history, best seen in the portrayal of Rosa Luxemburg, but also in the stylistic inconsistencies between the parts that relate real historical events, primarily in a satirical manner, and those in which a more melodramatic tone is used to convey the protagonists' religious experiences. The work thus makes high demands on the reader in terms of both aesthetic and religious tolerance.

Understandably, the critical response was rather muted, which meant that this extraordinary "Erzählwerk" did not achieve its deserved place among contemporary or successive generations of readers. Nevertheless, in 1978, when the paperback edition came out, it found an admirer in the renowned literary critic Hans Mayer, who wrote a lengthy article in the widely read magazine *Der Spiegel* in an attempt to garner a wider audience, including the political elite. Mayer's article ends with the passage, "Dies Buch erscheint heute wahrlich zur richtigen Zeit. Ein Buch für Bundeskanzler, Gewerkschaftsführer und Unternehmer, für die Hardthöhe [i.e. the Ministry of Defense] wie für Rudi Dutschke [the well-known spokesman of the student movement]." "Aber," Mayer added, "sie werden es nicht lesen" (128).

— Translated by Kurt A. Beals

Notes

[1] The definitive edition of *November 1918* in *Ausgewählte Werke in Einzelbänden*, ed. Werner Stauffacher (1991) divides the work into three parts, with the second part divided into two volumes, the numbering will be as indicated: *N-I* (*Bürger und Soldaten*), *N-II/1* (*Verratenes Volk*), *N-II/2* (*Heimkehr der Fronttruppen*), and *N-III* (*Karl und Rosa*). In this essay the quotations are taken from the dtv paperback edition.

[2] Rilke, *Sämtliche Werke I*, 315.

[3] Döblin uses passages from Rosa Luxemburg, *Die Russische Revolution* (1917).

Works Cited

Althen, Christina. *Machtkonstellationen einer deutschen Revolution: Alfred Döblins Geschichtsroman "November 1918."* Frankfurt am Main: Lang, 1993.

Dollenmayer, David B. *The Berlin Novels of Alfred Döblin*. Berkeley, Los Angeles, London: U of California P, 1988.

Dollinger, Roland. *Totalität und Totalitarismus im Exilwerk Döblins*. Würzburg: Königshausen & Neumann, 1994.

Haffner, Sebastian. *1918/19: Eine deutsche Revolution*. Reinbek bei Hamburg: Rowohlt, 1981; previously Munich: Kindler, 1969.

Hannover-Drück, Elisabeth, and Heinrich Hannover, eds. *Der Mord an Rosa Luxemburg und Karl Liebknecht: Dokumentation eines politischen Verbrechens*. Frankfurt am Main: Suhrkamp, 1979.

Kiesel, Helmuth, "Döblins Konversion als Politikum." *Hinter dem schwarzen Vorhang: Die Katastrophe und die epische Tradition. Festschrift für Anthony W. Riley*. Ed. by Friedrich Gaede, Patrick O'Neill, and Ulrich Scheck. Tübingen: Francke, 1994. 193–208.

———. *Literarische Trauerarbeit: Das Exil- und Spätwerk Alfred Döblins*. Tübingen: Niemeyer, 1986.

Kobel, Erwin, *Alfred Döblin: Erzählkunst im Umbruch*. Berlin and New York: de Gruyter, 1985.

Kuhlmann, Anne. *Revolution als "Geschichte": Alfred Döblins Roman "November 1918": Eine programmatische Lektüre des historischen Romans*. Tübingen: Niemeyer, 1997.

Lukács, Georg, *Die Theorie des Romans: ein geschichtsphilosophischer Versuch über die Formen der großen Epik.* Darmstadt and Neuwied: Luchterhand, 1971.

Mann, Thomas. *Essays (in 6 Bänden).* Ed. by Hermann Kurzke and Stephan Stachorski. Frankfurt am Main: Fischer, 1994.

Mayer, Hans. "Eine deutsche Revolution. Also keine": Über Alfred Döblins wiederentdecktes Erzählwerk 'November 1918.'" *Der Spiegel* 33 (1978): 124–28.

Nietzsche, Friedrich. *Sämtliche Werke. Kritische Studienausgabe in 15 Bänden.* Ed. by Giorgio Colli und Mazzino Montinari. Munich: dtv, 1980.

Osterle, Heinz D. "Alfred Döblins Revolutionsroman." *Alfred Döblin: November 1918.* Vol. 4: *Karl und Rosa.* Munich: dtv, 1978. 665–95.

Rilke, Rainer Maria. *Sämtliche Werke.* Ed. by Rilke-Archiv, in Verbindung mit Ruth Sieber-Rilke. Besorgt durch Ernst Zinn. Frankfurt am Main: Insel, 1955.

Rosenberg, Arthur. *Geschichte der Weimarer Republik.* Ed. by Kurt Kersten. Frankfurt am Main: Europäische Verlagsanstalt, 1977 (first edition 1935).

Sander, Gabriele: *Alfred Döblin.* Stuttgart: Reclam, 2001.

Winkler, Heinrich August. *Weimar 1918–1933: Die Geschichte der ersten deutschen Demokratie.* Munich: Beck, 1993.

Ziolkowski, Theodore. "Der Hunger nach dem Mythos: zur seelischen Gastronomie der Deutschen in den Zwanziger Jahren." *Die sogenannten goldenen Zwanziger Jahre: First Wisconsin Workshop.* Ed. by Reinhold Grimm and Jost Hermand. Bad Homburg: Gehlen, 1970. 169–201.

Döblin and Judaism

Klaus Müller-Salget

THE RELATIONSHIP BETWEEN Alfred Döblin and Judaism was the subject of vehement controversies during the 1930s and 1940s. These became even more intractable after Döblin's November 1941 conversion to Catholicism became public, a step that many people perceived as a betrayal. The Israeli author Schalom Ben-Chorin, who had emigrated from Munich, for example, signaled his disapproval in 1949 in a newspaper article entitled "Abschied von Alfred Döblin" (Farewell to Alfred Döblin). In contrast, in 1978 Erich Gottgetreu published in the "Mitteilungsblatt" for German-speaking immigrants in Israel an appreciation of Döblin in honor of the centennial of his birth under the title "Auch er trug die Fackel" (He too carried the torch); Gottgetreu endeavored in the article to understand Döblin's position.

Also in 1978, Rowohlt published the largely untenable Döblin monograph by Klaus Schröter, which put forth the assertion that Döblin had been, at least for some time, a racist and even an anti-Semite. This slander, which Winfried Georg Sebald took over unexamined in his book *Der Mythus der Zerstörung im Werk Döblins,* is based on falsified citations and other manipulations that I exposed and refuted point for point in 1984. Nevertheless, neither Schröter nor Sebald felt the need thereafter to retract their statements with the appropriate expression of regret. Their negative assessment was based on the accusation that Döblin was a renegade, by which however they did not mean from Judaism but from socialism.

Now as ever it is well to subject these distortions to a sober assessment of the facts. Much pertinent research on the topic exists. The essay by Louis Huguet, "Alfred Doblin et le judaïsme" (1976), is highly informative but unfortunately not easily accessible. The excellent catalogue *Alfred Döblin 1878–1978,* compiled by Jochen Meyer in collaboration with Ute Doster for the special exhibition of the Deutsches Literaturarchiv in Marbach in 1978, contains a very informative chapter, "'Zion und Europa.' Alfred Döblins Verhältnis zum Judentum" (357–75). Klara Pomeranz Carmely's approach in the chapter on Döblin in her book *Das Identitätsproblem jüdischer Autoren im deutschen Sprachraum* (1981) is one of paraphrase rather than analysis. Hans-Peter Bayerdörfer focused on Jewish narrative motifs and modes in his article in the collection *Im Zeichen Hiobs* (1985).[1] In 1995, the volume *Schriften zu jüdischen Fragen* (*SjF*) appeared within the Döblin edition of the Walter Publishing House, with an extensive commentary and a highly competent afterword by Hans Otto Horch.[2]

Döblin's parents, the master tailor Max Döblin and Sophie Freudenheim, originally from the Prussian province of Posnan, moved westward and settled in Stettin. They were only superficially connected with the Jewish religion (belonging to the so-called "twice-a-year Jews" who attended the synagogue only on high holidays). The young Döblin, due to what he considered a completely inadequate religious education, never developed an emotional affinity to Judaism. Nonetheless, he did experience anti-Semitism from childhood on, without, however, developing a feeling of inferiority or self-hate (*SLW*, 63). In 1912, he married Erna Reiss, who came from an even more assimilated family; his first son was baptized as a Lutheran, and Döblin himself left Judaism (*B I*, 259). However, anti-Semitism and, more generally, the situation of Jews in the Diaspora continued to concern him. This is shown in the novels *Die drei Sprünge des Wang-lun* (1915) and *Wallenstein* (1920), where persecution, expulsion, and even the killing of people of different faiths appear as important motifs (Huguet, 56–62).

Döblin expressed himself directly on anti-Semitism for the first time in 1920 in "Revue," one of the commentaries he wrote pseudonymously as "Linke Poot" (= left hand or paw) for Samuel Fischer's magazine *Die Neue Rundschau* (*DMB*, 74–84). He had nothing but mockery for what he called a "kulturhistorische Dämonopathie" (*DMB*, 77), which he placed in the same category as fear of ghosts and belief in witchcraft. As to the frequent allegations that Jews were superior in economic and intellectual matters, Döblin wrote that this was simply a "Druck- und Verdrängungssymptom" which would disappear by itself once the pressure was removed. He refuted racial theories then as well as later, as he considered the natural and social environment far more influential than "das sogenannte Blut" (*DMB*, 78).[3] The aphoristic essay "Zion und Europa" which appeared in 1921 in the *Neue Merkur*, was written in a similarly light, mocking tone (*KS-1*, 313–19). At this time, Döblin regarded Western European Zionism as "eine Form jüdischer Verärgerung und Nervosität"(*KS-1*, 318). Regarding the situation of the East European Jewry, he maintained that the right to self-determination of peoples would offer a completely adequate solution. The goal should not be to return to Palestine but national autonomy in the East; a Jewish state in Galicia, for example, would be a logical solution. He derided anti-Semitism as mental weakness of the upper and middle classes, asserting that anti-Semitism was non-existent "in der Praxis, unter den Realien" (*KS-1*, 317).

Two years later events forced Döblin to reexamine his optimistic views. Pogrom-like attacks occurred in Berlin's Scheunenviertel, where the Eastern European Jewish immigrants had concentrated, and Döblin woke up from his indolence.[4] He began to attend Zionist events, although he did not accept an invitation to visit Palestine. He considered Palestine a destination suitable only for retrogressive Jews bound to the old religion and, moreover, an area too small for the entire Jewish people. In a draft for a lecture that can be dated to March 1924, entitled "Zionismus und westliche Kultur," he again stated: "Das Ideal: eine jüdische Ostrepublik" (*SjF*, 267). This insistence on the attainment of autonomy for Eastern European Jews in places where they already lived has to do with Döblin's own origins in this region. He now felt the need to investigate this origin and to get to know the nature and way of life of East European Jews.[5] He had already come to appreciate Yiddish theater during the Berlin visits of the Vilna theater group.[6]

Döblin undertook a journey to Poland in the fall of 1924, financially supported by the S. Fischer publishing house and by the *Vossische Zeitung*, for which he wrote his travel reports. The trip was significant for him in many respects: philosophically and religiously, as well as in terms of his theory and practice of the novel, and particularly with regard to his estimation of Judaism. Only on this trip did he become fully conscious of the fact that Jews are a people. Hans-Peter Bayerdörfer has shown how the book *Reise in Polen* (1925), which grew out of the earlier reports, follows Döblin's path from the mere recording of a confusing multiplicity toward a dialogic understanding, culminating in a conversation with the rabbi of the Strickov Hasids that he perceived as "vollkommenes Labsal" (*RP*, 330; Bayerdörfer, 165). Döblin was impressed by the fact that the frequently humiliated Polish people now finally lived in a state of their own, and he drew a hopeful conclusion for the Jewish people: the Poles "sitzen in ihren eigenen Häusern. Den Juden kann es nicht entgehen" (*RP*, 99).

He concluded that a *spiritual* renewal of Judaism was necessary, an uplifting from the humiliating experience of the Diaspora and, as he put it, the terrible and hopeless belief in the Messiah. He articulated this view in *Unser Dasein*, which he began writing in 1927 but which was not published until April 1933 (and was then immediately burned by the Nazis). Hans-Peter Bayerdörfer has shown that Jews, Jewish tradition, and Jewish narrative modes also play an important role in Döblin's most famous novel, *Berlin* Alexanderplatz (Bayerdörfer, 168–71). In book seven of *Unser Dasein*, bearing the title "Wie lange noch, jüdisches Volk-Nichtvolk?," Döblin implored the Jews to turn to a full life, which also means: to their own land, and to their own responsibility. He expressed the danger to Jews in prophetic sentences:

> Aus der Geschichte müssen die Juden wissen, daß keine Leistung, keine Willfährigkeit und Ergebenheit schützt, sondern nur Kräfte, Macht und ihre kluge Anwendung. [...] Von Zeit zu Zeit treten Massenbewegungen auf, die auf ihre direkte Vertreibung oder Ausrottung ausgehen [...]: es ist in allen Ländern nur ein kleiner Schritt von der Papierstaatsbürgerschaft zum Pogrom oder neuen Ghetto. [...] Glaube sich keiner, keiner, der Jude ist, irgendwo seines Bürgerrechts oder auch seines Lebens sicher! (*UD*, 385, 389, 399, 400)

In the face of these strong (and justified) warnings, Döblin's suggestion to create a Jewish world organization and his warning not to call for a nation state too soon appear rather weak. But one must recognize that he was above all concerned with a change in consciousness, a renewal of the Jewish religion through the reaffirmation of the original strong belief in God (without the hope for the Messiah that he saw as paralyzing), and a recognition of the obligation to a full, active existence. These thoughts were actually a special aspect of Döblin's philosophical concept of humanity as both "Stück und Gegenstück der Natur": man as a seemingly inconsequential particle within the whole of the universe ("Stück der Natur") on the one hand, and on the other, as a knowing and active center of power ("Gegenstück der Natur").[7] Accordingly, he concludes book seven with the following assertion: "Die Religion, von der hier geredet wurde, ist keine Religion der 'Juden,' sondern der Menschen" (*UD*, 413). According to Döblin's views, Jews should play an exemplary historical role. They were supposed to set an example to Western nations with their "new religion" and by becoming a people without nationalism.[8] Döblin's subsequent disappointment over the actual course of events after 1933 comes as no surprise.

However one may evaluate the ideas expressed so far, it is clearly not true that Döblin concerned himself with questions of Jewish politics and rejected assimilation only in exile, as Sebald maintains (38). Nonetheless, his ideas became considerably more concrete in exile. Even before he left Berlin, he had begun to write the novel *Babylonische Wandrung oder Hochmut kommt vor dem Fall*, which he later interpreted as a premonition of exile. The fact that the curse of the prophet Jeremiah forces the guilt-laden Babylonian god Marduk on an arduous descent to Earth and eventually to repentance may also be read as an anticipatory fantasy of revenge of the Jew Döblin.

While still in Berlin, Döblin had made contact with representatives of neo-territorialism. This attempt to revive the territorialist movement, which had dissolved in 1925, was aimed at establishing settlements for the threatened European Jews. Territorialism differed from Zionism on the one hand in its willingness to consider areas other than Palestine (Angola, Uganda, and even Peru were discussed) and, on the other, in the intention to make Yiddish and not Modern Hebrew the general language; for this reason, the territorialists were also called Yiddishists. By this name Döblin had already mentioned the territorialists approvingly in *Unser Dasein*. The movement seemed to him more liberal, more open than Zionism (Huguet, 83). In Zurich, his first place of exile, he also became acquainted with representatives of the O.R.T., the Society for the Promotion of Handicrafts, Industry, and Agriculture among Jews. Founded in 1880 in St. Petersburg, it also worked to acquire settlement areas outside of Europe.[9] The O.R.T. was later responsible for the professional advancement of Döblin's son Peter and the survival of his son Klaus. Döblin was actively engaged in this organization as well as with the territorialists until 1937.

In exile, Döblin saw the need to revise book seven of *Unser Dasein*. He added a chapter titled "Jüdische Massensiedlungen und Volksminoritäten," which was pre-printed in September of 1933 in the first issue of Klaus Mann's magazine *Die Sammlung*. The entire text was then published a month later under the title *Jüdische Erneuerung* by Querido in Amsterdam. In the face of the Nazi takeover in Germany, Döblin recognized that his earlier call for the creation of a Jewish world organization was no longer adequate. He now demanded the "Gewinnung des Minoritätenrechtes für die Juden" and the "Vorbereitung der großen außereuropäischen Massensiedlungen," capable of receiving "das Gros der gesamten Judenheit" (*SjF*, 56, 58, and 59). In keeping with his reservations against Zionism, he suggested Angola, Peru and Australia as possible settlement areas and stated: "Es wird, grade um den Nationalismen zu entgehen, gut sein, sich mehreren Territorien zuzuwenden" (*SjF*, 59). Two years later, in *Flucht und Sammlung des Judenvolks: Aufsätze und Erzählungen* (*SjF*, 79–263), his position moved distinctly closer to that of Zionism. Döblin retracted his reservations against a Jewish national state, arguing that "ein Ding, welches für Staaten von heute 'reaktionär' ist, für die flüchtigen jüdischen Massen 'progressiv' sein kann" (*SjF*, 178). He even recognized that Palestine was the superior choice and called the earlier discussion favoring Uganda over Palestine "auf dem Hintergrund der jüdischen Geschichte kindlich" (*SjF,* 181). At the same time, he continued to criticize the practical applications of the Zionist idea as both elitist and provincial (*SjF,* 182–83).

During his Paris exile, Döblin was active as a lecturer and organizer. In November 1933 he became one of the founders of the Paris-based "Liga für jüdische Kolonisation," which became a section of the international "Freiland-Liga" in 1935; Döblin served on its board until 1936. A number of his essays appeared in Jewish journals in Yiddish; and he began to learn Yiddish (*B I,* 207) but did not make much more progress with this language than he did with learning French. In June 1935, he edited the only German-language issue of the magazine *Freiland,* which also contained his programmatic essay "Grundsätze und Methoden eines Neuterritorialismus" (*SPG,* 309–38). The following month, he participated in the conference of the European "Freiland-Ligas" in London, where he gave the opening speech, "Ziel und Charakter der Freiland-Bewegung,"[10] as well as the concluding remarks; but he was deeply disappointed by the course of the proceedings. Instead of the debates on fundamental principles that he had hoped for, the main concern was over organizational matters and quarrels between the different groups. In 1938, after his separation from the territorialists, he expressed his dissatisfaction in an article for the Paris magazine *Ordo,* reproaching the organization for "erbärmliches Intrigantentum, Faulheit, Doppelzüngigkeit und den erschütterndsten Unernst" and castigating the people in charge as "Ränkeschmiede, Maulhelden, Politikaster, Stellenjäger" (*SjF,* 351–52 and 354).

Feelings that had accumulated in Döblin over many years culminated in this attack. Already in December 1934 he had written to Isidor Lifschitz: "Ich selber habe nur eine halbe Freude an der Liga, weil sie zu einseitig sich auf 'Land' verlegt und nicht das nach meiner Meinung centrale Thema der Menschen, der jüdischen allgemeinen Erneuerung aufgreift" (*B I,* 199). At that time he had still held out hope for the London conference, although he was already toying with the thought of leaving the organization and founding a "Bund Neues Juda" (*B I,* 200). He was unwilling to give up his fundamentally utopian ideas (utopian particularly considering the historical situation) and kept hoping, on the one hand, to be able to bring about a concrete realization of his view of mankind and, on the other, to find a spiritual community and a home for himself.

There were further irritations. Döblin's involvement in territorialism did not meet with understanding by many of his fellow emigrants. The communist exile press even accused him of having become infected by fascism.[11] Even the writer, critic, and philosopher Ludwig Marcuse (1894–1971), for example, reacted to the "Freiland" issue, edited by Döblin, with vehement polemics.[12]

Despite such negative experiences, Döblin held fast to the "Freiland" movement until 1937, not least because of his friendship with Nathan Birnbaum, the advocate of a religiously tinged territorialism. Döblin published several articles in Birnbaum's magazines *Der Ruf* (Rotterdam) and *Der jüdische Volksdienst* (London), and he and Birnbaum also carried on a lively correspondence.[13] Döblin deeply admired Birnbaum's moral and intellectual integrity, and this helped overcome all other differences between the two men. Birnbaum's death on April 2, 1937 deprived him of an important source of support, and he wrote a moving memorial to this friend.[14]

Concurrent with his engagement on behalf of the persecuted Jews, Döblin was also at work on the novel *Amazonas,* a trilogy in which he reflected on the history of the Occident since the Age of Discovery. He thought he had discovered the cause for the descent into fascism in what he called "Prometheism," by which Döblin meant the total autonomization of man and the development of instrumental thinking. The largest part of the trilogy is dedicated to the history of the Jesuit republic in Paraguay, the attempt, ultimately destined for failure, to create a community and a refuge removed from the frantic conquests, displacement, and extermination of the native Indians. What Döblin really meant, at least in part, is shown in a passage in *Flucht und Sammlung des Judenvolks* and in "Grundsätze und Methoden eines Neuterritorialismus." There he formulated (and rejected) the criticism of the "Realisten, Historiker, Sozialisten" that the efforts of territorialism were unrealistic and completely idealistic: "Wir haben an den Jesuiten in Paraguay ein Beispiel. Es gibt keine Inseln mehr auf der Erde" (*SjF,* 172 and *SPG,* 327). In the South America trilogy, however, Döblin agreed with his critics.

In 1935 Döblin also discovered the writings of Sören Kierkegaard and the mystic Johannes Tauler in the National Library of Paris. This opened up for him on a personal level a new path in his search for a way to make concrete that which in 1927 he had called "das Ich über der Natur" or the "ewigen Urgrund." It is striking to see the frequent mention of God in the writings on Jewish problems, in particular in *Flucht und Sammlung des Judenvolks,* which concludes with a prayer.[15]

The attentive reader of Döblin's works should not be surprised that the formerly pugnacious atheist eventually turned to religion. The religious undercurrent is unmistakable from early on, and his rebellion against the authority of the father stemmed from his yearning for just such an authority. But why Catholicism of all things? This, too, is not all that surprising. The Jewish religion in the form known to him[16] and Jewish rituals[17] had remained alien to him. The figures of the Mother of God and the Crucified Jesus on the other hand fascinated him from early on (a fascination which can be explained biographically).[18] The trip to Poland reinforced his feelings. The Polish worship of the Madonna, the Church of the Virgin Mary in Cracow, and the Veit Stoß crucifix over the middle aisle of the church made a deep impression on him (*RP*, 239–41, 326). He later evoked this scene again at the beginning of the third volume of *Amazonas*. It also reappeared transformed before his eyes when he was stranded in a refugee camp in 1940 on his flight through France. On the verge of succumbing to despair, he recognized before the crucifix in the cathedral of Notre Dame et St. Privat in Mende that his previous worldview could not help him. In his notion of humanity as "Stück und Gegenstück der Natur" a central problem had remained unsolved: that of suffering in and from temporality. Now in 1940 he realized: "Der Mangel an Gerechtigkeit in der Welt beweist, dies ist nicht die einzige Welt," and: "Es ist unmöglich, den 'Ewigen Urgrund' zu empfinden. Es muß, damit es ganz an uns herankommt, das Wort 'Jesus' hinzutreten" (*SR*, 135, 169). In Los Angeles, he made contact with fathers of the Societas Jesu, whose efforts to create gentle Indian missions he had already described in the second volume of the *Amazonas* trilogy. He did not even consider a conversion to Protestantism, to which his wife and oldest son already belonged; this version of Christianity was too abstract for him and lacked the visual richness that fascinated him so much in Catholicism (Huguet, 111). His turning to the Catholic confession is thus a very personal decision that we should not attempt to judge. It is comprehensible from the point of view of his biography and the development of his worldview.

The fact that he kept this decision a secret until the end of the war in 1945 is a different matter. Two motives play a role here, and their respective weight is difficult to assess. On the one hand, Döblin did not want his conversion to become a political issue, to awaken the impression that he was abandoning the persecuted Jewish people. On September 17, 1941 he wrote to his friends, the Jewish couple Elvira and Arthur Rosin in New York:

> Würde ich, was gar nicht der Fall ist, heute oder morgen katholisch oder protestantisch werden, warum sollte ich es nicht, — wofern es "in meinem Busen" bleibt? Es wird jetzt bekannt, daß der Philosoph Bergson, bekanntlich ein Jude, schon jahrelang Katholik war; er behielt es aber als seine Privatsache bei sich und wußte, daß in dieser Zeit ein

Hervortreten damit bedeuten würde, dem eigenen Volk in den Rücken fallen. (*B I*, 259)[19]

And, with reference to himself:

> Würde ich mit irgendwelcher christlicher Haltung und entsprechenden Worten an die Öffentlichkeit treten, und gar jetzt, so würde das ein "Verrat" sein, nämlich an dem, was ich ja auch bin, am Jüdischen. (*B I*, 258)

On the other hand, Döblin was at that time dependent on financial support from Jewish aid committees and individuals, such as the Rosins, and therefore fearfully avoided any publicity about his conversion. On December 6, 1943 he asked his son Peter once again for "absolute Diskretion": "ich hätte sonst massenhaft Schwierigkeiten und Unannehmlichkeiten dadurch; ich will es *während des Krieges* absolut zurückhalten" (*B I*, 298).

It is not easy to assess Döblin's tactics in this regard. Elvira Rosin, who had reacted to the first rumors of Döblin's conversion with the reproach of betrayal, apparently changed her mind after reading his conversation on religion *Der unsterbliche Mensch* (1946). At least Döblin seems to have thought so, as he wrote her on September 30, 1948: "Der gute alte Ton hat mich wirklich sehr gefreut, liebe Frau Elvira: Sie haben wieder so aufrichtig, aber diesmal versöhnt geschrieben" (*B I*, 393, also 406).

There are many testimonies that Döblin retained ties with Jews and the fate of the Jewish people even after his conversion. Hans-Peter Bayerdörfer refers to the figure of Rosa Luxemburg in the tetralogy *November 1918* (Bayerdörfer, 173). The title of Döblin's last novel *Hamlet oder Die lange Nacht nimmt ein Ende* is an explicit reference to the Jewish day of atonement, Yom Kippur, the evening before which is called "the long night." In his radio commentary "Kritik der Zeit," which he read over the Südwestfunk between 1946 and 1952, Döblin commented sympathetically on the problems and struggles surrounding the establishment of the state of Israel, expressing his hope for a peaceful solution.

Two letters to his colleague Arnold Zweig (1887–1968), who returned from Israel to East Berlin in 1948, show Döblin's fundamental ambivalence toward his own Judaism and toward Zionism. He wrote on June 16, 1952:

> Ich denke auch öfter, sehr oft an Palästina und an das Judentum. Sie waren ja drüben, aus welchem Grund Sie zurückkehrten, weiß ich nicht, aber mir scheint auch, so positiv man zu vielen [*sic*] drüben steht, so sehr man die Heimstätte begrüßt, es dürfte drüben kaum der rechte Platz für unsereins sein, das Judentum ist längst geistig aus dem nationalen und lokalen Rahmen herausgetreten, und wie können dann gerade die Geistigen und Intellektuellen wieder in den alten Rahmen,

den eine andere Geistigkeit geformt hatte, zurücktreten: wir haben die Pflicht und den Willen, für eine größere und neue Gesellschaft den Rahmen zu formen [. . .]. (*B I,* 453)

On October 6 of the same year, however, after Zweig had tried to explain the reasons for his return, Döblin wrote to Zweig as a postscript to a tirade against the reactionary tendencies in the Federal Republic of Germany the following:

> Sie werden staunen über das, was ich Ihnen über Ihre Israelsätze sage: Sie hätten besser drüben bleiben sollen, dort genau die Sache, die Sie jetzt vertreten, dort vertreten sollen. Dort drüben waren Sie ein lebendiges und aktives Element, in Deutschland macht man Sie zu Schutt und Asche. (*B I,* 456)

More generally, and not just from the perspective of the current opportunity for action, he expressed himself in a letter of May 4, 1950 to Martin Buber:

> Es ist etwas Schönes und Neues und wahrhaft Gutes, das Sie dort ins Leben gerufen haben, eine Zufluchtsstelle für große Massen schuldloser und gejagter Menschen. Und mehr: Die Sicherung dieser Menschen im Zusammenhang mit einem Boden, der ihnen dann wirklich Heimat wird. [. . .] Dies haben Sie begonnen, und dies führen Sie jetzt weiter, und ich freue mich darüber, wie ich mich über Ihren Staat freue, daß er da ist. Mich selbst hat meine Geburt, mein Wachstum, mein Schicksal, auf einen anderen Weg geführt, der auch nicht zufällig und neuartig ist. [. . .] Für mich steht die Frage [. . .] nicht nach Land und Staat und politischer Heimat, sondern nach Religion, nach Diesseits und Jenseits und nach dem ewigen Urgrund, den Sie und ich Gott nennen. Ich kann darum Ihre Haltung und alles, was Sie betreiben, segnen und kann doch für mich selber sagen, hier im Lande: Ich spreche nicht von Staat und nicht von der Heimat, aber so ist es geworden, und hier stehe ich und kann nicht anders. (*B I,* 411–12)

In conclusion we can say that Judaism, Jewish heritage, Jewish tradition, and that which is euphemistically called "the fate of the Jews in the twentieth century" are of great significance for Döblin's life and work. He derived fundamental aspects of feeling, thinking, and writing from Judaism, and in the years from 1924 to 1937 he was not lacking in personal involvement as well. The fact that he took the step from Judaism to Christianity, a step which he perceived as being anticipated in history,[20] must be considered a personal decision and respected as such.

His last dictations, published under the title *Von Leben und Tod, die es beide nicht gibt,* bear witness to the fact that he did not find serenity even as a Catholic and that he continued to ask questions and to doubt his own position.[21] Since there obviously was a mental affinity between them, the words he had written in 1937 about his mentor Nathan Birnbaum apply also to Döblin himself and his relationship to the Catholic church:

> Auch für die Orthodoxie ist er unbequem geworden. Das Ewig-Rebellische ist ihm im Blut gelegen. Wie ein Ahasver hat er alle, alle noch existierenden, jüdischen Positionen durchlaufen, vom Atheismus und Liberalismus bis zu der Agudat.[22] Bei der Orthodoxie aber ist er geblieben, allen Widersprüchen zum Trotz. An jenem Ort also, wo überschäumende, sich verzehrende und gehetzte Naturen sich noch am ehesten geschützt und geborgen fühlen. Da ist er in einem jahrhundertealten Hafen angekommen. (*SjF*, 344–45)

For the inscription on his gravestone, Döblin, simultaneously crafty and modest, chose a sentence from the Paternoster: "Fiat voluntas tua." He is buried at the side of his son Wolfgang, who committed suicide in the Vosges village Housseras so as not to be captured by the Germans. Döblin confided to his friend Robert Minder the reason for not wanting to be buried in Germany under any conditions: he foresaw that in the future "unsere Gräber" would be once again desecrated in Germany (Minder, 51).

— *Authorized translation by Detlev Koepke*

Notes

[1] Bayerdörfer's insights have been extended in the meantime by Thomas Isermann. See also Claudia Sonino.

[2] Horch's essay "Alfred Döblin und der Neo-Territorialismus" was largely integrated into his afterword (*SjF*, 523–80).

[3] See also the article "Expressionismus, Altertumskunde und Fräulein Alomis" of January 19, 1922 (*KS-2*, 18–22): "Es gibt aber Mulatten. Das ist eine Kreuzung von Weißen und Negern. Also ist etwas vorhanden, sprich 'Natur,' was sich um die aufgeblasene Gesellschaftstheorie nicht kümmert. Es gibt Kreuzungen von Romanen und Germanen, von Eseln und Pferden; die Kreuzungen von Schafen, Hornochsen und Kanarienvögeln nennt man Rassetheoretiker" (21).

[4] See his report "Während der Schlacht singen die Musen." Originally published in *Prager Tagblatt*, November 11, 1923. Now in *KS-2*, 329–33.

[5] "Schließlich wurde mir deutlicher, was ich tun mußte und tun wollte: einmal feststellen, wer eigentlich das ist: die Juden. [. . .] Nun wollte ich einmal eine reale Reise in das Land meiner Väter machen" (*SLW*, 65–66).

[6] See the articles "Deutsches und jüdisches Theater" (December 28, 1921) in *KS I*, 362–67; "Expressionismus, Altertumskunde und Fräulein Alomis" (January 19, 1922) and "Palästinensisches Theater in Berlin" (June 20, 1924) in *KS II*, 18–22 and 406–10.

[7] Müller-Salget, *Alfred Döblin*, 241–47.

[8] Müller-Salget, "Herkunft und Zukunft," 266–68, 277.

[9] The original Russian name of the society was later translated into English (Organization for Rehabilitation through Training) and into French (Organisation, Reconstruction, Travail). Its present-day headquarters are in Jerusalem.

[10] Published at the time in Yiddish as "Cil un charakter fun der Frajland-bawegung." (Warsze: Frajland-lije far teritorjalistizer kolonisazije, 1935). The German translation in *SjF*, 312–22.

[11] See, for example, the articles by Otto Heller, "Das dritte Reich Israel" and Maria Lazar, "Die Infektion des Doktor Döblin."

[12] Ludwig Marcuse, "Döblin greift ein," *Das Neue Tagebuch*, vol. 3, no. 33 (August 17, 1935): 783–85. Döblin's reply "Jüdische Antijuden" also appeared in *Das Neue Tagebuch*, no. 42 (October 19, 1935): 1000–1004); now in *SjF*, 323–28.

[13] Döblin's letters from 1934 and 1935 (copies from Louis Huguet's collection), now published in *B II*, 86–106 and 108–11.

[14] "Zum toit fun Nosn Birnbaum." *Naie Stimme* (Warsaw) no. 2 (1937): 12–13. German translation in *SjF*, 344–47.

[15] According to a review by Birnbaum, cited by Horch, 36 (note 22), it consists of paragraphs of the Jewish "eighteen prayers." Döblin was drawn to a religious Judaism under the influence of Birnbaum, but this remained a relatively brief episode.

[16] See *B I*, 275: "Eine Religion muß für alle Völker und alle Menschen gleich sein, und da giebt es kein 'ausgewähltes Volk'"; "Die jüdische Religion ist eine Nationalreligion" (259); and "Ich konnte mit dem Nationalen, das am alten Judentum in der Religion noch hängt, schon lange nichts anfangen" (406).

[17] See *SLW*, 62.

[18] See Müller-Salget, *Alfred Döblin*, 20–26.

[19] Bergson, however, like Franz Werfel, did not even consent to be baptized, for the reasons mentioned in the quote.

[20] "Ich spreche von Christentum, und dieses ist natürlich erwachsen aus dem Jüdischen. Es läuft ja, wie tausendmal festgestellt, auch objektiv eine einzige Linie von einem Bekenntnis zum anderen" (*B I*, 406).

[21] First published (revised and with errors) in *Sinn und Form* 9 (1957), no. 5: 902–33. Now in *SLW*, 465–508.

[22] He means the international organization of orthodox Jews founded in 1912 in Kattowitz ("Agudat Israel"), of which Birnbaum had become the first general secretary in 1919. See *SjF*, 509.

Works Cited

Alfred Döblin 1878–1978. Special exhibitions of the Schiller Nationalmuseum. Ed. Bernhard Zeller. Catalogue Nr. 30. Exhibition and catalogue: Jochen Meyer in collaboration with Ute Doster. Munich: Kösel Verlag, 1978.

Bayerdörfer, Hans-Peter. "'Ghettokunst.' Meinetwegen, aber hundertprozentig echt.' Alfred Döblins Begegnung mit dem Ostjudentum." *Im Zeichen Hiobs: Jüdische Schriftsteller und deutsche Literatur im 20. Jahrhundert.* Ed. Gunter E. Grimm and Hans-Peter Bayerdörfer. Königstein: Athenäum, 1985. 161–77.

Ben-Chorin, Schalom. "Abschied von Alfred Döblin." *Hakidmah,* Jerusalem, July 1, 1949.

Gottgetreu, Erich. "Auch er trug die Fackel." *Mitteilungsblatt* of the Irgun Olej Merkas Europe 46, no. 31 (August 11, 1978): 5 and 7.

Heller, Otto. "Das dritte Reich Israel." *Neue deutsche Blätter* 1, no. 5 (Jan. 1934): 304–13.

Horch, Hans Otto. "Alfred Döblin und der Neo-Territorialismus. Mit bisher unveröffentlichten Auszügen aus Briefen Döblins an Nathan Birnbaum." *Internationales Alfred-Döblin-Kolloquium Paris 1993.* Ed. Michel Grunewald. Bern: Lang, 1995. 25–36.

Huguet, Louis. "Alfred Doblin et le judaïsme." *Annales de l'Université d'Abidjan,* Series D (Lettres), vol. 9 (1976): 47–115.

Isermann, Thomas: *Der Text und das Unsagbare: Studien zu Religionssuche und Werkpoetik bei Alfred Döblin.* Idstein: Schulz Kirchner, 1989.

Lazar, Maria. "Die Infektion des Doktor Döblin." *Neue deutsche Blätter* 1, no. 6 (Feb. 1934): 380–83.

Minder, Robert. *Wozu Literatur? Reden und Essays.* Frankfurt am Main: Suhrkamp, 1971.

Müller-Salget, Klaus. *Alfred Döblin: Werk und Entwicklung.* Bonn: Bouvier, 1972 (2nd. ed. 1988).

———. "Neuere Tendenzen in der Döblin-Forschung." *Zeitschrift für deutsche Philologie* 103 (1984): 263–77.

———. "Alfred Döblin und das Judentum." *Deutsch-jüdische Exil- und Emigrationsliteratur im 20. Jahrhundert.* Ed. by Itta Shedletzky and Hans Otto Horch. Tübingen: Niemeyer, 1993 (= Conditio Judaica. Studien und Quellen zur deutsch-jüdischen Literatur- und Kulturgeschichte, vol. 5), 153–63. Also in *Internationale Alfred-Döblin-Kolloquien Münster 1989–Marbach a.N. 1991.* Ed. Werner Stauffacher. Bern: Lang, 1993. 251–61.

———. "'Herkunft und Zukunft.' Zur Wiederentdeckung des Judentums in den zwanziger Jahren (Arnold Zweig, Döblin, Feuchtwanger)." *Conditio Judaica, Part 3: Judentum, Antisemitismus und deutschsprachige Literatur vom Ersten Weltkrieg bis 1933/1938.* Ed. Hans Otto Horch and Horst Denkler. Tübingen: Niemeyer, 1993. 260–77.

Pomeranz Carmely, Klara. *Das Identitätsproblem jüdischer Autoren im deutschen Sprachraum: Von der Jahrhundertwende bis zu Hitler.* Königstein: Scriptor, 1981.

Prangel, Matthias. "Alfred Döblins Konzept von der geistigen Gesamterneuerung des Judentums." *Interbellum und Exil.* Ed. Sjaak Onderlinden. Amsterdam: Rodopi, 1991 (= Amsterdamer Publikationen zur Sprache und Literatur, Vol. 90): 162–80.

Schröter, Klaus. *Alfred Döblin in Selbstzeugnissen und Bilddokumenten.* Reinbek bei Hamburg: Rowohlt, 1978.

Sebald, Winfried Georg. *Der Mythus der Zerstörung im Werk Döblins.* Stuttgart: Klett, 1980.

Sonino, Claudia. "Eine andere Rationalität: Döblins Begegnung mit den Ostjuden." *Internationales Alfred-Döblin-Kolloquium Bergamo 1999.* Ed. Torsten Hahn. Bern: Lang, 2002. 141–56.

Robinson the Castaway: Döblin's Christian Faith as Reflected in His Autobiography *Schicksalsreise* and His Religious Dialogues *Der unsterbliche Mensch* and *Der Kampf mit dem Engel*

Christoph Bartscherer

ALFRED DÖBLIN SUBTITLED his autobiography *Schicksalsreise*[1] with remarkable accuracy as "Bericht und Bekenntnis."[2] The book is first of all a detailed memoir of those troubled wanderings that began in May 1940 for the writer exiled in Paris since 1933. Fleeing the advancing Wehrmacht, Döblin arrived in Hollywood four months later, returning temporarily to the wreckage of postwar Germany in November 1945. Accordingly, his *Robinsonade* is divided into three parts, subtitled "Europa, ich muß dich lassen" (Farewell, Europe), "Amerika," and "Wieder zurück" (Back Again). It should be noted that although the first book was written in America between 1940 and 1941, the second and third came to be only seven years later, in his homeland. While Döblin felt compelled immediately upon his arrival in California to record the events of his flight in a book called "Robinson in France," which was based on his notes from exile and supplemented with current observations pertaining to postwar Germany, he did not finish the work until 1948.[3] In addition to this frame of documentary reporting, in which Döblin assumes the role of a contemporary commentator, *Schicksalsreise* has the characteristics of a religious manifesto, and here he reveals himself openly to his readership as a devout Christian. On this level, the first-person narrator presents the ideas and processes by which his flight became a spiritual adventure, in the course of which Döblin the Jew not only came to believe in Christ as the Son of God, but also fulfilled this recognition by his formal conversion to Catholicism.

The Catastrophe

As Döblin sat at work on his novel *November 1918,* the pen was literally struck from his hand by the radio report on 16 May 1940 that German troops had broken through the northern flank of the 9th Division of the French army between Sedan and Namur (*SR*, 17). The inconceivable defeat occurred with frightening speed. Hardly any doubt as to the outcome remained. Within a few weeks, France, which after the First World War had become the strongest European military power, was overrun and faced the humiliating occupation by its German archenemy. The mortal danger in which Döblin found himself was obvious to anyone familiar with his life. He was on the most-wanted list of his German persecutors not only as a Jew who in exile had strongly advocated an independent Jewish state. Long considered part of the political left, Döblin, after his election to the "Sektion für Dichtkunst" of the Prussian Academy of Fine Arts, had sided with Heinrich Mann (1871–1950) in fighting the advance of *völkisch*-nationalist trends by openly opposing the literary partisans of the Nazi movement, such as Erwin Guido Kolbenheyer (1878–1962), Josef Ponten (1883–1940), and Wilhelm Schäfer (1868–1952) (Meyer, 315 and 326–27). Finally, the indomitable Döblin became an even greater thorn in the side of the National Socialists when, beginning in October 1939, he accepted a position in the French Ministry of Information, whose mission was to produce counterpropaganda against Hitler's Germany (Prangel, 90–91). It was obvious that should he fall into the hands of the German occupiers, he would fare no better than his books, which with the exception of the novel *Wallenstein* had been included in the Nazi book burning of May 1933.

At first Döblin hesitated to turn his back on Paris, only sending his wife and youngest son to safety. As the danger of the German invasion of Paris grew by the hour, however, he could no longer postpone his flight. Along with the order for evacuation of other Paris officials, he left his post and Paris on June 10 with members of his department. What had begun as an orderly retreat of a like-minded group, buoyed by optimistic hopes of soon returning, eventually turned into a chaotic flight into the unknown, governed by fear, depression, and desperation. Searching vainly for his wife and child, Döblin was swallowed up into the rolling mass of fleeing refugees, where he was tossed about, disoriented and alienated, at the mercy of historical forces.

A Voyage between Heaven and Earth

In his refuge in America, Döblin began recording the turbulent experiences of his flight, which became a turning point in his personal development. The most important stations of the journey are recapitulated in the first part of the *Schicksalsreise*. However, as the title suggests, the narrative was from the beginning intent on going beyond empirical description and documentation. The emphasis of what is portrayed clearly lies within the subjective sphere of experience of the first-person narrator. "Die Reise verlief zugleich an mir, mit mir und über mir. Nur weil es sich so verhielt, begebe ich mich daran, die Fahrt, ihre Umstände, aufzuzeichnen" (*SR*, 65). Often the confessional nature of the text requires external events to appear as a mere backdrop for the internal authorial perspective and to be subordinated to spiritual currents. In a letter to the painter and writer Karl Jakob Hirsch (1892–1952), Döblin stressed that this type of religious autobiography required less the factualness of definite events and occurrences than the personal experiences of the author, whose inner development gives direction to things.[4]

Although Döblin presents the reader of *Schicksalsreise* with a relatively continuous and detailed account of the route taken, the various stages and stops, the endless train rides and the miserable emergency shelters, the indifference of most of the refugees and the inhumanity of officialdom, he thwarts any attempt at a realistic assessment by pointing out the dreamlike, imaginary character of his "journey of destiny." With the confidence of one familiar with mystical revelations, he writes that this was "keine Reise von einem französischen Ort zu einem andern, sondern eine Reise zwischen Himmel und Erde" (*SR*, 65). As his wanderings become a traumatic struggle for survival, followed by unforeseen rescue, the author is intent on demonstrating the presence of a providential destiny. This destiny, by means of almost miraculous strokes of luck and "Arrangements" (*SR*, 100), brought about the improbable reunion in Toulouse with his lost family amid a million refugees. It was furthermore responsible for the continuation of their flight, successful despite obstacles and dangers, through Spain and Portugal, and the eventual arrival in Hollywood. Döblin denied any principle of blind chance (*SR*, 111), believing instead in his own ability to read supernatural "Winke und Zeichen" (*SR*, 147); these ranged from the mysterious, telepathic connection with his wife (*SR*, 62–63) to the circus poster he interpreted as a personal sign (*SR*, 85), and were seen by Döblin as evidence for the Christian concept of predestination, cautiously paraphrased at first as "Ursinn" (*SR*, 135).

Döblin's subordination of his refugee experiences to an interpretation of divine salvation occurs in several stages. During his stay in the refugee camp La Vernière at Mende in Southern France, the negative and rather remote perception that one should not oppose the obscure forces governing human fate still dominates Döblin's thinking (*SR*, 143). Then, immediately following a dramatic example of aid from a stranger, comes the turn toward a personally-centered concept of events. At literally the last minute, a school official makes available a considerable sum of money, enabling the Döblins to leave France before the necessary *visa de sortie* expires (*SR*, 228–29). Under the impression of this extraordinary assistance, Döblin breaks with his earlier notion of an impersonal, primal order governing history and nature, replacing it with the Judeo-Christian image of a god actively involved in the course of world events (*SR*, 229).

The Experience of Jesus Christ in Mende

The decisive event in Döblin's "journey of destiny" happened between 22 June and 8 July 1940 during his internment in Mende, seat of the southern Département Lozère. His experience of Christ, so crucial for his later conversion, happened there during his repeated visits to the cathedral of Mende and took the form of an encounter with the "person" of Christ. Döblin presents a remarkably sober rendition of the thoughts, daydreams, and sensations that were to culminate in his conversion.

Like a prelude, the voice of the former natural scientist and psychiatrist is heard first. To counter the charge of religious delusions and autosuggestion, Döblin stresses that his mental condition at the time was normal (*SR*, 99–100). Although he had lost some fifteen pounds and even suffered a breakdown (letter to his son Peter, 12 August 1940, *B I*, 241) during his stay in the refugee camp, he vigorously rejects any claim that he had arrived at his "theology" solely because of physical or nervous exhaustion. Even if he was overwhelmed with strange, waking fantasies (*SR*, 140), he was not willing to let his susceptibility to spiritual vibrations and force fields be dismissed by psychological or physiological arguments. On the contrary, his hallucinatory agitation forms the basis for receiving the supersensory frequencies radiating to him — the clues, the signs, the wavelengths and forces that so dominated his life at the time (*SR*, 147, 154). He went so far as to welcome the purifying power of his predicament that had sharpened his perception (*SR*, 146).

However, despite Döblin's sensitization for the transcendental, *Schicksalsreise* does not document a conversion experience in the sense of a calling. Unlike the epiphanies of the Apostle Paul at Damascus, Augustine's Ostia vision, Martin Luther's "tower experience," or Pascal's "fiery night," Döblin makes no claim of having undergone a climactic conversion experience, a sudden seizure and surrender to God's presence (Biser, 20–21), but describes the process in *Schicksalsreise* as a "creeping conversion" (Baden, 14 and 164), a long-term cognitive approximation and shift of position, revealing to the converted author its intrinsic providential meaning only in retrospect. Even in the cathedral in Mende, where Döblin first acknowledged Christ as the crucified Son of God, he retained full conscious control despite his deep suffering, and was concerned about how convincing his arguments would be. In place of a euphoric outburst, a dithyrambic hymn, an exclamation of ecstatic thrall, there is in Döblin's text only a single laconic sentence, in which the divinity of the crucified Christ, now recognized at last, is crystallized: "Er ist Gott, er ist ein- und dasselbe mit dem ewigen Urgrund" (*SR*, 169).

The Mystical and the Rational Perspective

Döblin chose a mode of expression so intent on factuality because he wanted his struggle with the problem of the divine to be understood as an act entirely consonant with his powers of rational thought. He emphasizes that his encounter with Christ occurred entirely within the bounds of reason, an essential factor in evaluating and explaining his complex and protracted struggle toward acceptance of the divine.[5] The price for his emphasis on the rational character of his faith was that of every natural theology committed to underpinning religious experience with empirical credibility and connecting belief to a process of intellectual consent. Logical inconsistencies and aporias follow. As a result, *Schicksalsreise* is permeated by contradictions, such as the dichotomies of the individual and the world, man and God, Son of God and eternal first cause (*Urgrund*). Döblin's questioning intellect ferrets out contradictions and weak spots in Christian doctrine and unavoidably runs firmly aground on them. Theodicy, in view of the ruins of the Second World War and the author's personal crisis becomes particularly relevant, and takes center stage. God's passivity toward the National Socialist aggressors seems to Döblin as absurd as his flight through France, experienced as a "dämonisches" (*SR*, 107) cat-and-mouse game, irreconcilable with the idea of a numinous concept of salvation. At the same time, Döblin did not intend, aside from the argumentative elucidation of the experience in Mende, to support a positivistically diluted religion of rationality, a *religio rationis*. Under no circumstances was belief to be subordinated to reason or much less degraded to a second-order form of knowledge (Kolakowski, 116–17). Döblin was concerned with balancing the possibilities of speculative and spiritual awareness of God, rather than the rationalistic deconstruction of traditional revealed truths. He differed from other modernists of the early twentieth century who were committed to a symbolic concept of belief and a phenomenalistic theory of knowledge (Kolakowski, 121). Thus it is hardly surprising that he accompanied the rational narrative with a mystical commentary to account for the intuitive dimension of the processes involved in his religious conversion. This is evident above all in a narrative peculiarity of *Schicksalsreise*. For even though Döblin's autobiography lacks any supernatural experience as origin of his conversion, the text does not dispense with the transformation typical of many of his novels, in which an old pattern of existence is superseded by a new one. The metaphorical language of the mystic Johannes Tauler, whose sermons accompanied Döblin during his flight, is adapted and used as a device for expressing in words the spiritual experience of conversion.

The image of the "gestrandeten Robinson" (*SR*, 93), whose ship proved too unseaworthy for an ocean crossing (*SR*, 133) and who now, overtaken by a storm, lies shipwrecked and naked on the beach (*SR*, 109) stands for Döblin's own fate and provides the reader with a first indication of the text's intent. It suggests the author's realization that he has failed in his life. He unmasks the vanity, weakness, and worthlessness (*SR*, 109) of his old self, which up to now had been drifting indifferently on the surface of existence, while at the same time studiously avoiding any serious self-analysis (*SR*, 125), thereby neglecting his social responsibilities. The defeat of France serves as a symbol of personal guilt and culpable omission with regard to the National Socialist "hydra": "Aber was, frage ich mich, habe ich selber eigentlich aufgeboten, oder hätte ich heute aufzubieten, um sie zu vernichten. [. . .] Ich hatte immer gefragt; ich sah keine Waffen" (*SR*, 124). This severe self-questioning renders Döblin psychologically alert to the realization that he must abandon the intellectual "Umbau" that had deceived him for so long (*SR*, 109, 124). Mystical "Beraubung" (*SR*, 124) and "Entselbstung" must act to accomplish the necessary reversal in his consciousness. As so often in Döblin's novels, it is the proximity of death, the frightful "Todesdruck" (*SR*, 108) that also brings about the change in the isolated writer.

In the chapter "Ich prüfe und befrage mich," which, incidentally, was composed only after 1945 in Baden-Baden,[6] the author looks back on his life and gives the reason for the present emergency: "Ich fühle mich gezwungen, ein Fazit meines ganzen Lebens zu ziehen, abzurechnen mit mir, als ob ich vor dem Tode stünde. Es gilt nun zu ermitteln, was mich in diesen Stand gebracht hat, was ich getan und was ich unterlassen habe" (*SR*, 125). The various identity patterns that Döblin had assumed are critically examined, phase by phase, and exposed as insufficient sham solutions, as more or less interchangeable provisional modes of existence. For apart from the working-class milieu familiar to him from his youth and its association with a "menschlichen Brüderschaft" (*SR*, 133), neither Kleist nor Hölderlin, neither Nietzsche nor Dostoyevsky, neither Freud nor Marx, neither medicine nor the other sciences, neither Judaism nor socialism, could offer him an intellectual home (*SR*, 125ff.). After all, there remained always only the frustrating awareness of being without roots and remaining suspended in a position of idle indifference. "Die Fahne, um die Fahne geht es. Welche Fahne habe ich aber gehalten? Welche Fahne halte ich?" (*SR*, 131).

In view of the triumph of the National Socialists, Döblin therefore views his reluctance to be resolutely partisan as a personal deficiency. However, this outwardly defective design for life, which neglected the opportunity for religious self-discovery, may in the process of mystical transformation be converted into insightfulness. From a mystical perspective, it is precisely the outward failure that may allow the recovery of that primal state of human open-mindedness required for a new beginning. With the help of this comforting thought Döblin succeeds in extracting from the catastrophe a meaning suitable to his own individual fate, one that also correlates with the idea of divine justice. By this means, spiritual impoverishment can be interpreted as discovery, inner lack as gain (*SR*, 135). In support of this encouraging insight there accrues also a sense of God's presence and concern. Through an extraordinary softening of reality, the utterly disconcerted and uprooted refugee becomes aware of the obscured "Gestaltungswillen" of the "Urgrund," which reshapes the random nature of earthly events under the aspect of salvation and confers meaning (*SR*, 135).

Döblin recognizes in Mende that his fate too partakes in this transcendental guidance. For the first time, the uprooted writer sees a way to overcome his internal apathy by finding refuge in the idea of Christ. A breakthrough to a new sense of life follows, however, only upon leaving the refugee camp, when his "ausgehöhltes Inneres" (*SR*, 174) begins to fill with the experience of his suffering in Mende. It now becomes clear to Döblin that there can be no return to his previous state of consciousness. His breakdown has helped him attain a different, "unbekannte Ich" (*SR*, 174), which becomes the foundation for a new identity. In accordance with the laws of the mystical conversion process, the author emerges, after a phase of inner purification and religious reflection, from this most important stage of his "irdischen-überirdischen Abenteuer" (*SR*, 174) as a newly transformed human being.

From this juxtaposition of mystical and rational thought processes it may be concluded that Döblin conceived *Schicksalsreise* quite intentionally as bifurcated, as a "report" and as a "confession," both of which he presented as equally legitimate. In its mystical dimension, the experience in Mende provided him with a Christian motive for writing, characteristic of Catholic apologia, which fulfill their spiritual mandate by way of autobiography and conversion, in emulation of the Pauline apostolate (Doppler, 27). In their rational dimension, they function as a weapon of self-defense against the charge of religious irrationality. For although Döblin stood firmly by his Christian belief, he also wanted to secure for himself a voice in matters of reason. Thus he seemed to share in the optimism of Thomism and the scholastic tradition, according to which secular and spiritual knowledge are in agreement, permitting both approaches to penetrate through to God. The many years of intensive study Döblin devoted to the writings of Thomas Aquinas serve as evidence for this.[7]

Baptism

Döblin's conversion was, to be sure, not only a consequence of his encounter with Christ in Mende and the miracle of his escape. Its substantiation by baptism of November 1941 was prompted in part by concern for the religious education of his youngest son Stefan. Döblin wanted his son to have what had been denied to him and his generation growing up with the values of rationalism and the Enlightenment. A religious upbringing seemed to him the sole antidote to the demonic spirit of militarization of his epoch. "Woran sollte eine junge Pflanze sich hochranken? [. . .] Wir hatten Sprachen, Mathematik und Naturwissenschaften geschluckt, mit welchem Ergebnis? Wie hatte es uns geformt? Der Junge sollte besser geführt werden. Wir sprachen vom Christentum" (*SR*, 276–77). The desire to make available to his child a "wirkliches Koordinatensystem" (*SR*, 277) for the future compelled Döblin to think in terms of his own conversion. This meant giving up his caution and hesitance and confessing his Christian belief openly: "Mir war sicher, obwohl ich nicht wußte warum: es war das Christentum, Jesus am Kreuz, was ich wollte.[. . .] Ich empfand eine große Wärme, eine unbedingte Sicherheit in mir, wenn diese Dinge in mir auftauchten" (*SR*, 277–78).

Contrary to expectations, Döblin's choice of a confession proved to be exceedingly difficult. Tenacious research in local libraries did not help him come to a decision. The difficulty of choosing from among the many Christian denominations by means of reason alone drove the seeker to the edge of resignation and even threatened to choke off the first budding of his still rather tenuous piety. At this critical moment there occurred in Döblin's eyes once again a miracle of divine intervention, which helped him in his decision by directing him toward Catholicism.

> Wie sich aber schon auf der Reise, bei der Flucht, so oft der Finger Gottes gezeigt hatte, so tat er es jetzt. Und nachträglich meine ich: es war eigentlich selbstverständlich, nein, naheliegend und zu erwarten, daß er sich hier einmischte, der Himmlische, wo es sich um den Weg zu ihm selber handelte. (*SR*, 279)

The "finger of God" — this is how Döblin described it in *Schicksalsreise*. But what was really going on? The comments with which Döblin followed the above passage reveal that this directive was a relatively mundane event. The divine intervention consisted of a suggestion by his friend, the art historian Alois Schardt, that there was a church close by where sympathetic Jesuit fathers might be able to help. And that is what in fact happened. The firm faith of his Jesuit instructors endowed Döblin, plagued by doubt, with the confidence he so badly needed. The first purely informative consultations with the Jesuits gradually became catechetical dialogues which at last inculcated in Döblin and his wife the desire for membership in this Catholic community (*SR*, 281). But according to Döblin's account, what ultimately led him and his wife to take the step was the hitherto unknown sensation of joy and spiritual expansiveness exuded by the doctrine: "Der Finger Gottes! Das Zeichen! Nun wurde das Zeichen in dieser Form gegeben, in dem Glücksgefühl. Wie noch zweifeln, ob man auf dem rechten Weg war. Wir zögerten nicht, den Weg zu gehen" (*SR*, 281).

But although Döblin received a thorough catechesis from the Jesuit fathers of the Blessed Sacrament Church of Hollywood from January until his baptism on 30 November 1941, the conversion cannot be attributed to their teaching alone. By no means, as scholarship sometimes maintains,[8] did Döblin permit himself to be taken in by the polished rhetoric and dialectical superiority of his instructors. In answer to a query by Anthony W. Riley, Harold E. Ring, the last surviving of the four Jesuit fathers who advised Döblin, wrote that Döblin not only brought considerable prior knowledge to their sessions, being already rather well-versed in Catholic doctrine, but had probably already made the decision to convert. He writes: "It seemed to me that Doctor [Döblin] had on his own read much about the teachings of the Catholic Church. He had very few questions to ask. He sat quietly giving his assent to what was said [. . .] I thought that he had already made his resolve to seek baptism when he came for the instructions."[9]

Döblin apparently concealed from the fathers that he had studied the literature of Christian mysticism during his Paris exile. He had read Pascal (1623–62) in 1934 (*B I*, 194) and about the same time also come upon the works of Kierkegaard in the Bibliothèque Nationale. But being also immersed in research for his novel *Amazonas,* he had temporarily neglected these readings. After completing *Amazonas,* he was so captivated by Kierkegaard that he copied out whole passages from his writings (*SLW*, 314 and 316). This was followed by the discovery of the mystic Johannes Tauler (ca. 1300–1361),[10] a disciple of Meister Eckhart (before 1260–1328), whose book of sermons accompanied Döblin on his flight through France (Minder, 62). Much seems to indicate that Tauler sensitized Döblin's latent mystical tendencies. Certain passages in *Schicksalsreise* attest to Döblin's affinity for Tauler's mode of thought, especially his use of the *leitmotiv* of deprivation and nakedness (Kiesel, 437).

The reason that Döblin chose Catholicism over Protestantism was not only the result of providential inspiration. It had to do with the critical attitude toward Protestantism he had developed over several decades after repeated, intellectually rewarding, but religiously unsatisfactory overtures. Nevertheless, Döblin's religious sensibilities about 1912 agreed with Protestant doctrine to the extent that he had his sons Peter, Klaus, and Wolfgang educated and confirmed as Protestants.[11] In the 1920s, his reservations evolved into outright criticism, as the phenomenon of "cultural" Protestantism, then widespread in Germany, convinced him that it meant the surrender of religious fervor in favor of a rationalized Christian faith. As Döblin states in the 1926 *Ostwart-Jahrbuch,* this form of symbolically diluted Christianity so sorely lacked the specific essence of faith, the "produzierende, expansive, ausgreifende, sich ausgliedernde Seelengewalt," that it could bring forth only an ethically enlightened, liberally-schooled kind of person indistinguishable from other well-meaning individuals with no religious convictions.[12] Therefore, rediscovering the vital nucleus of Christianity, "das ungeheuere fabelhafte Faktum des Jesus von Nazareth"[13] was indispensable in retrieving the revolutionary force of faith capable of transforming human existence.

Nonetheless, Döblin's selection of Catholicism is not at all an expression of religious fanaticism that would denigrate or disavow validity of other confessions or religions. His understanding of what makes up the kernel of divine mystery is distinguished by a high degree of tolerance and intellectual farsightedness:

> Und es täte mir leid, wenn irgendwann und irgendwo das, was ich schreibe oder geschrieben habe, den Eindruck hervorbrächte, ich wäre intolerant und hätte die Ideen der Inquisition. Keine Spur. Ja, nicht ein einziges Mal nenne ich das Wort katholisch und römisch-katholisch. Ich spreche vom Christentum und dieses ist natürlich erwachsen aus dem Jüdischen. (*B I*, 408)

The Sequel to Döblin's Conversion

When Döblin's conversion became known in the first postwar years, the German press received the returnee coolly and uncomprehendingly. It defamed Döblin's declaration of faith as a flight from reality or even as the consequence of psychological derangement, without considering his difficult internal struggles and years of confrontation with questions about the meaning of religion.[14] The literary left, above all, with which Döblin had been identified, did not forgive their former comrade a credo that looked to them like a betrayal of socialism. The fact that a scientifically trained, supposedly enlightened writer committed "treason" by going over to the Catholic archenemy amounted for leftist critics to an inexcusable affront that could not go unpunished. On 14 August 1943 the artistic elite of the German exile community gathered in a small theater in Santa Monica, near Los Angeles, for a fitting observance of Döblin's sixty-fifth birthday. Invited guests besides Bertolt Brecht and Helene Weigel were also Heinrich and Thomas Mann, Hanns Eisler, Arnold Schönberg, and Fritz Kortner. Döblin apparently saw in this ceremonial gathering the occasion to make public his new religious convictions in a birthday address. But reactions to his speech were quite different than he evidently had expected. Instead of good wishes and understanding, the confused audience rewarded their honoree with rejection and indignation.[15] Then, immediately following the festivities, Brecht set about portraying Döblin's performance in his poem "Peinlicher Vorfall" as befouling and desecrating the "Plattform, die dem Künstler gehört."[16] With that he had put precisely into words the reproach that had resonated unspoken among his writer colleagues. Döblin, as Karl-Josef Kuschel put it, had broken the rules artists play by, had perverted the stage of art into an ecclesiastical pulpit, and had adulterated the realms of art and religion so strictly segregated ever since the Enlightenment. "Hence Brecht's arousal. A great artist like Döblin, by turning religious, had betrayed art and deceived his audience.

He had abused the purview of art to stage religious propaganda" (Kuschel, 24–25). Thus the celebrated author of *Berlin Alexanderplatz*, by confessing himself a devout Christian, had become for many of his guild of writers an artist no longer to be taken seriously. Döblin later remarked laconically on his speech: "Ich nahm mich und uns alle von dem großen Gericht nicht aus, das sich an der Welt entlud. Man lehnte mich schweigend ab" (*SR*, 274).

All the reproaches and denunciations that rained down upon Döblin when he returned to Germany after the war appear to share unconsciously in Brecht's judgment. In so doing, from a present-day perspective, they are all the less justified insofar as they betray crude ignorance of Döblin's literary legacy and distort the continuity of his philosophical and religious development. Superficially, public opinion had narrowed Döblin's authorship to *Berlin Alexanderplatz*, a book, as he trenchantly observed, only few had really read. As a person he was "auf eine Formel gebracht: Schriftsteller des Milieus, der Unterwelt, der Berliner Unterwelt" (*SR*, 349). The fact that Döblin had prefaced each of his major epic works with a "geistige Fundamentierung" and pursued in his thinking a "metaphysische Linie" (*SLW*, 215) was ignored. It was a foolish misconception to label him a materialist and atheist because after the First World War he, like Carl von Ossietzky (1889–1938), Egon Erwin Kisch (1885–1948), Johannes R. Becher (1891–1958), Brecht, and others, belonged to the "der Gruppe des Aufbruchs, der Menschlichkeit" (*B I*, 437) and now, by extension of these false premises, to misunderstand him as an apostate. Döblin had not suddenly gone ideologically over the edge, had not refused a rational theory of reality and, faced with the absurdity of the war, sought refuge in religiosity out of senility. "Wozu ich nur zu sagen habe, daß ich keine Zeit meines Lebens antireligiös war. Es wird mir schriftlich gegeben, daß ich 'als Denker vor der Mystik kapitulierte.' Ich sehe in der Anerkennung der Rätselhaftigkeit und des Geheimnisses dieser Welt nichts von Kapitulation" (*SR*, 351). Thus, Döblin defended himself against the accusation of escapism from this world and from irrationality with which he was repeatedly charged.

Had German literary criticism reacted to Döblin's religious conversion more perspicaciously, it would not have failed to understand that the author's conversion symbolized not a spontaneous genuflection before the institution of the church, but reiterated what he had repeatedly made the central theme in his literary works and defended by argument. Whoever, like Döblin, had since his youth had been interested in religion and metaphysics (*SLW*, 306), did not need to break with his convictions and commit betrayal (*B I*, 406) in order to adopt Christianity. The Christ motif permeates Döblin's entire work and is employed repeatedly as a parameter of orientation, as a positive or negative coordinate. Still, the now "secular," now "spiritual" value of Döblin's concept of religion before and after his conversion requires further explanation. For if Döblin's fascination with the Christ figure is evident as early as in his first literary text "Modern," and thereafter appears in many variations — in *Reise in Polen,* in *Unser Dasein,* in *Babylonische Wandrung* — as an indication of the depth of human suffering and the impotent subject of creation, the significance of the Crucified One as the resurrected Son of God was revealed to the writer only during his visit to the cathedral of Mende.

Döblin's Religious Dialogues: *Der unsterbliche Mensch* and *Der Kampf mit dem Engel*

In order to evaluate the firmness of his new belief, Döblin went to work writing his first religious dialogue *Der unsterbliche Mensch* shortly after arriving in America. The Christian worldview had become for the exiled castaway such an anchor and an axis (*B I*, 364) that he subjected it now to a kind of rational verification, in the form of an intellectual trial by fire. Translating it back into his own personal language, which amounted to integrating his belief into the Döblinian flow of language and ideas, served as the main criterion of truth.

> Nach einer Pause gab ich mir Rechenschaft, wo ich stand und was ich wirklich aufgenommen und mir einverleibt hatte, was also "mein" geworden war. Und um es ganz zu meinem Besitz zu machen, mußte ich es vor mich stellen und in meine Sprache übersetzen. Ließ es sich so vortragen, fragte ich? Der Eintritt in meine Sätze, in meine Sprache würde die Probe sein, und indem die Gedanken in meine Sätze eingingen, würden sie noch stärker und fester in mich eindringen. Also die aufgenommenen Gedanken sollten sich bewähren und beweisen, indem sie unter meiner Flagge kämpften. (*SR,* 289)

The Impulse to Dialogue

From a formal point of view, Döblin's religious dialogues are conceived according to the ideal model of "absolute discourse." Both are configurations of the Platonic or Socratic dialogue still current in the eighteenth century. As a literary genre or literary-philosophical art form, the dialogue places the highest priority on the principle of "reasoned discourse" (Wertheimer, 7–14). Two essential aspects of this tradition are the power of speech as an organ for reproducing and giving form to reality and verbal exchanges as a means for understanding and decision-making. In the twentieth century the philosophical dispute as a genre largely lost its function as an instrument for discovering truth (Wertheimer, 15–22).

Nevertheless, attempts to revive this genre in the modern literary period were not unusual, and Döblin's use of the Socratic dialogue was not unique. During the frightful days of the Second World War, as the saber-rattling language of violence threatened to swallow up peaceful communication, the dialogue was revived. Brecht's *Flüchtlingsgespräche* (Conversations among Refugees, 1940/41), André Gide's *Interviews imaginaires* (1942), and Cesare Pavese's *Dialoghi con Leucò* (1947) represent the generally felt need for interchange and expression in an age of distrust, undisguised hatred, and silenced conversations. In contrast, Gottfried Benn's prose dialogue *Drei alte Männer* (Three Old Men, 1949) is an attempt at safeguarding human awareness from resignation and meaninglessness in the face of the absurd reality of history.

The Two Protagonists

Döblin's religious dialogues receive their vital force from the tension between the two discussants, designated simply as "the Elder" and "the Youth." The contrast in their worldviews, the polarity of belief and unbelief, serves to advance their inquiry into the existence and nature of God. Initially, the two actors are clearly in the position of rivals, but, as the dialogue progresses — with the conversion of the youth — their differences are one by one abandoned: the positions of defense and prosecution, of devout Christian and enlightened atheist, of teacher and student, of physician and patient, of helper and convalescent (Bartscherer, 167–75).

Both the specific historical point of departure and Döblin's personal situation left their mark on the religious dialogues. The first one, *Der unsterbliche Mensch*, was written in or about 1942, while the firestorm of war was raging over Europe, and the screams of its dying victims echoed in Döblin's ear like an irrepressible accusation against God. The second, *Der Kampf mit dem Engel*, came into being almost a decade later (1951/52) in West Germany.

The dialogues reflect the changes that had taken place in Döblin's physical and spiritual constitution. Whereas *Der unsterbliche Mensch*, especially at the beginning, has the character of a contentious battle of words, long passages in *Der Kampf mit dem Engel* are marked by the peaceful climate of meditation and reverie. In striking parallel to the deterioration of Döblin's own health over the intervening decade, the Elder in the second dialogue no longer commands the resilience and intellectual swiftness necessary for carrying through a dispute on religious philosophy. He lives on the edge of death, has forsaken his earlier learnedness and withdrawn into the healing silence of a solitary life in nature. In general, the relation between the two speakers in *Der Kampf mit dem Engel* bespeaks the altered consciousness of the seventy-two-year-old Döblin, in whose thinking the conflict of belief and unbelief has yielded to the problem of the Christian religion as such. The focus has shifted to the question of the meaningfulness of a life in Christ and the inherent and implicit dangers of religious deviation. Thus it is the Youth who renews the debate with the question as to whether Christianity is a disease that wrecks human existence (*UM*, 294).

The Intellectual Heritage of Franz von Baader and Blaise Pascal

Döblin's focus in the religious dialogues revolves around the three main themes of God, humankind, and Christ. They are at the same time theology, anthropology, and Christology, which is to say knowledge of God's existence, knowledge of man's being, and the belief in the personhood of Christ. The line connecting and encompassing these themes is found in the dichotomy of self and nature or the body-soul problem, long a central concern in Döblin's thought. He was intent on illuminating and resolving the riddle of man's physical-spiritual double nature, his dual form as "Stück und Gegenstück der Natur" (*UD*, 475).

As was the case in his earlier philosophical writings, *Das Ich über der Natur* and *Unser Dasein*, in the religious dialogues man is viewed in terms of body-soul ambivalence and polar disunity, trapped in the paradox of being imprisoned in the organic and yet distinct from it. Thus he remains an incomplete creature eternally struggling for its own resolution and inner unity (Bartscherer, 177–80). In contrast to his earlier philosophy of nature, where philosophical monism allows for the unity of body and soul by equating the free spirit with the organic-unconscious, after his conversion, Döblin shifts the focus toward a personal approach, to a solution stressing the unmistakable individuality of the subject. In the religious dialogues, man is no longer merely an evolutionary sub-type of the great comprehensive being of nature and a sentient animal within the order of primates. Rather, man is the key figure of creation who, although bound to the material world, is able to distinguish himself from all other organic forms of life. Döblin clearly emphasizes the independence and superiority of the individual over his physiological dependency (Bartscherer, 236–37).

This transfer from the objective to the subjective area, from nature to the self, required a different, non-monistic solution. Aided by Judeo-Christian historical theology, Döblin found the answer in his new faith: the biblical account of man in paradise, his transgression and fall, and his salvation and restitution through Christ became for Döblin the indispensable mental clue capable of providing insight into the mysterious imbalance of our human nature. Since for Döblin Christian man is fundamentally a being of body-soul identity, the disproportion of mind and matter can be explained most plausibly as the consequence of a historical fall from grace. Accordingly, the triadic concept of body-soul unity in its original paradisical state, its disastrous destruction brought on by human error, and the possibility of restitution through the redemptive act of the Son of God by harmonizing ego and nature forms the unorthodox revision of the Christ theme in Döblin's cosmos of belief.

An important forerunner to Döblin's three-stage historical theory was one of the most notable representatives of Munich Romanticism, the Catholic theologian and anthropologist Franz von Baader (1795–1841), whose works Döblin had read. His theory of a "positive" salvation history transmitted by Christian dogma forms the background of Döblin's religious philosophy. Baader's doctrine describes the stages that the relationship of man to God underwent in the course of history, corresponding to the three great biblical phases of development: creation, fall, and redemption. It reconstructs man's original mission, to cooperate in completing creation, his inability to manage this task, and his failure in the resulting fall (Koslowski, 310–13). In the person of Christ it offers the prospect of redemption to the fallen sinner, who can regain his original ideal state through an inner rebirth.

In this respect, Baader's Christian historical theory unmistakably intersects with the theoretical ideas of a holistic conception of man. For the original or immortal human being was an androgynous being, uniting without contradiction masculine and feminine, interior and exterior, the eternal and temporal world. Only his fall brought about the diadic existence, splitting creation into the extremes of an incorporeal spirit and a soulless matter. With the advent of Christ, who, according to the dogma of hypostatic union, is at the same time true man and true God, the androgynous archetype is revived and an escape from the dualism of body and soul becomes possible (Deghaye, 255–67).

In addition to the historical-theological thought of Baader, Blaise Pascal's dialectical image of man appears to have significantly influenced

Döblin's religious dialogues. Pascal's inner disintegration of mankind finds its counterpart in Döblin's ideas. For the author of the *Pensées sur la religion* (Thoughts on Religion, 1670), man in his present state is an ambivalent, self-contradictory being (Küng, 18), a double nature tossed between misery and greatness, an existential intermediate between all and chaos, who harbors equally the capacities for divine and carnal being. Indeed, for Pascal the individual stands in such sharp contrast to himself that within him a ceaseless "internal war" rages between his reason and his passions (Pascal, *Pensées*, fragment 413, 119). So inextricably are nobility and baseness conflated in him that it is impossible to assign him to either of his two alternate beings. "What sort of freak is man! How novel, how monstrous, how chaotic, how paradoxical, how prodigious! Judge of all things, feeble earthworm, repository of truth, sink of doubt and error, glory and refuse of the universe" (*Pensées*, fragment 434, 34). In the radical uncertainty and dissolution of this existence man is an incomprehensible mistake ("a monster that passes all understanding," *Pensées*, fragment 420, 32), whose striving for an inner equilibrium will always fail, condemning him to pursue it in desperation. "Man is neither angel nor beast, and it is unfortunately the case that anyone trying to act the angel acts the beast" (*Pensées*, fragment 358, 215); this is the unappeasable law of existence for this dissonant being. For Pascal the destructive tensions of the *vérités opposées*, which prevent man from attaining repose, are discharged exclusively between the extremes of the sensual and the divine, of beast and angel, of body and spirit.

Prefiguring Döblin, Pascal viewed the loss of the paradisiacal unity of spirit and body in the fall from grace. Subsequently the negative dialectic between beast and angel, *misère* and *grandeur*, darkens human life and casts it into hopelessness. However, Pascal finds escape in a remedy (*Pensées*, fragment 526, 106) that simultaneously embraces the two poles of humanity, bestiality and divine omnipotence, and returns them to equilibrium. In Pascal's view none other than Christ can be the true healer of mankind. For "in Christ all contradictions are reconciled" (*Pensées*, fragment 684, 77). Only knowledge of him "strikes the balance, because he shows us both God and our wretchedness" (*Pensées*, fragment 527, 57).

Jesus Christ, the Personification of the Divine

Döblin too raises the Son of God to the center in the process of redemption. The presence and wholeness of his personhood can silence all contradictions, and his ability to synthesize and provide meaning guarantees mankind's restitution to an existence where body and soul are reintegrated.

For a world separated from God would, according to Döblin, inevitably succumb to the forces of dissolution and be irretrievably exposed to the endless strife and conflict between self and nature. Man would be subjected forever to the blindly raging mechanism of the dialectic between consciousness and matter and remain in a state of incessant contradiction with himself. However, in Döblin's eyes, the Creator is not merely an impartial observer of the human drama, of man's "Todesfahrt in die eigene Selbstherrlichkeit" (*UM*, 224) or the fall from Grace, but rather participates "mit der allerherzlichsten und schmerzlichsten Liebe" in man's fate; he assumes through his son an identification with the condemned, an "*imitatio hominis*" (*UM*, 236) in order to save the apostate rebel. In this way a new beginning, unique in world history, is presented; it liberates creation from the bondage of body-soul polarity and affords mankind the prospect of stability in an existence reconciled in Christ. For Jesus Christ emblemizes for Döblin a wholeness never before attained. He thus becomes the essence of a successful incarnation, realized through dialogue with the paternal primal cause. Or to put it differently, he is the prototype of an identity achieved through dialogic orientation, which is the equivalent of saying he is a wholly integrated person.

But what does Döblin mean when he posits the person as a central category? Existence as a "person" describes for Döblin a mode in which any kind of disjointed dialectical discontinuity is obliterated and the conflict of spirit and matter no longer exists (*UM*, 158). Only as a person can the Son of God become the promising index of repentance and change for man, who has fallen short of his destiny. Only as a person can he bridge the body-soul split. For as a person Jesus Christ incorporates the ideal type of an identity in which all conflicts are resolved and harmonized (Bartscherer, 281–87). This, however, requires that the submerged personal center in mankind be retrieved. According to Döblin, the suffering that assails us seemingly without our participation derives from man's frivolous abandonment of this personal center in his being and his inability to recall his original destiny: "Die Ursache des schrecklichen, unfaßbaren [. . .] Irrtums der ganzen Weltgeschichte [besteht] unverändert darin: statt aus [seinem] göttlichen Kern das Zentrum [seines] Daseins zu machen, war das Menschengeschlecht weiter und weiter im Protest gegen sich gewachsen. Man hatte sich gekrümmt und verbogen und war trocken und kümmerlich geworden" (*UM*, 558).

The true mission of the Son of God mingling with mankind thus consists for Döblin in exploding the degenerative hardening of man's worldly selfishness and "den [personalen] Kern neu einzubetten" (*UM*, 558). As though excavating a temple sunken far below the surface during the course of history, Christ, acting on behalf of human beings, has undertaken to resurrect angelic man from the darkness of oblivion and reestablish him in human consciousness. "Wenn der Mensch ein Gebäude ist, Christus zeigt den Grundriß" (*UM*, 559). According to Döblin's holistic understanding, Christ, by exposing his divine heart to mankind, reveals so vast a double nature that it reaches from his earthly reflection all the way to the divine.

> Berührt durch die aus dem göttlichen Wort Christi entstammenden Kräfte [. . .] dehnt und realisiert sich nun das menschliche Zentrum, welches heißt: "Bild und Ebenbild Gottes," so wie es [. . .] geschaffen wurde am sechsten Tage, als Gott in seine Tiefe stieg. So rief Jesus in jenen Tagen den Menschen abermals ins Dasein, um ihn seinen Weg durch die von der Liebe hervorgebrachte Schöpfung vollenden zu lassen. [. . .] Wieder wird der göttliche Kern des Menschen in seine Rechte über den lebenden Menschen eingesetzt. Und wieder fängt damit [. . .] alles von vorne an! (*UM*, 559)

These were philosophical cornerstones of Döblin's comprehensive Christology. The principle of the person becomes the key concept in a future holistic order of existence. Only when man has regained his humanity in the sense of Jesus Christ will the wounds of his one-sided worldliness heal, enabling him to find his way back to the primal state of the image of God.

Discovery of the Personality Principle

Döblin's insistence on the concept of person was the consequence of a shift in consciousness in the 1930s influenced by Martin Buber's (1887–1965) dialogic philosophy and Max Scheler's (1874–1928) value-immanent philosophy. Döblin found himself in the company of a number of leading representatives of Jewish and Catholic anthropology, almost all of whom, simultaneously with him, discovered the central significance of the principle of personality for the modern concept of humanity (Schmidinger, 78–102).

An important reason for this unprecedented emergence of Christian personalism can be found in the fact that only in the first decades of the twentieth century did the intellectual barricades fall which for over two centuries had stood in the way of the Christian principle that "man is person." Contrary to the generally accepted view, the notion of the personhood of man had not been one of the church's established articles of faith, but was instead the result of a protracted process of adaptation (Schmidinger, 30–38).

In its way stood above all Kant's new concept of personhood and that of German Idealism. It collided with the neoscholastically oriented concept of personhood of the Church, which meant by "person" a "mode of being." Kant's new concept called this tradition into question, by defining the "person" as an "autonomous subject conscious of itself" (Schmidinger, 46). In the eyes of the Church, the idea of the autonomous person conscious of him/herself took the place of a concept of person, where self-determination is possible only in reference to the higher order of God (Schmidinger, 42 and 56–60). This precarious situation changed only when the philosophy of value succeeded in combining Kant's autonomous concept of person with the Christian one through the non-systematic attitude of a "dialogic personalism" (Schmidinger, 78). For Scheler's philosophy of values defined "person" as an "a priori value" and as a "superconscious being" that exists independent of one's own consciousness (Schmidinger, 78–88). The philosophy of dialogue initiated by Ferdinand Ebner (1882–1931) and Martin Buber, on the other hand, considered the person the result of relationships in which the self is formed through the encounter with a divine Thou (Schmidinger, 89–102). These ideas made it possible to gradually modify the dominant constants of the Kantian idealistic discourse on man and to view them more appropriately. Not only the perception of unlimited autonomy, but also the subjectivist equation of "person" with "ego consciousness" had lost to a considerable degree their function as a premise for the concept of "person."

The main reason for Döblin's turn to the Christian principle of person, however, can be seen in the hegemonic intrusions of Fascism and Stalinism that menaced the private sphere in those years. The totalitarian claims of Hitler's and Stalin's dictatorships aimed to break the resistance of every individual by incorporating them into a uniform collective subject to manipulation or silenced by a state-organized mob-law. At a point in time when the language of repression and propaganda of the Bolsheviks and National Socialists brought about the *Gleichschaltung* of entire groups of people, when language, adulterated through ideology, inculcated an anonymous collective consciousness, when the voice of the individual was drowned out by the hysterical screams of the masses, and when the specter of a society infected by militarism threatened to eliminate the personal sphere, Döblin discovered the source of a subjective, autobiographical flow of speech, whose inner drive was the defense, confirmation, and conservation of personal freedom and dignity (Bartscherer, 147–49 and 207–10). Döblin became convinced that the victorious march of political totalitarianism would bring about a deadly struggle for the preservation of the personal sphere of the individual against the collectivist claims of the new dictatorial systems. In the final section of *Unser Dasein*, the last book that Döblin published before fleeing Germany, he had warned of the dangers of an omnipotent state machinery with its anonymous organizations and collectives. In reality, these structures concealed power-obsessed tyrants and violent rulers, who used their smoke-screen tactics only to devour the individual: "Wer heute dem Ich, dem Einzelnen, der Person, dem Individuum die Pflicht gegen das Dasein, die Verantwortung für sein Leben abnehmen will, ja, frecherweise behauptet, erst in diesen räuberischen und unwahren, hohlen Kollektiven und Einrichtungen werde das Ich zum Ich und könne unbesorgt sein, der übt ein bösartiges Täuschungs- und Fälschungsmanöver" (*UD*, 418–19).

Döblin's defense of human personality was the result of a shift in perspective from the object area to the subject area. Especially his Christian-inspired late works are characterized by a striking turn to the human subject and an increasingly personal style. In this respect, *Schicksalsreise* marks both a religious and a linguistic turning point with its first-person narrator: the changeover from an "object language" participating in the large movements of historical and natural processes to a "subject language" entering the microcosm of thought of the single human being. In the course of his artistic development, Döblin had gradually moved away from the "steinerne Stil" of historical facticity and his stylistic attitude of "depersonalization" (Kleinschmidt, 383–401) and transformed himself from the virtuoso reporter of large mass movements and collective forces to an illustrator of the individual and his/her existence.

Döblin acknowledged in an interview, dated 10 August 1948, that in his epic writings, the center of gravity in the valuation of the collective and the individual personality had shifted with increasing age. Whereas in his first epic projects — specifically until his utopian novel *Berge Meere und Giganten* — he had attempted to create a historical tableau or a sociopolitical totality, where the single individual played only a subordinate role, this "collectivist" artistic view had undergone a fundamental change in his subsequent works, in which the individual moved increasingly into the center of his creative interest.

> Und in meiner ersten Zeit des Schreibens habe ich mich völlig von dem Individuellen abgewandt, ja sogar, ich erinnere mich, ich habe Aufsätze geschrieben, wo ich gegen den Individualismus geschrieben habe, gegen das Private, gegen die Betonung des Psychologischen, das mir bis heute noch in gewisser Hinsicht unsympathisch ist, weil ich die tieferen und eigentlichen Zusammenhänge, die über-privat und über-psychologisch sind, viel genauer sehe. Aber richtig bleibt, daß ich im Laufe der Jahrzehnte, also von 1912, als ich anfing, bis jetzt, bis 1948, immer mehr eine Neigung

habe und hatte, zum Ich und zur Bedeutung des Ichs, über das Kollektive hinweg zu dringen. Und so ist auch in der Mitte ein Buch von mir bemerkenswert, das heißt "Das Ich über der Natur." Und wenn sie den "Unsterblichen Menschen" an das Ende dieses Weges setzen, so erkennen Sie, es geht da eine Linie, und mein "Hamlet"-Roman, [...], der stellt überhaupt nur drei, vier Personen hin und sieht ab völlig von der sozialen Situation und betrachtet nun nur ihre Ich- und Du-Gliederung und Position zueinander und sucht ihrer Herr zu werden. (*KdZ*, 157)

— *Translated by Lee Stavenhagen*

Notes

[1] The first edition was published by Josef Knecht Verlag in 1949 in Frankfurt, with an initial print run of 5,000 copies.

[2] See Anthony W. Riley, "Nachwort des Herausgebers," in Alfred Döblin, *SR*, 484.

[3] On the genesis of *SR* and the text versions, see Riley, 395–407.

[4] See Riley, "'... zwischen Himmel und Erde.' Zu Alfred Döblins *Schicksalsreise*," 318.

[5] See Riley, "Nachwort" in Alfred Döblin, *DUM*, 668.

[6] Riley, "... zwischen Himmel und Erde," 321, footnote 16.

[7] Bartscherer, 371, endnote 307.

[8] See Robert Minder, "Alfred Döblin zwischen Osten und Westen," 201.

[9] Riley, "Christentum und Revolution," 96.

[10] Döblin's reading of Tauler's works is documented by Louis Huguet only for 1939, without a precise date (Huguet, 127). This agrees with the fact that the figure of the mystic appeared for the first time in the opening volume "Bürger und Soldaten" of *November 1918*.

[11] "Alfred Döblin — sein Leben, sein Wesen, sein Werk — gesehen mit den Augen seines Sohnes Claude." Interview by Lutz Meunier of Claude Döblin on 2 September 1987 for RIAS Berlin, as part of the series "Gespräch zur Zeit, Sunday, 20 September 1987." Unpublished typescript at Deutsches Literaturarchiv, Marbach, 6.

[12] Döblin, "Dichtung und Christentum," an answer to a survey, in *Ostwart-Jahrbuch* 1 (1926): 148.

[13] Döblin, "Dichtung und Christentum," 149.

[14] For a survey of the negative echo evoked by Döblin's conversion, see the "Nachwort" by Anthony W. Riley in *SR*, 485–91, as well as his "Nachwort" in *DUM*, 665–72. The lack of resonance of Döblin's exile and late works is documented also in Helmuth Kiesel's *Literarische Trauerarbeit*, 1–10.

[15] See Kiesel 188–92 for a detailed account of the negative reactions to Döblin's speech on the occasion of his sixty-fifth birthday, where he hinted at the existential consequences of his conversion.

[16] Bertolt Brecht, *Gesammelte Werke*, vol. 10, *Gedichte 3*, 861–62.

Works Cited

Auer, Manfred. *Das Exil vor der Vertreibung: Motivkontinuität und Quellenproblematik im späten Werk Alfred Döblins.* Bonn: Bouvier, 1977.

Baden, Hans-Jürgen. *Literatur und Bekehrung.* Stuttgart: Klett, 1968.

Bartscherer, Christoph. *Das Ich und die Natur: Alfred Döblins literarischer Weg im Licht seiner Religionsphilosophie.* Paderborn: Igel Verlag Wissenschaft, 1997.

Biser, Eugen. *"Glaubenszeugnis. Kunst — Kritik — Mystik": Beiträge zum Jahr der Kultur.* Akademie-Publikationen Nr. 89. Augsburg: Katholische Akademie, 1991.

Deghaye, Pierre. "Baader und Böhme. Der anthropologische Standpunkt." *Die Philosophie, Theologie und Gnosis Franz von Baaders: Spekulatives Denken zwischen Aufklärung, Restauration und Romantik.* Ed. by Peter Koslowski. Vienna: Passagen Verlag, 1993. 243–71.

Doppler, Bernhard. *Katholische Literatur und Literaturpolitik: Enrica von Handel-Mazzetti. Eine Fallstudie.* Klagenfurt: Hain, 1980.

Emde, Friedrich. *Alfred Döblin: Sein Weg zum Christentum.* Tübingen: G. Narr, 1999.

Huguet, Louis. *Pour un centenaire (1878–1978): Chronologie Alfred Döblin.* Abidjan: Université 1978 (= Annales de l'Université d'Abidjan, 1978, Serie D [Lettres], Tome 11) (Copies available in Deutsches Literaturarchiv Marbach/ Neckar).

Kiesel, Helmuth. *Literarische Trauerarbeit: Das Exil- und Spätwerk Alfred Döblins.* Tübingen: Niemeyer, 1986.

Kleinschmidt, Erich. "Depersonale Poetik. Dispositionen des Erzählens bei Alfred Döblin." *Jahrbuch der Deutschen Schillergesellschaft* 26 (1982). 383–401.

Köpke, Wulf. "Die Irrfahrt durch Frankreich 1940 und die Identität des Exils." *Internationales Alfred-Döblin-Kolloquium Lausanne 1987.* Ed. by Werner Stauffacher. Bern: Lang, 1991. 25–35.

Koslowski, Peter. "Religiöse Philosophie und spekulative Dogmatik — Franz von Baaders Theorie der Gesamtwirklichkeit." *Die Philosophie, Theologie und Gnosis Franz von Baaders: Spekulatives Denken zwischen Aufklärung, Restauration und Romantik.* Ed. by Peter Koslowski. Vienna: Passagen Verlag, 1993. 289–325.

Küng, Hans. "Religion im Aufbruch der Moderne, Blaise Pascal: *Pensées.*" *Dichtung und Religion.* Ed. by Walter Jens and Hans Küng. Munich: Piper, 1992.

Kuschel, Karl-Josef. *"Vielleicht hält Gott sich einige Dichter...": Literarisch-theologische Porträts.* Mainz: Matthias-Grünewald-Verlag, 1991. 21–25.

Meyer, Jochen, and Ute Doster, eds. *Alfred Döblin 1878–1978: Eine Ausstellung des Deutschen Literaturarchivs Marbach am Neckar.* Munich: Kösel-Verlag, 1978.

Minder, Robert. "Alfred Döblin zwischen Osten und Westen." *Dichter in der Gesellschaft: Erfahrungen mit deutscher und französischer Literatur*. Frankfurt: Suhrkamp, 1972. 175–213.

———. "Begegnungen mit Alfred Döblin in Frankreich." *text + kritik* 13/14: Alfred Döblin (1972): 57–66.

Niggl, Günter. "Antwort auf das Inferno der Zeit. Das Spätwerk Alfred Döblins." *Christliches Exil und christlicher Widerstand: Ein Symposion an der Katholischen Universität Eichstätt*. Ed. by Wolfgang Frühwald and Heinz Hürten. Regensburg: Friedrich Pustet, 1985. 263–74.

Pascal, Blaise. *Pensées*. Trans. by A. J. Krailsheimer. Revised Edition. London: Penguin Books, 1995.

Prangel, Matthias. *Alfred Döblin*. Stuttgart: Metzler, 1987.

Riley, Anthony W. "Christentum und Revolution. Zu Alfred Döblins Romanzyklus *November 1918*." *Leben im Exil: Probleme der Integration deutscher Flüchtlinge im Ausland 1933–1945*. Ed. by Wolfgang Frühwald and Wolfgang Schieder. Hamburg: Hoffmann und Campe, 1981. 91–102.

———. "Nachwort," in *Schicksalsreise. Bericht und Bekenntnis*. 1993. 483–502.

———. "Nachwort," in *Der unsterbliche Mensch. Der Kampf mit dem Engel*. 1980. 661–98.

———. "Zum umstrittenen Schluß von Alfred Döblins *Hamlet oder Die lange Nacht nimmt ein Ende*." *Lit. Wiss. Jb*. 13 (1972): 331–58.

———. "'. . . zwischen Himmel und Erde.' Zu Alfred Döblins *Schicksalsreise*." *Begegnungen mit dem "Fremden." Grenzen — Traditionen — Vergleiche*. Akten des VIII. Internationalen Germanisten-Kongresses Tokyo 1990, vol. 9, section 15. Munich: iudicium, 1991. 317–26.

Schmidinger, Heinrich. *Der Mensch als Person: Ein christliches Prinzip in theologischer und philosophischer Sicht*. Innsbruck/Vienna: Tyrolia, 1994.

Weissenberger, Klaus H. "Alfred Döblin im Exil. Eine Entwicklung vom historischen Relativismus zum religiösen Bekenntnis." *Colloquia Germanica* (1974): 37–51.

Wertheimer, Jürgen. *"Der Güter Gefährlichstes ist die Sprache": Zur Krise des Dialogs zwischen Aufklärung und Romantik*. Munich: Wilhelm Fink, 1990.

Weyembergh-Boussart, Monique. *Alfred Döblin: Seine Religiosität in Persönlichkeit und Werk*. Bonn: Bouvier, 1970.

The Tragedy of Truth: Döblin's Novel
Hamlet oder Die lange Nacht nimmt ein Ende

Wolfgang Düsing

THE NOVEL *Hamlet oder Die lange Nacht nimmt ein Ende* (first published in 1956), like the whole of Döblin's late work, was long overshadowed by his middle period, which reached its pinnacle in *Berlin Alexanderplatz* (1929). Because of its bold structure and avant-garde narrative technique this novel, on which Döblin scholarship continues to focus primarily even today, came to be the standard by which his entire oeuvre was judged. This led to an underestimation of the later works, especially the *Hamlet* novel.[1] Döblin's troubles with this novel began with the search for a publisher. Finding no one in the Federal Republic, he published it in the GDR, although he had to change the ending: a protagonist who at the end of a long story retreats to a monastery, as in the original version, was unthinkable in the GDR, Döblin was informed (Graber, 591–93). In the revised version, the protagonist enters the "wimmelnde und geräuschvolle Stadt" (*H*, 573). Having existed mostly in the past, he awakens, after the death of his parents, to a new life.

When Döblin's work found a wider audience in the 1970s, also indicated by the regular symposia of the International Döblin Society, *Hamlet* received more attention. Scholarly concern centered around three problems: the alternate ending of the novel; its unusual structure, which combines a novel with a cycle of numerous novellas inserted into the main text; and the role of psychoanalysis, which defines the narrative perspective and the formation of the characters. The present study will also address these three problems and explore the tensions between the literary and theological content, between the aesthetic character and the theological tendency that emerges plainly in this text, written after Döblin's conversion. Having stood politically on the left during the Weimar Republic, although remaining at a critical distance from the Communist left and the leftist Union of Proletarian-Revolutionary Writers, Döblin had converted to Catholicism in 1941, during his American exile. This step, long anticipated in his personal development, caught his friends by surprise. When Döblin revealed his religious orientation at the celebration of his sixty-fifth birthday, it was misunderstood and criticized as a retreat from political engagement.[2] Within the context of the fundamental religious attitude of the *Hamlet* novel, we also have to deal with the question of whether the work must be seen as a Christian tragedy, which appears at first sight to be a contradiction, since the concept of a Christian tragedy contains both a theological and an aesthetic component that seem to be mutually exclusive rather than complimentary.[3]

The Double Ending

Scholarship soon began to deal with the consequences arising from the double ending for understanding the novel as a whole. Heinz Graber, who was co-editor of the novel for the Walter publishing house, showed that Döblin does not simply replace the first version with the second, but rather that the second arises from a critical confrontation with the first. The first version develops organically out of the course of the action. The ending has been prepared long before, since in entering the monastery Edward follows a pattern present in many variations in the inserted stories. The main figures in the stories "Die Prinzessin von Tripoli," "Erzählung vom Knappen, der seinen Ring verlor," and "Theodora" all go into monastic retirement and inspire Edward to emulate them. In the second version, Edward frees himself from precisely these precedents. Only by liberating himself is he able to overcome a state of self-alienation and attain his true identity (Graber, 594–95). When Edward remarks that he has until then been only an object and has had no real life, he stresses his newfound personal identity, which he has reached after a long healing process. This is confirmed by the fact that the stories told within the family circle, which contain earlier models of identification, have now lost all attraction for him. "Jetzt ist das Bild ein Bild," he says (*H*, 571), but, one might add, *only an image*. In the light of the new truth, the stories narrated earlier pale. Yet we should not jump to the conclusion that in this late period Döblin renounced the stories, or story-telling in general (and hence literature), for Edward's new truth is not given a specific form. It remains a utopia made possible only by passage through the long series of stories.[4] If this "truth" were to become more specific in Edward's new life, the literary result would be only that new stories supplant the old. For Döblin these are ever and again stories in which the essence of a biography and history as a totality is rendered.

The problems of the two versions dissolve when they are regarded against the background of Döblin's development. The conclusions sketch two modes of living for the recovering war veteran Edward. The conflict arising here between a *vita contemplativa,* monastic retreat, and a *vita activa,* the drive into the metropolis, expresses a dualism that marked Döblin's work from the beginning, except that now the contrast is viewed from a Christian perspective. To suppose that only the first version with its monastic motive can be seen as Christian is mistaken. The second version is Christian as well, because Edward distributes what he realizes from his inheritance among the poor, thus showing a conviction not substantially different from that in the first version. Therefore, the second conclusion cannot be connected with a crisis of faith, as Graber does.[5] Both conclusions reflect Döblin's conversion. The distinction is that in the first version, the protagonist rediscovers his war-damaged identity by withdrawing from the world, concentrating on a personal, internalized world, while in the second, he joins the world, or becomes absorbed into the whole. This dualism can be seen in Döblin's work as early as in the novel *Die drei Sprünge des Wang-lun;* it defines also the rhythm of Franz Biberkopf's development in *Berlin Alexanderplatz.*

This contrast in the structure of the self as "Stück und Gegenstück der Natur" is also one of the fundamental ideas in Döblin's writings on the philosophy of nature (*UD,* 30).[6] In *Wissen und Verändern!,* published in 1931 as a series of open letters in reply to questions asked by the student Gustav René Hocke, Döblin tries to arrive at a definition of the contemporary period. He stresses that human beings never obtain stability and harmony and thus are never identical with themselves (*WuV,* 151). Thus the search for identity, not possession of it, becomes the prime mover in human existence, an oscillating back and forth between two extremes, between a total "communion" in which the self threatens to dissolve into the whole and be lost in anonymity, and a radical "individuation," which trades off loss of the world for retreat into a fortress of self-awareness, where the isolated self also runs the risk of obliteration. Thus the self is essentially characterized by its "incompleteness." Döblin's description of the antagonistic tendencies within the self betrays the influence of Nietzsche. The isolation of the Dionysiac underpinnings from the Apollonian "principium individuationis" reappears in Döblin's analysis of the fundamentals of the self, the synthesis of which man strives for in vain (*UD,* 68–69). Döblin sees the archetypical image of human action in the destiny of the prophet Moses. Not even the utmost effort leads to the desired goal. The chapter in which Döblin describes the fundamental situation of human action is entitled "Immer vor dem gelobten Land." That human existence can never reach fulfillment is a mark of its finiteness, which Döblin affirms. This, however does not exclude "ein Gefühl von Tragik" (*UD*, 220, 223).

The basic situation of human existence as outlined above reveals that Döblin, faced with the decision whether and how the close of *Hamlet* could be changed, remained true to his convictions. He opted for the opposite of the first version with its contemplative individuation, namely, for a "communion" with all living beings, for participation in the whole. The first version leads to a concentration on the self and loss of the world. "Ich habe gelernt: ich bin von aller Welt entfernt," as he puts it in *Unser Dasein*. But then he says of the second version, "Ich suchte mich und fand die Welt" (*UD*, 273, 279).

The protagonist's search for the self is motivated by the story line. Edward Allison, a soldier on an American warship, has been severely wounded in a Japanese *kamikaze* attack. One of his legs has to be amputated, but that is not the worst of it. His friend has been killed, he is in shock himself, and the trauma of combat threatens to destroy him. He is first treated at a clinic. When his symptoms abate, he is sent home at his mother's insistence, in the hope that familiar surroundings will hasten his recovery. He feels that he has lost more in the war than this one leg, and wants to understand what has happened to him. He realizes that he must go farther back to discover the causes of his dilemma. As other family members become involved, the confrontation with his own past intensifies. His quest for identity is connected with the question of war guilt, which faces primarily the older generation. This investigation intersects with another, having to do with the novellas. Gordon Allison, Edward's father, a well-known writer, suggests telling stories in the evening for entertainment. He hopes that this will have a therapeutic effect and also mute Edward's unwelcome inquiries about the older generation's accountability for the war.

The Structure of the Novel

The complex structure of the novel is explained in part by how it evolved. Döblin states in his *Epilog* that a number of stories formed the nucleus of the Hamlet novel. "Ich kam darauf, sie zusammenzufassen und auszuführen. Man müßte sie, dachte ich, formal für jemanden erzählen wie in 1001 Nacht" (*AzL*, 396). The figure to whom the stories are addressed is Edward, the novel's protagonist. In this novel, as in the great novella cycles Boccaccio's *Decamerone* (1349–51), Margarete de Navarra's *Heptameron* (1559), and Goethe's *Unterhaltungen deutscher Ausgewanderten* (Conversations of German Refugees, 1795), we have a group of storytellers who contribute their tales to the general entertainment. The reason for storytelling in the *Hamlet* novel as in these other great novella cycles is first of all diversion. Additionally, it is connected with the hope for a therapeutic effect. Edward, the afflicted war veteran "will erkennen, was ihn und alle krank und schlecht gemacht hat [. . .]. Die Wahrheit, nur die Wahrheit kann ihn gesund machen. Und aus vielen Zerstreuungs- und Ablenkungserzählungen werden indirekte und immer mehr direkte Mitteilungen, schließlich Bekenntnisse und Geständnisse" (*AzL*, 396). Although the stories are supposed to be for diversion and amusement, they lead indirectly to the discovery of a hidden truth. And what they reveal is anything but entertaining. Behind the slick façade of familial harmony, the marks of bitter confrontation appear. At stake is the longstanding battle between the parents, which had had a harmful effect on Edward's childhood. The famous, widely respected, middle-class writer Gordon emerges as a dubious figure with questionable honor and a past bordering on the criminal, who with his former accomplice the shadowy Hazel Crocker narrowly escaped arrest. Behind the refined, angelic Alice, Edward's mother, hides his father Gordon's formidable adversary, a passionate, hate-driven woman who has forgotten no humiliation, whether intended or not, and now will stop at nothing to have her revenge.

From Döblin's remarks in the *Epilog* we can see first of all that a series of novellas forms the nucleus of the novel, which is composed by a process of embedding the stories in a frame and then integrating the interpolations and their frame into a dense epic structure. In so doing a thematic connection is established between the frame and the inserted stories, together with an interlinking of the action in the frame and the stories and numerous correlations between the figures on both narrative levels. It seems that for Döblin this structure came about spontaneously. He was not aware that he was not the first to compose a novel out of a series of novellas. Familiar examples in German literature are *Die Schuldlosen* (The Guiltless, 1950) by Hermann Broch (1886–1951) and *Nachts unter der steinernen Brücke* (By Night under the Stone Bridge, 1953) by Leo Perutz (1882–1957). Since these novels are not structurally identical with novella cycles, they should be seen as a distinct genre. They could be called "Novellenromane," a designation invented by Broch, who considered Goethe's *Wilhelm Meisters Wanderjahre* (1829) to be the first modern novel of this kind.[7] Ironically, Döblin had encountered this novel form earlier, without recognizing its artistic potential. In his essay, "Reform des Romans" of 1919, he reviewed the novel *Die Stadt des Hirns* (The City of the Mind, 1919) by Otto Flake (1880–1963) which can also be considered a Novellenroman. As early as 1915, Döblin had declared in his "Bemerkungen zum Roman," "Zehn Novellen machen keinen Roman. Nichts im Roman darf sich zur Novelle auswachsen." But then he admitted: "Es gibt trotz alledem Zusammenhänge. Man muß balancieren zwischen der Ariensammlung der alten Oper und der unendlichen Melodie Wagners" (*AzL*, 22). That might have led to a fairer assessment of Flake's novel, which Döblin dismissively called a "Mosaikroman." "Eine Art Rahmenerzählung, fünf Novellen eingeschoben, unerhört viel Reflexion." He admits that he first read the framing action then the novellas, and finally the commentaries within the novel (*AzL*, 45). "Browsing" in this fashion in Döblin's *Hamlet* would also leave a rather disturbing impression, although it must be admitted that Flake's novel, even if one strives for fairness from our historical perspective, is rather tough going. It is above all Flake's lofty philosophical ambition that aroused Döblin's justifiable mistrust and led him to overlook the originality of the structure.

Later, in his *Epilog*, Döblins says of the Hamlet novel: "Das Buch könnte eine neue Reihe einleiten, die dritte, wäre ich jünger. Aber einmal endet alles Fragen" (*AzL*, 397). If one sees in the *Hamlet* novel a third phase of his creativity, as Döblin did, then the preceding phase must be taken to have culminated in *Berlin Alexanderplatz*. This second phase must be distinguished in turn from the early works by its reaffirmation of the self, and by the appearance of a narrator who begins to interfere in the story. In the first phase, the epoch of the "steinernen Stil," the narrator remains invisible behind an impenetrable wall of facts and phenomena that are meant to speak for themselves. In his 1913 essay "An Romanautoren und ihre Kritiker," Döblin states categorically: "Die Hegemonie des Autors ist zu brechen." He requires of the writer an ascetic "Fanatismus der Selbstverleugnung" (*AzL*, 18). This depersonalization yields in *Berlin Alexanderplatz* to role-playing by the author, who appears in a minstrel's mask, thus ironizing himself, but nevertheless sharing intensively in the action and intervening with comments.

Another remark in the *Epilog* deserves particular attention: the comparison of the novel to a tragedy and its ending with a tragic catharsis. "Schließlich ist die Tragödie da, aber mit ihr die Katharsis" (*AzL*, 397). That is to say, the long-suppressed problems revealed by Edward's inquiries, which unveil the crisis in the family's interrelationships and end in the family's dissolution, are to be understood as a tragedy according to Döblin's notion of the tragic. The sister leaves home, father and mother die, although not without having first become reconciled. When the son returns from the war severely wounded the family is confronted with the past. The parents must come to terms with their own failure, with their egotistical tendency to look away that led not only to private guilt, but also beyond the personal sphere to shared culpability for the war. The Allison family consists of "innocents," who, like the characters in Broch's *Die Schuldlosen,* made no attempt, in their escapism, to prevent developments that led to the Second World War. The issue is one that goes beyond the private sphere and becomes one of collective guilt of "innocents," who in their self-absorption neither combated nor took seriously the approaching catastrophe.

The revelation, evolving step by step as a result of an analytical process, exposes with a suspense worthy of a crime thriller a childhood trauma behind the trauma of the war. Edward is detective and judge in one. He was a victim of paternal violence in the parental battle, just as he later falls victim to military violence. These are the issues he wants to clarify, for which he demands justice.

As the successor to Shakespeare's Hamlet, the hero Edward seeks to clear up a state of crisis and thus save himself and his family, an attempt that ends in failure. Numerous lines of action and narrative modes are interwoven. There is on one hand a Freudian psychoanalytical approach that determines the novel's structure down to its analytical narrative technique. The protagonist does not develop through new experiences, as in the traditional novel of development, but through reflection and dealing with matters long forgotten and repressed. A secret buried in the past captivates Edward, drives him to analysis and thus forward. This characterizes the action within the frame of the novel. The inserted novellas, however, are told in a synthetic manner.[8] In these novellas the characters of the novel respond to the changing situation by defending themselves and attacking others. The group of narrators forms the novel's center and characterizes its structure. It is Gordon who offers the first story. His troubadour story is brilliantly related, yet it does not receive only acclamation. Edward sees through his father, who created for himself an ivory tower where others cannot disturb him. Edward appeals to his father's sense of responsibility, although the man's escapist behavior has walled him off from all claims made upon him by his family and society.

While this technique of recollection used to reveal the past — reaching beyond the war trauma into remote childhood — may be unthinkable without the influence of psychoanalysis, the search for the truth is marked by a further component, namely existentialism. Combining these two trends, the appeal to both Freud and Kierkegaard is made possible by Döblin's interpretation of the Shakespearian Hamlet model. Edward is Döblin's Hamlet in the family tragedy, whereby the connections to Freud and his Oedipus complex and to Kierkegaard's theory of tragedy are obvious. Döblin's remarks in the *Epilog* imply that the whole may be regarded as a tragic process in which tragic guilt is not rooted in myth but is psychologically and religiously motivated. The catharsis is not that of antiquity but a Christian reconciliation, uniting Alice and Gordon, after much erring, in death.

Edward's Search for Truth

While the protagonist Edward/Hamlet legitimizes his search for truth by quoting entire passages from Kierkegaard, the novel constructs Edward's destiny with reference to Freudian psychoanalysis and the philosophy of Kierkegaard. The narrative structure of the novel is defined by an analytic technique of recollection and a considerable number of interpolated stories in which the characters project their images of self and others. The narrative is thus fragmented into a kaleidoscope of stories, all having the function of advancing the characters' search for the roots of their identities. The characters' reflection in a number of stories will be examined later in more detail. Meanwhile, the question arises as to the function of the psychoanalytical narration. Certain situations cause Edward to recall shocking memories that exist on two levels of consciousness. One series of memories is of his war experiences: the aerial attack, being wounded, and his friend's death. These belong to what Freud called "Deckerinnerungen," memories that conceal a more remote childhood trauma.[9]

The novel, however, including the line of action concentrating on Edward, goes beyond a psychoanalytic case study, since Edward's struggle to shed light on the past has several motives. There is first the search for identity, since Edward has returned from the war, as he says, "nicht bloß mit diesem dummen abgerissenen Bein, sondern — ohne mich" (*H*, 155). In this search, the two aspects of "I" and "me" can be distinguished according to G. H. Mead's *Mind, Self and Society* (1934) where the "I" serves as the subject of memory, as personal identity, and the remembered "me," the "I" as object, as social identity, which corresponds to the roles and patterns of behavior assigned by society. Proust's monumental *A la recherche du temps perdu* (1913–27) is built also upon this division of the self and the distance between the remembered and the remembering "I" which the novel bridges in memory in rediscovered time. In the *Hamlet* novel, this process of remembering is more psychoanalytically structured. Added to this are the stories, where the figures drawn from myth and literature result in an almost infinite variety of identification patterns and masks. This reflects the uncertainty, instability, and susceptibility to crisis of modern identity.

In connection with the problem of identity, Edward is faced also with the question of the older generation's responsibility for the war and its causes. With the insights achieved over his father's resistance, it becomes ever clearer that he is not a neurotic patient confronting an intact family, but that the family needs therapy, symbolizing in turn a general crisis of society. The closer Edward gets to the memory of the original conflict, the more dramatic his fears become. It consisted of a violent dispute between the parents in the attic of the house, which he experienced as a child and which triggered his father's outburst of hate against him. He was also directly involved, although at the time he did not understand it, since his mother had suddenly claimed that Edward's father was not Gordon, but Glenn, a much-revered friend of Alice. As Gordon's rage falls upon the son, his mother has difficulty shielding him from her husband's attack. This early childhood experience of a life-threatening attack is repeated in the *kamikaze* attack and causes the trauma. In this confrontation, Edward suffers ever more from a compulsion to repeat, a "Wiederholungszwang." "Die Träume rücken immer wieder von neuem gegen die schreckliche Situation an und suchen sie zu beseitigen," Döblin wrote in "Metapsychologie und Biologie" (1922).[10] Since the family is deeply involved, they too feel the pull of the past. This is evidenced by the reappearance of various items from earlier years. They begin wearing dresses and suits from that epoch again, and Alice is struck by a sudden awareness: "Oh, wir sinken alle in die Vergangenheit zurück" (*H*, 379). The characters fall ever more under the influence of old patterns of thought and behavior. A compulsive repetition connected with repressed, unresolved experiences indicates a sharpening crisis in the life of Döblin's characters. This is similar to the three blows of fate that strike Franz Biberkopf in *Berlin Alexanderplatz*, which are also the expression of such a compulsive repetition.

The story advances not only by means of Edward's striving for discovery but also by the novellas told and debated at the nightly get-togethers. The novellas are closely related to the destinies of the characters who use them to portray themselves and others from their perspective. Gordon's story about the troubadour, for example, is told in two versions, and Alice's Theodora legend is related in segments in order to show the particular state of development of the respective narrator. The stories can be read either as independent narratives or as continuations of the novel's action on another level. With the tale of the troubadour Jaufie (i.e. Jaufré),[11] the father constructs in the shape of the old knight who frees himself from the *minne*-obsession of his time a positive, humorous self-image, while at the same time characterizing his son as a naïve, dependent young man attached to his mother or his lover Petite Lay. Edward, who sees through this projection, criticizes his father's portrayal of a weak son and his masquerade as a lusty *bon vivant*. Above all he rejects his father's reduction of all values to ideologies behind which hide tangible interests. In his father's view, men are victims of false ideas who do not act in their true interest but allow themselves to be manipulated. Only he who sees through this is free. Not only Edward protests against his father's perspective. Miss Virginia counters with a pious tale of pure love, which fails to convince the skeptical Gordon. In the course of the family's discussions the father grows ever more chimerical; he comes to resemble Lord Crenshaw, a character in one of his stories who goes by the name of a bus stop instead of his own name, a man without a personality, but therefore infinitely changeable. Whether there is a real face behind the masks he wears remains an open question.

The stories offer numerous identity models that give the characters temporary stability, only to be superseded by others as the action of the novel proceeds. Every figure has by means of the stories a number of possible ways to project his own ego and his roles. Thus Gordon, the father, assumes on the one hand the role of the old crusader, the father of Jaufie, a modestly successful minstrel who nevertheless sees through the trickery of a *minne*-ideology concocted by women and leads a comfortable life in the orient, far from his tyrannical consort. But Gordon also presents himself as the demonic artist in his tale of Michelangelo. In the Lear fable by James Mackenzie, Alice's brother, Gordon appears as a tragicomic figure. In Alice's stories he is compared with Pluto, god of the underworld. He rejects this comparison, as well as his representation through the image of an archaic, wild boar from a Celtic legend retold by James Mackenzie. New projections are created when Edward recognizes himself in the image of the wild boar because of his own incessant and destructive questioning of others, and Gordon, in the second version of the story of Jaufie Rudel, assumes the role of the minstrel who only in death catches sight of his unknown beloved, a role which Edward had first taken to refer to himself. The revision of the story and the change in projection result from the progress in the novel's action and the development of the characters. In time, Alice is no longer the domineering mother of Jaufie, as Gordon had seen her, and no longer the mother awaiting the son lost in the war, as she had seen herself, nor Lady Imogen Persh, the equally strong adversary from James Mackenzie's story, but, after her reconciliation with the dying Gordon, the longed-for, unattainable beloved, the Princess of Tripoli. She also identifies herself with the penitential Theodora, thus renouncing her earlier existence as *femme fatale* and regretting the licentious life she led after her break with the traditional role as housewife and mother. In a farewell letter to Edward she finishes by telling the legend of Theodora and thus her own life. These suggestions may suffice to show what a wealth of interpretive possibilities Döblin elicits from the interreflecting stories, so that with every turn of the action, the stories and their characters appear in a new light.

The web of communication relating the stories and the action of the novel become even denser with a scene bearing the title "Ein Theaterstück." The play is performed on Gordon's birthday for the family circle. The guests themselves are presented in a rather disturbing way: "Die eleganten Damen [. . .]: die Wäsche, die Röcke, die Blusen, die Jacken und Mäntel, der Haarschmuck, die Hüte. Sie waren noch mit viel mehr bekleidet und wußten es nicht, wie bei der Zwiebel, Schale um Schale" (*H*, 398). Dress is no longer an expression of the individual's style, for there is no individual. "Layer after layer" can be peeled off without reaching any nucleus. Even the presence of these figures is only illusory considering the weight of history that each one bears. It goes back from the First World War to the St. Bartholomew's Night Massacre, to the invasion of William the Conqueror, to the destruction of Carthage. The retreat into the distant past is surpassed by references to the history of evolution, to epochs in development long before humankind appeared. "Ihre Kehlen vibrierten. Es sangen Vögel. Stiere brüllten. Tiergeschlechter lebten, Quallen, Pflanzen, Korallenverbände. Da lebten alte Erdperioden und Katastrophen" (*H*, 399). A gigantic historical and an evolutionary past reaching even farther back is still present within those living today. The tiny self of every-day life, the autonomous personality, becomes an arsenal containing an unlimited wealth of shapes from the present and past reaching back into early and primeval history to the very beginnings of life. The infinite metamorphoses of life through evolution until the appearance of man, which the narrator sees as still functioning and influencing behavior, correspond to the reflections of the figures in history and in the stories. This is realized anew in the play. The play "Lord Crenshaw," based on one of Gordon's novellas, presents an allegorical bus ride from Crenshaw to Wilshire and back. The passengers are characters from the stories who get off at the last stop, while others board. Only a single unknown figure and his companion, who hides behind changing masks, make no move to get off. The masks indicate stories that contain projections of Gordon. The figure appears now as a crusader, referring to the story of Jaufie Rudel, now with a wild boar's head, reminiscent of the Celtic legend and the Lear story by James Mackenzie, Alice's brother. The tragic mask with its broken nose refers to the Michelangelo story. While the other passengers are replaced, Lord Crenshaw, who wears these masks, continues to travel back and forth with his companion, never getting off, a simile for the senseless repetition of the same, the meaninglessness of the journey of life, from which Edward later distances himself.

The Consequences of Truth

In the play, presented at a birthday party and closely related to the worsening conflict within the family, the interpretative models developed thus far culminate in a dramatically significant moment. The premonitions of the characters multiply and, in the next chapter, titled "Die Enthüllung," the novel moves inexorably toward the discovery of the truth, which, however, leads to a new life only for Edward, while bringing death for the parents. And yet the catastrophe, within the framework of the Christian interpretation, contains the possibility of reconciliation, since the parents depart from life reconciled with each other and with God.

By the time of the birthday party, the novel's focus is no longer primarily on Edward but on the entire family. Alice had brought Edward home not only to accelerate his recovery, but also because she saw in him an ally in her reckoning with Gordon. The tension in the novel depends on the one hand on the discovery of a hidden past and, on the other, on the dramatic process of the impending catastrophe. Edward's search for the truth, meant to promote his healing, sets in motion the self-destruction of the family: an astonishing ending for a novel that uses psychoanalysis as a narrative technique. The ending is furthermore surprising because the novel's author was a psychiatrist, who appreciated the contributions of Freud and psychoanalysis, even if he was not a Freudian himself. *Hamlet,* however, is not only a psychoanalytic case study but also a Christian tragedy, as Döblin, influenced by Kierkegaard, understood it. That Döblin had studied Kierkegaard's theory of the tragedy in *Either/Or,* is also clear from the novel *November 1918.*[12] A psychoanalytic investigation of a repressed past finds its goal in a Kierkegaardian search for truth. This, however, takes an altogether tragic course, foreshadowed by the many stories based on tragic myths.

Edward, the Hamlet figure, thus appears in an irksome double perspective. He himself brings up Kierkegaard at the moment his father tries to withdraw elegantly from his responsibility and evade Edward's unwelcome questions with his Jaufie Rudel story. He freely quotes Kierkegaard's categorical demand: "Ich will Redlichkeit."[13] Edward interprets Kierkegaard's statement and identifies himself with his search for truth.

Above all, however, Edward recognizes himself in Kierkegaard's restless passion for questioning. Edward is not interested in the outcome of Kierkegaard's thinking or his philosophical position, but his way of seeking, the modern restlessness, that quickly casts doubt on any result. "Wie Kierkegaard von Frage zu Frage springt, von einer auf die andere herunterspringt, an jedem gewonnenen Resultat rüttelt und nie gewiß wird, wie er weiterspringt, und nichts zustande bringt und nichts weiß — das hat etwas von einer Angst, von einem Schwindel, von einem Sturz ins Bodenlose an sich" (*H*, 173).

A second aspect of Kierkegaardian influence can be seen in Döblin's use of Kierkegaard's notion of an aesthetic, an ethical, and a religious state determining the relationship of the characters to one another. Initially, Gordon represents the aesthetic state. Kierkegaard's description of the aesthetic conscience shows striking parallels to Gordon's behavior: "'Das Leben ist ein Maskenspiel,' belehrst Du uns, und dies ist Dir ein unerschöpflicher Unterhaltungsstoff, und noch immer ist es niemand gelungen, Dich zu erkennen, denn jegliche Enthüllung ist stets eine Täuschung [. . .] Deine Maske ist von allen die rätselhafteste [. . .], Du selber bist ein Nichts, eine rätselvolle Gestalt."[14] The similarity to Gordon's behavior is obvious. When Alice asks why, as Lord Crenshaw, a figure with interchangeable personalities, he wears ever new masks, Gordon answers, "Weil es mir Spaß macht und weil ich es kann" (*H*, 416). Edward, on the other hand, initially represents the ethical state. But the clearer the metaphysical character of Kierkegaard's "unconditional requirement" becomes, the more the ethical state tends toward the religious one. This is true also for Gordon and Alice, who attain in death the religious state and reconciliation with God.

The Christian catharsis, however, cannot conceal that the conclusion of the novel with the death of the parents, the sister's flight, and Edward's decision to separate himself from the family history is not easy to understand emotionally. It was Edward who had given the impetus for a comprehensive confrontation with the past, and it was he who had also insisted that the older generation accept responsibility for the war. But then this same Edward declares that he had nothing to do with all that has happened. He distances himself from the play that he himself had organized by saying: "Wie fahren nicht in der Runde, nein, wir fahren nicht in der Runde," essentially rejecting history as a senseless circular movement. He also wants nothing more to do with the play, with anything that has gone before, with the stories, and with the action of the frame: "Ich bin nicht im Spiel" (*H*, 571–72). He sees himself above all as a victim, a war casualty and a casualty of his parents' conflict. In the course of his recovery he becomes more and more the active agent who demands an accounting with Kierkegaardian logic. In the background stand his experiences in the Second World War, the memory of the victims, the "Trauerarbeit" (Kiesel, *Trauerarbeit*, 489–98), and his indignation over the behavior of the older generation. But this grief would be fitting also with regard to the family's fate, in which Edward is innocently implicated. When it is said that the bomb that destroyed the ship, wounding Edward and triggering the trauma, continued to fall (*H*, 24), then not only Edward, but also his family were struck by the events of the war. The family catastrophe is therefore at least partially, caused by the war, which does not exclude the complicity of those involved, but mitigates it. The family could not sustain the great stress connected with Edward's treatment and was shattered by it.

Edward's sudden determination to deny all responsibility for these events is probably connected also with Döblin's problem of how to untangle the labyrinth of relationships and end the novel with an unequivocal conclusion. But Döblin rarely succeeded in doing so. Unambiguity in two different conclusions is in itself a paradox. After finishing *Berlin Alexanderplatz*, Döblin wrote resignedly: "Bisher sehe ich: der Dualismus ist nicht aufzuheben" (*B I*, 165). Since Edward has overcome his war neurosis and emerges with his health restored from the family's collapse, any tragic compassion would have to be felt for Gordon and Alice rather than for him, who has found a future. Döblin himself felt that tragedy derived from the fact that the tragic hero is persecuted relentlessly for pardonable weaknesses and mistakes and disproportionately punished. That is the fate of Gordon and Alice, who become each other's *nemesis* and who, although "innocent," still bear some tangential responsibility for the political developments, and have little with which to counter Edward's condemnation.

As to the two variant conclusions already mentioned, it can be stated in retrospect that the first is preferable, making possible as it does a more reasonable ending of the very complex action of the novel. In distinction to the second version, the action prepared for it. Most of all, Edward's monastic retreat from the world follows naturally from his previous behavior, from his unconditional religiously motivated search for truth. It is a reaction appropriate to his war experiences, the death of his younger friend, for which he feels responsible, and to the family tragedy, including his parents' death. The moment of reconciliation, the catharsis, lies in a life of meditation, in Edward's memory, notwithstanding its Christian aspect, not in a new beginning that breaks with the past.

This is not to denigrate the second version of the conclusion. It is moving that the last great novel of the terminally ill Döblin closes with an affirmation of his faith in life. A "neues Leben" begins in vernal nature as it does for Edward. He is entirely overcome by the vital power of nature: "Die Maikäfer waren den Winter über tot, jetzt kriechen sie herum und fressen die grünen Blätter." Everything he has experienced earlier belongs to winter, a lifeless period succeeded by spring. He has the feeling of being "noch im Entstehen," of being a fetus (*H,* 571–72). Although the first conclusion follows logically from the novel's design as a Christian tragedy and from the experiences of its protagonist, the second conclusion, embedded in the living power of nature and indestructible hope that a new beginning remains a possibility, corresponds more closely to Döblin's fundamental outlook, as is manifest in many of his works.

I would like to conclude with some thoughts of a perhaps rather venturesome nature. Döblin's four-volume narrative work about the Weimar Republic, entitled *November 1918,* which preceded the *Hamlet* novel, is a historical portrayal with distinct references to the time of the writing. The collapse of the Weimar Republic, which did not succeed in dispersing the shadows of the lost war and building a democratic society, was meant by Döblin as a warning for the new start after 1945. This suggests examining *Hamlet* also for a perspective pointing toward the future,[15] although Döblin does not portray the Second World War or the question of guilt from a German point of view, while the few events referred to stand as representations for the misery of any war. And yet one may assume that Döblin could not and would not for a moment forget the German situation and his own exile with its crushingly painful experiences, the concern for his sons, above all the sorrow at the loss of his son Wolfgang, who died as a French soldier. He brooded in self-accusation to such an extent, as Brecht reports in his *Arbeitsjournal* (published 1973; 605) that he perceived the advent of the Nazi regime as his own personal failure and guilt. This renders Edward's insistence on the question of war guilt and his harsh condemnation of the older generation in *Hamlet* understandable from a Christian viewpoint. On the other hand, Döblin was among the first to return from exile after the collapse, in order to take an active role in building a democratic society.

As to the question of a perspective reaching beyond the war's end, the novel affords the answers already discussed — severe penance for the older generation tainted by guilt, while in the first version the younger generation is left with the duties of grief and remembrance. In the second version, Edward's answer is a radical forsaking of a fateful past and a new beginning. These two mutually exclusive paths toward a confrontation with the past were repeatedly discussed in Germany and also repeatedly chosen. Each path is justified in its own way, and each in itself is one-sided. The goal must be to combine them, which is easy to call for but difficult to realize. It speaks for Döblin's realism that he did not attempt a synthesis, but left the two conflicting paths adjacent, the imperfection of humankind and the tragedy of truth.

— *Translated by Lee Stavenhagen*

Notes

[1] To give one example: Günther Blöcker writes in his *Kritisches Lesebuch* that Döblin "[vermag] die Botschaften, die ihn bewegen, nicht mehr zu formulieren" (30). Among others, Klaus Müller-Salget, in his *Alfred Döblin*, shares the negative evaluation of the works written after 1933 (see especially 379).

[2] See Kiesel, "Döblin's Konversion als Politikum," 193–208 and Kiesel, *Literarische Trauerarbeit*, 145–200 and 215–20.

[3] This explains why theoreticians have had problems with this concept, with the exception of a few writers like Schopenhauer. See his *Die Welt als Wille und Vorstellung*, vol. 1, 353–56 and vol. 2, 556–62.

[4] Leo Kreutzer reads Edward's liberation from the role of Hamlet as the establishment of a distance between the narrator and his own story: "Ein unaufgelöster Widerspruch, auch im Poetologischen" (131).

[5] See Graber, 593ff. That both endings must be understood in a Christian sense is emphasized by Anthony W. Riley in "Der umstrittene Schluss von Alfred Döblins *Hamlet*," 352.

[6] See Düsing, *Erinnerung und Identität*, 103–27.

[7] Broch's letter to Dr. Brody, 17 July, 1933. Hermann Broch, *Werke. Kommentierte Werkausgabe*, ed. Paul Michael Lützeler, vol. 13/1, 243. On the genesis of *Die Schuldlosen* from a series of novellas, see Richard Thieberger, "Hermann Brochs Novellenroman und seine Vorgeschichte." On this topic see also Düsing, "Der Novellenroman: Versuch einer Gattungsbestimmung" and "Döblins *Hamlet oder Die lange Nacht nimmt ein Ende* und der Novellenroman der Moderne."

[8] On the change between the analytic and synthetic mode of narration see Kümmerling.

[9] Sigmund Freud, "Über Deckerinnerungen," *Gesammelte Werke*, vol. 1, 531–54. On Döblin's memorial technique, see my *Erinnerung und Identität*; also, with an informative survey of scholarship, Thomas Anz, "Döblin und die Psychoanalyse." Döblin's connection with psychiatry and psychoanalysis has been examined more thoroughly recently by Wolfgang Schäffner in *Die Ordnung des Wahns*. See also Eva Horn, "Versuchsanordnung Roman." In her analysis, informed by Freud and Foucault, the ambiguous *Hamlet* novel leads to a single consistently pursued thesis: "Die ultima ratio, auf die alles hinausläuft, ist denn auch das gemeinsame Lieblingsthema aller Erzählungen im Roman: Sexualität" (29). On Döblin's relation to Freud, especially his theory of trauma, see also Ingrid Maaß.

[10] *Neue Rundschau* 33 (1922), 1224. Döblin refers to Freud's treatise *Jenseits des Lustprinzips* (Beyond the Pleasure Principle, 1920). See my study "Döblins *Hamlet oder Die lange Nacht nimmt ein Ende* und der Novellenroman der Moderne," 275.

[11] Döblin's typing error. He refers to the troubadour Jaufré Rudel. See Anthony W. Riley, "Jaufré Rudel und die Prinzessin von Tripoli."

[12] Kiesel, *Literarische Trauerarbeit*, 475–76.

[13] He quotes Kierkegaard's essay "Was ich will?" *Gesammelte Werke* 34, Section: "Der Augenblick," 48. See Monique Weyembergh-Boussart, *Alfred Döblin*, 296 (endnote 14).

[14] *Entweder/Oder, Gesammelte Werke,* 2nd and 3rd Section, 169–70; see also Monique Weyembergh-Boussart, 349.

[15] A similar idea is indicated by Helmuth Kiesel's observation of parallels between the ending of the novel and Alexander and Margarete Mitscherlich's thoughts on the problem of "Vergangenheitsbewältigung" in *Grundlagen kollektiven Verhaltens*. See Kiesel, *Literarische Trauerarbeit*, 498.

Works Cited

Anz, Thomas. "Döblin und die Psychoanalyse." *Internationales Alfred-Döblin-Kolloquium Leiden 1995.* Ed. by Gabriele Sander. Bern: Peter Lang, 1997. 9–31.

Auer, Manfred. *Das Exil vor der Vertreibung: Motivkontinuität und Quellenproblematik im späten Werk Alfred Döblins.* Bonn: Bouvier, 1977.

Bauer, Werner M. "Gegensatz und Ambivalenz. Überlegungen zu Alfred Döblins Roman *Hamlet oder Die lange Nacht nimmt ein Ende.*" *Sprachkunst* 6 (1975): 314–29.

Blöcker, Günther. "Die lange Nacht der Lüge. Zu Alfred Döblins *Hamlet*-Roman." *Kritisches Lesebuch: Literatur unserer Zeit in Probe und Bericht.* Hamburg: Leibniz, 1962. 29–32.

Broch, Hermann. *Kommentierte Werkausgabe.* Ed. by Paul Michael Lützeler. Vol. 13/1: *Briefe.* Frankfurt: Suhrkamp, 1981.

Düsing, Wolfgang. "Döblins *Hamlet oder Die lange Nacht nimmt ein Ende* und der Novellenroman der Moderne." *Internationales Alfred-Döblin-Kolloquium Münster 1989– Marbach 1991.* Ed. by Werner Stauffacher. Bern: Peter Lang, 1993. 271–82.

———. *Erinnerung und Identität: Untersuchungen zu einem Erzählproblem bei Musil, Döblin und Doderer.* Munich: Fink, 1982.

Durzak, Manfred. "Flake und Döblin. Ein Kapitel in der Geschichte des polyhistorischen Romans." *Germanisch Romanische Monatsschrift* 20 (1970): 286–305.

Freud, Sigmund. *Gesammelte Werke*. Chronologisch geordnet. 18 vols. Ed. by Anna Freud et al. Vol. 1–17: London: Imago, 1940–42. Vol. 18: Frankfurt: S. Fischer, 1968.

Graber, Heinz. "Nachwort des Herausgebers." Alfred Döblin, *Der deutsche Maskenball von Linke Poot — Wissen und Verändern! Offene Briefe an einen jungen Menschen*. 305–18.

———. "Nachwort des Herausgebers." Alfred Döblin, *Hamlet oder Die lange Nacht nimmt ein Ende*, 583–99.

Grand, Jules. *Projektionen in Alfred Döblins Roman "Hamlet oder Die lange Nacht nimmt ein Ende."* Bern: Lang, 1974.

Horn, Eva. "Versuchsanordnung Roman. Erzählung und Wissen vom Menschen in Alfred Döblins *Berlin Alexanderplatz* und *Hamlet oder Die lange Nacht nimmt ein Ende*." *Internationales Alfred-Döblin-Kolloquium Leipzig 1997*. Ed. by Ira Lorf and Gabriele Sander. Bern: Lang, 1999. 117–34.

Kierkegaard, Sören. *Gesammelte Werke*. Trans. by Emanuel Hirsch, Hayo Gerdes, and Hans Martin Junghans. 36 Sections in 26 vols. Düsseldorf/Cologne: Diederichs, 1950–66. Section 2 and 3: *Either/Or* I (1956), II (1957), Section 34 *Der Augenblick* (1959).

Kiesel, Helmuth. "Döblins Konversion als Politikum." *Hinter dem schwarzen Vorhang: Die Katastrophe und die epische Tradition. Festschrift für Anthony W. Riley*. Ed. Friedrich Gaede, Patrick O' Neill, and Ulrich Scheck. Tübingen, Basel: Francke, 1994. 193–208.

———. *Literarische Trauerarbeit: Das Exil- und Spätwerk Alfred Döblins*. Tübingen: Niemeyer, 1986. 489–98.

Köhler, Erich. *Marcel Proust*. Göttingen: Vandenhoeck & Ruprecht, 1967.

Kreutzer, Leo. *Alfred Döblin: Sein Werk bis 1933*. Stuttgart: Kohlhammer, 1970.

Kümmerling, Beate. "Analytische und synthetische Erzählweise: Zur Struktur von Döblins Roman *Hamlet oder Die lange Nacht nimmt ein Ende*." *Internationales Alfred-Döblin-Kolloquium Lausanne 1987*. Ed. by Werner Stauffacher. Bern: Lang, 1991. 165–80.

Links, Roland. *Alfred Döblin: Leben und Werk*. Berlin: Volk und Wissen, 1965.

Maaß, Ingrid. *Regression und Individuation: Alfred Döblins Naturphilosophie und späte Romane vor dem Hintergrund einer Affinität zu Freuds Metapsychologie*. Bern: Lang, 1997.

Mead, George H. *Mind, Self, and Society: From the Standpoint of a Social Behaviorist*. Chicago: U of Chicago P, 1934.

Morherndl, Stephanie. *Alfred Döblin: "Hamlet oder Die lange Nacht nimmt ein Ende."* Graz: Phil. diss. (Masch.), 1963.

Müller-Salget, Klaus. *Alfred Döblin: Werk und Entwicklung*. Bonn: Bouvier, 1972.

Nietzsche, Friedrich. *Werke in drei Bänden*. Ed. by Karl Schlechta. Munich: Hanser, 1960.

Riley, Anthony W. "Ein deutscher Lear? Zu einigen Quellen in Alfred Döblins 'Erzählung vom König Lear' in seinem *Hamlet*-Roman." *Jahrbuch für Internationale Germanistik*. Bern: Lang, 1976: 475–82.

———. "Jaufré Rudel und die Prinzession von Tripoli. Zur Entstehung einer Erzählung und zur Metamorphose der Legende in Alfred Döblins *Hamlet*-Roman." *Festschrift Beißner*. Ed. by Ulrich Gaier and Werner Volke. Bebenhausen: Rotsch, 1974. 341–58.

———. "Zum umstrittenen Schluß von Alfred Döblins *Hamlet oder Die lange Nacht nimmt ein Ende*." *Literaturwissenschaftliches Jahrbuch* NF 13 (1972): 331–58.

Schäffner, Wolfgang. *Die Ordnung des Wahns: Zur Poetologie psychiatrischen Wissens bei Alfred Döblin*. Munich: Fink, 1995.

Schopenhauer, Arthur. *Die Welt als Wille und Vorstellung*. 2 vols. Darmstadt: Wissenschaftliche Buchgesellschaft, 1968.

Steinmetz, Horst. "Hamlet oder die lange Nacht der Intertextualität." *Internationales Alfred-Döblin-Kolloquium Leiden 1995*. Ed. by Gabriele Sander. Bern: Lang, 1997. 237–46.

Weyembergh-Boussart, Monique. *Alfred Döblin: Seine Religiosität in Persönlichkeit und Werk*. Bonn: Bouvier, 1970.

Select Bibliography

Döblin's Works

[Döblin's texts are cited in chronological order according to the *Ausgewählte Werke in Einzelbänden*, published by the Walter Verlag. Whenever a work is not or not yet a part of this edition, it is cited according to its first edition. Almost all the volumes are also available in the dtv paperback edition.]

Literary and Philosophical Works

Die Ermordung einer Butterblume. Sämtliche Erzählungen. (First edition: 1913.) Ed. Christina Althen. Düsseldorf/Zürich: Walter, 2001.

Die drei Sprünge des Wang-lun. (First edition: 1915/16.) Ed. Walter Muschg. Olten, Freiburg i. Br.: Walter, 1960.

Wadzeks Kampf mit der Dampfturbine. (First edition: 1918.) Ed. Anthony W. Riley. Olten, Freiburg i. Br.: Walter, 1982.

Jagende Rosse. Der schwarze Vorhang und andere frühe Erzählwerke. Ed. Anthony W. Riley. Olten, Freiburg i. Br.: Walter, 1981

Wallenstein. (First edition: 1920.) Ed. Erwin Kobel. Olten, Freiburg i. Br.: Walter, 2001.

Berge Meere und Giganten. (First edition: 1924.) Olten, Freiburg i. Br.: Walter, 1977.

Die beiden Freundinnen und ihr Giftmord. (First edition: 1924.) With an epilogue by Jochen Meyer and two handwriting samples. Düsseldorf/Zurich: Artemis and Winkler, 2001.

Reise in Polen. (First edition: 1925/26.) Ed. Heinz Graber. Olten/Freiburg i.Br.: Walter, 1968.

Manas. Epische Dichtung. (First edition: 1927.) Ed. Walter Muschg. Olten/Freiburg i. Br.: Walter, 1961.

Das Ich über der Natur. Berlin: S. Fischer, 1927.

Alfred Döblin: Im Buch — Zu Haus — Auf der Straße. Presented by Alfred Döblin and Oskar Loerke. (First edition: 1928.) With an afterword by Jochen Meyer. Marbach: Deutsche Schillergesellschaft, 1998.

Berlin Alexanderplatz. Die Geschichte vom Franz Biberkopf. (First edition: 1929.) Ed. Werner Stauffacher. Zürich/Düsseldorf: Walter, 1996.

Berlin-Alexanderplatz. A screenplay by Alfred Döblin and Hans Wilhelm for Phil Jutzi's 1931 film. With an introductory essay by Fritz Rudolf Fries and accessory materials to the film by Yvonne Rehhahn. Munich: edition text & kritik, 1996.

Unser Dasein. (First edition: 1933.) Ed. Walter Muschg. Olten, Freiburg i. Br.: Walter, 1964.

Babylonische Wandrung oder Hochmut kommt vor dem Fall. (First edition: 1934.) Ed. Walter Muschg. Olten, Freiburg i. Br.: Walter, 1962.

Pardon wird nicht gegeben. (First edition: 1935.) Ed. Walter Muschg. Olten, Freiburg i. Br.: Walter, 1960.

Amazonas. Romantrilogie. (First edition: 1937/38.) Ed. Werner Stauffacher, Olten, Freiburg i. Br.: Walter, 1988.

Der Oberst und der Dichter oder Das menschliche Herz. (First edition: 1946.) *Die Pilgerin Aetheria. Zwei Erzählungen.* Ed. Anthony W. Riley. Olten, Freiburg i. Br.: Walter, 1978.

Der unsterbliche Mensch. (First edition 1946.) *Der Kampf mit dem Engel.* Ed. Anthony W. Riley. Olten, Freiburg i. Br.: Walter, 1980.

November 1918. Eine deutsche Revolution. Erzählwerk in drei Teilen. (First edition: 1939; 1948/50.) Ed. Werner Stauffacher. Olten, Freiburg i. Br.: Walter, 1991.

November 1918. Eine deutsche Revolution. Vollständige Ausgabe in vier Bänden, mit einem Nachwort von Heinz D. Osterle. Munich: Deutscher Taschenbuch Verlag, 1978.

Drama, Hörspiel, Film. Ed. Erich Kleinschmidt. Olten, Freiburg i. Br.: Walter, 1983.

Schicksalsreise. Bericht und Bekenntnis. (First edition: 1949.) Ed. Anthony W. Riley. Solothurn/Düsseldorf: Walter, 1993.

Hamlet oder Die lange Nacht nimmt ein Ende. (First edition: 1956.) Ed. Walter Muschg. Olten, Freiburg i. Br.: Walter, 1966.

Essays, Letters, and Journalistic Writings

Aufsätze zur Literatur. Ed. Walter Muschg. Olten, Freiburg i. Br.: Walter, 1963.

Autobiographische Schriften und letzte Aufzeichnungen. Ed. Edgar Pässler. Olten, Freiburg i. Br.: Walter, 1980.

Briefe. Ed. Heinz Graber. Olten, Freiburg i. Br.: Walter, 1970.

Briefe II. Ed. Helmut F. Pfanner. Düsseldorf/Zürich: Walter, 2001.

Der deutsche Maskenball. Von Linke Poot. (First edition: 1921.) *Wissen und Verändern!* (First edition: 1931.) Ed. Heinz Graber. Olten, Freiburg i. Br.: Walter, 1972.

Kleine Schriften. Bd. 1: 1902–1921. Ed. Anthony W. Riley. Olten, Freiburg i. Br.: Walter, 1985.

Kleine Schriften. Bd. 2: 1922–1924. Ed. Anthony W. Riley. Olten, Freiburg i. Br.: Walter, 1990.

Kleine Schriften. Bd. 3: 1925–1933. Ed. Anthony W. Riley. Zürich/Düsseldorf: Walter, 1999.

Kritik der Zeit: Rundfunkbeiträge 1946–1952. Im Anhang: Beiträge 1928–1931. Ed. Alexandra Birkert. Olten, Freiburg i. Br.: Walter, 1992.

Schriften zu Ästhetik, Poetik und Literatur. Ed. Erich Kleinschmidt. Olten, Freiburg i. Br.: Walter, 1989.

Schriften zu jüdischen Fragen. Ed. Hans Otto Horch in association with Till Schicketanz. Solothurn/Düsseldorf: Walter, 1995.

Schriften zu Leben und Werk. Ed. Erich Kleinschmidt. Olten, Freiburg i. Br.: Walter, 1986.

Schriften zur Politik und Gesellschaft. Ed. Heinz Graber. Olten, Freiburg i. Br.: Walter, 1972.

Works Translated into English

Alexanderplatz, Berlin: The Story of Franz Biberkopf. Trans. Eugene Jolas. New York: Ungar, 1931.

Confucius. The Living Thoughts of Confucius. Presented by Alfred Döblin. New York, Toronto: Longmans, Green and Co., 1940.

Men Without Mercy. Trans. Trevor and Phyllis Blewitt. New York: H. Fertig, 1976.

November 1918: A German Revolution. Includes *Volume 1: A People Betrayed* and *Volume 2: Karl and Rosa.* Trans. John E. Woods. New York, NY: Fromm International, 1983.

Tales of a Long Night: A Novel. Trans. Robert and Rita Kimber. New York: Fromm International, 1984.

Journey to Poland. Trans. Joachim Neugroschel. New York: Paragon House Publishers, 1991.

Destiny's Journey. Trans. Edna McCown; introduction by Peter Demetz. New York: Paragon House, 1992.

The Three Leaps of Wang Lun: A Chinese Novel. Trans. with an introduction by C. D. Godwin. Hong Kong: Chinese UP, 1991.

Secondary Literature

Bibliographies and Conference Proceedings
(In chronological order.)

Schuster, Ingrid, and Ingrid Bode, eds. *Alfred Döblin im Spiegel der zeitgenössischen Kritik.* Bern/Munich: Francke, 1973.

Huguet, Louis. *Bibliographie Alfred Döblin.* Berlin/Weimar: Aufbau, 1972.

Schuster, Ingrid, ed. *Zu Alfred Döblin.* Stuttgart: Klett, 1980.

Stauffacher, Werner, ed. *Internationale Alfred-Döblin-Kolloquien Basel 1980–New York 1981–Freiburg i. Br. 1983.* Bern: Peter Lang, 1986.

———, ed. *Internationale Alfred-Döblin-Kolloquien Marbach a. N. 1984–Berlin 1985.* Bern: Peter Lang, 1988.

———, ed. *Internationales Alfred-Döblin-Kolloquium Lausanne 1987.* Bern: Peter Lang, 1991.

———, ed. *Internationale Alfred-Döblin-Kolloquien Münster 1989–Marbach a.N. 1991.* Bern: Peter Lang, 1993.

Grunewald, Michel, ed. *Internationales Alfred-Döblin-Kolloquium Paris 1993.* Bern: Peter Lang, 1995.

Sander, Gabriele, ed. *Internationales Alfred-Döblin-Kolloquium Leiden 1995.* Bern: Peter Lang, 1997.

Lorf, Ira, and Gabriele Sander, eds. *Internationales Alfred-Döblin-Kolloquium Leipzig 1997.* Bern: Peter Lang, 1999.

Hahn, Torsten, ed. *Internationales Alfred-Döblin-Kolloquium Bergamo 1999.* Bern: Peter Lang, 2001.

Prangel, Matthias, ed. *Materialien zu Alfred Döblin Berlin Alexanderplatz.* Frankfurt am Main: Suhrkamp, 1975; 2nd ed. 1981.

Sander, Gabriele. *Alfred Döblin.* Stuttgart: Reclam, 2001. 347–80.

Biographical Studies
(In alphabetical order.)

Anders, Günther. "Erinnerung an Döblin." *Neue Rundschau* 94 (1983): H. 4. 5–9.

Beyer, Manfred. "Alfred Döblin und Robert Minder." *Internationales Alfred-Döblin-Kolloquium Paris* (1993): 53–65.

Döblin, Claude. "Alfred Döblin in Berlin — und nachher." *Internationale Alfred-Döblin-Kolloquien Marbach/Berlin* (1984/85): 118–26.

Haehling von Lanzenauer, Reiner. "Alfred Döblins Baden-Badener Jahre." *Die Ortenau* 70 (1990): 403–9.

Huguet, Louis. "La jeunesse d'Alfred Döblin. Heritage et election." *Revue d'Allemagne* 5 (1973): 728–45.

———. *Pour un centenaire (1878–1978): Chronologie Alfred Döblin.* Annales Université: Abidjan, 1978.

Kesten, Hermann. "Alfred Döblin. 'Wie lange werden wir uns noch auf unserm Floß halten?'" Hermann Kesten. *Lauter Literaten: Porträts — Erinnerungen.* Vienna: Desch, 1963. 405–22.

Lüth, Paul E. H., ed. *Alfred Döblin zum 70. Geburtstag.* Includes homage to and reminiscence of Döblin by H. Mann, W. v. Mob, H. Kasack, H. Kesten and others. Wiesbaden: Limes, 1948.

Mayer, Hans. "Besuch bei Alfred Döblin." Hans Mayer. *Zeitgenossen: Erinnerung und Deutung.* Frankfurt am Main: Suhrkamp (1998): 158–66.

Meyer, Jochen. *Alfred Döblin 1878–1978: Eine Ausstellung des Deutschen Literaturarchivs im Schiller-Nationalmuseum.* Munich: Kösel, 1978.

Minder, Robert. "*Alfred Döblin zwischen Osten und Westen.*" *Dichter in der Gesellschaft: Erfahrungen mit deutscher und französischer Literatur.* Frankfurt am Main: Insel, 1966. 175–213.

———. "Begegnungen mit Alfred Döblin in Frankreich." *Text & Kritik. Alfred Döblin* 13/14 (1966, 2nd ed. 1972): 57–66.

Müller-Salget, Klaus. "Alfred Döblin." *Deutsche Dichter des 20. Jahrhunderts.* Ed. Hartmut Steinecke. Berlin: Erich Schmidt, 1994. 213–32.

Neumann, Harald. *Leben, wissenschaftliche Studien, Krankheiten und Tod Alfred Döblins.* St. Michael: Bläschke, 1982.

———. "Alfred Döblins Beziehung zu den Exilzeitschriften *Das Neue Tage-Buch* und *Die Zukunft* 1937–1940." *Internationales Alfred-Döblin-Kolloquium Paris* (1993): 37–51.

Stephan, Alexander. "Personal and Confidential. Geheimdienste, Alfred Döblin und das Exil in Südkalifornien." *Internationales Alfred-Döblin-Kolloquium Leiden* (1995): 192–209.

———. *"Communazis": FBI Surveillance of German Emigré Writers.* Trans. Jan van Heurck. New Haven: Yale UP, 2000. 166–68.

Thieberger, Richard. "Begegnung mit Alfred Döblin." *Internationales Alfred-Döblin-Kolloquium Paris* (1993): 3–6.

Weissenberger, Klaus. "Döblins Exil in Amerika." In Schuster, ed., *Zu Alfred Döblin.* Stuttgart: Klett, 1980. 57–81.

Wetzel, Jürgen. "Sozialismus ohne Faszination. Drei Briefe Alfred Döblins im Landesarchiv Berlin." *Mendelsohn Studien, vol. 8: Festschrift für Cecile Lowenthal-Hensel zum 3. Okt. 1993.* Berlin: Duncker & Humblot, 1993. 237–56.

Selected Criticism
(In alphabetical order.)

Althen, Christina. *Machtkonstellationen einer deutschen Revolution: Alfred Döblins Geschichtsroman, "November 1918."* Frankfurt am Main/New York: Peter Lang, 1993.

Auer, Manfred. *Das Exil vor der Vertreibung: Motivkontinuität und Quellenproblematik im späten Werk Alfred Döblins.* Bonn: Bouvier, 1977.

Bartscherer, Christoph. *Das Ich und die Natur: Alfred Döblins literarischer Weg im Licht seiner Religionsphilosophie.* Paderborn: Igel, 1997.

Becker, Sabina. "Alfred Döblin im Kontext der Neuen Sachlichkeit (I/II)." *Jahrbuch zur Literatur der Weimarer Republik.* St. Ingbert (1995/96): Vol.1 (1995): 202–29. Vol. 2 (1996): 157–81.

Belhalfaoui, Barbara [= Köhn, Barbara]. "Alfred Döblins Naturphilosophie — ein existentialistischer Universalismus." *Jahrbuch der Deutschen Schillergesellschaft* 31 (1987): 354–82.

Berman, Russell A. *The Rise of the Modern German Novel: Crisis and Charisma.* Cambridge, MA: Harvard UP, 1986.

Birkert, Alexandra. "Das Goldene Tor. Alfred Döblins Nachkriegszeitschrift — Rahmenbedingungen, Zielsetzung, Entwicklung." A special edition of the *Archiv für Geschichte des Buchwesens* 33 (1989): 201–317.

Demetz, Peter. *Worte in Freiheit: Der italienische Futurismus und die deutsche literarische Avantgarde 1912–1934. Mit einer ausführlichen Dokumentation.* Munich: Piper, 1990.

Dollenmayer, David B. *The Berlin Novels of Alfred Döblin: "Wadzek's Battle with the Steam Turbine," "Berlin Alexanderplatz," "Men without Mercy" and "November 1918."* Berkeley: U of California P, 1988.

Dollinger, Roland. *Totalität und Totalitarismus im Exilwerk Döblins.* Würzburg: Königshausen & Neumann, 1994.

Düsing, Wolfgang. *Erinnerung und Identität: Untersuchungen zu einem Erzählproblem bei Musil, Döblin und Doderer.* Munich: Fink, 1982.

Hake, Sabine. "Urban Paranoia in Alfred Döblin's *Berlin Alexanderplatz.*" *The German Quarterly* 67 (1994): 347–68.

Hüppauf, Bernd. "The Historical Novel and a History of Mentalities: Alfred Döblin's *Wallenstein* as an Historical Novel." *The Modern German Historical Novel: Paradigms, Problems, Perspectives.* Ed. David Roberts and Philip Thomson. New York: Berg 1991. 71–96.

Keck, Annette. *"Avantgarde der Lust": Autorschaft und sexuelle Relation in Döblins früher Prosa.* Munich: Fink, 1998.

Keller, Otto. *Döblins Montageroman als Epos der Moderne: Die Struktur der Romane "Der schwarze Vorhang," "Die drei Sprünge des Wang-lun" und "Berlin Alexanderplatz."* Munich: Fink, 1980.

Kiesel, Helmuth. *Literarische Trauerarbeit: Das Exil- und Spätwerk Alfred Döblins.* Tübingen: Niemeyer, 1986.

Kleinschmidt, Erich. "Döblin-Studien. I. Depersonale Poetik. Dispositionen des Erzählens bei Alfred Döblin." *Jahrbuch der Deutschen Schillergesellschaft* 26 (1982): 383–401.

———. "Döblin-Studien. II. 'Es gibt den eisklaren Tag und unseren Tod in den nächsten 80 Jahren.' Alfred Döblin als politischer Schriftsteller." *Jahrbuch der Deutschen Schillergesellschaft* 26 (1982): 401–27.

Klotz, Volker. "Agon Stadt. Alfred Döblins Berlin *Alexanderplatz* (1929)." In Volker Klotz, *Die erzählte Stadt: Ein Sujet als Herausforderung des Romans von Lesage bis Döblin.* Munich: Hanser, 1969. 372–418.

Koopmann, Helmut. *Der klassisch-moderne Roman in Deutschland: Thomas Mann, Alfred Döblin, Hermann Broch.* Stuttgart: Kohlhammer, 1983. [On Döblin: 77–112.]

Koepke, Wulf. "Alfred Döblins Überparteilichkeit. Zur Publizistik in den letzten Jahren der Weimarer Republik." *Weimars Ende: Prognosen und Diagnosen in der deutschen Literatur und Publizistik 1930–1933.* Ed. Thomas Koebner. Frankfurt am Main: Suhrkamp, 1982. 318–29.

Kort, Wolfgang. *Alfred Döblin: Das Bild des Menschen in seinen Romanen.* Bonn: Bouvier, 1970.

Kreutzer, Leo. *Alfred Döblin: Sein Werk bis 1933.* Stuttgart: Kohlhammer, 1970.

Kuhlmann, Anne. *Revolution als "Geschichte": Alfred Döblins Roman "November 1918": Eine programmatische Lektüre des historischen Romans.* Tübingen: Niemeyer, 1997.

Lorf, Ira. *Maskenspiele: Wissen und kulturelle Muster in Alfred Döblins Romanen "Wadzeks Kampf mit der Dampfturbine" und "Die drei Sprünge des Wang-lun."* Bielefeld: Aisthesis, 1999.

Mayer, Dieter: *Alfred Döblins "Wallenstein": Zur Geschichtsauffassung und zur Struktur.* Munich: W. Fink, 1972.

Müller, Harro: "War and Novel: Alfred Döblin's *Wallenstein* and *November 1918*": *War, Violence, and the Modern Condition.* Ed. Bernd Hüppauf. Bern/New York: Walter de Gruyter, 1997. 290–99.

O'Neill, Patrick. *Alfred Döblin's "Babylonische Wandrung": A Study.* Bern: Herbert Lang, 1974.

Reid, James H. "*Berlin Alexanderplatz* — A Political Novel." *German Life & Letters* 21 (1967/68): 214–23.

Ribbat, Ernst. *Die Wahrheit des Lebens im frühen Werk Alfred Döblins.* Münster: Aschendorf, 1970.

Riley, Anthony W. "Zum umstrittenen Schluß von Alfred Döblins *Hamlet oder Die lange Nacht nimmt ein Ende.*" *Literaturwissenschaftliches Jahrbuch im Auftrag der Görres-Gesellschaft* N.F. 13 (1972): 331–58.

Ryan, Judith. *The Vanishing Subject: Early Psychology and Literary Modernism.* Chicago/London: U of Chicago P, 1991.

Sander, Gabriele. *Alfred Döblin.* Stuttgart: Reclam, 2001.

———. *Alfred Döblin: Berlin Alexanderplatz. Erläuterungen und Dokumente.* Stuttgart: Reclam, 1988.

Schäffner, Wolfgang. *Die Ordnung des Wahns: Zur Poetologie psychiatrischen Wissens bei Alfred Döblin.* Munich: Fink, 1995.

Schoonover, Henrietta S. *The Humorous and Grotesque Elements in Döblin's "Berlin Alexanderplatz."* Bern/Las Vegas: Peter Lang, 1977.

Sebald, Winfried Georg. *Der Mythus der Zerstörung im Werk Döblins.* Stuttgart: Klett, 1980.

Stegemann, Helga. *Studien zu Alfred Döblins Bildlichkeit: "Die Ermordung einer Butterblume" und andere Erzählungen.* Bern/Las Vegas: Peter Lang, 1978.

Tatar, Maria. *Lustmord: Sexual Murder in Weimar Germany.* Princeton: Princeton U P, 1995.

Tewarson, Heidi Thomann. *Alfred Döblin: Grundlagen seiner Ästhetik und ihre Entwicklung 1900–1903.* Bern/Las Vegas: Peter Lang, 1979.

Voss, Dieter. *Ströme und Steine: Studien zur symbolischen Textur des Werkes von Alfred Döblin.* Würzburg: Königshausen & Neumann, 2000.

Weyembergh-Boussart, Monique. *Alfred Döblin: Seine Religiosität in Persönlichkeit und Werk.* Bonn: H. Bouvier, 1970.

Weiler, Inge. *Giftmordwissen und Giftmörderinnen: Eine diskursgeschichtliche Studie.* Tübingen: Niemeyer, 1998. [On Döblin: 228–47.]

Wichert, Adalbert. *Alfred Döblins historisches Denken: Zur Poetik des modernen Geschichtsromans.* Stuttgart: Metzler, 1978.

Žmegač, Viktor. "Alfred Döblins Poetik des Romans." *Deutsche Romantheorien. Beiträge zu einer historischen Poetik des Romans in Deutschland.* Ed. and introduced by Reinhold Grimm. Frankfurt am Main: Athenäum, 1968. 297–320.

Contributors

CHRISTOPH BARTSCHERER is Assistant Professor in the Department of Senior Studies at Ludwig-Maximilians-Universität in Munich. He is the author of *Das Ich und die Natur: Alfred Döblins literarischer Weg im Lichte seiner Religionsphilosophie* (1997) and has just finished *Der Abtrünnige: Heinrich Heines blasphemische Religion* (2003).

DAVID DOLLENMAYER is Professor of German in the Department of Humanities and Arts at the Worcester Polytechnic Institute in Worcester, Massachusetts. He is the author of *The Berlin Novels of Alfred Doeblin* (1988) and co-author (with Thomas Hansen) of the first-year college textbook *Neue Horizonte* (6th edition, 2003).

ROLAND DOLLINGER is Associate Professor of German and Chair of the Department of Modern Foreign Languages at Sarah Lawrence College. He is the author of *Totalität und Totalitarismus im Exilwerk Döblins* (1994), of articles on contemporary German literature, and co-editor of *Philosophia Naturalis* (1996).

NEIL H. DONAHUE is Professor of German and Comparative Literature, and Chairperson of the Department of Comparative Literature & Languages at Hofstra University on Long Island, where he has taught since 1988. He is author of *Forms of Disruption: Abstraction in Modern German Prose* (1993), *Voice and Void: The Poetry of Gerhard Falkner* (1998), and *Karl Krolow and the Poetics of Amnesia in Postwar Germany* (2002).

WOLFGANG DÜSING is Professor of German Literature in the Deutsches Institut at Johannes Gutenberg-Universität, Mainz, Germany. He has written numerous articles on German literature from the eighteenth to the twenty-first century. He is the author of *Schillers Idee des Erhabenen* (1967), *Schiller: Über die ästhetische Erziehung: Text, Materialien, Kommentar* (1981), and *Erinnerung und Identität: Musil, Döblin und Doderer* (1982). He has edited *Experimente mit dem Kriminalroman* (1993), *Traditionen der Lyrik* (1997), and *Aspekte des Geschichtsdramas. Von Aischylos bis Volker Braun* (1998).

VERONIKA FUECHTNER is Assistant Professor of German at Dartmouth College. She has published articles on Herbert Marcuse, Alfred Döblin, and on the state of German Studies in the US. She is presently working on a book on the relation between psychoanalysis and culture in Berlin during the Weimar Republic.

HELMUTH KIESEL is Professor of Modern German Literature at the University of Heidelberg. His book *Literarische Trauerarbeit* (1986) was the first comprehensive study of Döblin's works after 1933. He has edited editions of Kafka, Ernst Jünger, and Erich Kästner, and he has just finished his book *Geschichte der literarischen Moderne* (forthcoming 2004).

ERICH KLEINSCHMIDT is Professor of Modern German Literature and Cultural Studies at the University of Cologne. His recent publications include *Gleitende Sprache: Sprachbewußtsein und Poetik in der Moderne* (1992) and *Autorschaft: Konzepte einer Theorie* (1998). He has just finished *Labyrinthe der Intensität: Modulative Kulturpoetik um 1800* (forthcoming).

WULF KOEPKE is Distinguished Professor of German Emeritus at Texas A&M University. He has published widely on German Classicism, Romanticism, and twentieth-century German literature. He is author of *Lion Feuchtwanger* (1983) and *Understanding Max Frisch* (1990). *The Critical Reception of Alfred Döblin's Major Novels* appeared with Camden House in 2003.

KLAUS MÜLLER-SALGET is Professor for German Language and Literature at the University of Innsbruck, Austria. He is the author *of Alfred Döblin: Werk und Entwicklung* (1972; 2nd ed. 1988), *Max Frisch* (1996), *Heinrich von Kleist* (2002), and co-editor of *Heinrich von Kleist: Sämtliche Werke und Briefe* (1987–1997).

HELMUT F. PFANNER is Professor of German in the Department of German and Slavic Languages at Vanderbilt University in Nashville, Tennessee. He is the author of *Hanns Johst: Vom Expressionismus zum Nationalsozialismus* (1970), *Oskar Maria Graf: Eine kritische Bibliographie* (1976), and *Exile in New York: German and Austrian Writers after 1933* (1983).

GABRIELE SANDER is a lecturer at the University of Wuppertal and is working on the critical edition of Kafka's letters. She is the author of *Alfred Döblin* (2001) and *Studien zu Alfred Döblin's "Berge Meere und Giganten"* (1988), and editor of *Blaue Gedichte* (2001), an anthology of poetry.

HEIDI THOMANN TEWARSON is Professor and Chair of the Department of German Language and Literatures, Oberlin College. She is the author of *Alfred Döblin: Grundlagen seiner Ästhetik und ihre Entwicklung, 1900–1933* (1979); *Rahel Varnhagen mit Selbstzeugnissen und Bilddokumenten* (1988, 5th ed. 2003); and *Rahel Levin Varnhagen: The Life and Work of a German Jewish Intellectual* (1998) as well as over twenty articles.

Index

Abraham, Karl, 116, 119, 130
Adler, Alfred, 124
Aeschylus, works by:
　Oresteia, 66, 157
aestheticism, 34, 220, 221
Alexander, Franz, 129
Allert de Lange, 13
Alsace-Lorraine (Saargemünd,
　Hagenau), 2, 8, 118, 184, 216,
　217, 219, 220
Althen, Christina, 223
America, 14, 66, 69, 71, 216,
　222, 247, 249, 259
apposition (epic), 84, 88
Arndt, Ernst Moritz, works by:
　Lied vom Feldmarschall, 152
Auernheimer, Raoul, 162
Augustine, 251
Aurora-Bücherei, 14

Baader, Franz von, 262
Baden-Baden, 175, 252
Bahr, Hermann, 185
Bahr, Hermann, works by:
　Der Meister, 185
Bayerdörfer, Hans Peter, 144,
　158, 234, 235, 236, 241
Bebel, August, 26, 27
Bebel, August, works by: *Die
　Frau und der Sozialismus*, 26
Becher, Johannes R., 11, 146,
　187, 258
Ben-Chorin, Schalom, 233
Benjamin, Georg, 121
Benjamin, Walter, 11, 121, 147
Benn, Gottfried, 1, 17
Benn, Gottfried, works by:
　Drei alte Männer, 260

Berlin, 1–13, 24, 25, 32, 36, 56,
　59, 62, 66, 67, 72, 94, 95, 97,
　99, 112, 113, 115, 119, 120,
　122, 127, 129, 141, 142, 146,
　151, 152, 161, 162, 164, 170,
　174, 175, 183, 184, 186, 217,
　220, 221, 222, 224, 225, 227,
　235–37
Berlin Psychoanalytic Institute,
　117, 119, 122, 123
Berliner Tageblatt, 10, 12
Biha, Otto, 146
Bildungsroman, 150, 154
Bing, Max, 173
Birnbaum, Nathan, 239, 243
Blei, Franz, 163
Bloch, Ernst, 187
Boccaccio, works by:
　Decamerone, 274
Bonhöffer, Karl, 114
Braun, Alfred, 173
Brecht, Bertolt, 1, 3, 4, 7, 9, 10,
　12, 15, 17, 23, 66, 78, 146,
　173, 187, 257, 258
Brecht, Bertolt, works by:
　Arbeitsjournal, 285;
　Flüchtlingsgespräche, 260;
　Mann ist Mann, 144
Breitenfellner, Kirstin, works by:
　Lavaters Schatten, 150
Breuer, Joseph, 116
Broch, Hermann, 1, 19, 275
Broch, Hermann, works by:
　Die Schuldlosen, 277
Brod, Max, 163
Buber, Martin, 55, 65, 66, 67,
　242, 265, 266
Bucovich, Mario von, 142

Bumke, Oswald, 113
Bund Proletarisch-Revolutionärer
  Schriftsteller (BPRS), 11, 271

caricature, 48, 84, 219, 225
Carmely, Klara Pomeranz, 233
catharsis, 15, 276, 278, 283
Catholicism, 2, 20, 189, 229,
  230, 233, 240, 247, 255, 256,
  271
Cervantes, 148
Cervantes, works by:
  Don Quixote, 67, 228, 229
Christ, figure of, 25, 27, 30, 247,
  250, 251, 253, 254, 258–65
Christianity, 220, 222, 240, 242,
  256, 258, 261
collage, 78, 145, 147, 152, 174
conversion, 15, 20, 62, 64, 97,
  189, 211, 216, 229, 230, 234,
  240, 241, 247, 250–61, 271,
  273
Courths-Mahler, Hedwig, 156
Cracow (Poland), 187, 196, 240

Dada, 147
Dahn, Felix, 7
Dahn, Felix, works by:
  Ein Kampf um Rom, 7
Dix, Otto, 82
Döblin, Alfred, works by:
  *Alfred Döblin: Im Buch — Zu
    Haus — Auf der Straße*, 10
  Amazonas, 1, 13, 15, 17, 20,
    55, 191, 193–214, 215, 239,
    240, 256
  "An Romanautoren und ihre
    Kritiker: Berliner Programm,"
    36, 56, 71, 75, 94, 114, 163,
    276
  Babylonische Wandrung, 13,
    169, 215, 236, 259
  *Die beiden Freundinnen und ihr
    Giftmord*, 20, 87, 124–28

Berge Meere und Giganten, 1,
  5, 10, 13, 17, 19, 20, 55,
  93–107, 147, 170, 193, 267
Berlin Alexanderplatz, 1, 3,
  4, 5, 6, 10, 11, 12, 14, 15,
  17, 19, 36, 55, 62, 66, 78,
  87, 127, 128, 141–58, 167,
  168, 169, 172, 173, 175,
  176, 188, 217, 228, 230,
  236, 258, 271, 273, 276,
  279, 284
"Buddho und die Natur," 129
*Die deutsche Literatur
  (im Ausland seit 1933)*, 13
*Der deutsche Maskenball (Linke
  Poot)*, 8, 184, 190, 224, 234
Die drei Sprünge des Wang-lun,
  1, 5, 6, 17, 18, 20, 50, 55–74,
  77, 94, 147, 164, 234
Die Ehe, 9, 12, 168
"Die Enteisung Grönlands," 170
Epilog, 193, 274, 275, 276, 277
*Die Ermordung einer Butter-
  blume*, 5, 18, 23, 37–50
"Die Ermordung einer Butter-
  blume," 38, 45–48, 77, 114
*Flucht und Sammlung des
  Judenvolkes*, 13, 237, 239
*Gedächtnisstörungen bei der
  Korsakoffschen Psychose*, 33,
  113–14
*Die Geschichte vom Franz
  Biberkopf* (radio play), 173,
  174
*Gespräche mit Kalypso. Über die
  Musik*, 18, 34–36, 38, 148
"Die geweihten Töchter," 165,
  166
Giganten, 10
*Hamlet oder Die lange Nacht
  nimmt ein Ende*, 1, 3, 16, 17,
  19, 23, 55, 69, 241, 268,
  271–86
"Die Helferin," 42

"Der historische Roman und wir," 13, 78. 206, 218
Das Ich über der Natur, 13, 93, 103, 104, 105–7, 129, 141, 239, 261, 268
Jüdische Erneuerung, 13, 237
Der Kampf mit dem Engel, 259, 260, 261
The Living Thoughts of Confucius, 14
Die Lobensteiner reisen nach Böhmen, 5
Lusitania, 9, 172
Manas, 10, 13, 23, 141
"Natascha macht Schluß," 169
Die Nonnen von Kemnade, 9
November 1918, 1, 13, 14, 15, 16, 17, 20, 23, 55, 170, 190, 191, 215–32, 241, 248, 282, 285
   Vol. I: Bürger und Soldaten 1918, 13, 16, 215, 216, 219
   Vol. II: Verratenes Volk, 216, 221
   Vol. III: Heimkehr der Frontruppen, 216, 221
   Vol. IV: Karl und Rosa, 216, 224
Der Oberst und der Dichter, 15
Pardon wird nicht gegeben, 13, 14, 55, 71, 72, 215
Reise in Polen, 9, 187, 235, 259
"Der Ritter Blaubart," 42, 43, 44
Schicksalsreise, 14, 15, 170, 247–52, 254, 255, 256
Der schwarze Vorhang, 7, 28–32, 33, 34, 43, 49
"Die Segelfahrt," 38, 40–42, 44
"Staatsanwalt *Fregus*," 170
"Das Stiftsfräulein und der Tod," 38–40, 41, 42, 44

"Die Tänzerin und der Leib," 38, 43–45
Unser Dasein, 13, 105, 148, 191, 235, 236, 237, 259, 261, 267, 274
Der unsterbliche Mensch, 15, 241, 259, 260
"Die Verwandlung," 42, 44, 49
Wadzeks Kampf mit der Dampfturbine, 6, 7, 18, 55, 64–72, 77, 152
Wallenstein, 1, 5, 7, 8, 18, 20, 55, 75–89, 94, 147, 206, 234, 248
Wissen und Verändern!, 2, 12, 127, 188, 189, 190, 191, 273
Döblin, Erna (Reiss), 71, 122, 234
Döblin, Klaus, 237, 256
Döblin, Max, 71, 234
Döblin, Meta, 118
Döblin, Peter, 71, 237, 240, 241, 250, 256
Döblin, Sophie (Freudenheim), 2, 234
Döblin, Wolfgang, 243, 285
Dos Passos, John, 1
Dos Passos, John, works by: *Manhattan Transfer,* 1
Dostoevsky, Fedor M., 148–50
Dostoevsky, Fedor M., works by: *Crime and Punishment,* 150; *The Idiot,* 149

Ebert, Friedrich, 217, 219, 221, 223, 225, 226
Ebner, Ferdinand, 266
Eckhart (Meister Eckhart), 256
Edschmid, Kasimir, 23
Eggebrecht, Axel, 10, 13
Eichendorff, Joseph von, works by: *Mondnacht,* 82
Eisler, Hanns, 257
Elshort, Hansjörg, 67
Ewers, Hans Heinz, 162

exile, 2, 3, 4, 11, 13–15, 17, 19, 23, 78, 129, 169, 175, 191, 205, 206, 210, 211, 215, 236–38, 247, 248, 256, 257, 271, 285
Expressionism, 5, 18, 93, 163

Fallada, Hans, 1
Fassbinder, Rainer Werner, 4, 12
Federal Republic of Germany (West Germany), 16, 242, 260, 271
Feuchtwanger, Lion, 1, 7, 23, 78
First World War, 1, 2, 4, 7, 9, 18, 19, 64, 72, 82, 94, 100, 102, 118, 122, 165, 183, 184, 215, 216, 229, 248, 258, 281
Fischer, Samuel + publishing house, 5, 10, 17, 143, 149, 234, 235
Flake, Otto, works by: *Die Stadt des Hirns*, 275
Flaubert, Gustave, works by: *Salambô*, 211
France, 13–15, 86, 97, 102, 129, 167, 193, 194, 216, 225, 240, 247–51, 256
Frankfurter Zeitung, 128, 143, 184
Freiburg im Breisgau, 32, 71, 112, 126
Freikorps, 102, 215, 225, 227
Freytag, Gustav, 7, 206
Freytag, Gustav, works by: *Die Ahnen*, 7
Freud, Sigmund, 113, 117, 118, 120, 123–25, 127, 253, 277, 278, 282
Freud, Sigmund, works by: *Beyond the Pleasure Principle*, 123; *Das Ich und das Es*, 125; *Zur Psychopathologie des Alltagslebens*, 116
Froeschel, Georg(e), 169, 170
Fromm, Erich, 119, 134
futurism (Futurismus), 18, 19, 36, 55–58, 75, 94, 165

George, Heinrich, 12, 168, 174
George, Stefan, 1, 176
German Democratic Republic, 16, 271
Die Gesellschaft, 11
Gide, André, works by: *Interviews imaginaires*, 260
Giraudoux, Jean, 175
Goethe, Johann Wolfgang von, 67, 151, 155
Goethe, Johann Wolfgang von, works by: *Die Leiden des jungen Werther*, 150; *Wilhelm Meisters Lehrjahre*, 154; *Wilhelm Meisters Wanderjahre*, 275; *Unterhaltungen deutscher Ausgewanderten*, 274
Das Goldene Tor, 15
Goll, Yvan, 165
Gottgetreu, Erich, 233
Graber, Heinz, 17, 271–73
Graf, Oskar Maria, 7, 209
Grass, Günter, 3
Gruppe 1925, 9, 11, 187

Haffner, Sebastian, 224, 226
Hauff, Wilhelm, works by: *Reiters Morgengesang* (poem), 152
Hauptmann, Gerhart, 5, 185
Hauptmann, Gerhart, works by: *Hanneles Himmelfahrt*, 185
Herzfelde, Wieland, 14
Hesse, Hermann, 5
Heym, Georg, 1
Hirsch, Karl Jakob, 249
Hirschfeld, Georg, works by: *Die Mütter*, 185
Hirschfeld, Magnus, 119, 121
historical novel, 7, 20, 77–79, 88, 205–7, 218
Hitler, Adolf, 2, 190, 191, 206, 207, 215, 248, 266
Hoche, Alfred Erich, 33, 35, 113–14

Hocke, Gustav Rene, 12, 188, 190, 273
Hölderin, Friedrich, 27, 32, 253
Hölderin, Friedrich, works by: *Hyperion*, 27
Hofmannsthal, Hugo von, 24
Hofmannsthal, Hugo von, works by: *Ein Brief,* 24; *Der Tor und der Tod,* 39
Hollywood (Los Angeles), 3, 169, 170, 216, 247, 249, 255, 257
homosexuality, 125, 155, 156
Horch, Hans Otto, 234
Horkheimer, Max, 100, 209
Horst, Karl August, 16
Huch, Ricarda, works by: *Der große Krieg in Deutschland,* 7
Huguet, Louis, 67, 233, 234, 237, 240

Ibsen, Henrik, works by: *Wenn wir Toten erwachen,* 185
Ihering, Herbert, 23, 145, 167
intertextuality, 147, 158

Joyce, James, works by: *Ulysses,* 1, 10, 142
Judaism, Jewish, Jews, 2, 9, 13, 20, 25, 71, 142, 144, 187, 191, 197, 207, 233–43, 247, 248, 253, 265
Jünger, Ernst, 1
Jünger, Ernst, works by: *Der Arbeiter,* 104; *Blätter und Steine,* 102
Jutzi, Phil, 168

Kafka, Franz, 1, 3, 17, 48, 49, 164
Kafka, John, 169
Kaiser Georg, 1, 23, 166, 187
Kaiser Georg, works by: *Von Morgens bis Mitternachts,* 166
Kant, Immanuel, 266
Kasack, Hermann, 187
Kästner, Erich, 183

Keck, Annette, 44
Keller, Evelyn F., works by: *Reflections on Gender and Science,* 106, 107
Keller, Gottfried, works by: *Der grüne Heinrich,* 150, 151
Kemper, Werner, 120
Kerr, Alfred, 12
Kesten, Hermann, 1, 14, 216
Keyserling, Hermann Graf von, 119
Kierkegaard, Sören, 210, 220, 239, 256, 277, 278, 282, 283
Kierkegaard, Sören, works by: *Either-Or,* 210
Kinostil, 12, 162, 163, 164
Kisch, Egon Erwin, 258
Klein, Melanie, 119
Klein, Melanie, works by: *The Psychoanalysis of Children,* 123
Kleist, Heinrich von, 155, 156, 253
Kleist, Heinrich von, works by: *Germania und ihre Kinder,* 155; *Penthesilea,* 155; *Der Prinz von Homburg,* 155, 226
Klöpfer, Eugen, 185
Kobel, Erwin, 84, 87
König, Eberhard, works by: *Stein,* 186
Koeppen, Wolfgang, 3
Körber, Hilde, 174
Koestler, Arthur, 190, 209
Kolbenheyer, Erwin Guido, 187, 248
Kommunistische Partei Deutschlands (KPD), Communists, 8, 9, 11, 14, 105, 146, 184, 188, 190, 238, 271
Kort, Wolfgang, 83
Kortner, Fritz, 257
Kracauer, Siegfried, 169
Kraepelin, Emil, 113, 115, 117
Kronfeld, Arthur, 120, 121
Kropotkin, Peter, 188

Kunke, Frieda, 71
Kuschel, Karl-Josef, 257

Lang, Fritz, works by:
　Metropolis, 10
Lasker-Schüler, Else, 1, 163
Lautensack, Heinrich, 163
Le Bon, Gustave, works by:
　La psychologie des foules, 6
legend, 228, 229, 279–81
Lenin, Leninist, 63, 188, 221, 225, 227
LeRoy, Marvin, works by:
　Random Harvest (film), 170
Liebknecht, Karl, 184, 217–29
Lifschitz, Isidor, 238
Die Linkskurve, 11, 146
Lipps, Theodor, 113
Die Literarische Welt, 166
Loerke, Oskar, 187
Lukács, Georg, works by:
　Theorie des Romans, 230
Lustig, Jan, 169
Luther, Martin, 189, 251
Luxemburg, Rosa, 184, 217–30

madness, 32, 33, 49, 82
Mann, Heinrich, 1, 17, 187, 248, 257
Mann, Klaus, 237
Mann, Thomas, 1, 3, 4, 5, 12, 17, 24, 49, 170, 209, 211, 224, 226, 257
Mann, Thomas, works by: *Essays,* 224, 226; *Joseph* tetralogy, 59; *Tod in Venedig,* 56; *Tristan,* 44
Mannheim, Karl, works by:
　Ideologie und Utopie, 189
Marcuse, Herbert, 13
Marcuse, Ludwig, 14, 239
Marinetti, Tommaso, 18, 56–58, 60, 75, 165
Marinetti, Tommaso, works by:
　Mafarka le futuriste: roman africain, 56, 58

Martin, Karl-Heinz, 166, 168
Marxism, Marx, 186–91, 218, 253
Mauthner, Fritz, 30–31
Mauthner, Fritz, works by:
　Beiträge zu einer Kritik der Sprache, 30
Mayer, Dieter, 87
Mayer, Hans, 224, 230, 231
Mead, G. H., works by:
　Mind, Self and Society, 278
Mehring, Walter, 146, 169, 187
Meidner, Ludwig, 82
Mende, 15, 240, 250, 251, 253, 254, 259
Meng, Heinrich, 119
Meyer, Jochen, 71, 118, 233, 248
Milton, works by:
　Paradise Lost, 229
Minder, Robert, 16, 119, 243, 256
modernism, modernity, 11, 18, 19, 25, 28, 34, 36, 56, 93, 148, 165, 252
monism, scientific, 35, 36, 226, 261, 262
montage, 12, 19, 142, 145, 147, 149, 152, 154, 155, 157, 158
Müller, Georg (publishing house), 5
Müller, Harro, 78, 84, 87
Münzenberg, Willi, 190
Muschg, Walter, 16, 17, 63, 211
Musil, Robert, 1, 10, 23
Musil, Robert, works by:
　Nachlaß zu Lebzeiten, 82
myth, mythical, mythic, 12, 19, 29, 41–43, 50, 66, 102, 145, 173, 228, 229, 278, 282
mythology, mythological, 10, 141, 145, 146, 155, 157, 158, 198, 200, 209, 228–30

National Socialism, Nazism, National Socialist, 1, 3, 8, 20, 113, 174, 187, 188, 190, 207,

215, 216, 218, 224, 248, 251–53, 266
Naturalism (Naturalismus), 24, 75, 76
Der Neue Merkur, 234
Die Neue Rundschau, 5, 8, 93, 184, 234
New Objectivity, objectivity, Neue Sachlichkeit, sachlich, 18, 36, 69, 76, 106
Niclas, Yolla, 2
Nietzsche, Friedrich, 27, 29, 30, 220, 253, 273
Nietzsche, Friedrich, works by: *Also sprach Zarathustra,* 28; *Genealogie der Moral,* 29; *Vom Nutzen und Nachteil der Historie,* 218
novella cycles, 274, 275
Novellenroman, 1, 19

Pabst, G. W., works by: *Geheimnisse einer Seele,* 119
Paris, 13, 14, 16, 41, 169, 190, 193, 216, 221, 238, 239, 247, 248, 256
parody, 151, 154, 156
Pascal, Blaise, 251, 256, 262
Pascal, Blaise, works by: *Pensées,* 263
Pavese, Cesare, works by: *Dialoghi con Leucó,* 260
Petersen, Julius, 187
Perutz, Leo, works by: *Nachts under der steinernen Brücke,* 275
Photography, 19, 24, 169, 175, 176
Pinthus, Kurt, 5, 163
Piscator, Erwin, 12, 168
Poland, 2, 9, 20, 187, 235, 240
Polgar, Alfred, 169
polyphony, polyphonic, 145, 147, 223
Ponten, Josef, 187, 248

Prager Tagblatt, 9, 185
Proust, Marcel, works by: *A la recherche du temps perdu,* 278; *Du côté de chez Swann,* 56
Prussian Academy of the Fine Arts, 9, 171, 187, 248
Puccini, Giacomo, works by: *La Bohème,* 44
pychoanalysis, 20, 113, 118–29, 271, 277, 278, 282

Querido (publishing house), 13, 210, 215, 216, 237

Radio, 9, 12, 15, 19, 171–75, 183, 187, 241, 248
Radio Play, 9, 12, 172–75
realism, 36, 56, 228, 286
Regensburg, 38, 114
Reich, Wilhelm, 119, 127
Remarque, Erich Maria, 1
Reuchlein, Georg, 45
Ribbat, Ernst, 63, 68, 156
Riley, Anthony W., 17, 255
Rilke, Rainer Maria, 1, 3, 222
Ring, Harold E., 255
Rosenberg, Arthur, 224
Rosin, Elvira and Arthur, 240, 241
Roth, Joseph, 1
Rubiner, Ludwig, 6, 163
Ruttmann, Walter, 142
Ruttmann, Walter, works by: *Die Sinfonie der Großstadt* (film)

Sachs, Hanns, 119
Die Sammlung, 237
Sander, August, works by: *Antlitz der Zeit,* 175, 176
Schäfer, Wilhelm, 187, 248
Scheler, Max, 265, 266
Schiller, Friedrich, works by: *Die Bürgschaft,* 155; *Lied von der Glocke,* 155; *Wallenstein,* 7, 156; *Wilhelm Tell,* 186

Schmidt, Arno, 3
Schmiedel, Hans Peter, 172
Schnitzler, Arthur, 26
Schönberg, Arnold, 257
Schröter, Klaus, 233
Schuster, Ingrid (and Bode, Ingrid), 6–8, 10–13, 15, 16, 23, 55, 167, 190
Schutzverband deutscher Schriftsteller (SDS), 9, 186
Sebald, Winfried Georg, 3, 183, 236
Sebald, Winfried Georg, works by: *Der Mythos der Zerstörung im Werk Döblins,* 233
Second World War, 15, 63, 169, 175, 187, 190, 215, 251, 260, 277, 284, 285
Sengler, Elli, works by: *Erkenntnis,* 156
Shakespeare, 277
Simmel, Ernst, 119, 120, 121, 127, 128, 130
Social Democrats, 8, 188
Sophocles, works by: *Antigone,* 220, 226, 227, 229
Sozialdemokratische Partei Deutschlands (SPD), 184, 190
Spartacus, Spartacist, 216, 217, 221, 223–25, 227
Sperber, George Bernard, 211
Sperber, Manes, 190
Stalin, Josef, 266
Stauffacher, Werner, 205, 210, 211
"steinerne Stil," 76, 164, 267, 276
Sternberg, Fritz, 187
Sternheim, Carl, 24
Sternheim, Carl, works by: *Bürger Schippel,* 186; *Der Student von Prag* (film), 162
Stöcker, Helene, 119
Der Sturm, 5, 23, 32, 37, 55–57, 163

Suhrkamp (publishing house), 17
symbolism, 40, 67, 228

Tauler, Johannes, 220, 222, 239, 252, 256
Thomas Aquinas, 254
Toller, Ernst, 1
Tolstoy, Leon, works by: *War and Peace,* 7
tragedy, 151, 157, 276, 277, 284, 286
tragedy (Christian), 272, 282, 285
tragedy (family), 277, 284
tragedy (Greek), 158, 204
Trakl, Georg, 1
Tucholsky, Kurt, 8, 183

Uhland, Ludwig, 152
Uhland, Ludwig, works by: *Der gute Kamerad* (poem), 153
United States, 14, 169, 170
Unabhängige Sozialdemokratische Partei Deutschlands (USPD), 8, 184

Verdi, Giuseppe, works by: *La Traviata,* 44
Verein Sozialistischer Ärzte (VSÄ), 121
violence, 2, 7, 29, 49, 50, 56, 63, 64, 82, 96, 100, 121, 127, 128, 129, 144, 152, 215, 227, 260, 277
Voltaire, François Marie Arouet de, works by: *Candide,* 210

Wagner, Richard, 229, 276
Wagner, Richard, works by: *Tristan und Isolde,* 220
Walden, Herwarth, 5, 23, 24, 55, 163
Wedekind, Frank, 26, 146
Wegener, Paul, works by: *Der Golem* (film), 162, 166
Weigel, Helene, 257

Weimar Republic, Weimar period, 2, 6, 8, 17, 20, 50, 93, 94, 102, 103, 105, 119, 127, 168, 173, 183, 184, 186, 188, 190, 191, 208, 217, 271, 285
Die Weltbühne, 7, 8
Werfel, Franz, 1
Weyrauch, Wolfgang, 174
Wilhelm, Hans, 168
Winkler, Heinrich August, 226
Wolf, Friedrich, works by:
   Cyankali § 218, 121
Women, portrayal of, 26, 27, 28, 29, 31, 56, 60, 69, 72, 99, 115, 124, 126, 144, 151, 153, 197, 200, 280
Das Wort, 78
Wundt, Wilhelm, 113, 117
Wyler, William, works by:
   Mrs. Miniver (film), 170

Ziolkowski, Theodor, 228
Zech, Paul, 163
Zeit-Echo, 6
Zeitschrift für Sozialforschung, 13
Ziehen, Theodor, 113, 114, 116, 117
Zuckmayer, Carl, 1
Die Zukunft, 190
Zweig, Arnold, 119, 165, 166, 241, 242
Zweig, Stefan, 119

Alfred Döblin (1878–1957) was one of the great German-Jewish writers of the twentieth century, a major figure in the German avant-garde before the First World War and a leading intellectual during the Weimar Republic. Trained as a psychiatrist, Döblin greatly influenced the history of the German novel. His best-known work, the best-selling 1929 novel *Berlin Alexanderplatz*, has frequently been compared in its use of internal monologue and literary montage to James Joyce's *Ulysses* and John Dos Passos's *Manhattan Transfer*. Döblin's oeuvre is by no means limited to novels, but in this genre, he offered a surprising variety of narrative techniques, themes, structures, and outlooks, from his first-published "Chinese" novel *The Three Leaps of Wang-lun* (1915/16) to his last "Novellenroman" *Hamlet* (1956), which deals with the question of personal responsibility for catastrophic historical events. Döblin's impact on German writers after the Second World War was considerable: Günter Grass, for example, acknowledged him as "my teacher." And yet, while *Alexanderplatz* continues to fascinate the reading public, it has overshadowed the rest of Döblin's immense oeuvre.

A Companion to the Works of Alfred Döblin seeks to do justice to such important texts as Döblin's early stories, his numerous other novels, his political, philosophical, medical, autobiographical, and religious essays, his experimental plays, and his writings on the new media of cinema and radio. This volume gives the reader a well-rounded portrait of the life and works of a highly complex modern author as yet not well known in the English-speaking world.

ROLAND DOLLINGER is associate professor of German and chair of the Department of Modern Foreign Languages at Sarah Lawrence College. He is the author of *Totalität und Totalitarismus im Exilwerk Döblins* (1994) and co-editor of *Philosophia Naturalis* (1996), in addition to having authored articles on contemporary German literature.

WULF KOEPKE is Distinguished Professor of German Emeritus at Texas A&M University. He has published widely on German Classicism, Romanticism, and twentieth-century German literature. he is the author of *Lion Feuchtwanger* and *Understanding Max Frisch*. His *The Critical Reception of Alfred Döblin's Major Novels* was published by Camden House in 2003.

HEIDI THOMANN TEWARSON is professor and chair of the Department of German Language and Literature at Oberlin College. She is author of *Alfred Döblin: Grundlagen seiner Aesthetik und Ihre Entwicklung, 1900–1933; Rahel Levin Varnhagen: The Life and Work of a German Jewish Intellectual,* and over twenty articles.

Camden House brings its usual high standards to this assemblage of essays by 13 noted scholars. Comprehensive and well-researched. . . .
CHOICE

Many non-specialists would be hard pressed to name a single work of Döblin's beyond his great novel *Berlin Alexanderplatz*. . . . The current volume attempts to address this imbalance and does an excellent job of introducing readers to the full range and at times baffling variety of Döblin's production.
GERMAN QUARTERLY

A comprehensive and informative introduction to the difficult work of a central author of the 20th century.
MONATSHEFTE

A Companion to the Works of Alfred Döblin succeeds in its plan to illuminate Döblin's work from the most varied standpoints. . . . This volume can be recommended both for the expert on the secondary literature to Döblin and to the reader new to the works of this great author.
SEMINAR

www.ingramcontent.com/pod-product-compliance
Lightning Source LLC
Chambersburg PA
CBHW031705230426
43668CB00006B/118